Heidegger, Hölderlin, and the Subject of Poetic Language

John D. Caputo, *series editor*

JENNIFER ANNA
GOSETTI-FERENCEI

Heidegger, Hölderlin, and the Subject of Poetic Language
Toward a New Poetics of Dasein

FORDHAM UNIVERSITY PRESS
New York ■ 2004

Perspectives in Continental Philosophy No. 38
ISSN 1089-3938

Library of Congress Cataloging-in-Publication Data

Gosetti-Ferencei, Jennifer Anna.
    Heidegger, Hölderlin, and the subject of poetic language : toward a new poetics
of dasein / Jennifer Anna Gosetti-Ferencei.—1st ed.
    p. cm.—(Perspectives in continental philosophy ; no. 38)
    Includes bibliographical references and index.
    ISBN 0-8232-2360-4 (hardcover)
    1. Heidegger, Martin, 1889–1976—Views on poetics. 2. Heidegger, Martin,
1889–1976—Views on German poetry. 3. Hölderlin, Friedrich, 1770–1843—
Language. 4. German poetry—History and criticism. 5. Poetics—History.
6. Phenomenology and literature. I. Title. II. Series.
    B3279.H49G593 2004
    193—dc22

                                                                    2004011586

Printed in the United States of America
07 06 05 04 5 4 3 2 1
First edition

For Arthur Milan Alexander Ferencei

"Auch, dass Kinder sind, so bleibet eine Gewissheit des Guten"

—Hölderlin

Contents

Preface

Martin Heidegger's theory of language, in particular in his interpretations of the poet Friedrich Hölderlin, has brought poetry to the forefront of philosophical thought after more than two millennia of nearly unanimous, but also highly problematic, philosophical ejection of poetry from the realm of knowledge and truth. This alone makes Heidegger's poetics worthy of serious study. Heidegger's interpretations have dominated the reception of Hölderlin's poetry and have established Hölderlin as the philosopher's poet, yet one who rightly forces a reengagement and critique of the metaphysical tradition to which he is wedded. The aim of this book is to develop a theory of poetic language and of the subject of poetic speech in light of Heidegger's interpretations, one that engages a critical study of Heidegger's philosophy and yet attends to Hölderlin as a thinker and practitioner of poetics in his own right. Contrary to the received scholarship on Heidegger's Hölderlin, and contrary to Heidegger's severance of language from the notion of the subject, I develop a competing theory of the subject of poetic language, a theory of poetic *Dasein* or poetic existence, drawing from several distinct illuminations of subjectivity in Continental thought, including Hölderlin's roots in Kantian philosophy. My subject of poetic language is to be disentangled from the metaphysical determinations of the model Heidegger criticizes. This book aims to provide a needed contribution to the study of poetics in light of Heideggerian philosophy, since it takes on the problem of the absence of subjectivity in Heidegger's theory of language; and I believe it is the only account to counterpose, in significant philosophical detail, Heidegger's interpretations of Hölderlin to the latter's own incipient theory. Thus I aim in part toward a revivification of Hölderlin, in the case that his work has been too decisively overshadowed by — and even confounded with — Heidegger's readings. The theory of poetic subjectivity I suggest remains nonetheless advanced by Heidegger's philosophical intuitions about the importance of poetic language.

With regard to Heidegger, while aiming to avoid distortion of the unity of his thought, I argue that the phenomenological impulses of his engagement with language can be distinguished from the domination of its ontological-historical aspects — Heidegger's theory of the history of Being, to which his model of the poet is tethered. Against Heidegger's eschatological tendency to lift the poet out of mundane concerns, and in particular against his argument that the poet heroically "founds" truth and thus plays a privileged role in the destiny of humanity and of the German people in particular, I attempt to reclaim Heidegger's earlier account of Dasein's being in the world, and his earlier conception of the facticity of human existence. These aspects of Heidegger's thought, I argue, are consistent with a Hölderlinian poetics, in that the radical finitude of the subject of poetic speech is made apparent by the nature of that speech, which, precisely because of that finitude, offers a poetic shelter for that which is. By virtue of involvement in a unique relationship to language, the poet's perspicacious insight into the depths of reality and into the possibility (and loss) of the divine leaves him or her painfully aware of the limitations of the standpoint of consciousness. The subject of poetic language is itself not a unified anchor of cognition from which to analyze the world; it is, rather, analeptic, that is, an effort at self-restoration in light of radical limits, a restoration realized only in and through the illimitable process of sheltering engagement with what is.

Although the primary aim of this book concerns the theory of poetic language and its attendant subject, it is no less important that the political entanglements of Heidegger's reading of Hölderlin be taken on directly. The subject of poetic language, for all its fragility — emphasized, for instance, in the revolutionary poetics of Julia Kristeva, which I treat in the penultimate chapter — unravels the heroistic founding of truth that Heidegger, in the troubling context of his involvement with German fascism, attributes to Hölderlin. That poetry is to found and institute Being in a thrust against the historical-ontological crisis, is challenged by the theory I propose, which is, then, much closer to the tenor of Heidegger's later theory of *Gelassenheit*, loosely defined as a poetical letting-be. The notion of *Gelassenheit*, I argue, contributes to dismantling the more heroic strain that overtakes Heidegger's thinking about the relation of Dasein to Being, and returns to the more phenomenologically rooted insights of Heidegger's early work.

Heidegger is right that an instrumental view of language lacks the resources to address the profundity of human existence. If poetic language can be shown to uniquely illuminate the human situation, as I believe it does, and offer, as I also believe, a palliative resource for the ailments of modernity and for human life in the wake of its failures, then what we make of our most significant poets is indeed not only a scholarly and aesthetic issue, but rather one that pertains to the very possibilities of our being and dwelling which Hölderlin so courageously, yet unheroically, examined. It is also possible that poetic thinking, when tethered to an account of the poetic self—or a poetic account of the self—puts us in a position to overcome the seemingly irreparable rift between modernism, with its belief in subjectivity and truth—and postmodernism, which has yet to fully articulate an account of the subject in the wake of its deconstruction. A new poetics of Dasein, I hope, can do for philosophy what string theory has aimed to do for theoretical physics, that is, reconcile convincing but incompatible and incomplete models of the universe. It is toward these possibilities that my thinking here, and the poetic theory that emerges, are aimed. This book is an effort to think through a theory of poetic language and a model of poetry, on one hand in affirmation of the possibilities of poetic thought and dwelling and on the other in light of the fragile conditions of poetic life and engagement that resist the heroism of the founding of truth, yet might offer its shelter. The new poetics of Dasein I set forth in the final chapter aims to offer an original account of the poetic self. This might provide a phenomenological scaffolding from which to view the structures of poetic experience and understand the unique form of truth that belongs to poetic language. Beyond Hölderlin, poets such as Arthur Rimbaud, Rainer Maria Rilke, and Miklós Radnóti are considered in light of a radically revised poetic phenomenology of being in the world.

Acknowledgments

Some of the material treated in this book appeared in earlier formulations as articles in *International Studies in Philosophy* and *Philosophy Today;* articles related to my work here were published in *International Philosophical Quarterly* and in *Feminist Interpretations of Martin Heidegger,* ed. Nancy Holland and Patricia Huntington (Bloomington: Indiana University Press, 2001).

I would like to thank the Delores Zohrab Liebmann Fund for fellowship support that afforded work on this project during a stay at the Humboldt University in Berlin, and the German Academic Exchange Service (DAAD), without whose assistance I would not have been able to achieve the fluency in German requisite for this kind of engagement with Heidegger and Hölderlin. About the topics treated in this book, I have learned much from too many people to name, but a few mentions are necessary. John D. Caputo has provided much counsel for this project, as well as enthusiastic encouragement, for which I gratefully thank him. I am indebted to Richard Howard of Columbia University, from whom I have learned a great deal about the special vivacities of poetic language. Thanks to Patricia Huntington at Loyola University of Chicago for her helpful comments on the manuscript.

Friends, colleagues, and students, too many to name, have offered various kinds of support and discussion. I should like to thank specifically Bill Parrigin; Victoria Pitts at Queens College; Angela Pitts at Mary Washington University; and Eric Charles LeMay at Harvard

University, who have been longtime interlocutors in my engagements with these topics. Above all, I am grateful to Milan Ferencei, whose love for poetry is eclipsed only by his insights into being, and who has been able to afford my life a sustained conversation about the subject(s) of poetic language. This book, however, is dedicated especially to my son Arthur Milan Alexander Ferencei, whose wondrous existence bespeaks the very source at which poetry and thinking are always grasping.

Abbreviations of Frequently Cited Works

General

CJ   Immanuel Kant, Critique of Judgment

Heidegger's Writings

Note: In cases where I rely primarily on available English translations, the abbreviation will be given according to the English translation; yet in some cases I have altered the translations slightly. Where I have altered the given translations significantly, I provide also the German reference after the English reference. In the case of references to *Being and Time* I provide the English, then the German, reference. For volumes not available in translation at the time of this writing, and for those for which I do not give an English reference, the translations are my own (these include GA 60, GA 52, GA 13, and GA 39). In some cases individual essays were published in English translation in volumes that do not correspond to their appearance in German volumes; in these cases I use abbreviations for the essays (LH, OWA) as given below. See the bibliography for full citations.

EB   *Existence and Being*
EHD   *Erläuterungen zu Hölderlins Dichtung*
EM/IM   *Einführung in die Metaphysik* (EM)/ *An Introduction to Metaphysics* (IM)
EP   *The End of Philosophy and the Task of Thinking*
G / DT   *Gelassenheit / Discourse on Thinking*
GA 60   *Phänomenologie des religiösen Lebens, Gesamtausgabe 60.* (*The Phenomenology of Religious Life*)
GA 24   *Die Grundprobleme der Phänomenologie, Gesamtausgabe 24.* (*The Basic Problems of Phenomenology*)
GA 63   *Ontologie (Hermeneutik der Faktizität), Gesamtausgabe 63.* (*The Hermeneutics of Facticity*)
GA 53 / DI   *Hölderlins Hymne "Der Ister," Gesamtausgabe 63.* (*Hölderlin's Hymn "Der Ister"*)

GA 13	*Aus der Erfahrung des Denkens, Gesamtausgabe 13.*
GA 52	*Hölderlins Hymne "Andenken," Gesamtausgabe 52.*
GA 39	*Hölderlins Hymnen "Germanien" und "Der Rhein," Gesamtausgabe 39.*
HW	*Holzwege*
LH	"Letter on Humanism," in *Basic Writings*
OWA	"The Origin of the Work of Art," in *Basic Writings*
PLT	*Poetry, Language, and Thought*
QT	"The Questions Concerning Technology," in *The Question Concerning Technology and Other Essays*
ST	*Schelling's Treatise on the Essence of Human Freedom*
SZ / BT	*Sein und Zeit / Being and Time*
T	"The Turning," in *The Question Concerning Technology and Other Essays*
US / OWL	*Unterwegs Zur Sprache / On the Way to Language*
W / P	*Wegmarken / Pathmarks*
ZSD/ OTB	*Zur Sache des Denkens / On Time and Being*

Hölderlin's Works

Note: In-text citations are given for theoretical writings and for *Hyperion* only. All poems quoted are found in *Werke und Briefe,* I and II. Other references are given in endnotes. Except where otherwise noted, translations of the poems are my own. Existing translations I have consulted are cited in the bibliography.

ELT	*Essays and Letters on Theory*
H	*Hyperion*
TS	*Theoretische Schriften*
WB I	*Werke und Briefe, Band I*
WB II	*Werke und Briefe, Band II*

Kristeva's Works

Note: In-text citations are given for these frequently-cited works. References to other writings are given in endnotes. Translations of essays not marked individually in the bibliography are found in *The Kristeva Reader.*

ACW	*About Chinese Women*
AKI	"A New Kind of Intellectual"
DL	*Desire in Language*
RPL	*Revolution in Poetic Language*
WT	"Women's Time"

Introduction
The Dialogue Between Poetry and Thinking

Martin Heidegger's thinking, from the beginning, anticipates a turn to poetic language and to Hölderlin. Although Heidegger became seriously occupied with Hölderlin in his writings and lectures in the 1930s, he had read him decades earlier, even before the publication of Hellingrath's edition of Hölderlin's collected works, which began to appear in 1916.[1] Still, in *Being and Time*, Heidegger shows little sensitivity to poetic language, though he admits that "poetical discourse" (*"dichtende" Rede*)[2] amounts to "a disclosing of existence" (BT 205/162),[3] and announces the necessity of "the task of *liberating* language from logic" (BT 209/165). In *Being and Time*, it is necessary to ask, "What kind of Being does language have?" (BT 209/166), though later Heidegger will effect a reversal and ask the question of the "language of Being." While in *Basic Problems of Phenomenology* (1927) Heidegger approaches poetic language — here, a page from Rainer Maria Rilke's *Notebooks of Malte Laurids Brigge* — he quickly shies away from this as an insight into a phenomenological account of truth.[4] Yet long before the notion of a "turn"[5] is treated in the *Beiträge zur Philosophie* (1936–38) (GA 65, 407–409) and later in the essay "Die Kehre,"[6] Heidegger's writings foreshadow in many ways the "turn" from philosophy to what he called the experience of thinking, one which is guided, from *Being and Time* to "Time and Being,"[7] by a "listening"[8] to poetry. Already in 1923, Heidegger begins a lecture course

in phenomenology with the claim that, "it is my conviction that philosophy is at an end" ("Es ist meine Überzeugung, dass es mit der
Philosophie zu Ende ist") (GA 17, 1). What emerged out of this conviction—out of the "end of philosophy" itself—is more than an oeuvre of a single thinker. For what Heidegger establishes is not a "new
philosophy" of Being, not only a phenomenological and fundamental ontology as outlined in *Being and Time*, but a radical revaluation
of philosophy itself—its "overcoming" (*Überwindung*), as he put it,
its "destruction" (*Abbau*)—one that employs the reserves of earlier
thinkers, from Heraclitus and Parmenides to Nietzsche, Aristotle,
and Kierkegaard, to name only a few. But Heidegger employs above
all a recuperation of the thinking he finds implicit in Hölderlin, who
for Heidegger belongs essentially to the law of movement of that
thinking that is, as essentially historical, yet to arrive, to the *Bewe-
gungsgesetz des Künftigen* that Heidegger then aims to bring to thoughtful word.[9] After the nascent insight of the *Basic Problems of Phenomenology*, Heidegger comes to understand in a "primordially" thoughtful
way that a phenomeno-ontological understanding of truth can no
longer ban poetic language, as metaphysics had, from the realm
theretofore reserved for logical concepts. Heidegger comes to see
that "poetry and thought, each needs the other" (OWL 70), that the
liberation of language from logic was not only a task to be relegated
to a future project but also the only proper ground for a thinking of
Being. Thus Heidegger provides both a theorization of philosophy's
end and a point of departure for rethinking its long and elusive history; but both the "end" and the inceptive (*anfänglich*) beginning[10]
(GA 39, 3–4; GA 65, 55–57) are guided by an account of language
that takes its guide from poetic language. "A properly unique beginning," Heidegger writes, "lies in whatever is said poetically" (DI 8).
Heidegger draws his formulation of the *Seinsgeschichte*, the history
of Being's self-disclosure and withdrawal, from Hölderlin's notion
of the absent gods, from the Hölderlinian notions of *Andenken* or
remembrance and preparatory awaiting (which Heidegger takes up
as *Vordenken*), and weaves them into a theory of the ontological "founding" (*Stiften*) of the poetic word.

For Heidegger, what arrives in the wake of philosophy's end is above
all the demand to requestion the meaning of language—of that which
makes us human; for we are, endowed with language, the site of transcendence, wherein beings can appear in their Being. To be of language
is to have a particular relation to beings—to be the projective horizon,
the openness of possibility, against which they emerge into appearance

as beings; but it is also to be able to ask the question of Being *per se*, to have a relation to the presence and withdrawing that for Heidegger characterizes a "world"—to which he adds, after *Being and Time*, *physis*, nature, and "earth." Hölderlin occupies a preeminent place in Heidegger's departure from philosophy and revisitation of thinking not only because he is a poet but also because he thematizes this demand to think language in its relation to our strange, even estranged, what Heidegger calls "uncanny" (*unheimlich*) humanness.

Poetic language has been an incipient source for the critique and self-address of philosophy since Plato banned the poets from the *polis* and Aristotle relativized this expulsion by granting poetry a philosophical, cathartic social function[11]; it surfaced in Kant's notion of "aesthetic ideas" in the *Critique of Judgment,* which, Kant claims, are best expressed in poetry; in the "Earliest System-Program of German Idealism" attributed to Hegel, Schelling, and Hölderlin wherein poetry is to survive philosophy; in Schlegel's fragments; in Kierkegaard's journals and in his pseudonymous acknowledgment in *Philosophical Fragments* to be writing poetry; in Nietzsche's attempt to search for a writing that "sings"; in Adorno's arguments for the critical and utopian "truth content" of art; finally in Kristeva's investigations into poetic language as revolutionary for thought. For Heidegger, poetic language harbors a promise for thinking. This promise is one that confronts above all Hegel's claim, which Heidegger cites in *The Principle of Reason* (PR 61), that "the sequestered nature of the universe cannot resist the power of absolute cognition"—it confronts and overcomes what Heidegger understands as the *completion* of the rational, willing subject itself. Poetry's alternative is a promise for the liberation of that which is ruthlessly inscribed within, reduced to, or forgotten by the language of concepts—by the demand, as Heidegger claims of Leibniz, to render everything rational—of that which is forgotten by the subject who, in modernity, emerges as the ground and measure of truth, reality, world, and nature. Poetic language shelters what René Char names an "immensity," this "density" of the world and of existing, echoing what Heidegger calls "facticity" (*Faktizität*). Facticity, it must be said, is for Heidegger in no way irrelevant to the generalities of philosophy, but is rather the ground thereof; in factical life, "the way to philosophy is made possible" (GA 63, 11). Heidegger shows that since conceiving does not exhaust the possibilities of thought, the conceptual does not exhaust the realm of the thinkable (PR 18); the concept excludes what it cannot render transparent, thereby exiling it from the sphere of truth and meaning (PR 17). For Hölderlin, the limits of philosophy are the limits of sayability and meaning, and constitute a both philosophical and poetological[12] problem — the grounds for a unique skepticism that is to be weaved out of and into a theory of poetic language; and this is precisely the problem of the relation between thought or consciousness — having or being of language — and world. Hölderlin, occupied with hopes that for Heidegger will sound far too humanistic, asks in a letter what room is left in the rationalism of philosophy and political thought for human harmony — by which he means the joy of life, wonderment in nature's beauty, communal celebration of life as such — all of which cannot be granted truth by concepts that demand necessity. Joy, wonderment, and even, in the wake of Schiller, love can be thought according to Hölderlin only poetically, according not to a conceptual but to a poetic logic (ELT 109). Insofar as this poetic logic involves, as I shall argue, a poetic subjectivity, Hölderlin's theory of poetic language is to be brought into dialogue with Heidegger's critique of the subject.

Heidegger was not the first to declare philosophy at an end, but his task was to overcome its completion in what he called the last metaphysics of Nietzsche and in the technological will to power Heidegger associates with the modern subject (LH 218). What Heidegger first illuminates, particularly after *Being and Time,* is what metaphysics has forgotten, and the crisis that philosophical thought had effected in its demand to think according to laws that reduce truth, and thereby Being, to static actuality and presence. To historical experience and lived experience — which had occupied Heidegger, as a student of Husserl, already before 1920 and had a century before been the problem of Kierkegaard's notion of existence — was now added the experience of nature, and the earth itself, as that forgotten, enframed, consumed by metaphysics, which, Heidegger argues, begins with Plato and takes its upsurge in modernity.

Heidegger's insights into poetic language — and thus into the poetic nature of language as such — promise a rehabilitation of thinking in the wake of the end of metaphysics and in the failure of philosophies of consciousness and subjectivity to secure what Hölderlin calls a harmonious — that is, nondominating — relation between subject and world. Heidegger's thinking about and with language is then his radicalization of thinking as such, a thinking of what Heidegger claims language itself promises when listened to outside the logic of conceptual-rational truth-claims or the mere transmission of information that characterizes the technologization of language. Phenomenological ontology is thus brought to word in a way that admits — even shelters — the livingness of that to which it refers; poetic language, furthermore, is shown to be an access to truth neither as correctness nor as the correspondence between thought and actuality but as a process of partial, and therefore finite, disclosure. That we are bearers of language and therefore privy to this disclosure—to Being itself—becomes the matter for thinking. What is most erroneous in technological thinking and in the technological domination of beings—namely, the forgetting of Being, or *Seinsvergessenheit*—is overcome, illuminating the finitude of all disclosure of what is. Since for Heidegger poetic language admits this finitude—that it is a revealing—it becomes the most compelling source for a phenomenological-ontological account of truth. It is, among others, the aim of this project to draw out Heidegger's phenomenological-ontological insights into poetic language insofar as they are indebted to and further Hölderlin's poetic thought.

This privilege granted to poetic language in the disclosure of beings is, moreover, tethered in Heidegger's account to an historical, even destinal, sending (*Geschick*) of Being itself, and functions as the remembrance (*Andenken*) of that silenced by *Seinsvergessenheit*. The silent convergence of subjectivity and humanism—that is to say, of what Heidegger calls metaphysics—with modern technology in this forgetting becomes the site of Heidegger's overcoming and of his engagement with poetic language and with Hölderlin. Yet while Heidegger's thoughtful dialogue with poetic language offers a pressing alternative for thinking, it is also the case that, as is well known, Heidegger's engagement with Hölderlin and poetic language involves two interweaving tendencies—a struggle for thinking fought on two fronts, as two possible turns for thought: one in the reverence of a quiet, sheltering, *Gelassenheit* listening to poetry, the other in a violent, yet likewise poetic founding of truth. This twofoldedness (*Zwiefalt*) accounts for the heightened critical sensitivity required to address the inheritance of Heidegger's turn to poetic language (*Dichten*) as the entrance into thinking (*Denken*), but especially to address Heidegger's engagements with Hölderlin.

My focus here is on the structure of poetic subjectivity implied by a Hölderlinian poetics, rather than on providing at length an alternative phenomenology of poetic creation. Yet the weighing of a *Gelassenheit* model over one of the founding of truth sets the tone, if not also the foundational structure, for an account as well of creative production, which I address in the final chapter. Between Heidegger's theory of letting-be and his violent poetics, I aim to present here a new poetics of Dasein. The stance of the poet and the special nature of poetical truth cannot be adequately articulated without a discussion of Dasein's creative life, an element I argue is essential to a poetical notion of existence.

But first it is necessary to account for, and disentangle, the duality within Heidegger's account of poetic language. For one is confronted by what at first appears as an ambivalence, and sometimes as a contra-diction,[13] and what is certainly a twofoldedness, in Heidegger's theory of poetic language. Heidegger's thought with regard to poetic lan-guage has radically reoriented the nature of phenomenological ontology and has found an alternative source for the redirection of thought as such, one that responds to the destruction of the earth and of our rela-tion thereto in a uniquely nonrepresentational kind of thinking. In "Dia-logue with a Japanese," in his interpretation of Stefan George's poem "The Word," in the many lecture courses and essays on Hölderlin and in the reading of Rilke, Heidegger finds in poetic language an alterna-tive to the violence of technological rationality, which defines, reduces, manipulates, and exhausts its object, its "other." One finds in many of these writings, particularly those essays in *Unterwegs zur Sprache* of the 1950s, a critique of subjectivity as a critique of violence, at least of the violence of representation and manipulation, of possession and use-rela-tions. Heidegger imagines a *Gelassenheit* inherent in a poetic response to the world and to earth—a letting-be of things as a letting-go of repre-sentational consciousness, of the exclusivity of rational, conceptual truth-claims. As Heidegger outlines in "Origin of the Work of Art," attendance to things in their own elusive self-unfolding becomes possible outside their reduction to metaphysical-technological measures. Such a *Gelassen-heit* involves the resignation of subjectivity as will, as the desire to mas-ter and define, and requires a more imaginative, perhaps more difficult, more phenomenologically genuine, kind of thinking. One can then ask about technology's essence, how to live with technology and at the same time preserve a critical distance from it; one can ask what might other-wise now be considered the nostalgic, or at least romantic, question of nature. Heidegger's thought poses these questions, ones, it has been argued, that are of urgency for our own attempts to think philosophi-cally if that implies finding other modes of being-in-the-world: are there not truths and meanings, possibilities and experiences, textures and processes of factical life that are ignored, or even destroyed, by the monopoly that technological rationality holds on truth-claims and exerts over reality and over us? Is there not something more at stake in the destruction of nature than the loss of natural resources, something that might be essential to what we call our humanity and our humaneness?

Do we not have a relationship to language that is other than merely instrumental, and can we not learn other ways of thinking in listening to language differently? Does not poetic language, long neglected by philosophical thinking, hold a source for that thinking, a source for a possible liberation?

Yet while these questions, as well as contemporary continental philosophical traditions and the liberation of thinking from metaphysics, are opened up by Heidegger's thought, his readers encounter at the same time — in the "Origin of the Work of Art," *Introduction to Metaphysics*, and the lecture courses on Hölderlin — other dimensions of the poetic relation to truth and Being. One finds here a theory of decision and founding, and, as I will argue, a sometimes phenomenologically questionable preference for the "essential"; one finds not only a quiet sheltering of truths but their violent instigation. One cannot help but notice, in Heidegger's discussion of strife and struggle, on belligerence and instigation, on the "either/or" of historical decision, that, as Werner Marx claims, Heidegger's theory of a Hölderlinian-poetic alternative to technological subjectivity "proceeded in a deliberately violent way." In reading Hölderlin after Heidegger, and with sensitivity to the philosophical and political dimensions of that engagement, one must account for the fact that "the violently active kind of essential thinking is particularly evident in the 'dialogue' with Hölderlin's poetry."[14]

Wherefrom this ambivalence, this contradiction — *Gelassenheit*, on the one hand, *Streit* and instigation on the other, a fluctuation that does not strictly follow a chronological shift in Heidegger's tone — particularly in reading the writings on Hölderlin in the 1930s and 1940s — but rather an oscillation in the approach to the relation of poetic language to truth and "origin" (*Ursprung*)? One might isolate it, as have some of Heidegger's recent critics, in Heidegger's approach to poetry, in his method of listening.[15] Heidegger himself describes his method in vacillating ways. On one hand, it is a "thinking dialogue," a "listening," a thinking of the "unthought" that could not be brought to full expression in the poem itself. Heidegger insists that thinking cannot add anything to the poem, cannot attempt to demand its insertion into a system of thought or a philosophy (GA 52, 5–6; GA 39, 4–6; DI 26). The remarks on Hölderlin's poetry are "merely an accompaniment to the poem," "merely provide a few markers" (DI 2). Heidegger grants the poem itself, the poem's word, an unprecedented philosophical dignity, a singularity (DI 14). The poem is an "enigma" we should not wish to solve (DI 35), but that nevertheless gives direction to thinking. Thus his method is presented as an example of *Gelassenheit* itself:

letting poetry, other to thought, speak to thinking. On the other hand, Heidegger claims that, particularly in the case of Hölderlin, the poet demands thinking conquest (*denkerische Eroberung*), to be thoughtfully dominated by the thinker (GA 39, 5), that thinking wins entrance into the "*Machtbereich*" of the poem only through "*Kampf*," just as the poet himself, in *Kampf*, becomes "master and slave" (GA 39, 19, 22). For this we need "weapons of thinking" (*denkerische Waffen*) that are still lacking (GA 39, 23). We must let Hölderlin's poetry have force (*walten*) over us, in order that our existence involves the *Macht* of poetry (GA 39, 19). Hölderlin's own "thinking listening" becomes then what Heidegger calls "destiny" (*das Schicksal*), which is to be spared from all randomness (GA 52, 2–3); its equivocity (*Vieldeutigkeit*) is strictly "gathered" (*versammelt*) (GA 52, 10; EHD 192).

In this context, Heidegger's thinking then defines, according to the law of an "essential" destiny, the essence of the poem, indeed of poetic language itself. It has been pointed out that Heidegger both comes closer to Hölderlin than any other reader ever has to any poet, and, at the same time, that "Hölderlin says exactly the opposite of what Heidegger makes him say" (Paul de Man)—that "Hölderlin's poetry is turned into its opposite by the use Heidegger makes of it" (Otto Pöggeler).[16] Derrida has suggested that Heidegger's interpretations are a "catastrophe,"[17] and the reader who takes note of the political undercurrents in Heidegger's interpretations—particularly in the lecture courses on Hölderlin—is puzzled in comparing Heidegger's political gestures to Hölderlin's largely ignored—and in Heidegger's reading almost entirely silenced—political thinking; this difference, furthermore, has not yet been given an audible voice in philosophical accounts of their *Zwiesprache*.[18] Heidegger mentions Hölderlin's own worldview (*Weltanschauung*)—which includes an unwavering hope for democracy, a peaceful, "feminine," even "defenseless" (GA 39, 17) image of Germania, and what Hölderlin calls "human rights" (*menschliche Rechte*)—only in order to dismiss it, in mid-1930s Germany,[19] as "untimely for our hard times" (GA 39, 17–18). Hölderlin's "my love is the human race" ("meine Liebe ist das Menschengeschlecht") (WB I, 813), belongs to a humanism left behind even by Heidegger's later critique of technology, for all its merits.

While Heidegger's political engagements have been understood as relevant to his Hölderlin interpretations,[20] it must be said that Heidegger remained critical of National Socialism's biologism and racism (GA 69, 71, 88; GA 52, 27–28), was "not an anti-Semite," as Karl Jaspers argues.[21] Yet Heidegger never disputed having seen at least some convergence between his own philosophical, "Hölder-linian" hopes and the revolution invoked by the National Socialist reign. Long after he had been proven wrong about this convergence, he nevertheless remained critical of democracy and saw, after the war, the confrontation with technology as the singularly important political issue — one that, he thought, could not be taken on within the political sphere. Though I would argue that Heidegger's critique of technology is philosophically unsurpassed and is not to be dismissed as masking an ideological agenda, the historical-ontological apparatus of thinking that supports it cannot be spared from a critical assessment even if we grant Heidegger regrettably naive intentions; and it is no longer possible — not only from our historical vantage-point but in the wake of recent publications of *Gesamtausgabe* volumes and a sharpened philosophical reception of Heidegger's later thought[22] — to set aside historical events entirely in favor of the event of thinking and its singular historicality, even as efforts are rightly devoted to the radical and liberating, *Gelassenheit* dimensions thereof. In *What Is Called Thinking?* (1951) Heidegger still claims that World War II had decided nothing essential, nothing that "pertains solely to the destiny of the essence of humanity upon earth." In my view, this claim presses one to question whether or not Heidegger, when he claims that a thinking of Being "must abandon the attempt to understand Being from the viewpoint of beings"[23] — when he is compelled to argue that "Being alone is" (EP 79) — is successful in joining the later *Ereignis* ontology to the phenomenological bastions of his thought, which always involve not only occurrence itself and its process but also what occurs.[24] Is Hölderlinian poetic language genuinely "beyond beings" in a recollection of origin, as Heidegger often hopes despite his insights (particularly in reading Stefan George and Rilke) into the relation between word and beings, or does poetic language merely open a way toward a thinking of the *Ereignis*, Being in its self-withholding granting, without being capable of following that thought "beyond beings"? In 1941 Heidegger himself suggests, in a text of compositions he calls *"Winke,"* that poetic language remains too tethered to images (to beings) to free thought for the *Ereignis* entirely (GA 13, 33). There Heidegger attempts a thinking beyond even poetic language, a thinking that is, unlike poetic language, imageless (*bildlos*), and that, unlike the poeticized (*das Gedichtete*) in the poem, has no point of departure in beings — *"hat im Seienden keinen Anhalt."* The answer to these questions might be implicated in the effort to disentangle *Gelassenheit* from the vestiges of violence that haunt the founding and decision that Heidegger claims poetic language instigates; for the historically real violence which, as Lyotard argues, Heidegger "forgets,"[25] is overlooked precisely in favor of origin and essence — in favor of the disclosure and withdrawal that issues disclosure — as opposed to "that which is."

Yet major dimensions of Heidegger's account of poetic language, particularly in the essays of *On the Way to Language* (*Unterwegs zur Sprache*) in the 1950s, are far removed from the distressing moments of Heidegger's thinking, and it is indeed his turn to Hölderlin's poetry that, it is argued, affords Heidegger's turn away from political engagements and toward the *Gelassenheit* thinking. This is not to deny other influences on Heidegger's thought. There is, for instance, Heidegger's attention to other poetic verse, such as that of Angelus Silesius (Johannes Scheffler, the contemporary of Leibniz), whom Heidegger sees as usurping Leibniz's "principle of reason." Still more, Heidegger inherits his understanding of dwelling from Meister Eckhart's notions of detachment (*Abgeschiedenheit*) and letting-be (*Gelassenheit*), which denote for Eckhart a detachment, for instance, from worldly goods and influences.[26] Yet it is Heidegger's readings of Hölderlin — most of which appear in the lectures between 1934 and 1942, and in the essays of *Erläuterungen zu Hölderlins Dichtung*, which appears in 1951 — far more so than those of Eckhart, Rilke, George, or Trakl, that press again the political question, for it is in the lecture courses on Hölderlin that Heidegger articulates the poetic thinking of German historical destiny. Hölderlin is for Heidegger not only the "essential poet" but also "the poet of the Germans" and the "most German of all German" poets (GA 52, 119), who determines for the Germans the "essence of history" (GA 52, 77) and of the *Vaterland* (GA 52, 132–135, 140–142). Despite this brief political contextualization of Heidegger's readings of Hölderlin, my project here concerns not Heidegger's politics but — and even this only secondarily — the ways in which his theory of language and interpretations of Hölderlin become philosophically-ontologically political or counterpolitical, and the ways in which this political or counterpolitical element transforms the relation between phenomenological revealing and ontological founding throughout Heidegger's reading of poetic language.

It must further be said that although Heidegger's reading of Hölderlin, as his most important source for a thinking of "origin," is infused within Heidegger's later philosophy in both sides of what we have called its ambivalence or twofoldedness, Heidegger is not solely responsible for the interpretation of Hölderlin that emerges in our century, nor is Heidegger's the only prevailing one, particularly in Europe.[27] If Heidegger, as it has been argued, essentializes and nationalizes Hölderlin, the way for this—scarcely noted by either critics or advocates of Heidegger's Hölderlin interpretations—was long prepared for by a nationalist and even racialist *Literaturwissenschaft*, by Norbert Hellingrath's editorial interpretations upon which Heidegger relies (GA 52, 16–17, 44–6; EHD 152; OWL 78),[28] and by the then only recent adoption of Hölderlin into the German canon. Wilhelm Scherer was among the first in 1874 to take up Hölderlin during the formation of the notion of "national" literature.[29] He was followed, in 1894, by August Sauer[30] and later by Josef Nadler, who, as the rector of the German University in Prague, organized a "literary science" according to a regionalist theory of the *Stämme* and *Herkunft* of the author.[31] Long before Heidegger, the move to set up Hölderlin as the "voice of the people" of early-twentieth-century Germany was in process and it was not a uniformly affirmative one[32]; and if Heidegger is credited with discovering the "essential" and the "pure" in Hölderlin's poems, it was already anticipated in Dilthey's 1906 *Das Erlebnis und die Dichtung*.[33] Hölderlin had been ignored as a "German" poet since Goethe's complaint about Hölderlin's *"heftige Subjektivität"*[34] (a surprising criticism next to Heidegger's claim that Hölderlin poetizes beyond subjectivity) and did not, until almost the turn of the century, enter into the ranks of national literature with Schiller and Goethe. Hölderlin had been adopted by National Socialism quite independently of Heidegger's interpretations[35]—an appropriation tethered to the heroism of the George school[36] around the time of World War I. Lukács protested against the Nazification of Hölderlin before Heidegger's elaborations on the "poet of the Germans,"[37] and Hölderlin was furthermore employed after the war as a mantra for leftist student protests and celebrated for his humanism.[38] Nevertheless, Heidegger—following Hellingrath's elaboration of the *"vaterländische Umkehr"*[39]—takes Hölderlin significantly out of context; for whatever the complexities of Heidegger's understanding of the national, Hölderlin's aim for revolution is democratic, which Heidegger's is not, and Hölderlin's aim involves furthermore a utopian longing for community "beyond the state."[40]

Yet Heidegger finds in Hölderlin as well the mourning promise for a recovery—if only in awaiting the new gods—from the ills and technological violence of modernity, and from belligerently reductive forms of thinking. If Heidegger's political entanglements do not exhaust his contributions to the radical reorientation of thinking in the wake of metaphysics, they furthermore do not exhaust his readings of Hölderlin. Having at least indicated some of the complexities of reopening the dialogue between Heidegger and Hölderlin, we can now say that this project takes up primarily the *Gelassenheit* realm that Heidegger aimed to achieve for thinking by attending with an unprecedented gravity to poetic language and to the language of Hölderlin. The liberation of this realm from the troubling dimensions I have heretofore outlined requires, moreover, an attendance to the phenomenological function of poetic language as the self-showing finitude of disclosure, and, furthermore, of the limits and even fragility of poetic saying. If the violent dimensions of Heidegger's reading give way to a nonaggressive, *Gelassenheit* dwelling, the writings of Hölderlin underlie and guide that account of dwelling, and provide the philosophical-poetological underpinnings for this fragility, which itself calls into question the "original violence" Heidegger has argued poetic language is. Heidegger employs Hölderlin in overcoming the metaphysical-technological subject and in imagining a thinking beyond subjectivity, and in this Heidegger elucidates the unique virtues of language rendered poetic and understood poetically, and the relevance of this for a thinking he once called phenomenological.[41] At the same time, Heidegger's overcoming of subjectivity involves both *Gelassenheit* receptivity and the obedience (DI 124) of historical founding beyond the concerns of a subject. Thus Heidegger's discussion of Hölderlin is not merely of literary[42] and not only of political[43] significance, but is also rather a matter of philosophical significance, if not urgency. When this thinking meets up with the phenomenological texture of poetic language, and its aforementioned fragility—its even self-refuting character, as we shall see in chapter 3, on Hölderlin's poetics—the issue of subjectivity, or of the self found within that fragile texture of disclosure, reemerges despite Heidegger's critique.

It is then, in particular, the critique of subjectivity and the abandonment of humanism[44] in favor of a thinking beyond subjectivity that opens itself to examination with regard to Heidegger's dialogue with Hölderlin. For if, as I shall outline in chapter 1, the turn to poetic language involves an overcoming of subjectivity and humanism, particularly in the danger of the technological domination of the earth, this move nevertheless preempts an insight Heidegger might have found in Hölderlin, and which might guide the relation between poetic-phenomenological revealing and ontological founding in ways incompatible with resolution, decision, and strife found in "The Origin of the Work of Art" and elsewhere, and perhaps incompatible with the gathering of

Schicksal to which Heidegger tethers Hölderlin's language. This insight is nothing less than a subjectivity not grounded exclusively in rationality, not secured as the anchor of nature's secrets, not the gaze of absolute cognition, not a technological will to power. A close reading of Hölderlin's thought about language, consciousness, and Being might reveal that an entanglement in beings need not be rendered according to that absolute gaze or to a technological-metaphysical fixation upon static presence, a fixation which would obscure Being as a process of emergence and self-withdrawal. Entanglement in beings might also be the "thrownness" (*Geworfenheit*) of a subject understood poetically, one haunted as well as enlivened[45] by the openness of the possible. Heidegger's thought, then, might take a somewhat different turn if Heidegger's interpretations of Hölderlin's poems are joined with a reading of Hölderlin's poetological writings, his essays and letters, in which, as I shall argue, such a subject is to be retrieved.

In his lecture courses and essays on Hölderlin, Heidegger often cites and refers to these writings, but admits to neglecting Hölderlin as a thinker — even as a thinker of poetic theory (GA 39, 5–6, 40–41). Passages from Hölderlin's essays and letters are employed by Heidegger to support his interpretations (for example, EHD 33–35, 157–158, 183; GA 39, 66–67; 74–75; 84–87) and Heidegger admits the dialectical complexity of Hölderlin's thought and Hölderlin's importance as a philosopher in the ranks of Hegel and Schelling (GA 39, 6) — a view that is now supported by copious research into Hölderlin's importance for the birth of speculative philosophy[46] and is made more accessible to philosophical readers by recent versions of Hölderlin's collected theoretical writings.[47] In several instances Heidegger admits the philosophical difficulty of Hölderlin's theoretical writings. In reference to one such essay Heidegger claims, "It requires the highest gathered force of thought and the longest breath of a metaphysical-dialectical grasping, to follow the thinking poet in his treatise" ("Es bedarf der höchsten denkerischen gesammelten Kraft und des längsten Atems eines metaphysisch dialektischen Begreifens, um dem denkerischen Dichter in seiner Abhandlung zu folgen") (GA 39, 85). The thesis of the *"vaterländische Umkehr"* indeed arises in one such essay (ELT 114) to which Heidegger refers but upon which he does not elaborate.

Hölderlin's theoretical writings are indeed fragmentary and difficult, and they involve complex critiques of transcendental and Idealist philosophy, an exhaustive exegesis of which is beyond the scope of this project.[48] Yet I hope that it becomes clear in the following analyses of these writings that the question of subjectivity must be taken up in a different light from what Heidegger's critique affords. Heidegger recognizes that Hölderlin's thought—for example the essay "Operations of the Poetic Spirit" ("Über die Verfahrungsweise des poetischen Geistes") (ELT 62–82; TS 39–62) cannot be understood without its philosophical context: "The treatise cannot be grasped without real understanding of the innermost core and the fundamental questions of the philosophy of Kant and, above all, of German Idealism" ("Die Abhandlung ist ohne wirkliches Verständnis des innersten Kerns und der Grundfragen der Philosophie Kants und vor allem des deutschen Idealismus nicht zu begreifen") (GA 39, 84).) This understanding is, however, alluded to but elucidated nowhere in Heidegger's Hölderlin interpretations, despite that in this essay Hölderlin offers a poetological critique of transcendental idealism. One must credit Heidegger with not subordinating Hölderlin's poetry and even theoretical essays entirely to the tenets of Idealist philosophy, according to the "usual method" of claiming that "Hölderlin metaphorphosed Schelling's or Hegel's philosophy into poetry" (GA 39, 84), and grant that his *Seinsgeschichte*-oriented interpretations open up a reading of Hölderlin wherein questions of truth and Being, as well as the relation to nature or earth, are granted precedence. Insofar as Heidegger achieves a unique proximity to certain elements of Hölderlin's poetry, this requires the rejection of just such a subordination to philosophical systematicity, and indeed respects Hölderlin's difference from Hegel and Schelling. Yet Heidegger, though quoting Hölderlin's essay at length, silences Hölderlin's own philosophical-poetological voice—Hölderlin's own answer to the questions of truth and Being—by immediately retreating to an account of the poetic *leitmotiv* of the "holy" (*das Heilige*) (GA 39, 86) which Heidegger has already laid out as the poet's wholly non-subjective reception of Being, beyond the poet's own experience or feeling (GA 52, 5–6; GA 39, 42–43). (I note here that Heidegger's rejection of the terminology of "experience"—*Erfahrung*, as experience in general, and *Erlebnis*, as indicating a specific experience of an event—is not absolute, for he does refer to "poetic experience," as I discuss in chapter 3. I retain it in this book because it is of integral significance for understanding Hölderlin's poetics.) Moreover, the passage from Hölderlin's essay that Heidegger cites takes up the grounds of this very subjective feeling or perception (*Empfindung*) of unity—the feeling of the holy—"in the subjective state" ("in einem subjectiven Zustande") of the human being's conscious reflection. Hölderlin writes in the passage cited by Heidegger of the relation and harmony between subject and object—their "harmonious opposition" (*das Harmonischentgegengesetzte*)—and the loss and reinscription of this harmony, a movement that for Hölderlin is the relation between consciousness and the operations of poetic language (GA 39, 84–85).

Heidegger treats similarly Hölderlin's difficult philosophical essay "Becoming in Dissolution" (ELT 96–100; TS 33–39), wherein Hölderlin takes up the relation between possibility and actuality; but Heidegger argues that Hölderlin "by no means philosophizes too much" ("keineswegs zu viel philosophiert"), and that Hölderlin is rather here only contemplative (*nachdenklich*) with regard to the concealed beginnings of the (not yet written) poem "Andenken," which Heidegger calls "this most German of all German poems" ("dieser deutschesten aller deutschen Dichtungen") (GA 52, 119). Where Heidegger admits the relation of Hölderlin's thinking here to that of Fichte, Hegel, and Schelling,[49] in fact admits that Hölderlin's thinking is "still metaphysical," Hölderlin's poetry—and his illumination of poetry as the matter for thinking—is to be thought otherwise: "but he poeticizes differently" ("aber er dichtet anders") (GA 52, 120). What Heidegger does not illuminate is that Hölderlin's thought already contains a radical, poetological critique of metaphysics without fully leaving it behind. Heidegger claims of Hölderlin that "a world divides him from Schiller's 'Philosophical Poems,'" overlooking Hölderlin's own self-admitted dependence on Schiller's aesthetics—a dependence against which Hölderlin struggled by leaving Jena, where Schiller's influence was too great.

While Heidegger aims to think the "belonging together of poetry and thinking,"—what he calls the "philosophical truth" rendered by poetic language (DI 11, 110)—in Hölderlin's case Heidegger in some sense divides them. Hölderlin himself articulated not only poetically but poetologically/philosophically the grounds for his turn to poetic language and the form that this was to take. Despite the delicate nuances that belong to the poetry-thinking dialogue, and the varying descriptions of what "happens" therein,[50] in the lecture course on Hölderlin's *Der Ister*, Heidegger claims: "it is only the thinker who knows what thinking is. The poet alone decides about poetry, and the thinker alone decides about the realm of thought, no one else" (DI 146). In Heidegger's account, Hölderlin becomes a poet and only a poet, thus making room for the thinker who is to retrieve the "unthought" that could not be brought to expression in the poem. Not only is this separation challenged by Hölderlin's philosophical-poetological writings, so too is the notion of "decision" that here still haunts Heidegger's understanding of thinking and poetizing despite their otherwise receptive character.

Yet it is of significance for our discussion that Hölderlin has his own theoretical account of poetic language, and of the poet's relation to Being. As Hans-Jost Frey tersely suggests, "Heidegger's understanding of language is different from Hölderlin's."[51] This difference is indeed the relation of poetic language to truth, thinking, and Being, a relation that can itself be brought, in certain respects, to further and even release Heidegger's ontology to its *Gelassenheit* dimensions.

It has been claimed that while interpretation of Hölderlin's work far surpasses that of all other early Romantic writers, that it "moves at dizzying heights," the scholarly account of German Idealism's formation has until recently left Hölderlin out—despite that, as Dieter Henrich argues, the history of its origins is illuminated by no text more than by another of Hölderlin's essays, "Judgment and Being."[52] While Hölderlin's thinking is exhausted neither by Idealism, from which he departs, nor by his associations with Romanticism, poetic language and a theory thereof constitute Hölderlin's response to the impossibility of self-grounded philosophical reflection; Hölderlin's aim to construct what he called a "poetic logic" (ELT 109) is the response to the subject's loss of harmonious union with the world or nature. Yet the scholarship on Hölderlin's theoretical writings has yet to alter the prevailing understanding of Hölderlin received largely through Heidegger's interpretation of the poems and other scholar's painstaking philological research thereof. The themes of Hölderlin's own thought are overshadowed by the poetic figure of Hölderlin borne of George,[53] Hellingrath, and Heidegger's interpretations; by theories regarding his madness; by the overwhelming grace of his late hymns and their reception by Hölderlin scholars; and by Adorno's paratactic reading of the late poems. Heidegger has been criticized, by and large, only from what Henrich calls a "respectful distance,"[54] and exceptions to this take on largely a rereading of the poems to which Heidegger had paid considerable attention.

If, in taking up Hölderlin, we now have the responsibility of asking to what extent, and how, Heidegger is indebted to Hölderlin for his insights, both those of *Gelassenheit* tenor and those of *Streit*, this can no longer be accomplished in neglect of Hölderlin's own philosophical-poetological projects. The available studies of Heidegger's Hölderlin—from Adorno's critique[55] to those of recent scholars[56]— begin to confront Heidegger with competing interpretations of Hölderlin's poems and with philosophical challenges about the nature of poetic language, but do not yet bring about a dialogue between Heidegger's thought and Hölderlin's *thought*. It is perhaps only now, with the relatively recent publication of Heidegger's Hölderlin lectures in the *Gesamtausgabe*, after decades of philological and philosophical research on Hölderlin's writings and in the emergence of a renewed account of his philosophical importance for Idealism and Romanticism, and in the growing discussion of Heidegger's theory of poetic language, that the *Zwiesprache* Heidegger aims to have had with Hölderlin might involve two fully engaged thinkers of poetic language. If there is a difference to be marked between Heidegger and Hölderlin, one not restricted to a single preempted, but vastly important insight into the problem of the subject, is this difference not to be marked in the sphere of the relation between thinking and poetic language, and therefore, for Heidegger, in the sphere of the *Ereignis* itself? The present project, initiating an examination of Heidegger's dialogue with poetic language—and thereby of the transformations in Heidegger's thinking—through an engaged interpretation of Hölderlin's philosophical-poetological writings, is taken up with a view to this question.

In Heidegger scholarship, with the exception of a few critical studies of the poems, Hölderlin has been understood to be virtually identical, if not identically anticipatory, to Heidegger's own thought.[57] Hölderlin is often collapsed not only with Heidegger but also with Heidegger's other interpretations, particularly with those of Nietzsche and Heraclitus,[58] just as Heidegger sometimes conflates them (GA 39, 123–134; GA 52, 78). While Heidegger employs Hölderlin as a pillar of his critique of the modern subject, we have just begun to ask in this context about Hölderlin's own critique of this subject, the fact that Hölderlin, as has been argued, belongs "explicitly in modernity"[59]—as does his draw toward Greek antiquity—and thus belongs to the problems which emerge in response to the finitude of consciousness.

It is my aim that in this book the oscillating dimensions of Heidegger's readings of poetry and his theory of language—which I have marked here as the problem of *Gelassenheit* and *Streit*, phenomenological revealing and ontological-historical founding—become illuminated philosophically and thoughtfully as an examination of the character of poetic language and its relation to phenomenological disclosure. It is my contention that through an examination of the finitude and form, the special indirectness, of poetic language, a retrieval of the *Gelassenheit* dimension of Heidegger's theory is set to work upon, unravel, and distress the *Streit* and the insistence on founding which have in moments on Heidegger's path saturated the account of poetic language in its unique possibilities for disclosure. If Paul de Man has shown that Heidegger misinterprets the temporality of Hölderlin's writings—and therefore of Hölderlin's theoretical account of "poetic time"—that Heidegger has mistaken Hölderlin for an apocalyptic poet when Hölderlin's work in fact shows a precisely "non-apocalyptic structure,"[60] Heidegger has also missed the critique of hubris inherent in Hölderlin's work—one which, as I hope to show, is supported by Hölderlin's own critique of the subject. The capacities for ontological founding which Heidegger grants the poet are radically compromised by the loss of transcendental and epistemological certainty in Hölderlin's critique of Kant, Fichte, and transcendental philosophy, a loss that the form and procedure of poetic language reflects. I will engage the notion of loss in the chapters that follow insofar as it aids discernment of the Heideggerian-Hölderlinian difference on the question of the subject.

Heidegger's turn to poetic language, elucidating quiet preservation and shelter of what is forgotten or the latter's violent institution, thus mirrors, from this point of view, nothing less than the problem and status of subjectivity in Heidegger's overcoming of metaphysics after his thinking moves away from the self of *Being and Time*. For, it has been argued, in the writings after *Being and Time* the attempt to overcome subjectivity—the rational-technological subject of metaphysics and representation, its violence—nevertheless often employs, until the 1950s, the residue of a violent or decisive will that is attributed either to the essential decisions of history or to the original structure of Being itself.[61] In "The Origin of the Work of Art" this appears as both the "either/or" decision with which Hölderlin confronts the (essentially historical) German people and as the strife between world and earth—in the revealing-concealing of Being—that the work of art instigates. In *Introduction to Metaphysics* this is thought as the violent origins of poetry in its proximity to the lightning-clearing of Being. Heidegger's thinking with regard to poetic language both abandons subjectivity and, at times, ascribes its more aggressive dimensions to the movement of historicality or to poetic-artistic creations.[62] And yet the status of the subject or the self left behind in *Being and Time* reemerges as a problem in Heidegger's readings of poetry. Has poetry, as Heidegger asserts, no subject at all—has it abandoned subjectivity—or does it retain a Nietzschean, eschatological will?

It is pertinent here, at the outset of my argument, to define my terms "subject" and "self," and to clarify how they will be employed in the following chapters. In German philosophy, reference to the "subject" (*Subjekt*) had been in use since at least Kant and German Idealism to denote the conditions of possibility for knowledge and experience—consciousness regarded in its cognitive and universal structures. The subject had to be regarded in radical differentiation from its object, that which was known or experienced. The subject is then a determination of metaphysics, and in Heidegger will be rejected along with the whole "metaphysics of subjectivity" that pervades modern philosophy. For if the subject is, metaphysically speaking, radically differentiated from its object, Heidegger (like other later phenomenologists) wants to show the degree to which a being who experiences and knows the world is primordially involved in it, that its very structure or conditions of possibility are tethered to Being as such. Here are emphasized ontological, rather than primarily rational-cognitive, features, and so Heidegger will use the term *Dasein* in place of subjectivity or "the subject."

The term "self" affords a still richer sense of this involvement. While I will use the term "subject" for the site and structure of the conditions of possibility of experience, the "self" is what it is or becomes in and through this experience. While Heidegger rejects, along with the "'I' itself, the 'subject,'" all traditional connotations of the "self"–insofar as it is taken to mean "something selfsame in manifold otherness" (BT 150/114)–he nevertheless allows for reference to the self in the sense of Dasein's self. Thus the self is not, like Descartes's ego, a metaphysical given, but must be existentially won—for one can "lose" oneself, not be oneself. While its existential structures remain universal, the self is radically altered by the way in which one exists—for instance, authentically or inauthentically.

The term "self" (in German, *Selbst*), although scarcely appearing in Heidegger's later philosophy, also has an important place in his earlier writings. In *Phänomenologie des religiösen Lebens*, the lecture courses of 1919–20 (GA 60), the "self" is one of the three categorical points of analysis (self-world, communal world, and surrounding world–*Selbstwelt, Mitwelt, Umwelt*) of factical life experience, the source and subject matter of philosophy as Heidegger sees it. Both Paul's and Augustine's notions of self are analyzed in phenomenologically intimate terms. The self, as distinct from the subject, includes relational multiplicity, the multiplicity of what Heidegger terms its historical and factical connection to the surrounding world and to others (GA 60, 103–104, 192, 196); it is a "genuinely personal existence" (GA 60, 333). Heidegger's qualified retention of the term *Selbst* will finally erode along with the notion of *Dasein*, when Heidegger ultimately seeks to overcome humanism. He will explicitly reject, along with the metaphysical "subject," the too-humanistic notion of a "self," in particular when it comes to interpreting Hölderlin's poems, as I will make clear in chapter 2.

In Hölderlin's writings, however, both the "subject" and the "self" have a distinct place. If the subject and subjectivity are thought in metaphysical terms of conditions of possibility, Hölderlin poetically reconfigures, but does not reject, this kind of philosophizing. The "subject" will indeed be examined along Kantian lines in Hölderlin's writings, and the basic condition of its separation from the object will be accepted as a problem, to be overcome, too, with poetical or poetological means. The notion of the "self," likewise, does not fall away, but signifies the site of intense personal and historical involvement with the world, according to the conditions of subjectivity as Hölderlin reconfigures them. Thus both terms are needed to adequately render Hölderlin's treatment of the "subject of poetic language"—*subject* suggesting the conditions of possibility of knowledge, judgment, and experience, *self* expanding this notion to include the personal, that is, historical and existential, connection to the world, which compromises the a priori self-certainty of a transcendental subject.

Indeed, in this book I retrieve from Hölderlin a dimension of the "subject of poetic language" that Heidegger left behind in his critique of the modern subject, the presence of which in Hölderlin's writings is a significant, even grounding element of his theory of language and of his critique of philosophy in its epistemological, transcendental, and ontological truth-claims. Although it has been said that Hölderlin's writings resist interpretation, that "the fundamental significance of Hölderlin is not yet understood,"[63] the problem of subjectivity—of what Hölderlin called the "poetic 'I,'" of uniting the "self and world, subject and object"—is found in nearly all of Hölderlin's philosophical-poetological writings, including the preface to and dimensions of *Hyperion*, the "Ground to Empedocles," the essays on Sophoclean tragedy, "Judgment and Being," "Operations of the Poetic Spirit," "On the Law of Freedom," "On the Concept of Punishment," and is addressed in many of Hölderlin's philosophical letters. This dimension of Hölderlin's thought is what I call here the subject of poetic language, the problem of subjectivity, which marks Hölderlin's departure from transcendental philosophy into poetic language. Although Hölderlin shares with Heidegger a critique of transcendental, rationalist subjectivity, particularly of the absolute idealist subject and its cognitive gaze, Hölderlin remains close to the grounds of experience which condition what he calls poetic "receptivity"—a term he borrows from Kantian philosophy, the study of which consumed much of his efforts at the *Tübingen Stift*.[64] This might diverge from Heidegger's attempt to think poetically toward Being as the *Ereignis*, a history of withdrawal in which it can be said that "Being alone is" (EP 79). Hölderlin argues for the possibility of a poetic receptivity to life, joy, the sacred, and earth, a receptivity that characterizes a subject denied transcendental foundations. The notions of the tragic, mourning, the infinite approximation, and consciousness—which in fact makes awareness of Being paradoxically emergent—involve a radical reorientation of philosophy's subject or "I" (*Ich*). Far from what Derrida calls Heidegger's "disqualification of the concept of the 'subject,'"[65] Hölderlin lays the groundwork for an incipient theory of poetic, even analeptic, subjectivity. To draw this out from Hölderlin's writings is thus to argue that between Heidegger's subjectless *Gelassenheit* and the residues of a violent, decisive subjectivity—for both of which Heidegger employs Hölderlin—is to be found a third possibility, one outlined in Hölderlin's philosophical-poetological writings and implicit in the fragile receptivity involved in the disclosure and shelter of poetic language.

To think through Hölderlin from this point of view is to reengage Heidegger's own thinking and to favor, perhaps further, its liberating elements at the expense of the resolute ones. Hölderlin's poetic, analeptic—we could say, *Gelassenheit*—subject not only preserves an element of humanism left behind by Heidegger's critique, but also challenges the capacity of poetic language to found or institute Being, to found or institute history. If this founding role is challenged, the phenomenological truth of poetic language which Heidegger first illuminates remains to reveal a poetic engagement with beings, to disclose beings without quantifying, possessing, and measuring them, and illuminates our poetic dwelling among things and other human beings as bearers of this disclosure which respects the inherent mystery of the world. The capacity of poetic language to disclose beings without rendering them statically present, to grant them their elusive character while bringing them into emergence, indeed constitutes a special relation to Being, if that is understood not as essential, destinal-historical founding but, more phenomenologically, as a granting of emergence into presence, as the elusive self-disclosure of things under the auspices and shelter of words, themselves fragile and elusive. Hölderlin, thus understood as a poetic thinker in his own right, might well have disappointed Heidegger in his attempt to overcome humanism, but he provides the beginnings of an account of subjectivity true to most phenomenological insights. This presses Heidegger's thought to a reconsideration of subjectivity, perhaps, in some sense, a return to some dimensions of the self of *Being and Time* (BT 351/303, 330/285, 370/323). If, as de Man shows, the notion of a self fundamentally belongs to an account of Hölderlin,[66] is there, moreover, not indeed a self who experiences the fragile, finite, elusive disclosure of world that Heidegger illuminates? Is it not this very account required by a Hölderlin's aim for a harmonious dissolution of opposition between "our self and the world, subject and object," which was to be the form of his proposed "New Letters on the Aesthetic Education of Man" (ELT 132)? Is this not, finally, what we would find if we joined Heidegger's phenomenological insights into poetic language—and poetic insights into phenomenology—to the self that inhabits *Being and Time?*[67] This jointure would involve not so much a resolute (*entschlossenes*) Dasein but a precarious one—Heidegger calls it *geworfen*—a self who is concerned as much with nature, art, and communal life as with work and equipment, and for whom history is less a totality of resolute repetition (*Wiederholung*) than an openness to loss, remembrance, and celebration.

Although there could be other points of departure for thinking through the dialogue between Heidegger and Hölderlin, this project is taken up primarily with regard to the subject of poetic language—what I will call in the following seven chapters an incipient theory of poetic subjectivity, initiated, in the main, by Hölderlin's theoretical writings. If Heidegger's adoption of Hölderlin as the poet for thinking issues in the wake of his critique and displacement of subjectivity, Hölderlin—perhaps more naive, perhaps more visionary, more utopian—did not attempt to overcome metaphysics but proposed its radical, poetic reformulation in an account of the subject poetically displaced. The relation of Heidegger's ontology to its phenomenological origins, its turns and transformations, will be taken up in a reengagement of Heidegger's dialogue with Hölderlin. In the penultimate chapter Hölderlin's poetic, *Gelassenheit* subject will be juxtaposed to a theory outlined by Kristeva, for whom any treatment of poetic language is a treatment of the subject, albeit one, in her terms, put "in process/on trial."

The structure of my analysis is thus: I analyze Heidegger's theory of poetic language within the context of his philosophy as a whole, but in particular with regard to the critique of subjectivity, which extends from the Dasein of *Being and Time* to the writings on *Gelassenheit* and technology, and is finally overcome, or set aside, in the thinking of *Ereignis*. Heidegger's phenomenological ontology in its various stages is presented as the context in which his theory of language arises, and Heidegger's lecture courses on Hölderlin,[68] as well as the essays in *Erläuterungen zu Hölderlins Dichtung* and in *On the Way to Language* (*Unterwegs zur Sprache*), are the principle texts of my analysis. I begin by examining the relation of Heidegger's critique of subjectivity as *Seinsvergessenheit* to his theory of language as remembrance, in which the poet appears as a "vessel" (DI 71) of Being's echo, beyond mere feeling and experience (*Erlebnis*) that characterizes the traditional-subjective account of the poetic "I." While the first chapter presents an analysis of the self in *Being and Time* as an alternative to the subject-ego of modern philosophy and Husserlian phenomenology, the penultimate chapter returns to this self in dialogue with Hölderlin and contemporary poetic theories, yet there I will also show the limitations of revolutionary poetics in light of a phenomenology of poetical experience and creation. The aim of chapter 1 is primarily to set Heidegger's turn to poetic language within the context of phenomenological ontology and his critique of the subject as forgetful of Being, such that the turn to poetic language as remembrance is contextualized according to its phenomenological and ontological transitions. The metaphysics of subjectivity is for Heidegger the basis of *Seinsvergessenheit*, and it is to Hölderlin that Heidegger turns for an account of *Andenken* or poetic, non-subjective remembrance of Being, origin, and historical essence, as we see in chapter 2. I show here in what ways Heidegger's path of thinking from the self of *Being and Time* to the history of Being to the *Ereignis* — and thus the transformations of phenomenological ontology — is indebted to his readings of Hölderlin.

If the problem of language is for Heidegger grounded in the relation of Being to subjectivity as its "forgetting," the relation of Being and the subject is for Hölderlin grounded in a theory of language. In chapter 3, I argue that for Hölderlin the elusiveness of Being — its ineffability in concepts — is thought according to a critique of Kant and transcendental philosophy. For Hölderlin this involves, furthermore, the analeptic character of the subject, a perhaps impossible restoration from the subject's loss of grounds, a loss implied by Hölderlin's notion of judgment (*Urtheil*) as the original separation of subject and object.

An account of the liberating elements of Heidegger's critique of humanism and of the modern subject requires, moreover, a consideration of his critique of technology, which comprises chapter 4. If Heidegger overlooks the complexities of Hölderlin's engagement with metaphysical problems — judgment, reason, and reflection — he situates Hölderlin's contributions nevertheless within a radical alternative to the technological domination of the earth, thus bringing to thinking Hölderlin's poetizing of the sacredness of nature. It is here discussed that Heidegger's critique of technology promises a poetic dwelling — a non-anthropocentric relation to earth and nature; I further suggest that while Heidegger releases thinking to a liberating relation to earth, he nevertheless overlooks a humanism, indeed a non-anthropocentric one, which Hölderlin's theory of language offers. Thus a Hölderlinian reformulation of the subject escapes the technological will Heidegger ascribes to subjectivity as such and opens up the subject of poetic language to *Gelassenheit* dwelling vis-à-vis the earth or nature. It is particularly the poetics of "life," drawn from Kantian aesthetics, that can articulate a poetical receptivity of the natural world.

In chapter 5 I investigate what Heidegger, after Hölderlin, calls "poetic dwelling," and take up the aforementioned "twofoldedness" which haunts this dwelling in Heidegger's account. The *Gelassenheit* thinking, as a nonaggressive listening, is seen to be complicated by a violent institution of truth that Heidegger, in the 1930s and 1940s, has ascribed to the poetic vocation and to the origins of poetic language. Here I outline Hölderlin's own political thought, though preserved only in letters and a few short essays. The faithfulness Hölderlin maintains to community and human social concerns presses his reader to confront political questions from an alternative stance than the nationalism in which Heidegger's thought became entrenched, and perhaps even from the form of what has been called Heidegger's "counterpolitical" turn. The question of Hölderlin as "poet of the Germans" is then to be taken up as both an ontological and a political one.

In chapter 6, the incipient subject of poetic language, which I have outlined according to my interpretation of Hölderlinian sources and which I have argued is to a considerable extent compatible with Heidegger's *Gelassenheit*, will be analyzed in terms of accounts of subjectivity in contemporary continental poetic theory. The most compelling of such accounts is to be taken up with regard to Kristeva's "subject in process/on trial." Albeit less extensively, I will also examine some articulations pertaining to poetic subjectivity by Valéry and Blanchot. For Kristeva, the subject is illuminated in poetic language, and is shown to be transcendentally ungroundable, compromised in its self-possession, a fluctuation between identity and alterity. Thus an engagement with her theory of poetical revolution is called for. Kristeva's notion that the poetic subject admits alterity from within, and is thus revolutionary, can add nuance to the Heidegger-Hölderlin dialogue on the notions of the foreign and the proper, the uncanniness of the human being's relation to Being and the wandering induced by that relation. Nevertheless, I will claim that the negative dimensions of Kristevian poetical revolution, in its conscription to Freudian notions of repression and negative drives, limits Kristeva's contribution to a new theory of the poetic subject. The view I will advance as a new poetics of Dasein, rather, will emphasize the spontaneity of poetical creation, which, I argue, far exceeds and thus ought not be reduced to Kristeva's notion of the semiotic drives. Moreover, the subject of poetic language that she proposes is always one broken down and shattered; while this speaks to a major aspect of the Hölderlinian-inspired subject I have outlined throughout this book, namely loss and the tragic, it neglects the analeptic or restorative element of poetical creation. Such an account, as I hope to provide in sketch in the final chapter, requires a reconception of the poetical imagination, which is neglected in the post-metaphysical poetics of both Kristeva and Heidegger.

In the final chapter I am able to propose what I hope is an original poetics of Dasein sketched out in the wake of the analysis of the subject of poetic language throughout this book. Here I draw in outline a new theory of poetical Dasein, a theory of poetic language rooted in an understanding of the self poetically conceived. Beyond the poetics and poetry of Hölderlin, I propose a theoretical structure—a continuum of poetical stances that I mark between interpretations of Arthur Rimbaud on one hand and Rainer Maria Rilke on the other—that can articulate the possibilities for the subject of poetic language and thus make phenomenological sense of the subject of much of modern poetical language since Hölderlin. In order to do so I engage Heidegger's notion of the self in *Being and Time* and first suggest that this self, given Heidegger's critique of humanism or anthropocentrism, can be rehabilitated in poetic, *Gelassenheit* fashion. I am especially concerned to show how poetical experience is relevant for the disclosure of "world," now poetically rather than practically conceived, and how the self's experience and structure is always implied in this disclosure. Yet history and the relation of the self to historical truth are to be unlocked from the totality of Dasein's authentic resoluteness, its return to itself— and thus from a people and its destiny. The elusiveness of poetical truth renders poetical founding and totality impossible, since it implies the vulnerability of human existence to loss and finitude. This vulnerability is, however, also emblematic of a unique kind of poetical cognition and an access to what I call poetical truth. From Rimbaudian disorientation to Rilkean clarity, a layer of the self's experience can be glimpsed through poetic language, and it is the structure of this experience, and the poetical truth to which it attests, of which I aim to give an account. I argue, contrary to most current post-Heideggerian poetics, that the imagination must be phenomenologically rehabilitated in order to understand poetic language as a site of genuine creation.

Heidegger's thought—in its sensitivity to that which exceeds the limits of conceptual sayability, in its phenomenological-ontological alternative to a world grasped as mere presence and actuality, in its redirection of philosophical thinking to a unique, rigorous kind of listening, and in its insights about the phenomenologically disclosive possibilities of poetic language—is thus to be engaged in a dialogue with the philosophical-poetic thought of Hölderlin and to be brought beyond it toward a new possibility of conceiving the subject of poetic language. This engagement is to lead beyond their dialogue toward a poetics of existence that is not only ontologically profound but also phenomenologically convincing. My theory of the poetic subject confirms not the resoluteness or decision, *Streit* or *Stiften,* but rather a radical *Gelassenheit.* For the specific nature of truth inherent in poetic language reveals the fragility of both self and world. This a new poetics of Dasein must address.

1

Heidegger's Critique of Subjectivity and the Poetic Turn

The Context of Phenomenological Ontology

Heidegger's poetics, especially its Hölderlinian elements, can be understood only within the context of a consideration of his theory of Being in its broader development. Important here is that the trajectory of Heidegger's ontological concerns spans several stages from his early treatments of facticity to his later theory of language, and at each stage the strategies of phenomenological engagement shift accordingly. At each stage, however, it can be said that a continuity with the whole of Heidegger's thought—despite the well-known notion of the "turn" and the suggestion of a radical break with his earlier work—is maintained by the persistence of a dual concern: a critique of the modern model of subjectivity, and the analysis of the subject's "forgetting" of Being. What ontological profits Heidegger aims to yield from his interpretations of Hölderlin must be situated in this continuity; for it is to Heidegger's conviction that the metaphysics of subjectivity has exhausted itself in the near-final oblivion of Being that Hölderlin's poetry is said to offer a radical alternative. This alternative of a poetics beyond subjectivity will be examined in chapter 2, insofar as Heidegger eliminates subjective elements from interpretation of the poems. In the present chapter I trace Heidegger's philosophy through the guiding motif of the subject's "forgetting" and its relationship on one hand to facticity and on the other to artistic-poetical creation. My claim is that there is an ever-evolving tension between Heidegger's phenomenological and ontological aims, a relationship that undergoes substantial revision throughout the transformations in his thought.[1] Ultimately I will argue that Heidegger's poetic theory loses phenomenological clarity when Being is articulated as an historical destiny. In later chapters of this book I aim to restore phenomenological principles to the study of poetic language and the structure of its subject.

Heidegger's poetic theory, and his view of the work of art in general, articulates an instigation of truth and its disclosure, marking a radical turn away from "forgetting." What makes his articulation worthy of critical scrutiny is, further, the way in which such instigation is said to require inevitable error. Such error is concordant with Heidegger's understanding of fate (*Schicksal*), also inseparable from the notion of the history of Being (*Seinsgeschichte*) that Heidegger articulates as the ontological complex of forgetting and remembrance. The relationship between freedom and error must be taken into account if we can answer the political and methodological questions that arise in poetics beyond subjectivity, as well as posit an alternative account of the subject of poetic language. Both freedom and error (in the form of a critique of hubris) arise as concerns in Hölderlin's own poetic theory—albeit with residues of Enlightenment and Romantic thinking Heidegger seeks to overcome, as I will show in chapter 3. Error is inevitable for Heidegger because poetic language, as he sees it, is a dangerous task of venturing beyond the bounds of humanism; freedom is collapsed into the fate of this venturing. While Heidegger is right to highlight error as possibly attending poetical articulation, given the partiality of the latter, such error is ascribable not to destinal sending but to the fragility of the relationship between poetical experience and truth. Freedom as Heidegger sees it is intertwined with the notion of destiny; I will argue, in chapter 7, for a notion of freedom that pertains to the spontaneity of poetic language.

In order to outline the phenomenological and ontological movements in Heidegger's thought, we begin with a brief outline of what Heidegger calls phenomenological ontology (BT 62/38): a method of uncovering what grounds our experience but is forgotten when we articulate it. For Heidegger the human being is characterized as having a familiarity with Being, which determines how we encounter the world. This familiarity also constitutes our transcendence; for as familiar with Being, human life structures a horizon against which beings appear, and the ecstatic temporality of our history, our present engagements, and our projects render that horizon one of temporal disclosure. In his early writings, Heidegger names the process and texture of this life "factical life experience," or facticity (*Faktizität*); in *Being and Time* it is tethered to the existential self (*Selbst*) and its unity in care (*Sorge*); in the later writings it is taken up, beyond the subject or self, in a theory of language. In contradistinction to Heidegger's aims, the philosophy of subjectivity—Heidegger's emblem for the philosophy of modernity from Leibniz to Hegel and Husserl—accounts for the relation between thinking and world on the basis of a presumed opposition between the subject of reason/cognition and its object; the philosophy of subjectivity thus fails to grasp this relationship as disclosure—of the presence and absence of beings on the part of the human being as transcendence, a relation that belongs not to the subject's faculties (or even, after *Being and Time*, to the self's ecstatic temporality) but to Being itself. The world is for the Heidegger of *Being and Time* comprised not merely of entities or objects constituted by consciousness or cognition, but of structures of concern that determine how entities come to be present for us. This coming to be present is a *process* of coming into presence; but this process is conditioned by the structure of our making-present, which in turn presupposes our unique relation to Being. To presence means "letting that which has environmental presence be encountered"[2]; and this letting-be encountered is precisely what poetic language will accomplish. Contrary to Husserlian phenomenology, the world is not constituted by a transcendental ego, but is rather relative to the existing self for whom this existence, its own Being, is a matter of concern (*Sorge*). Heidegger must then pose the question of Being as such in an analysis of how these concerns structure the self (*Dasein*, Heidegger's term for human existence). After *Being and Time*, Heidegger shifts the focus of phenomenological ontology from an analysis of Dasein to that of Being as such. Ontology is to become more radical, a thinking of Being without its being grounded in beings or in Dasein. It is no longer Dasein but language that discloses beings; and language is not considered a possession or a capacity, but rather involves the human beings in the emergence into presence of beings and in what Heidegger will call the "happening" (*Geschehen*) of truth. That is to say, Being is understood according to a history of its own self-disclosure and withdrawal, a history that comes to utterance in language. If the history of metaphysics has forgotten Being—and the technological objectification of the world is the counterpart of this forgetting, as we will discuss in chapter 4—the task at metaphysics' end is its recollection, one that takes on historical dimensions.

In the writings after *Being and Time*, the historical dimension of Being concerns no longer the historicality (*Geschichtlichkeit*) of Dasein's own temporality (*Zeitlichkeit*), but rather the *Seinsgeschichte*, and the task of thinking a "history of Being" concerns overcoming the forgetting of Being on the part of subjectivity—both in philosophy, as metaphysics, and in the world of engagement, as technological manipulation that "enframes" (*Ge-stell, stellt*) the earth. Heidegger's task becomes the discovery of the unclaimed, silent ground of Western thought, one that this history has forgotten, one that remains unthought. Heidegger abandons the structural argumentation found in *Being and Time* in favor of a hermeneutic interpretation—a *Wiederholung* or repetition—of the history of philosophy, one that becomes a meditation, a sojourn into this unthought—into what for Heidegger is a "path of thinking" that, as Heidegger claims, remains under way as a preparation for a "new beginning" of thinking.[3] This new beginning takes on an intensely poetical tenor, for Heidegger now claims that "all reflective thinking is poetic, and all poetry is in turn a kind of thinking" (OWL 136).

Heidegger's turn to a theory of poetic language as the source for ontological truth attends his formulation of the *Seinsgeschichte*, which aims at recollection, or remembrance, of the origin in the commencement of a new, other history. Heidegger employs the notion of gathering (*Versammlung*) to render historically dimensional the remembrance, *Andenken*, of Being. *Andenken* institutes a commencement of thinking after the completion of metaphysics and in its wake. *Andenken* is not the intentional recollection of a subject but occurs beyond the realm of that subject or self, occurs for a being—poet or thinker—who has transcended subjectively grounded, metaphysical, representational thinking. Being, as historical, is the groundless ground of all philosophical utterance; as historical, it is grounded in its own self-sending, destined, throughout its transformations, its decay in the history of metaphysics, toward the crisis that for Heidegger defines modernity and the technological situation to which it has led. It is this crisis that allows the commencement to appear.[4] The self-concealing of Being becomes a forgetting (ZSD 55–57), one that, Heidegger thinks, is nearly complete; yet at this near completion, a time of "extreme danger," Heidegger's reorientation for thinking aims as a "turning around" (*Umwendung*) of forgetting, a recollecting. Heidegger discovers, in poetry and particularly the poetry of Hölderlin, the saying of Being that guides us to a "saving"—to the finding of a way just when it becomes apparent that we are, with all of our technological achievements, lost.

Thus it can be said that Heidegger's adoption of Hölderlin as the poet of the "new beginning"[5] is issued in the critique of subjectivity as the forgetting of Being. Although the critique of subjectivity does not exhaust Heidegger's overcoming of metaphysics, it is informed by every factor of his critique, conceptualizing Being as what he calls the metaphysics of presence: technological thinking, scientific rationality, humanism, and anthropocentrism. The history of the subject—culminating in various essential historical-philosophical moments, for instance in Descartes, Hegel, Nietzsche—is, according to Heidegger, a history of forgetting, at the end of which philosophy has exhausted its capacities for a thinking of Being. Subjectivity appears to be self-given and immediate and does not have to ask the question of its own being; it is "more than any other entity 'certain' (of itself)" and "assures itself by positing itself as the foundation of beings"; it is "conceived of as the true a priori"; finally the subject "is conceived of in the context of its opposition to objects."[6] In Heidegger's account the human being, as subject, reduces the world to an object at its own disposal, forgetting to wonder at the presence of things. What Heidegger calls thinking (*denken*) as "thanking" (*danken*) for such presence is not an ontological religiosity[7] but a phenomenological sensitivity to the twofold dimension of appearances, a twofoldedness grounded in the ontological structure of truth, which Heidegger names *aletheia*.[8] Phenomenology has provided the insight that the appearance of things is always only partial, that beings appear only against the background of a horizon that does not; Heidegger's ontology adds that this partiality is rooted not merely in the transcendental conditions of rational subjectivity, as in Kant, but in the structure of presence and absence that truth, as *aletheia*, is. Not only is Being self-withdrawing in the appearance of beings, it appears and withdraws throughout the epochs of a history that can be "read" in the progress or regress of philosophical ontology, which remembers what has withdrawn or forgets it in obliviousness (PR 91). It is this history that has wandered into a crisis of withdrawal. Poetry, and most essentially the poetry of Hölderlin, provides a way out of this withdrawal, out of the "darkness of the world's night" (PLT 94) of forgetting, for Hölderlin's poetry is a courageous venture into that darkness—an investigation of that withdrawal—in order to uncover poetically a new beginning, beyond subjectivity (DI 165). Poetry offers a language in which beings are revealed in a relation to Being, which ordinarily withdraws itself in the very appearance of things; as historical, it is, for Heidegger, a collecting of lost traces, a gathering of signs, which provides the way for a thinking not grounded in subjective conditions but, Heidegger thinks, in Being itself, to which we might "listen."

I have claimed that Heidegger's analysis of forgetting in our relation to Being is found long before his explicit turn to Hölderlin. Heidegger diagnoses "forgetfulness" in his early writings on facticity and in *Being and Time*, both of which provide conceptual categories for the later poetics, albeit ones that will be significantly transformed. We now turn to these works in order to place Heidegger's turn to Hölderlin in the context of his phenomenological ontology as a whole, and to account for the depths of connection between Heidegger's poetic "turn" and the continuities along his path.

Forgetting and the Analysis of Facticity

Let us trace then the notion of facticity, an early anchor of Heidegger's analysis of forgetting that is carried through the principal currents of Heidegger's thought. One incipient thematization of forgetting (*vergessen*) is found in the 1920–21 lectures, *Phänomenologie des religiösen Lebens*, which are concerned directly with the problem of facticity. These lectures are particularly helpful for our thesis because here Heidegger takes up phenomenology as the method for investigating the "lifeworld" (*die Lebenswelt*), wherein phenomenology is not to remain theoretically distanced from its object of study, but indeed to effect a "turning around" of the forgetting tendencies that belong to factical life experience. Heidegger finds in the phenomenological method (altered, certainly, from its Husserlian form) an access to the realm of the pre-theoretical, what is original to factical life experience but is forgotten in its scientific articulation. It is in such access that phenomenology, Heidegger claims, "is not a preliminary science of philosophy but philosophy itself" (GA 60, 22); that is to say, phenomenology is already conceived as a kind of remembering, a prefiguration—still within the philosophical terminology he will later set aside—of the turn to Hölderlin as the poet of *Andenken* or remembrance.

In these lectures of winter 1920–21 (GA 60), and further in those of the summer of 1923 on the "hermeneutics of facticity" (GA 63), phenomenology *is* for Heidegger the phenomenology of factical life. Before philosophical concepts, before the theorizing of life on the part of science and philosophy, the world is experienced as facticity. "Facticity" is a term that arose in theology in a "dispute over faith in the Resurrection," but for Heidegger refers to life in its process and performance, "to the fact of its being a fact," to the elements of experience "behind which one cannot go."[9] Giorgio Agamben has shown that the category of facticity plays a significant role in Heidegger's displacement of Husserl's notion of intentionality.[10] Facticity, moreover, "marks Heidegger's reformulation of the question of Being in an essential manner."[11] In factical life experience we have a tendency to forget the performance-nature of our being; and philosophy, as a higher-order reflection of this tendency, and in its struggle to define itself as the origin of the sciences, has forgotten its origins in factical life; the latter, Heidegger thinks, should be philosophy's point of departure (*Ausgangspunkt*) (GA 60, 10–11, 16). Phenomenology is factical life's own address to itself, but one that runs counter to factical life's own attitudinal tendencies; for forgetting, which Heidegger will associate with the notion of fallenness, is a fundamental trait of facticity.[12] This is not yet described as a problem of subjectivity, a problem of one who experiences, but rather as a reflection of the experience itself; for the rich texture of the lifeworld resists thematization.[13]

The hermeneutics of facticity acknowledges that "life" and "life experience" can be an object of analysis only by threatening to reduce its performance or process to a content. A phenomenology of factical life experience begins by acknowledging that "I myself experience not even my own ego in isolation, but I am as such always caught up in the surrounding world ["der Umwelt verhaftet"]" (GA 60, 13). This experience of self is not merely theoretical reflection or an inner perception, since the "experience itself has a worldly character" (GA 60, 13). Philosophy's aim is not to exhaust factical life experience by clarifying it as object for a subject, but rather to point, in what Heidegger calls a "formal indication,"[14] to this experience, such that it becomes accessible without being reduced to the transparency and fixity of philosophical concepts.

Yet if philosophy heretofore has tended to forget its origins in factical life experience, has adopted the scientific prejudice of objectivity, has attempted to reduce factical life experience to its philosophical cognition, this tendency does not come, as it were, from above. The tendency to forget factical life experience belongs, Heidegger thinks, to factical life experience itself. He writes: "The falling tendency of factical life experience ["die abfallende Tendenz der faktischen Lebenserfahrung"], constantly tending toward the significant connections of the factically experienced world, its gravity, as it were, conditions a tendency of factically lived life toward the attitudinal determination and regulation of objects (GA 60, 17)." Just as Heidegger will later argue that Being has a tendency to hide itself in a logic of beings, factical life experience, Heidegger claims, "constantly strives toward articulation in the sciences and ultimately toward a scientific culture" (GA 60, 15); for its experience is the "taking-cognizance-of" (*die Kenntnisnahme*) objects with an indifference to the manner of the experiencing of those objects. It is indifferent because it has self-sufficiency (*Selbstgenugsamkeit*) in its concerns; it does not need to ask about the "how" of experience. It thus "falls into significance" (*Bedeutsamkeit*), in which it is absorbed in the complexes of significance (*Bedeutungszusammenhänge*) among things that appear, among its objects. In this "falling tendency," Heidegger claims, "a complex of objects [*Objecktszusammenhang*] increasingly forms and increasingly stabilizes itself. In this way one arrives at a *logic of the surrounding world* ["einer Logik der Umwelt"]" (GA 60, 17). Factical life experience is not only the point of departure for philosophy, it is also "what essentially hinders philosophizing itself ["was das Philosophieren selbst wesentlich behindert"]" (GA 60, 16), for philosophy has followed the prejudice (*das Vorurteil*) inherent to factical life experience in forgetting facticity (itself) in favor of the logic of objects.

Here Heidegger presents a template of his later thesis concerning the *Seinsgeschichte,* and the tendency of Being to elude the grasp of the metaphysical concepts that prevail throughout the history of philosophy. Philosophy, insofar as it is guilty of the scientific prejudice, is a transcendental forming of such object-domains (as in "Plato's world of ideas"), but "the attitude toward objects . . . remains identically the same" in scientific philosophy as in science proper (GA 60, 17). Whereas later Heidegger turns to poetic language, here Heidegger entrusts the phenomenological method with providing a turning around of this attitudinal falling.

Dasein's Forgetting

Fallenness and Inauthenticity

The falling tendency (*abfallende Tendenz*) that is a part of factical life experience anticipates the notion of fallenness (*Verfallen*) in *Being and Time.*[15] Fallenness is the tendency of Dasein to become absorbed in the world of beings within which it tarries, to become caught up in the details of life, in presence, without noticing its own Being-there. Of course, a certain kind of forgetting (*Vergessen*) is necessary to Dasein's Being-there, for the functioning of everyday life and Dasein's engagements therein. Heidegger writes:

> A specific kind of forgetting is essential for the temporality that is constitutive for letting something be involved. The Self must forget itself if, lost in the world of equipment, it is to be able "actually" to go to work and manipulate something (BT 405/354).

This practical necessity is, even if it is inauthentic, related to the ontological question that defines Dasein as a "Being-there."

Even the forgetting of something, in which every relationship of Being towards what one formerly knew has been seemingly obliterated, must be conceived as a modification of the primordial Being-in; and this holds for every delusion and for every error (BT 90/62).

The "ontological priority of the question of Being" (BT 32–35/11–16) means for Heidegger the posing of the question of Being as the question of fundamental ontology, upon which "all other ontologies can take their rise" (BT 32/11). *Being and Time* begins with the "Necessity for Explicitly Restating the Question of Being" (§1) and the first sentence of this paragraph is: "This question today has been forgotten" (BT 21/2). Because the forgetting of the question of Being is not only a philosophical prejudice but one that belongs to "everyday life," the question of Being can only be "sought in the *existential analytic of Dasein*" (BT 34/13).

The notion of forgetting thus introduces the problem of inauthenticity. Ontically, it is possible that Dasein, which "decides its existence" (BT 33/12), neglects its possibility to be itself, a possibility that is determined by its relationship to Being. But even in inauthenticity, even in neglecting the question of its own Being, Dasein is not far from this question. Both authenticity and inauthenticity are modes of factical life; but now Heidegger claims that forgetting the question of Being is a modification of remembering, even if it is ontically prior. For the question of Being, by virtue of the question of its own Being, is what distinguishes Dasein ontically as ontological. Even as inauthentic:

Dasein's Being is an issue for it in a definite way; and Dasein comports itself toward it in the mode of average everydayness, even if this is only the mode of fleeing *in the face of it* and forgetfulness *thereof* (BT69/44).

Forgetting is, moreover, the inauthenticity of Dasein's self-forgetting, wherein Dasein "gets dragged along" in its thrownness. Here Dasein's authentic "possibility of itself" is endangered by forgetting. As inauthentic, Dasein:

never arrives at any other ecstatical horizon ["ekstatischen Horizont"] of its own accord, unless it gets brought back from its lostness by a resolution ["im Entschluss aus ihrer Verlorenheit zurückgeholt"], so that both the current situation and therewith the primordial 'limit-situation' ["ursprungliche 'Grenzsituation'"] of

Being-towards-death will be disclosed as a moment of vision which has been held on to (BT 400/348–349).

In facing its own death as its own, in being-towards-death (*das Sein zum Tode*), Dasein is awakened from its slumber and distraction—from its forgetting—by the question of its own finitude, and therefore awakened to the question of its Being. Dasein is, as the one who experiences death, the being for whom its own Being, the "possibility of itself" (BT 33/12), is a concern (*Sorge*), one illuminated by the call of conscience, by uncanniness (*Unheimlichkeit*). If in inauthenticity, the "self of the self-forgetful 'I am concerned' shows itself as something simple which is constantly selfsame but indefinite and empty" (BT 322/277), in the call of conscience, "uncanniness pursues Dasein and is a threat to the lostness in which it has forgotten itself" (BT 322/277). This call (*Ruf*) of conscience, which turns Dasein away from forgetfulness, anticipates the poet's calling (*Beruf*) Heidegger will examine two decades later in the essay "Wozu Dichter?" ("What are Poets For?").

In keeping with Heidegger's critique of subjectivity, the structures of worldhood are irreducible to an absolute ego that is divorced not only from its world but also from the ecstatic temporality of worldhood and Being-in-the-world; Dasein signifies, then, Heidegger's destruction of the subject-object distinction of metaphysics, which relies upon the category of presence and "forgets" a prior relation to the world. This forgetting belongs not exclusively to Dasein but also to Being itself. Already Heidegger refers to Heraclitus in his understanding of the twofold character of forgetting that will come to dominate his later concerns: forgetting Being is not only our forgetting, but is Being's withdrawal; Being "sinks back into hiddenness" (BT 262/219). Heidegger claims that "withdrawal . . . must come to thinking as such; facticity must show itself in its concealment and opacity."[16] A relationship to Being turns out to have the structure of Being's own self-showing: the *aletheia*-structure of unconcealedness and hiddenness. Just as the tendency to forget in factical life experience belongs to the structures of factical life itself, the tendency to forget the unique relation to Being that makes up human Dasein is not a matter of Dasein's self-determination beyond a concern for Being but is grounded in Dasein's own thrownness (*Geworfenheit*). *Verfallen* is a mode of forgetfulness that is made possible by Dasein's finding itself amidst a world of beings; fallenness is then Dasein's forgetting, an ambiguity and a hazy idleness, a being distracted by the falling tendency of everyday life rather than "taking hold of" it as informed by its deeper, ontological structures. Thus fallenness is Dasein's mode of forgetting. In terms recalling

Kierkegaard's analysis of modernity, Heidegger defines its elements as "idle talk" (*Gerede*), "curiosity" (*Neugier*), and "ambiguity" (*Zweideutigkeit*) (BT §36–38). Idle talk, a kind of empty everyday speech, such as gossip or small talk, amounts to "perverting the act of disclosing" that belongs to an authentic relation to beings and their Being. Therefore idle talk has been "uprooted existentially" (BT 212–214/168–170). Curiosity is "concerned with the constant possibility of distraction," with novelty, seeing "*just* in order to see," with "abandoning itself to the world." It is characterized by "not tarrying alongside what is closest"—that is, the ontological origin—in a "never dwelling anywhere" (*Aufenthaltslosigkeit*) (BT 214–217/170–173). Ambiguity is determined in terms of discourse, wherein one pretends to disclose, but really covers over, an understanding of the world. Ambiguity demands that understanding be "accessible to everyone," in which it becomes impossible to decide "what is disclosed and what is not," and is juxtaposed by Heidegger to "reticence" (BT 217–218/173–174). In these aspects, fallenness is a tendency of Being-in-the-world, just as Heidegger had earlier characterized the falling attitudinal tendency as a tendency of factical life experience.

The Ontological Difference and the Facticity of Dasein's Relations Within the World

Yet authenticity affords a countermovement; authentic Dasein is not so much caught up with beings, in the manner of treating Being itself as a being, but asks the question of Being in a manner illuminated by Dasein's own ecstatic temporality. Heidegger's thinking here involves the ontological difference, the difference between Being and beings, which delineates Heidegger's ontology long after he leaves behind the existential analytic of Dasein in favor of language as the site of disclosure. Heidegger defines the ontological difference in the 1949 preface to the third edition of the 1929 essay "Vom Wesen des Grundes" or "The Essence of Ground." He writes:

The ontological difference is the "not" between beings and Being. Yet just as Being, as the "not" in relation to beings, is by no means a nothing in the sense of a nihil negativum, so too the difference, as the "not" between beings and Being, is in no way merely the figment of a distinction made by our understanding (ens rationis) (P 97).

In *Being and Time* the distinction between Being and beings, and that between Dasein and other entities, is crucial for understanding the problem of forgetting. Dasein's forgetting is grounded in both the fact that Dasein is unlike other entities—by virtue of its facticity and thrownness into a situation, or world—and that it has the capacity to ask the question of Being by means of the question of its own Being. The question of Being comes ontologically *prior to*—even if ontically posterior to—Dasein's absorption by everyday life, as a possibility illuminated by death. Thus Heidegger calls his analysis of Dasein's relation to Being one of "a priori" structures.[17] An authentic philosophy, as fundamental ontology, must not only lay out "the meaning [*Sinn*] of Being in general" (BT 31/11), but also investigate that being for whom these structures are a matter of special concern; such an ontology must take on both the disclosing and obscuring elements of the life of this being, and thus must take on the process of disclosure and withdrawal itself. This process *is* the concern of ontology per se. In *Verfallenheit*, or forgetting the question of Being, Dasein is caught up in the present, in beings of the world as present; Dasein does not yet understand itself as opened to the space of presencing as the clearing-movement of the "possible." Forgetting is in many stages of Heidegger's thought viewed as the state of being snagged up by particular beings; in the "Letter on Humanism," Heidegger writes that "forgetting the truth of Being in favor of the pressing throng of beings unthought in their essence is what *Verfallen* means in *Being and Time*" (LH 212).

We remember, however, that although the question of Being is ontologically prior to the absorption in everyday life wherein this question is forgotten, the latter is ontically prior. The specificity of Dasein's relations within the world ("innerhalb der Welt") (BT 33/13), and the particular singularity that defines Dasein ontologically, must be taken up within an analysis of Dasein's concerns, as a factical, finite being, that is to say, as a being who has a relation of possibility to beings, Being, and itself. For "the question of existence never gets straightened out except through existing itself" (BT 33/12). The question of Being for Dasein does not entail a divestment from the realm of particular beings, even if Heidegger's concern is the "turning around" from beings to the question of Being. For the question of existence is a question that Dasein harbors even in its inauthenticity and distraction. Dasein exists as facticity, and so cannot be thought outside its situation in the midst of beings. Dasein's facticity is its very freedom, being always in excess of beings and grounding them as what they are.[18] There is a "double life" of Dasein as absorbed in the world and "insofar as it constitutes the world," awakened to the temporal structure that underlies this world-constituting.[19] Nevertheless, Heidegger outlines an awakened

Dasein — Heidegger calls it a "rapture" (*Entrückung*) and a "moment of vision" (*Augenblick*) — not unlike Husserl's transcendental (if not more ecstatic) reduction wherein Dasein "becomes manifest to itself in an immediate manner, that is, independently of all reference to the world." As involved in the world of beings, Dasein is lost to itself; as "exiled from the world," Dasein finds itself authentically.[20] But in either situation, in the distraction in the world of entities or awakened to the ontological (groundless) ground of Dasein's ecstatic finitude, the ontological structures of Dasein's existentiality must be grounded in the ontic existence of Dasein and thus in the presence of beings. Heidegger writes, "can ontological Interpretation do anything else than base itself on *ontical possibilities* — ways of potentiality for Being — and project these possibilities upon their *ontological possibility?*" (BT 360/312). Thus there is no "exile" from the world after the moment of the "rapture" of the call of conscience. For this reason, Heidegger is able to maintain a formulation of the question of Being as the most concrete question (BT 29/9).

Yet in the essay-lecture "Time and Being," some three decades after the publication of *Being and Time*, the ontological difference — the grounding of beings in Being — is set aside altogether.[21] For Heidegger no longer attempts to think the "meaning of Being" according to the temporal unity of Dasein's ecstasis, but aims instead to think Being "without beings" (OTB, 24). Between *Being and Time* and "Time and Being," Heidegger's thinking turns to an interpretation and *Wiederholung* of Hölderlin. We will see a tension in Heidegger's poetics — a tension we will have to clarify in the chapters that follow — between its concrete rootedness in the earth and in things enfolded within the fourfold, and its striving to obviate any form of reduction of Being to the realm of beings. This is, I argue, the source of the tension between phenomenological insight and the reign of ontology.

From Forgetting to Remembrance in Poetic Language

Heidegger turns from Dasein's self-forgetfulness to *Seinsvergessenheit*, both as the forgetting of Being on the part of thinking and as Being's withdrawal. The "not" between Being and beings, which constitutes the ontological difference, is now the site of the interstice or "between" (PR 60; LH 229) of that withdrawal, which the human being experiences as an "uncanniness." This is no longer the uncanniness of Dasein's ecstatic self, but is attributed to Being's own self-concealing movement, which, beyond the space opened by the self's practical engagement with beings, is now thought according to the history of Being, the *Seins-geschichte* (EP 79; PR 64–66). In the "Letter on Humanism" Heidegger announces a turn from the "still dominant" metaphysics that had not yet been fully overcome in *Being and Time*, for there Heidegger had conditioned Being in the structure of presencing that constitutes Dasein's ecstasis. Thinking after *Being and Time* is to retain, he claims, "the essential help of phenomenological seeing" and dispense "with the inappropriate concern for science and research" that still inhabited Heidegger's earlier terminology; but we find a transfer of concern from the projective horizon of Dasein to the horizon of Being's own clearing (LH 235). The forgetting of Being, as both our forgetting and Being's own sending (*Geschick*) (PR 64–66), reaches its apogee in the philosophy of subjectivity and its humanism, in which Being is reduced to the objectivity of objects, to that presenced according to the conditions of a subject (EP 46–48). The subjectivity of the individual subject is only one moment in this greater "system, thought as the unity of order of knowledge" (EP 48). Thus it must be made clear, in the *Letter on Humanism*, that "Being is illumined for the human being in static projection [*Entwurf*]. But this projection does not create Being." (LH 217) Heidegger must remove the last traces of metaphysical humanism from his thinking of Being, for in humanism Being is thought of as the "most general" being that encompasses all beings or "as the product of a finite subject" (LH 219). The thought of Being as the whole of beings is, Heidegger argues, part and parcel of the philosophy of subjectivity (EP 48). In *The Principle of Reason,* Heidegger writes:

> Subjectivity is the essential lawfulness of reasons which provide [*zu-reicht*] the possibility of an object. Subjectivity does not mean a subjectivism, rather it refers to that lodging of the claim of the principle of reason which today has as its consequence the atomic age in which the particularity, separation, and validity of the individual disappears at breakneck speed in favor of total uniformity. Whether or not we want to look into and attest to it today, all this is based in the *Geschick* of Being as objectness for the subjectivity of Reason . . . its injunction unleashes the universal and total reckoning up of everything as something calculable (PR 80).

Subjectivity is opposed to *Gelassenheit,* for "it does not let beings: be" (LH 228). Language, and in particular poetic language, offers a different, radically nonsubjective relation between the human being and world, a nonobjectifying relation to earth (PR 96). For Heidegger, an attendance to language reveals that:

the human being is never first and foremost the human being on the hither side of the world, as a "subject," whether this is taken as "I" or "We." Nor is he ever simply a mere subject that always simultaneously is related to objects, so that his essence lies in the subject-object relation. Rather, before all this, the human being in his essence is ek-sistent into the openness of Being, into the open region that lights the "between" within which a "relation" of subject to object can "be." (LH 229)

Language and a listening to poetic language constitute an access to the *Geschick* of *Seinsvergessenheit,* a standpoint that "looks back" (PR 61, 75, 88) in remembrance (*Andenken*) (PR 94; EP 75–83). For, as Heidegger argues, "humans only speak inasmuch as they respond to language as the basis of the *Geschick*" (PR 98). Language determines (*be-stimmt*) human beings, such that "in this determining, humans are touched and called forth by a voice [*Stimme*] that peals all the more purely the more it silently reverberates through what speaks" (PR 50). More radically, "the world's destiny is heralded in poetry, without yet becoming manifest as the history of Being" (LH 219). For this manifestation, a thinking that "listens" to poetic language is needed (OWL 82).

The Turn to Language After Being and Time

In the wake of *Being and Time,* Heidegger's thought is characterized by several reformulations of his thinking, both returning to and stepping away from his original point of departure.[22] Language, and a poetic interpretation of the artwork (OWA; QT 35), become the place-site (*Ort, Ortschaft*) of Being; the human being is investigated in its essence not on the basis of its transcendental, a priori structures but in terms of its relationship to Being in language. The elusiveness of Being—its hidden, inexplicable, self-concealing character—is increasingly emphasized, for Being "gives itself and refuses itself simultaneously" (LH 215). In Heidegger's turn to language, the "history of Being now becomes the guiding thread and the primary condition for all phenomenology," though this move constitutes as well a "distance from phenomenology" as classically understood in favor of the "inclusion of the History of Being in every description of phenomena."[23] It remains to be seen to what extent this affords fair attention to phenomena as phenomena; for the emphasis here is on the urgency of Being's remembrance. Heidegger's turn to language articulates a sharpening of his critique of subjectivity, which is now understood as the historical "darkness" of forgetting. Against the philosophy of sub-jectivity and the history of metaphysics, and the maintenance, in *Being and Time*, of the question of Being as that of the Being of beings,[24] Hei-degger's attempt to think Being amounts to a remembrance or a rec-ollection of Being (PR 94; LH 215; EP 75–83); for, he writes, "the most profound oblivion is not-recollecting" (EB 63).

Language—not as the "expression of thinking, feeling, and willing" (OWL 34–36; T 41), not as the communication of speaking subjects (OWL 59, 96–97, 112, 117, 120, 125; LH 212–213), and not as the pos-session or faculty of the human being (OWL 107, 114–115, 121) or of human reason (LH 221)—takes the place of Dasein and marks the pas-sage to the self-giving of Being in its dual character of revealing-conceal-ing. Rather than of Dasein, Heidegger more frequently now writes in terms of *der Mensch*, the human being, or *Menschentum*. Language is now the "primal dimension within which human essence is first able . . . to belong to Being" (T 41). In the earlier thinking of the facticity of Being-in-the-world, Being is not a "what" but a "how," a formulation that involved an orientation not only to but within the world of human life and praxis; here Being is not a "what" but a "happening" (*das Geschehen*), an "event" (*das Ereignis*) (OTB; GA 65). This thought of *Ereignis* is said to be the "repetition and completion of the thought of facticity" we find in Heideg-ger's writings of the 1920s.[25] Yet Heidegger now clarifies that what is to be thought is Being removed from the "pressing throng of beings unthought in their essence" (LH 212).

In this vein, Heidegger formulates one possible mode of poetic dwelling, which Heidegger discovers in his interpretations of Hölder-lin's poetry, and which is characterized by what he names *Gelassenheit*. The latter means a "releasement toward things" (DT 54), a letting-be of beings—made possible by our being in excess of beings. This involves a recognition of Being's elusive, self-concealing, character, an "open-ness to the mystery" of things. Poetry, as the essence of the work of art, is to orient us toward a new listening; Hölderlin is, for Heidegger, the guiding flame of this new orientation. The poet is a preparing, a waiting, a recalling of Being's lost echo. The poet stands, in Heideg-ger, for the renunciation of subjectivity, the renunciation of will, and the acceptance of this task.

The Phenomenological Truth of Poetic Language

The relation to beings in Heidegger's later though is addressed in its full complexity only by outlining Heidegger's theory of the artwork. The engagement with art and poetic language reformulates beings according to a nonsubjectivistic, nonrepresentational account of their emergence into presence. The aim is to undo beings from their extrication in the leveling subject-object distinction of metaphysics, to release things into their relation to Being. The things of the world are accessed more essentially than subjective-metaphysical or technological accounts of reality afford. Heidegger aims to show that things are not merely objects for a subject, and furthermore have not only a worldliness (*Weltlichkeit*) as in *Being and Time,* but involve as well a rootedness in earth; they involve an "earthiness" (*das Erdige*) (OWL 101). Thus the "world" (*Welt*) of *Being and Time* — as the intersignifying sphere of human practical and existential concerns — is coupled in "The Origin of the Work of Art" and thereafter with an account of "earth" (*Erde*). The poetic mode of phenomenological disclosure responds to "the feeling that violence has long been done to the thingly element of things and that thought has played a part in this violence. . . . Can such an assault perhaps be avoided — and how? Only, certainly, by granting the thing, as it were, a free field to display its thingly character directly" (OWA 25). Thus phenomenology's demand "to the things themselves" is now formulated as a liberation from the reductive history of things in metaphysics — reduced to the matter-form distinction, substance-accidents, as the substrate of sense-data. The imposition of a propositional structure (for instance, substance-accidents) on the thing amounts to an "assault" on its thingly character. In contrast, an "attentive dwelling within the sphere of things" illuminates the "self-contained character" of a thing (OWA 157), which is forgotten when its unity is determined as a subjective accomplishment or on the basis of rational principles. Yet even Husserl, whose theory of intentionality resituates the subject in the lifeworld, attributes the thing to the ego's building up of unities, to *constitution.* Heidegger demands to account for beings in their Being, arguing essentially that things are closer to us than are sensations or perceptions or intentionally constituted unities — that, in the world, we hear the storm itself and not our own synthetic accomplishments that build it up. In the turn to poetic language, Heidegger defends the immediacy of the thing from a point of view opened out by the "showing" (*Zeigen*) he argues poetic language affords. In contrast, metaphysical "representation knows nothing immediately perceptual" because it is caught up in the calculation of the conditions of objectivity, wherein "what can be immediately seen when we look at things, the image they offer to immediate sensible intuition, falls away" (OWA 26–27).

Taking up the work of art as a model of a thing, anterior to its determination by metaphysical accounts of thingness, shows how inappropriate those accounts have been for attending to the thing in its phenomenal appearance. While the substance-accidents model "keeps things at arm's length from us, as it were, and sets it too far off," the sensations-model "makes it press too physically upon us. In both interpretations the thing vanishes" (OWA 26). In a phenomenological approach, we can yield ourselves to the "undistorted presencing of the thing." The thing must be "accepted in its own constancy" (OWA 26). While the matter-form distinction of traditional aesthetics comes closest to accepting this constancy, it is likewise "an encroachment upon the thing-being of a thing" in denying this thing its true worldliness. The work of art, on the other hand, as in van Gogh's painting of the peasant shoes, shows the thing in its worldliness and earthiness because it is itself grounded, for Heidegger, in the essence of language as showing. The artwork illuminates that "this equipment belongs to the *earth*, and it is protected in the *world* of the peasant woman. From out of this protected belonging the equipment itself rises to its resting-within-itself" (OWA 34).

While the revealing accomplished by the work of art allows things to be grasped in their Being, Being is itself the happening of truth as unconcealedness (OWL 53). "But perhaps it is only in the picture that we notice all this about the shoes" (OWA 34). The artwork is both the revealing and the founding of the truths that it shows, for "beings can be as beings only if they stand within and stand out within what is lighted in this lighting" (OWA 53). While the essence of things is closest to us, the thing "evades thought most stubbornly"; things "refuse themselves to us." This refusal recalls the resistance to philosophical formulation on the part of factical life experience, and the relation of this resistance to forgetting. The need for phenomenological revealing becomes clear, and in this context we recall, again, Heidegger's arguments in *Being and Time* about the phenomenological method. There the meaning of Being must be "wrested from" the appearance of things in their correlative capacity to be covered up: "the way in which Being and its structures are encountered in the mode of phenomenon is one which first of all must be wrested from the objects of phenomenology." In a linguistically playful way, Heidegger argues that the method of phenomenology is required by fundamental ontology as the point of departure (*Ausgang*) for an access (*Zugang*) to phenomena and for the passage (*Durchgang*) through "whatever is presently covering it up" (BT 61/36–37). Now the phenomenological approach must be yet more sensitive and far more radical, for things are not simply there in the world of Dasein and presenced by the ecstatic nature of Dasein's factical concerns; rather, the thereness of things, their belonging to a world, is accomplished by the work of art itself. At the same time, the work of art has the function of showing this very belongingness. If the thing itself is "strange and uncommunicative" (OWA 31), the painting "spoke" for the thing, both showing and founding the world in which it finds its worldliness (OWA 35). This is the dual task of revealing and founding that belongs to the work of art. Art is shown to be in its essence poetic because the showing, which both reveals and founds world, belongs to the nature of language as showing. For Heidegger this means that

> Truth happens in van Gogh's painting. This does not mean that something which is at hand is correctly portrayed, but rather that in the revelation of the equipmental being of the shoes beings as a whole—world and earth in their counterplay—attain to uncon-cealedness. . . . The more simply and essentially the shoes are engrossed in their essence, the more directly and engagingly do all beings attain a greater degree of being along with them (OWA 56).

In being shown in their essence things are bestowed Being; showing, even more so in poetic language itself than in the painting, shelters the thing's Being in revealing the latter as itself elusive. Language "echoes" the origins of this elusiveness or "twofoldedness," thus disclosing and founding at once. Thus Heidegger argues that the "truth of beings, happens in the work" of art (OWA 39), and it is Hölderlin's poetry that, awakened to the historical essence of that disclosive founding, is the quintessential moment of the happening of truth in the work (OWA 56–57). Although Heidegger attends to several examples of artworks—paintings, music, sculpture—they are all indebted to language for their capacity to show and found truth; poetic language is now the showing of beings "in an access which genuinely belongs to them" (BT 61/37). Because "language alone brings beings as beings into the open for the first time," art is quintessentially poetic, is granted its possibility by the showing that language is. Language is, as we have seen, not conceived as the utterance of a subject or of subjects, but the responding concealing-revealing movement of Being itself. Insofar as language belongs to Being and not to subjects, it shows beings in their essential origin; it is already a kind of remembrance. In "The Origin of the Work of Art," then, Heidegger moves from the revealing of a thing to the "open region" of beings as a whole (OWA 55), and moves back toward beings only after showing this region in its linguistic character, and language in its historical character, as the recollection of origin (OWA 74). This recollection of origin is presented as a decision: an "either/or" for which Hölderlin is an "infallible sign" (OWA 78). As the poeticizing things in their gathering proximity to Being, "poetic composition is truer than the exploration of beings" (LH 240). That is, the proper understanding of things or beings should lead us beyond them to the origin of Being's withholding revelation in language.

The Founding (*Stiften*) of Truth and Being

The Word as Essential (Wesentlich) and Original (Ursprunglich)

We have seen that for Heidegger art is fundamentally poetic, granted its disclosive nature by virtue of the revealing that belongs most essentially to language. For Heidegger, then, "the essence of art is poetry. The essence of poetry, in turn, is the founding of truth" (OWA 75). Yet Heidegger must demarcate poetry, as essential language, from its dangerous kinship with unessential language, or the language of representation that belongs to the metaphysical, subjectivistic naming, or objectification, of things. For if language is the disclosure of Being, this disclosure takes form in both poetic and conceptual or technical language. Poetic language, though essential, is kindred to a realm of inessential engagements characteristic of the forgetting of Being. For "even the essential word, if it is to be understood and so become a possession in common, must make itself ordinary."

> The pure and the ordinary [*Das Reine und das Gemeine*] are both equally something said. Hence the word as word never gives any direct guarantee as to whether it is an essential word or a counterfeit [*ein Blendwerk*]. On the contrary—an essential word often looks in its simplicity [*Einfachheit*] like an unessential one [*ein Unwesentliches*] (EHD 37/EB 276).

Since "language itself is poetry in the essential sense," it is, when it says the essential, a "setting into work of truth." As revealing, poetry "founds" truth, in the sense of bestowing, grounding, and beginning (OWA 74). Yet poetry accomplishes this, in contrast to the language of metaphysical concepts or everyday communication, in its relation to origin. A heeding of the essence of origin requires a nonsubjectivistic willing, what Heidegger conceives as the freedom of submission to a destiny articulated, in its apparent and hidden dimensions, within language itself. This is because language must be able to admit the presence of what is not only actual, graspable and communicable in concepts, but also the presence of what, as present, is bestowed within the clearing on the basis of something left unsaid. Being grants a stay or lingering within presence through language on the basis of a withdrawal, which itself makes this disclosure possible. Poetic language is then never a mere grasping hold of, never an expression of a meaning fully explicit, exchangeable between interlocutors.

Essential language, the language of the (essential) poem, articulates by virtue of its relation to truth the necessity of returning to the thinking of Being, a necessity brought about by the *Seinsgeschichte*. Heidegger's view is laden with political resonance: the poet participates in Being's disclosure, guides an "historical people" to this disclosure via the aforementioned decision, even if human "erring" also collaborates with Being's (own) self-concealment. Poetic recollection or remembrance is both ahead of itself, venturing toward the most extreme oblivion, and a return to the "original" sending—a movement echoing the *Wiederholung* executed by authentic Dasein in *Being and Time*. In this sense it is ontologically historical, for "recollection in the history of Being is a thinking ahead to the Origin, and belongs to Being itself" (EP 83). *Andenken* or remembrance, which Heidegger draws from Hölderlin's poem, is then an essential destinal recollection of origin. Heidegger writes:

> we . . . never find what is Original in the historical retrospect of what is past, but rather only in remembrance which thinks at the same time upon presencing Being (what has been in being), and upon the destined truth of Being. (EP 75)

Poetry is then involved in the founding of the truth of Being because it, like thinking, utters the "essential word." "Recollection in the history of Being" occurs in that moment wherein the human being not as individual but "in his decisive character" grants "the word of response to the claim of Being"; only as such "can a reflection of its dignity shine forth to Being" (EB 76).[26] The dignity of language is that it responds to the origin, that silenced possibility precluded by metaphysical thinking. Great poetry is for Heidegger "pure" because it is a pure reception, or remembrance, of what is essential—of this lost, but not irretrievable, possibility. In "Hölderlin and the Essence of Poetry," Heidegger associates this with the power [*Macht*] of poetry:

> it is precisely this essential element of the essence that we are searching for—that which compels us to decide whether we are going to take poetry seriously and if so how, whether and to what extent we can bring with us the presumptions necessary if we are

to come under the sway of poetry ["im Machtbereich der Dichtung zu stehen"]. (EHD 34/EB 270)

This essence is, as a thinking of origin, responsive to the *Seinsgeschichte,* as Heidegger writes in "Das Gedicht" ("The Poem") in *Erläuterungen zu Hölderlins Dichtung:*

> In Hölderlin's poetry we experience the poem poetically . . . distinct in that it alone concerns us destinally [*schicksalhaft*]. For it poetizes us, ourselves, the sending [*das Geschick*] in which we stand, whether or not we know it, whether we are prepared to send ourselves ["uns darein zu schicken"] into it or not. (EHD 182–183)

In the "Letter on Humanism," Heidegger again renders the relation of poetry to truth historical and links this to Hölderlin's poetry in particular.

> As the destiny that sends truth, Being remains concealed. But the world's destiny is heralded in poetry, without yet becoming manifest as the history of Being. The world-historical thinking of Hölderlin that speaks out in the poem "Andenken" is therefore essentially more primordial and thus more significant for the future than the cosmopolitanism of Goethe. (LH 219)

The contrast with Goethe is significant, for poetry's importance is, Heidegger argues, "essentially other than humanism" (LH 219).

This demarcation of the essential over the inessential is linked to Hölderlin's notion of the "holy"—in the poet's reception, gathering, and interpretation of the call of the gods, of historical Being (LH 230). The poet encounters beings as signs of the destiny of withdrawal and clearing. The poet's naming of the gods is his response to their address; the poet brings us into "the sphere of decision" as to whether or not to yield to their claim (EHD 40/EB 280). The poet's "releasement of things" to what they are essentially involves their releasement to the essential destiny. This releasement is now the formulation of what was once called facticity, Dasein's always being in excess of beings by virtue of a relation to the possible. Here responsibility is "responsibility of a destiny" ("Verantwortung eines Schicksals") (EHD 40/EB 279). The poet's relationship to "the people" is their releasement into what involves them essentially, that is, politically. Heidegger writes, "when Hölderlin composes 'Homecoming' he is concerned that his 'countrymen' find their essence . . . the homeland of this historical dwelling is nearness to Being" (LH 218). This historical and nationalist dwelling is to overcome the forgetfulness of Being to which Dasein was seen to be ontically susceptible.

Founding and Dwelling

Much needs to be said about these notions of "destiny" and "homeland" in the context of German nationalism. But a balanced view requires that we first take note of the way Heidegger's articulations of the truth of poetic language come to express a constellation of concerns in his thought that populate the writings after *Being and Time*. To acknowledge these constellations is to recognize, as Otto Pöggeler writes, that Heidegger's work "manifests changing perspectives" that do not lead one to a "developmental history" of his thought even if one finds a leitmotiv there. Thus it has been claimed that Heidegger's "ways can provide only different impulses which force one to come to terms with them."[27]

These different impulses are captured in the dual formulation of the poetic response to (participation in) the *Seinsgeschichte*, which I discussed in the introduction. Poetic dwelling in the later works is characterized by the nonviolence of *Gelassenheit*, a letting-be that escapes representational thinking and refuses the technological objectification of things in favor of a more essential, poetic revealing; this is the "turning around" that also motivates and arises from factical life. Dwelling here reflects Hölderlin's notion of peaceful dwelling; the "pondering, framing, loving is Saying: a quiet, exuberant bow, a jubilant homage, a eulogy, a praise" (OWL 148). "To dwell" means "to be set at peace, means to remain at peace within the free, the preserve, the free sphere that safeguards each thing in its essence" (PLT 149). Here is found Heidegger's discovery of the earth, for poetic language offers a different appreciation of nature than that offered by metaphysics. Because poetic language grants the elusive character of presence — that beings are never fully disclosed as actual but belong to the structure of Being's withdrawal — poetic language does not dominate nature as an object to be exhausted in mechanistic laws or in technological manipulation. The granting of the twofold essence of Being "promises the gentler twofold of humankind" (OWL 175) and just such a dwelling on earth. Heidegger writes:

> Poetry does not fly above the earth and surmount the earth in order to escape it and hover over it. Poetry is what first brings the human being onto the earth, making him belong to it, and thus brings him into dwelling. (PLT 218)

Here Heidegger develops a theory of listening (*Zuhören*) informed by his conception of Asian (more specifically, Japanese) ways of thinking about nature and language (OWL 1–54). Language is conceived as the "flowering" of Being[28] (OWL 47) and our role is to shelter the clearing. Here Heidegger's reformulation of the question and form of philosophy is a pressing confrontation with technological modernity and an attempt to offer a mode of critical reflection thereupon. The task of thinking and poetizing is the preserving and sheltering of things within an ontological abode. Heidegger's overcoming of metaphysics as a "receptive listening" (PLT 209) promises a saving grace — a remembering — in a time of crisis.

The constellation of Heidegger's concerns includes, however, a nationalist account of the historical-eschatological crisis, one that retains and projects its worst dimensions onto Being itself. This is the thinking of poetry as a "founding of truth" as in the second two-thirds of "The Origin of the Work of Art" (1935–36) and *Introduction to Metaphysics* (1935), a thinking that makes its way into the hero-istic Hölderlin interpretations in the 1930s and 1940s. As we have seen, "The Origin of the Work of Art" sets up a counter to the "violence" that metaphysical accounts of the thing have asserted against beings, and aims to uncover them more essentially-phenomenologically; yet Heidegger reinscribes this violence in the form of a struggle between the worldly and earthly dimensions of founding. This diverges significantly from his phenomenological point of departure, the attendance to things in their concrete appearance; while phenomenology is concerned with what appears, this violence is enlisted by Heidegger's increasing emphasis on concealment, by the claim that things "resist" showing, that they therefore need to be wrested into the clearing. Accordingly, we may now establish a connection among the dimensions of Heidegger's philosophy we have examined in this chapter: facticity's self-forgetting tendency; fallenness and inauthenticity; and concealment. Here the "thingly character" that shows itself "directly" gives way to an elusiveness that needs a belligerent, even violent unconcealment, for earth and world are argued to be "opponents" in the strife (*Streit*) of opposition (*Gegeneinander*) (OWA 61). The "setting-up" of world and the "setting-forth" of earth are the projects not of human subjects, but of Being's historical essence, which calls human beings into submission and decision. Heidegger abandons phenomenological insight into the nature of language as showing when founding is granted a belligerent onto-historical dimension. I argue that the phenomenological aspect of his thought needs be retrieved to counter this apparently totalizing onto-historical dimension. For it is my view that phenomenology, as attendance to the things themselves in their concrete and manifold appearances, is eclipsed when Heidegger attempts to define the destinal origin which founding recalls as a decision that confronts, via Hölderlin, the German people. Here art and poetry as the essence of art are not merely the phenomenological access to Being Heidegger promises, but the *instigation* of "battle" for unconcealment; earth and world, Heidegger writes, are to "fight the battle" between the revealing of a destiny and its self-concealing, such that the self-concealing opens a "clearing" in which the "destiny of an historical people" is "won." The work of art is this very battle and instigation, and thus art and poetic language, as essential showing, are, Heidegger claims, "belligerent." Heidegger's thematization of the crisis of the "German people" as an "essentially historical" people (EB 260, 268; 283–284; OWA 77–78; WM; GA 39; DI), and of Hölderlin's poetry as putting this people "in decision" (EB 279, 274, 271; OWA 78) eclipses Heidegger's phenomenological insights into the nature of poetic showing.

In "The Origin of the Work of Art," Heidegger's discussion of poetic founding takes on qualities that he associates elsewhere with the "will" and the destructiveness of the subject. This text belongs nevertheless to the corpus of Heidegger's critique of subjectivity; for Heidegger refuses subjective, Kantian categories—the artist as "source" of a work, aesthetics as the subjective reception of a work—as categories for understanding the work of art.[29] The human role in the disclosure that belongs to art is the "entrance into and compliance with the unconcealedness of Being" (OWA 67). To demand a category of genius in Heidegger's account of art is to miss precisely the character of what Heidegger calls the "sober resolution of that existential self-transcendence which exposes itself to the openness of Being as it is set into the work," and that for Heidegger, "in this way, standing-within is brought under law" (OWA 67). This resolution is a nonsubjective one, for it is the "submission" to a destiny, even if that submission is articulated as a free submission (OWL 57).[30] But with respect to the writings after *Being and Time*, it has been claimed that freedom appears "as only to be freed for a destiny always already sent"—that is, determined only by the singular unthought or origin of the history of Being, itself gathered as a unity from the point of view of its *Vollendung*.[31] The overcoming of subjectivity as will is the submission to a destiny even as a violent one, a destiny founded by the poet, who, introducing another beginning of the essence of truth, compels a decision to participate. This truth is an historical one that, at least in the "Origin of the Work of Art"—to which we return in chapter 5—confronts a historical people, a theme that appears in Heidegger's lecture courses on Hölderlin, at which we will look closely in the next chapter.

Freedom and Erring Beyond Subjectivity

If Heidegger's later theory of language has been celebrated for its attendance to human dwelling, it nevertheless issues questions that pertain to the nature of language as showing and founding. My approach has been to analyze how phenomenological revealing gives way—at least in moments in Heidegger's thinking—to founding in the sense of decision and submission. For Heidegger poetic language not only discloses phenomenologically, but also, at least in the 1930s texts, it founds and institutes essential historicality, founds and institutes a *Seinsgeschichte* in remembrance of the same. If founding and instituting involve both *Streit* and *Gelassenheit*— and if we are to avoid the simplistic diagnosis that there are simply two Heideggerian "philosophies" here—how is this ambivalence related to the nature of showing and founding? As we have seen in the case of "The Origin of the Work of Art," phenomenological showing is eclipsed by ontological-historical founding. This leaves us to ask about the relation of phenomenological and ontological truth insofar as they are located essentially in poetic language, and demands a reconsideration of Hölderlin, who has been enlisted in this poetic founding. The next two chapters will present such reconsideration. In the concluding section of this chapter, we take up the relation of this truth to freedom, error, and destiny in the wake of Heidegger's critique of the subject. For if remembrance of the *Seinsgeschichte* displaces a philosophy of the subject, in what sense is the human being ascribed freedom, and how does this address the question of responsibility for the "truths" that are founded in and through poetic-artistic acts?

Truth and Freedom

Heidegger's discussion of ontological "decision" and his ascribing its structure to the process of Being's historical self-withholding unconcealment brings up the problem of freedom. His critique of subjectivity is also a critique of the modern, Kantian account of freedom as autonomy.[32] In the writings of the 1930s and early 1940s, "decision" is neither autonomous, nor is it described as spontaneity, as in Sartre's *Transcendence of the Ego*, but rather as a form of submission to what the poet "instigates." When Heidegger then writes of freedom, it is to be understood not as the autonomy of a subject freed by virtue of its transcendental grounds from the causality of nature, but as the transcendence—as Dasein or as language itself—which marks Being's disclosure.

In the essay "Vom Wesen der Wahrheit" ("On the Essence of Truth"), freedom has a positive sense; Heidegger perhaps rightly defines freedom not as the capacity or "license" (*Ungebundenheit*) to do what we want to do (W 84); it is not mere "willing" but belongs to the unique situation of the human being in the revealing (*Entbergung*) of Being; freedom is the "letting-be of what is" (*das Sein-lassen des Seienden*) (W 86), and thus it is factical; it is of the human being's relation to the possible that grounds our access to beings. Heidegger here offers an alternative to the transcendental notion of freedom that situates the human being, as the representing consciousness, over and against its object, over and against nature. Freedom is thought here in relation to truth, to the disclosure and withdrawal of Being, and to the nature of the human being as "ek-sistence," standing in relation to the "open" (*das Offene*) (W 86), a notion employed in Heidegger's interpretations of Rilke (PLT 91–142). The disclosure of Being is this openness, which the human being does not constitute, but in which the human being finds its proper role of "letting-be." This resonates with the role of the poet as *Gelassenheit*—not so much as the founder or instigator of truth, but as letting-aiding truth into unconcealment, a process that is, in turn, the condition for the poet's language; this belongs, then, to a phenomenological account of the relation between language and revealing. Poetic language then differs radically from the violence of forgetting, from what Rilke called "parting against the Open" (PLT 112–116), a turning-against that allows human beings to represent nature to themselves according to the conditions of their own subjectivity; such representation is seen to be violent when it is the exclusive measure of the real. Heidegger's *Gelassenheit* freedom overturns the Enlightenment subject's transcendental grounding of objectivity, which consists in this objectifying representation of nature as what is other to subjective freedom.

Freedom is then tethered to the structure of disclosure and concealment of Being; in fact, it *is* this structure, or *is as* this structure. Thus Heidegger claims that "truth is in essence freedom" ("die Wahrheit im Wesen Freiheit ist") The human being ek-sists "only as property of this freedom" ("nur als Eigentum dieser Freiheit") (W 86). The human being ek-sists outside of the realm of beings — in the open of disclosure, and the freedom of this being is not a possession of truth, but is rather possessed by truth in its own process of disclosure and concealment.

It is difficult, then, to view Heidegger's concept of freedom according to any traditional model of ethics as self-responsibility. For the human being is also "essentially historical," because the human being is "sent" in the destiny of truth; the "rare and simple decisions of history" (W 86) belong to this truth and are the province of the essence of truth. In the context of Heidegger's nationalism, it is disturbing that freedom is indistinguishable from historical destiny. Freedom, as the standing-out in the disclosure of beings, is historical, and belongs to the history of Being, not merely "chaotic dissemination" but "gathered" in "sameness and simplicity" and in a "solid constancy" (PR 91, 45) as the destiny of the West from the point of view of a new departure in the wake of metaphysics' end. Freedom then is not only a relation to the disclosure of beings within Being's history but to the "gathering" itself. Freedom is freedom to ek-sist as this disclosure, a freedom marked by a particular historical demand or decision. If ek-sistence is itself brought into the clearing, from the point of view that the danger of Being's withdrawal itself illuminates, this disclosure is the historical disclosure of the essence of being human. This essence, disclosed historically, is also an historical essence; this disclosure, too, compels a historical "decision," either for instigation or submission or for the preparation of a way.

Freedom and Error

Heidegger's critique of subjectivity redraws the lines between thought and truth, and aligns truth not with correctness nor the affirmation of a community of subjects (agreement) but with the "open" as Being's disclosure. Error, too, belongs to truth because truth is disclosure that, pertaining to Being, always involves Being's withdrawal. Truth cannot be separated from error, because truth is always a matter of the twofold disclosure. Yet if truth is also historical, error belongs to history's essence. If the essence of truth compels a "decision" to submit to the new beginning, one announced by the poet's departure from metaphysics, this also involves error. Error is not a lack of disclosure but belongs to the process of disclosure as such. Just as freedom is not opposed to but rather confounded with destiny, error, grounded in freedom, is not opposed to truth; as a delimitation of truth, it is a necessary dimension thereof. Heidegger overturns models of truth as correctness, or as agreement of thought to reality, both of which belong to the metaphysics of presence. While the measure of scientific or technological truth is correctness or effectuality, phenomenological-ontological truth acknowledges the inherent incompletability of disclosure.[33] If freedom is not freedom of autonomy but the openness of disclosure, error is understood not as going astray from correctness or rightness but as the accompaniment to the process of disclosure. Since the human being does not direct the disclosure of Being but only participates—is "sent"—within this disclosure, human freedom is inescapably erroneous, just as it is inherently truthful in the essential sense. The remembrance of Being as an historical founding of truth affords an especial event of disclosure, and is thus also tied up with both freedom and error.

Heidegger's account of freedom decenters the human subject, and so too does his account of error. This must have been on the mind of Jean Beufret, who, in the letter to Heidegger that spurred the "Letter on Humanism," asked the question of the possibility of ethics,[34] to which we might add the question of historical decisions and errors. Keeping in mind that Heidegger's answer comes in the wake of mass murder, violence, destruction, and destitution in post–World War II Germany, this question is pressing, to say the least. In the wake of Heidegger's critique of the subject and his thinking of *Ereignis* as the "sole occurrence" beyond the subject's "entanglement" in beings (DI 165), one asks if it is possible then to give a content to the occurrence of error and to assign responsibility for specific and profoundly consequential errors. Heidegger's ontological rendering precludes this. Needed is an account of error not absorbed into the ontological structure of occurring, which renders silent any specific factical content. If poetic language not only shows but founds truth in the structure of its occurrence, can it not be said that erroneous "truths" are also founded and instituted, and thus that such truths are to be reevaluated by thinking?[35] These questions are not readily addressed by Heidegger's argument that truth is grounded as much in erring as in not erring, that Being is a disclosure and a concealment at once. For Heidegger error is inevitable:

> The errancy [*die Irre*], in which in each case historical humanity [*Menschentum*] must wander, so that its path is errant, essentially co-gives [*fuegt . . . mit*] the openness of Dasein. (W 92)

And again:

> The human being errs. He [sic] does not merely fall into error
> [*die Irre*]. He rather always wanders into error because he, ek-sis-
> tent, in-sists, and thus is already in error. . . . Error is part of
> the inner constitution [*Verfassung*] of Dasein, in which the histor-
> ical man [*der geschichtliche Mensch*] is involved [*eingelassen ist*]. . . .
> Errancy [*der Irrtum*] is not simply the singular mistake but the
> kingdom [*Königtum*], (the reign) [*die Herrschaft*] of history of
> the complicated entanglements of erring. (W 92)

Heidegger argues that historical humanity must wander into error
not because error is the sometimes negative consequence of human
freedom—that we abuse it consciously or not, that we make mistakes for which we are responsible, that we are guilty of our failures
to not err—but because erring is the possibility of ek-sisting itself. The
human being *must* err; his/her path is essentially, intrinsically erratic
(*irrig*) because it is this error that grounds the possibility of not erring
(W 92–93). The human being makes necessity of need (W 93) in the
very mystery of being-there. Only out of the necessity of erring comes
the possibility of "commanding" the forgotten mystery. Forgetting as
erring is here thought as a collaboration between the human being's
freedom—as one element of the twofold relation of openness—and the
concealing and self-disclosure of Being itself. The human being, essentially errant, can then turn necessity into a need to return to the essential, the need for remembrance and thus for poetry.

> Freedom, consisting in the in-sistent ek-sistence of Da-sein, is the
> essence of truth . . . only because freedom itself springs from the
> original essence of truth, from the reign of mystery in error. (W 93)

This "mystery of Dasein" is Dasein's original relation to error, and
it is a mystery that has been "forgotten" in the history of metaphysics
wherein the human being has been considered the measure for a (fallacious) notion of truth. Just as the forgetting of Being comes to be
understood as Being's own self-concealment, this

> forgetting gives the apparent disappearance of the forgotten a
> presence of its own. Inasmuch as the mystery denies itself in and
> for the sake of forgetfulness, it leaves historical man to rely on
> his own resources in the realm of the practical. (W 91)

In this realm, the human being builds up a world according to its
measures of correctness, which is taken to be opposed to error, thought

here inessentially as incorrectness. But the "forgotten essence of truth," the mystery that poetic language shelters, is that truth is not opposed, but rather originally related to, error (W 96). Thinking is then to uncover this heretofore "forgotten" essence of truth (W 91).

Error, Fate, and Phenomenological Disclosure

We return briefly back to "The Origin of the Work of Art," where the notion of freedom is related to a violent founding of truth, a "resolute" "decision" (OWA 187), the founding nature of which belongs neither to a subject as artist nor to a collective subject of decision, but to the work itself—which, as the *Streit* between earth and world in the coming-to-presence of truth, instigates decision. Beyond subjectivity, the human being gives itself over to destiny *(Schicksal)*, even in its errors; does Heidegger in effect grant very that destiny, or the work that institutes it, the role that was in metaphysics that of the subject?[36] The human being as subject abandons its will to destinal historical-ity, which itself, from the point of departure of its gathering-end, "sends" *(schickt)* the origin to be remembered. The artist or poet is no longer an aesthetic subject—a genius as the source of the work—and the Volk who is "confronted" by that work (OWA 187) is no longer a commu-nity of subjects of taste or of freedom in the sense rendered by Kant-ian aesthetics and its treatment of beauty in art as the symbol of moral goodness. Being—though without telos, will, or the logic of dialectic—is to be recollected in the "gathering" of its history, through which the unthought origin becomes manifest as a new possibility for thinking. The "errant course" (PR 46) of Being is its reduction to the principle of reason and subjectivity and the oblivion this fosters, and Heidegger calls this a "doubly errant" course (PR 45); but Heidegger renders this course according to a logic of decision, thus suggesting a singular, if in itself nuanced, view of history (EP 58).[37] Decision is the letting-hap-pen of truth not only in the sense of showing but as founding; as an historical and political event, this founding must be instigated by artis-tic-poetic works. It need be remembered that in "The Origin of the Work of Art" this decision concerns the embrace by the German peo-ple of their specifically German essential destiny. The founding of truth is a decision that is not the acting of free subjects, but the "free" respond-ing to a call. This radically limits individual or collective responsibil-ity for what might be founded politically or historically. Either poetic affirmation-remembrance-founding or subjective-technological forget-fulness of the Schicksal, the opening or closing of earth in the strife with world, is outlined as a possible option. Refusal, reformulation, resistance, or the pause of uncertainty are not.[38] The political context in which Heidegger writes "The Origin of the Work of Art" renders this omission immensely problematic.

Poetic language, as the errant-truthful historical founding and reception of *Schicksal,* is said to be opposed to subjectivity's egocentrism and will. Yet I argue that poetic language, when attended with phenomenological (rather than *seinsgeschichtliche*) fidelity, is incompatible with the decision and simplicity of founding and the totality of *Schicksal.* Poetic language indeed requires a special relation to truth as withdrawing disclosure; but errancy need not be inevitable and disclosure need not be confounded with fate. Phenomenological insight into the nature of poetic language as disclosure discords significantly with the notions of decision and *Schicksal,* both of which instigate a "gathering" of what is disclosed in fact more characteristic of the totalization of technological revealing. If technological revealing demands a revealing that is total and exhaustive, poetic language grants that things are brought into presence without demanding that they be fully present. Poetic language need not instigate a struggle to wrest into unconcealment; its capacity for indirect evocation, for withdrawing even as it declares, for abiding in uncertainties, is far more compelling than its capacity to gather or found political-historical truth, a capacity I will challenge in later chapters. Moreover, while it would be too simplistic to demand a simple retrieval of a moral subject, one that could absorb the question of responsibility for error, some kind of subject—a less heroic but also less submissive one—might be indeed found in an alternative theory of language, as I shall argue in the final chapter of this book. Let me here suggest that the problem of error might be analyzed more phenomenologically, highlighting Being's revelation as one that does not afford exhaustive illumination. In terms of the revealing of historical truth, poetic language is unfit to posit a fate, a sending, which could be so unambiguously interpreted, which could be linked to resoluteness as the "either/or" options of an instigated decision. The history of Being, if rendered in poetical language at all, would always echo shifting perspectives and multisignificance that reflect the inexhaustibleness and incompletability of remembrance. Such an account would be more faithful to Heidegger's phenomenological origins than to the structure of the *Seinsgeschichte.* Most important, error would be no longer wedded to decision that is gathered into a simplicity, and freedom would be no longer conceivable according to a fate that is unambiguous, gathered, and, as a *Vollendung* of metaphysics, totalized by thought. Drawing from the notion of *Gelassenheit*, as the letting-happen of that which unfolds itself, we could speak of the phenomenologically illuminable pause of indecision, uncertainty, and evasiveness that attends the inexhaustibleness of the real. Against Heidegger's notion of the history of Being, I will argue that poetic language is unique not in instituting Being in the sense of decision or *Schicksal*, but in rendering apparent the impossibility of its absolute univocity. If for Heidegger "Hölderlin utters the 'essential word' and thereby initiates Being into what it is,"[39] Heidegger has also shown that poetic language, and the language of Hölderlin, admits and introduces a radical *Gelassenheit*.[40] Hölderlin's poetry suggests to the German language not a "test to be stood," not a nationalist confrontation, but the irretrievability of the origin, one that echoes ineffable loss. It is this irretrievability that, I shall argue in chapter 3, governs Hölderlin's understanding of Being and its elusiveness; it renders Hölderlin's understanding of language compatible with a *Gelassenheit* sense of phenomenological disclosure but not with a history of Being. Yet it shall also be seen that this disclosure does not displace the subject, as does Heidegger's theory, nor does it abandon the concerns of humanism. As I will show, Hölderlin's understanding of the elusiveness of Being issues not from an "overcoming" of modern subjectivity, but rather from its radical poeticization.[41]

Heidegger's own thinking moves in significant ways beyond the notion of "decision" announced in "The Origin of the Work of Art." In Heidegger's writings on poetic language after the 1930s and early 1940s, the forgetting of Being on the part of metaphysics and technological subjectivity requires a redirection of thinking that can no longer be entrusted to the decisions and acts of an historical people. However, in the case of his Hölderlin-interpretations, Heidegger never drops the notions of "historical essence" and of the particular historical essence of the "Germans." Yet if the remembrance of Being is still a matter of historical urgency, Heidegger sees that it cannot be situated within the strife of "world and earth" or the violent institution of truth in the work of art; and the notion of the "German" or the "proper" (*das Eigene*) is brought into dialogue with the notion of the "foreign." Heidegger's overcoming of subjectivity turns from the resoluteness of decision to the thinking of *Ereignis* beyond beings, to a history wherein "Being alone is" (EP 79); and if this thinking, as Heidegger argues, offers the preparation for another "way," it must do so in a return to the "world,"[42] a return made possible by Heidegger's notion of dwelling. Poetic language, if it is to be articulated in terms of truth, involves a truth that eludes any word; its plurivocity implies the loss of a narrative thread[43] that would guarantee the essential-historical character of our relation to Being. If Being is brought to word in language, poetry affirms, after Hölderlin, not fate but "the gentle shyness of the accidental" (ELT 142).[44] Poetic language does not found truth but suggests what Heidegger resonantly called "the quiet power of the possible" (LH 238). A new poetics of Dasein will have to conceive of an alternative to an existential ontology of forgetting, and it will have to reinstate the specificity of Dasein as the locus of responsibility for the utterances and interpretations of poetic language.

2

Heidegger's Hölderlin
Anðenken anð Ereigniɕ Beyonð Subjectivity

We have seen that Heidegger's turn to poetic language and his theory of language are issued in a critique of subjectivity as forgetfulness of Being in favor of thinking that, in remembrance and recollection, recalls the *Seinɕgeɕchichte*.[1] Poetic language is not only the shelter of truth, but it also founds and institutes truth in radically recollecting an essential-destinal origin. As we will see in this chapter, Heidegger's interpretations of Hölderlin are both placed squarely within this schema and are pressed still further, such that the overcoming of subjective metaphysics yields a thinking of *Ereigniɕ* and the *"eɕ gibt"* that "sends" Being but withholds itself in that sending. If subjectivity constitutes a forgetting of Being, poetic language is its founding remembrance. I have suggested in the previous chapter that the role of poetic language in the *founðing* of truth demands serious philosophical scrutiny, but the poetic subjectivity I propose in light of Heidegger's critique of the subject, and for which I will draw upon a contending address to Hölderlin's poetics in the next chapter, can yet be described in Heidegger's terms as a *ɕhelter* of truth. It must then be seen in what ways poetic language involves truth without, however, obviating the question of subjectivity; and so a contrast must be demarcated between the *Ereigniɕ* ontology, which eschews all traces of subjectivism in posing language as the shelter of Being, and the model I will draw, culminating in chapter 7. But first we must outline in this chapter Heidegger's figuration of Hölderlin as the essential destinal poet.

Before laying out Heidegger's interpretation of Hölderlin, Heidegger's method of approach must be regarded in its unique philosophical aims. It must be noted that Heidegger does not aim at a philological or literary-theoretical accuracy in addressing Hölderlin, but engages rather in a philosophical confrontation to be sharply distinguished from ordinary *Literaturwissenschaft.* Attendance to Heidegger's polemical manner of interpretation, an *Auseinandersetzung* or confrontation, is useful here. *Auseinandersetzung,* Gregory Fried notes, "is an ontological concept for Heidegger," describing both "the way in which Being happens and how it concerns us" and our relationship to Being. The notion of *Auseinandersetzung* appears in many of Heidegger's interpretations — of Aristotle, Heraclitus, and Nietzsche — but also in Heidegger's readings of Hölderlin (GA 39, 6; EHD 60). This creative confrontation sharply differentiates Heidegger's style of interpretation, which he calls an "interpretive construction" (*auslegender Aufbau*) (GA 43, 279), from merely historiological or philological scholarship. Here *Auseinandersetzung* is Heidegger's strategy of addressing Being through Hölderlin. In fairness, then, Heidegger is not aiming for historical accuracy in interpreting Hölderlin's poems, and criticisms against Heidegger are insufficient if they merely point out his inaccuracies. To confront a great work for Heidegger "means to cast it in its most powerful light, so that both it and one's own position are most radically exposed to examination."[2] Only in a nonhistoriological confrontation, or "only in *Auseinandersetzung* does a creative interpretation arise" (GA 43, 275). Any interpretation, according to Heidegger, is polemical, because it is a confrontation with Being, and "our Being is polemical."[3] This can be linked to Heidegger's stance that Being is ever-concealing just as it reveals itself to us, and our facticity is such as to be a relationship to this twofold nature of truth, a point we have examined, and to which we will return.

Even within Heidegger's own strategies of interpretation, however, one can challenge both the configuration of themes he, as a creative thinker, draws from Hölderlin, and the figure he presents of Hölderlin as the poet of Being and of German destiny. What is needed, which I aim to accomplish, is an analysis of the dynamics of Heidegger's overall interpretation. To give, in preview, just one example of how this might be accomplished, we note that while Hölderlin is read by Heidegger as "deeply wedded in spirit to Heraclitus, the philosopher of the unity of opposites bound together in strife,"[4] we ought also consider, in our own confrontation with Hölderlin and with Heidegger's reading, Hölderlin's relationship to other Greek figures, like

Empedocles, and to the philosophy of Kant, a connection that, as I will discuss, compromises Heidegger's (literal-ontological) interpretation of the poet's founding of truth. It is indeed of *philosophical,* and not merely literary or historical, significance, to trace the turns that Heidegger is unwilling or reluctant to make in his engagement with Hölderlin; thus, we can take note of which texts Heidegger will not "undergo," or neglects, in his confrontation, and what other creative possibilities of thought might be offered by these texts. Thus I do not take issue with Heidegger's "interpretive construction" as such; for, after all, it is with such construction that the philosophical significance of Hölderlin is established and competing alternatives from Hölderlin are opened out; and it is with such construction that Heidegger's important destruction (*Abbau*) of the history of thought is possible. Yet I take issue with Heidegger's claim that the most powerful reading, as he notes in his interpretations of Nietzsche, requires "the setting in place of the antagonist in his highest . . . dangerousness."[5] For one question, among others, remains unanswered: dangerous to whom and for whom? And ought we take Hölderlin's own references to danger at face value, as Heidegger does in his heroicizing readings of the poetic calling? Answering these questions is a most complex endeavor, but in the case of the Hölderlin interpretations it concerns the German *Volk,* for whom Hölderlin is said to found and presence a world, to bring to light the polemical nature of their relation to Being, and, of course, those sacrificed to that ideology.[6] In the context of 1930s and early 1940s Germany, and of Heidegger's complicated association with fascism, what this founding entails is a disturbing question, and leaves us to reexamine the figure of Hölderlin, so instrumental in Heidegger's theories of language and Being at this time. No less important is it to ask whether there is not another creative, powerful reading to be drawn from Hölderlin that need not submit entirely to Heidegger's views, a reading in which the poet's courage is held radically in check by the elusiveness of what the poet addresses. Indeed, the very profundity of Heidegger's interpretations of Hölderlin, and their resulting influence, have so dominated philosophical interest in Hölderlin as to almost eclipse competing interpretations. However, such questions I pose here are pressing ones, if a general theory of language — a philosophical poetics — is to be drawn from the same region as that of Heidegger's insights. We begin with an account of Heidegger's specific attendance to the figure of Hölderlin, and in particular the means by which Heidegger rids the poet of subjective traces in order to submit to his figuration to the *Seinsgeschichte.*

Hölderlin and the Sending of Being

Hölderlin is taken up in Heidegger's writings as the "essential poet" who thinks essentially the poetic task as the renunciation of subjectivity (DI 165) and the recollection of Being in "destitute times" (EB 271, PLT 93–94). With this, Heidegger attempts to reorient the thinking of Being away from traditional philosophical argumentation—which tends to reduce Being to a category of presence disclosable, without remainder, in concepts; he finds in poetic language, along with the work of art in general, a source for rethinking ontology, no longer "fundamental" ontology, but ontology as the thinking of *Ereignis,* as historical disclosure and withdrawal, as topography of Being. If the human being's relation to Being is one of disclosive transcendence, the language of philosophy has nevertheless tended to obscure the question of Being. Poetic language is, however, suited to the disclosure of Being because what it makes present is not grasped in an all-illuminating clarity; poetic language reveals something of the world without failing to indicate that it is a partial revelation. This is the relation of poetic language to a phenomenological account of truth as *aletheia,* and to the "unthought" that underlies all saying (PR 71; LH 218; WN 56). Poetic language points to its own disclosive role and its own limits for disclosing; it thus makes evident that language itself is a revealing—in contrast to conceptual language, which aims at transparency and total exposure of the "real." According to Heidegger, technological "man," in contrast, follows scientific-conceptual language in obscuring its role in disclosure; defining beings as measurable or reproducible, it does not make apparent the relativity of that actuality to the process of disclosure itself. Heidegger finds Hölderlin particularly compelling because the task of the poet is an explicit question in both the philosophical writings and the poems. Heidegger locates Hölderlin's poetizing and poetic thinking at a privileged, and yet dangerously penurious, moment of Being's withdrawal. Hölderlin's own turn to the writing of poetry is situated in philosophical reflections on language and on the limits of conceptual language for articulating Being, and yet this "thinking" reflection is taken up in Hölderlin's poetic works. Heidegger writes, "Hölderlin has not been chosen because his work, one among many, realizes the universal essence of poetry, but solely because Hölderlin's poetry was borne by the poetic vocation to write expressly of the essence of poetry" (EB 271).

Heidegger's interpretations of the "poetic vocation" (*dichterischer Beruf*) nevertheless rely, for the most part, on meditative thinking with a selection of Hölderlin's poems rather than a sustained reading of Hölderlin's theoretical writings.[7] Heidegger argues in the 1941–42 lectures on Hölderlin's "Andenken" that what is to be thought is not Hölderlin's "experience," nor the truth of his historical situation (GA 52, 28); but this must be understood in the context of Heidegger's aims discussed earlier, which eschew historiography. According to Heidegger, we cannot interpret Hölderlin solely according to the tenor of his times. Rather, interpretation, as Heidegger remarks in reference to Aristotle, is always situated within the living present, what demands to be thought. In turning to poetry as the source for a thinking of Being, Heidegger preserves the distinction between thinking and poetry (GA 52, 2–5; GA 39, 41) even as he draws them into close relation (GA 52, 55). Thus Hölderlin's poetry is not to be incorporated into a current "system of philosophy" (GA 52, 5), and the aim of a genuine thoughtful laying-out (*Auslegung*) of the poems lies "in making itself superfluous" (GA 52, 38–39). Despite Hölderlin's own corpus of philosophical writings, Heidegger claims Hölderlin as "essential," as the "poet of poets," but explicitly *not* as a philosopher or even as a poetic theorist. It is the poeticized (*das Gedichtete*) in the poems, and indeed only in the essential poetry—*nur die wesentliche Dichtung* (GA 52, 7)—that is to be "thought." In the winter semester lectures in 1934–35 on Hölderlin's poems "Germania" and "The Rhine," Heidegger had claimed that Hölderlin is the choice for his thinking through poetry not because the poet also happened to be a philosopher ("auch philosoph") but rather on poetic-ontological grounds alone: "Hölderlin is one of our greatest, that is, our most futural, *thinkers* because he is our greatest *poet*. The poetic approach [*Zuwendung*] to his poetry is only possible as a *thinking* confrontation with the *revelation of Being* [*Offenbarung des Seyns*] won in this poetry" (GA 39, 5–6).

This confrontation is beyond subjective utterance or enunciation of a subject's intention, as linguistic acts would be described in the classical theory of expression. The poeticized in the essential poetic word is not invented by but overcomes the poet—as Heidegger writes, "*überdichtet den Dichter*" (GA 52, 6–8).[8] It is the thinker who is granted access to that "poeticized" in the poem; for this "poeticized" is not merely the "content" of a poem, what Benjamin indicated with "the poeticized," which maintains the poet's subjective, experiential element.[9] The poeticized is rather that to which the "listening" (*hörender*) poet responds, what calls the poet to what is called (*das Angerufene*) in the poem. Our access to this calling is not a matter of a literary science (GA 52, 2), which might attempt to locate the meaning of the work in a represented intentionality, experience, or feeling (*das Erlebnis, die Erfahrung*) on the part of the author (GA 52, 5–6, 22–24, 28–29, 36, 50, 54, 58, 61, 71). Representing the latter would require a re-creation according to historical facts and philosophical clarifications, or, as in Dilthey's *Das Erlebnis und die Dichtung*, which Heidegger implicates in the *Andenken* lectures (GA 52, 6) and elsewhere criticizes,[10] a theory of poetic "experience." Heidegger is critical of the terminology of both *Erlebnis* and *Erfahrung*, critical of an account of accumulated experience, the first-person standpoint as grounding an event, and the first-person interiority of witness. (As I will argue in chapter 7, this renders Heidegger's poetics unfit to address a realm of poetry, for instance by Miklós Radnóti and Anna Akhmatova, in which the strategies of poetical form enact a sustainment of self in the face of its threatened extinction). Dilthey's attendance to experience presupposes not only a merely historiographical re-creation of what is inaccessible, but also a theory of expression that Heidegger rejects. In "A Dialogue on Language," Heidegger criticizes the notion of language as expression because it implies a philosophy of inner experience, of "inwardness" or the "soul." It is worth outlining Heidegger's critique in brief. The dialogue takes up the problem of subjective expression in the context of the Japanese interlocutor's question about a 1931 essay that refers to "expression"; Heidegger aims to correct subjectivistic intonations in that essay and critique contemporary notions of subjective experience as found, for example, in Dilthey and Buber. The following passage from the dialogue is relevant here:

I: In the days of that lecture, everyone was talking about experience (*Erlebnis*), even with phenomenology.

J: A famous book by Dilthey has the title *Experience and Poetry*.

I: To experience in this sense always means to refer back—to refer life and lived experience back to the "I." Experience is the name for the referral of objective back to the subject. The much-discussed I/Thou experience, too, belongs within the metaphysical sphere of subjectivity.

J: And this sphere of subjectivity and of the expression that belongs to it is what you left behind when you entered into the hermeneutic relation to the twofold.

I: At least I tried. The guiding notions which, under the names "expression." "experience," and "consciousness," determine modern thinking, were to be put into question. (OWL 36)

Thinking the poeticized in the poem requires a rejection of any subjective experience behind, or preserved in, or expressed in the poem; the poetic word is to be thought beyond the subject, essentially, as a disclosure of Being. This requires rejecting subjective notions of experience, soul, inwardness, consciousness, and expression, for the poeticized is not a "meaning" in the sense of something "meant" (GA 52, 5) but rather the *essence of what is to be said*, for which the poet is not an agent or a subject but a conduit of reception.

Heidegger chooses Hölderlin as the "essential poet" because Heidegger learns from the latter that "the making of poetry, too, is a matter for thinking" (PLT 99–100). Hölderlin's poetry is a "thinking poetry" (PLT 95) because Hölderlin articulates, for Heidegger, the "essence of poetry" (EB 271). As a poet in destitute times, the destitution of Hölderlin's age — the age of Enlightenment rationality and the failure of that rationality, according to the Romantics, to address the true nature of life and of the divine — "made the whole being and vocation of the poet a poetic question for him" (PLT 94). Hölderlin is, still more strongly, a poet of the decay of the West (*Abendland*) who poses the question of Being as a question of the lost relation to the "holy." Heidegger writes, after Hölderlin: "To be a poet in destitute times means: to attend, singing, to the trace of the fugitive gods" (PLT 94). Heidegger illuminates the sense of lostness in Hölderlin's hymns, which thematize the relation of human beings to the gods who no longer appear in their world. "This is why the poet in the time of the world's night utters the holy," Heidegger writes. "This is why, in Hölderlin's language, the world's night is the holy night" (PLT 94).

For Hölderlin, this absence of the gods marks the failure of reason to grasp the holy — what he called the "soul of the world" (ELT 116). The decay of thinking in a time of crisis — the oblivion of Being — thus dominates the interpretations of Hölderlin's poetry; and therefore the "law that rules over" (PLT 95) Hölderlin's poetry is that of Being's self-concealing sending. The specificity of locale in Hölderlin's poems — landscapes, rivers, particular sites and experiences — is rendered by Heidegger as the intimacy of Being and its eschatological "coming."

The locality to which Hölderlin came is a manifestness of Being, a manifestness which itself belongs to the destiny of Being and which, out of that destiny, is intended for the poet.

But this manifestness of Being within metaphysics as completed may even be at the same time the extreme oblivion of Being. (PLT 95)

Heidegger thinks this time of ontological penury as one in which meaning must submit to rank and order. At this extreme point—between the forgetting of Being and its recollection, the lost gods and those yet to come (EB 289)—Hölderlin's poetry is highest "in its rank and position in the course of the history of Being" (PLT 98). Hölderlin's poetry is "the song that sings essentially" (PLT 141), a singing that "answers to the coming world era." This era, "as destiny . . . lies in Being and lays claim to the human being" (PLT 142). Hölderlin's poetry thus "arrives out of the future" as a pure arrival. Heidegger thus interprets Hölderlin's line that "where the danger is / there grows the saving power" as an ontological-historical announcement or message (QT, 28): "The more purely the arrival happens, the more its remaining occurs as present. The greater the concealment with which what is to come maintains its reserve in the foretelling saying, the purer is the arrival" (PLT 142).

Hölderlin, as "precursor of poets in a destitute time," therefore cannot be "overtaken" by another poet, as Heidegger writes in the essay "What Are Poets For?" For Hölderlin's pure arrival "overcomes from the start all perishability," and it is in this way that Hölderlin "partakes in destiny" (PLT 142). Heidegger wants to preserve Hölderlin as the announcement of and within a historical ontology, and thus he insists that the "time" for Hölderlin's poetry will never arrive as a popular appropriation of his poems, even if Hölderlin wrote in his letters extensively of a poetic "education" of the public, an education that was to breed therein sympathy and a love for freedom (ELT 136–140, 146). Heidegger's protectionism of Hölderlin as a "public" poet recalls both Kierkegaard's criticisms of the inauthentic public of the "present age," as well as Nietzsche's disdain for a philosophy for "everyman," for a "timely" kind of thinking. That Hölderlin is a destinal poet means for Heidegger precisely that his poetry "will never arrive in such a misshapen way" as to become "timely." "It would thus be mistaken to believe that Hölderlin's time will come only on that day when 'everyman' will understand his poetry" (PLT 142). That Hölderlin has indeed been appropriated in varying ways by (a likewise varying) public—from the pocketbooks, edited by Friedrich Beissner, printed in thousands for German soldiers at the front in World War II[11] to the employment of Hölderlin poems and the Hölderlin "figure" in the leftist student protests of the 1960s[12]—therefore does not concern Heidegger's notion of the poet's destiny. For poetry is a matter neither of popular consumption nor of mass production but of thinking, and indeed for the thinking of Being as remembrance.

If Hölderlin is never to become timely, cannot be overtaken in the destiny of Being, is an arrival of "pure coming," his poetry is fixed by Heidegger within an historical inheritance of Being's sending, one that cannot be derived from Hölderlin's chronological place within history nor from a teleological transition among continuous epochs, as in the logic of Hegelian dialectic.[13] For that to which Hölderlin appeals is the lost echo of that which, in the history of metaphysics, was always concealed (EP, 81). If Hölderlin hearkens to the Greeks in the "Origin of the Work of Art," and in the "Dialogue on Language," the "play" of epochs are rendered a certain relativity in the *Geschick* as the "play" of Being that eludes logic, a play that, as Heidegger argues in *The Principle of Reason*, is "without why."[14] "The epochs," Heidegger writes, "can never be derived from one another much less be placed on the track of an ongoing process." And yet the "sending" of Being is indeed an inheritance:

> Nevertheless, there is a legacy from epoch to epoch. But it does not run between the epochs like a band linking them; rather, the legacy always comes from what is concealed in the *Geschick*, just as if from one source various streamlets arise that feed a stream that is everywhere and nowhere. (PR 91)

This concealed is the "unthought" that issues in poetry as the lost origin. In "A Dialogue on Language," Heidegger argues that the origin of the Greek sense of phenomena is a lost one. "To enter into thinking this unthought, to see it in the source of its reality. To see it so is in its own way Greek, and yet in respect of what it sees no longer, is never again, Greek" (OWL 39).[15] That Hölderlin recalls-receives the "Greek" message does not entail an anachronistic repetition of what the Greeks actually thought, but the retrieval of a possibility for thinking that is lost, with Plato, when thinking becomes metaphysical.[16] In some form, "in an even more Greek manner," the poet is to think the "unthought"— that never-yet retrieved possibility of thinking that constitutes the origin to which the poet appeals. In "What Are Poets For?" destiny is the essential, singular destiny of the "pure"; it is not a "chaotic dissemination" but simple and self-same (PR 91).

This destiny requires a listening for the "essential." Yet language is a "dangerous possession" because it does not admit when it says the essential and when it says the inessential. As we will see in chapter four, this view reflects the twofold character of revealing in "The Question Concerning Technology," in which both *techne* and *poiesis* are modes of revealing; since their common origin as a bringing-forth is fractured in metaphysics, modern technology obscures the fact that it is a form of revealing at all. Thus language, as a revealing par excellence, contains the "danger" of technological revealing and the "saving power" of poetry. Because "the pure and the ordinary are both equally something said," language "necessary conceals in itself a continual danger for itself" (EB 275). This danger is read at face value by Heidegger, but is linked in Hölderlin to the threat of hubris[17] on the part of the human being, who, endowed with reason and the faculty of judgment (*Urtheil*), asserts himself over and against other beings and thinks himself to be the source of the unity of these beings. For Heidegger, this danger is an essential one belonging to the same destiny as the "innocent" word. Hölderlin admits this danger in his drama *Empedocles*,[18] where the poet takes on the violent domination of beings associated with metaphysical subjectivity, particularly, for Hölderlin, in the subjective idealism of Fichte.[19] Empedocles thinks he has given expression to nature that otherwise would be a "dead stringed instrument," a mere corpse without the unification of "life" granted by the language he utters; but for this hubris he is left bereft and, without nature's consolation, must perish. The danger for Hölderlin belongs to the paradox of subjectivity; for Heidegger, it is the threat that the unessential will obscure the essential and its unique destiny. Heidegger claims that "where there is to be a *single* conversation, the essential word must be constantly related to one and the same" (EB 278). Being and its self-withholding is the danger that is uttered in the word of the poet: the "abyss" of the time of the absent gods. History is the manifestation of Being as an historical sending, a history that becomes apparent as such only at its *Vollendung*, the end, "which shows itself in the discovery of the unity of Western thinking,"[20] a discovery Heidegger thinks himself as having made. The danger of oblivion is an historical one, and the "simple saying" of the poet is a responding address to this history. Although Heidegger also writes of the "play" of difference, Heidegger insists on the singularity of this history: "Both — existence as a *single* conversation and historical existence — are alike ancient, they belong together and are the same thing" (EB 279). This is not to ascribe to history a logic of transitions but to retrieve, from the point of view of its "completion," a possibility excluded by, but held as the unthought within, this history.

Heidegger's interpretation of Hölderlin marks the transition from the "first" beginning of philosophy to another beginning, one in which the poet, outside metaphysical constraints, can grasp the movements of the history of Being in their unity. Hölderlin's poetry marks a moment that itself "determines a new time" (EHD 44/EB 313); although not ready to be heard in Hölderlin's own historical moment, this is a movement beyond metaphysics, which for Heidegger is the turn from philosophy to "thinking." Yet if this transition is not one of logical or dialectical necessity, it has an eschatological structure. For Hölderlin's poetry as essential brings us to the "sphere of decision as to whether we are to yield ourselves to the gods or withhold ourselves from them" (EB 280). In Hölderlin's poetry, Heidegger argues, the poetic word grounds (*stiftet*) Being, establishes history by pressing on into the danger of metaphysical forgetting in order to gather the traces of remembrance (GA 52, 3). The poet thus responds to the fact that "Being must be opened out" (EB 281). This role, after the completion of metaphysics, affords a supreme power to the poetic word of founding truth, for, according to Heidegger, "What the poet says and undertakes to be, is the real" (EB 286). The decision into this opening and establishing of Being, a decision that issues only in the moment of danger. If there is in Heidegger "no privileged standpoint at the end of philosophy,"[21] there is nevertheless an urgent call to what the poet delivers. In "The Origin of the Work of Art," as we examined in the previous chapter, this is illustrated as the struggle between earth and world; "poetry is the foundation which supports history" (EB 283) because it "compels a decision" (EB 271) "to be involved in the proximity of the essence of things" (EB 282). Hölderlin, as the poet of the "purest poetry," stands out in the midst of this danger, "exposed to the divine lightnings" (EB 284). Though Heidegger rejects a biographical account of the poetry, Heidegger explains Hölderlin's madness as the consequence of this danger (EB 282, 285; ST 2; GA 52, 42–48). Yet poetry is itself not something "mad," nor is it "lawless" or "capricious," but "is itself essentially establishment — that is to say, the act of firm foundation" (EB 286). The poet, receptive of Being's sending-withdrawing call, intercepts the signs of the gods and interprets them for the people, thus founding truth.

> The poet himself stands between . . . the gods . . . and the people. He is one who has been cast out into the Between, between gods and human beings. But only and for the first time in this Between is it decided, who the human being is and where he is settling his existence. (EB 288)

Thus Hölderlin's poetry is the "inaugural act" and is thoroughly ontological.[22] The freedom that concerns Hölderlin philosophically and poetically[23] — as a reader of Kant[24] — finds its place in Heidegger's reading as the freedom, once again, of saying-response to a destinal sending, the freedom to found history (GA 52, 3) in bringing truth to work (GA 52, 91). Hölderlin's references to freedom are strictly curtailed by the interpretive construction. Hölderlin's line "poets are free as swallows" thus means for Heidegger "not undisciplined arbitrariness and capricious desire, but supreme necessity" (EB 287). Though the act of founding involves freedom, this freedom is not that of a subject with all its metaphysical entanglements, but freedom as a response to the determining of a new time as the time of necessity, a singular call: "The essence of poetry, which Hölderlin establishes, is in the highest degree historical, because it anticipates a historical time; but as a historical essence, it is the sole essential essence" (EB 290). The poet thus "fashions truth, vicariously, and therefore truly for his people" (EB 290); this fashioning, however, is a response and not the self-assertion of a will (PLT 213–228).[25]

Remembrance Beyond Subjectivity

The relation between this renunciation of subjectivity and destiny is articulated in Heidegger's interpretations of Hölderlin's poem "Andenken." In this poem Hölderlin recalls his sojourn in Bordeaux, France, to which he walked after having lost a position as private tutor and in the crisis of forced separation from his lover Suzette Gontard, who has died by the time Hölderlin wrote this poem upon returning home. The first stanza reads,

> Der Nordost wehet,
> Der liebste unter den Winden
> Mir, Weil er feurigen Geist
> Und Gute Fahrt verheißt den Schiffern.
> Geh aber nun und grüße
> Die schöne Garonne,
> Und die Gärten von Bordeaux
> Dort, wo am scharfen ufer
> Hingehet der Steg und in den Strom
> Tief fällt der Bach, darüber aber
> Hinschauet ein edel Paar
> Von Eichen und Silber pappeln

> The Northeast wind is blowing,
> To me the most beloved of winds
> Because it means for the sailors
> fiery spirit and safe passage.
> But go now and greet
> The beautiful Garonne,
> And the gardens of Bordeaux
> There, where the path cuts sharply
> Along the canal and the stream
> Falls deep into the river,

But a noble pair of oak and silver poplar
Looks on from above

Here Hölderlin recalls what he found during his sojourn, each element of which is interpreted by Heidegger—the northeast winds (GA 52, 31–32, 35–42, 48–49), the shore and gardens of Bordeaux and the trees, acorn and silver poppy (GA 52, 52), and in later stanzas the brown women (GA 52, 59, 79–83) and the city's holiday (GA52, 59–61), and then the loneliness, the absence of friends (GA52, 175–180). Heidegger argues that "Andenken" is not the remembrance of earlier experiences of a subject or self. "The poem, rather asks Andenken." The poet answers in that he "poetizes the essence of Andenken" (EHD 84), that is, the remembrance of Being.

If, at first glance, the poem appears to be about "personal experiences" (*persönliche Erlebnisse*) (GA 52, 28) the lyrical tenor of the poem seems to strengthen this impression:

Es reiche aber,
Des dunkeln Lichtes voll,
Mir einer den duftenden Becher,
Damit ich ruhen möge . . .

But one of the fragrant chalices
Full of the dark light
Would suffice to me
So that I might rest . . .

On the basis of Hölderlin's correspondence, we know of his departure, "perhaps forever" (ELT 151), from Germany to France, and his distraught return whereupon he finds his beloved has died, and whereupon his period of madness—which extends to the rest of his life—is said to have begun. Heidegger argues against reading the poem according to the "curiosities" (*Neuigkeiten*) of Hölderlin's biography (GA 52, 28). Yet if the biographical reference is at all of use—for example in the letters to Böhlendorff, which Heidegger will employ as the logic of the poem's journey (GA 52, 22–23, 68, 121–132) into the "foreign" and back home—it is so as of another language (*eine andere sprache*) than that of the poet's experiences (GA 52, 29).

The content (*Inhalt*) of the poem is rejected as the site of what is essential in the poem, for Heidegger criticizes the notion of "content" as a literary-theoretical, or even metaphysical, category divorced from the poem's essence. Heidegger aims to articulate not merely content of the poem but the "poeticized" (*das Gedichtete*), and such requires the dismissal of the operation of images (*Bilder*). Heidegger resists imagistic reading of the poems in part because images yield to ontological translation only with great difficulty. Heidegger argues in fact that the thoughts (*Gedanken*) of the poem are not to be located in the poem's images—they are not "of" those images; neither are the thoughts ornamentalized or illustrated through images. The poetical thoughts are not merely poetically "painted" in images, a view which Hölderlin, given his reference in the poem those who, "wie Mahler," gather the earth's beauty, apparently does not share. (GA 52, 61; GA 39, 16).[26] Such rejection is also contested by Rilke's poetics, wherein images, for instance in *The Book of Images (Das Buch der Bilder)*, provide structure for the 'clearing' in which inwardness can wander out among things of the world and find correspondences between self and world. Yet Heidegger dismisses images for additional reasons: firstly, because they evoke the subjectivistic notion of the imagination as articulated in the Kantian aesthetics he leaves behind. In the penultimate and final chapters I will argue that the image and the imagination are consistent with Hölderlin's poetics and essential to a new poetics of Dasein. But for Heidegger, the difference between thoughts and images is to be challenged through the essential unity (*Einheit*) of the poem (GA 52, 29), itself uncovered or unfolded by the thinker. If Heidegger often differentiates the roles of *Denken* and *Dichten,* here the role of the thinker is "almost a *Mitdichten*" (GA 52, 55) in displacing the power of images for the unsaid source underlying them.

Heidegger aims to usurp the power of images in the poem, secondly, because he wants to disqualify *literaturwissenschaftliche* notions of symbol and metaphor (GA 52, 34, 39–40), which traditionally provide access to the poem's content. Most importantly, though, he refuses images because they tend to guide the reader into an imagined world of the poet's "experiences," which then seems to constitute the poem's real subject matter. An imagistic interpretation would fail to reach the poem essentially-ontologically, and would mire the poet within an inessential entanglement in beings rather than the event of Being as such. Since Heidegger reads the elements of the poem according to the passage of *Andenken* toward the origin, the "source" (*die Quelle*) (GA 52, 169–175), he must wrest our thinking from fixation upon the poem's elements or entities, a wresting to which the poem's images pose a problem. It is worth noting that in the same year as this lecture course Heidegger attempts to achieve an "imageless" (*bildlos*) thinking, in composed passages he calls *"Winke"* (hints or gestures). These passages, which appear on the page in the manner of poems, are unlike poems in that they are *"bildlos,"* have "no point of departure in beings" ("keine Aufenthalt im seienden") (GA 13, 33). Heidegger himself makes a connection between his compositions and this interpretation of Hölderlin. For in the "Andenken" lecture course he suggests that a "hint" from thinking is necessary: "Aber ein Wink dahin ist hier nötig" (GA 52, 27; see also 41). Such a hint or gesture conducts access to the poem which avoids dependency upon images and the entities to which they refer. Such an access would bring interpretation to the pure source, so that poetic language can be opened out as the site (*Ort*) of *Ereignis*. If *Ereignis* is to be thought as pure "occurrence" (EP 79), such a nonimagistic thinking is necessary.

Again, in the lecture course on "Germanien" (1934–35), Heidegger likewise explicitly rejects the comparison of the images in the poem to those in a painting, wherein the "gods" are announced. The announcement of the gods in "Germanien" is achieved not through imagistic representation of a content, as in the representation of the proclamations of the angels to Mary in the *"Darstellung"* of Renaissance painting (*Malerei*) (GA 39, 15–16). It is worth noting that in 1955 in the essay "Über die Sixtina" Heidegger gives an interpretation of a painting by Raphael, in which *Bild* is treated differently.[27] One could speak of an "essence of the image" (*Bildwesen*). Here the image grants essence to what a "window" is: "its frame enborders [*eingrennzt*] the open of transparency [*des Durchscheinnens*], in order to gather [*zu ersammeln*] the window through the release of appearance [*Freigabe des Schienens*]" (GA 13, 120). The image "is nothing other than the affirmation of this appearance." The bringing of arrival announced in the painting's Mary and child "gathers its happening in the glancing look into the essence of both, out of which the look is formed" (GA 13, 121). Yet again here the image is not essential and does not provide symbolic meaning; it is "kein Sinnbild"—but rather "is the appearance of the time-play-space [*Zeit-Spiel-Raum*] as of the place [*des Ortes*], wherein the mass is celebrated." The image forms (*bildet*) the *Ort* of *aletheia* (GA 13, 121).

If the poem is here not to be read as a series of images representing or voicing the poet's experiences, the richness of the poetic word lies, for Heidegger, in its simplicity (*Einfachheit*), a simplicity which is not penurious, "inexact," or simplistic (GA 52, 26). The reading of the poem "Andenken" is thus introduced by the notion of simplicity as the poem's "poeticized" essence: to think and ask *Andenken* as historical remembrance (GA 52, 16). This is not merely recollection of beings encountered as past (*Vergangenes*) but an instituting or founding history wherein the word comes to truth (GA 52, 21). For "only the historically-founding [*geschichtestiftender*] poet allows what poetry is, and perhaps must be. Only the historically-instituting [*geschichtegründende*] thinker brings past [*gewesende*] thinkers to speak [*zum Sprechen*]'" (GA 52, 3). Interestingly, the editor of Hölderlin's poems upon whom Heidegger relies, Norbert von Hellingrath, understood this poem—in contrast to the more "hymnal" poem—as particularly tethered to Hölderlin's specifically personal experiences, the "persönliche Erlebnisse der Menschen Hölderlin (nicht des Dichters)" (GA 52, 23), and named the poem "lyrical." Heidegger argues against this account, claiming, again, that the poem is decisively not about the poet's experiences nor about remembrances of things past ("Erinnerung, Gedächtnis an Vergangenes") (GA 52, 24). According to Heidegger the poem is neither lyrical nor hymnal, and though it recalls the Bordeaux landscape, the sea, the people there, "the language is of founding, of the institution of what is coming." The poem's important closing line, the source of Heidegger's notion of founding—"was bleibet aber stiften die Dichter"— "gathers everything" (*alles sammelt*), and in this line the authentic (*das Eigentliche*) comes forth without mediation (*unvermittelt*) (GA 52, 24). Not the content, but the leap from the poem's title (remembrance) to this last line (remaining) "indicates the whole" of the poem and the poeticized (GA 52, 24). We must then hear the poem not in singular "images" but as a "dark," still opaque (*undurchsichtig*) poem that rings "in one" (*in Einem*), a "poeticized" that remains still concealed (*verborgen*): the recollecting-waiting for the arrival of the inceptive word (GA 25, 13–14). Just as the Raphael painting gathers the essence of the release of appearances, the poem gathers the "poeticized"—that is, its ontological-historical role in founding truth.

This rejection of images and the experiences they might evoke is linked to Heidegger's rejection altogether of the subjective dimensions of Hölderlin's language. This latter rejection is accomplished in the eclipse of subjective elements of the poet's wandering by a national destination to which this wandering ultimately submits. For Heidegger the landscape, trees, river, the brown women of Bordeaux (EHD 102) "do not have their original essence in the reported sojourn in France" but rather in the reflections upon what is proper to "home" (GA 52, 144–145, 178–182), a "principle" that Heidegger finds in letters Hölderlin wrote to his friend Casmir Böhlendorff on December 4, 1801, and December 2, 1802 (GA 52, 22–23, 121–132; EHD 82). It "is grounding principle of the poetizing of this poet, that to him wandering in the foreign remains essentially for going home into the own law of his poetic song" (EHD 83). This law is the response to destiny as a renunciation of will. "Andenken" is the "poetic truth of the essence of *Andenken*" (EHD 84) in which the "I" and the "me" of the poem (*ich, mir*) refer not to Hölderlin himself but to his renunciation (GA 52, 36, 170: GA 39, 42–43). The second stanza of the poem continues with reference to the speaker's own memory of the aforementioned landscape. Hölderlin's syntax allows memory to be intertwined with the landscape he has described and further articulates:

> Noch denket mir das wohl und wie
> Die breiten Gipfel neiget
> Der Ulmwald, über die Mühl,'
> Im Hofe aber wächset ein Feigenbaum.

> Still these thoughts come to me and how
> With broad tips nods
> The elm forest over the mill,
> But in the courtyard grows a fig tree.

Heidegger writes,

> Who speaks here? Hölderlin himself. But who, here and now, is Hölderlin himself? The one whose essence finds it fulfillment in "willing" that this wind is and should be as it is. (EHD 85)

A similar treatment is given in the interpretation of "Germanien," wherein Hölderlin as poetic subject is explicitly silenced:

> Who is this "I"? Hölderlin? . . . The poem as a whole is language and speaks (*ist sprache und spricht*) . . . actually no one speaks here. (GA 39, 42)

The wind Hölderlin recalls at the beginning of the poem, and which Hölderlin relates directly to the poem's speaker ("Der Liebste unter den Winden / Mir"), is not that of the landscape of Hölderlin's experience. Rather, "this wind calls upon the poets to find themselves in the destiny of their historical essence" (EHD 86). According to Heidegger, whenever Hölderlin says "I" (*ich*) or "me" (*mir*) he means the poet who finds his essence in the sending of Being. *Andenken* is therefore the "sending of the essence of this poet" ("Wesensschickung dieses Dichters") (EHD 87). The poet has overcome "will" in the metaphysical sense and adopts "will" in the sense beyond subjectivity (GA 52, 41). Just as freedom and destiny are collapsed, as we discussed in the previous chapter, here will and destiny are indistinguishable:

"Will" means here in no way the egoistic enforcement of a self-ishly calculated desire. Will is the knowing readiness for the belonging in destiny. This will wills only that which comes, because what comes already addressed this will towards a knowing and calls upon this will to stand in the wind of promise. (EHD 87)

Thus the subjective structure, the "I" of the poem, is thought by Heidegger as the reception of destiny: "What the poet wills is what is willed in essential wishing, that is, the destinal [*das Schickliche*]" (EHD 127).

For Heidegger, the poem and what it poetizes do not belong to a poetic subject but to the history of Being and its "founding." Heidegger connects Hölderlin's last line "Was bleibet aber, stiften die Dichter" to such founding rather than to the poetical memory which brings to mind beautiful but transient, and thus lost, things the way painters do. *Andenken*, and the poetizing-thinking thereof, is for Heidegger an historical act (*geschichtliches Handeln*).[28] As such, it is an event (*das Ereignis*) that does not merely belong to "culture." This act "does not require merely deeds [*Taten*] in order to effect [*wirken*], or effects [*Wirkungen*] in order to be [*um zu sein*]" (GA 52, 27). This destiny is what is in turn "founded" by the poet as what remains. In "Andenken," such memory is linked to the sea as the river's origin. Hölderlin's speaker claims:

> Es nehmet aber
> Und giebt Gedächtniß die See,
> Und die Lieb' auch heftet fleißig die Augen
>
> But the sea takes
> And gives our memories
> And love also diligently holds our eyes

With the reference to love Hölderlin suggests both the inwardness of subjective feeling and the painterly imagery of remembrance as that upon which we might gaze.[29] For Heidegger, that "which remains" is not an imagistic memory of fleeting experience, of finite thoughts (*sterblichen Gedanken*), which the sea, like love, withholds or restores. It is rather the destiny, the sending of the "origin," to which the poet is privy. "The founding dwelling near to origin is the original dwelling, wherein the poetic is first grounded" (EHD 149). This dwelling is of the "essence" that belongs to the poet alone. The "original" *Andenken*, as the "experience of the poet, rather takes the poet into the sphere of his essence which is opened in the poem" (EHD 51).

Heidegger takes up the first line of the poem, "Der Nordost wehet," in which, according to Heidegger, "already begins a secret"—the turn homeward toward the homely source in the poem's time-space (*der Zeit-Raum der Dichtung*) (GA 52, 32, 53). This time-space realm will be articulated again as the structure of *Ereignis* in the essay "Time and Being" some two decades later, and this articulation arises again in *Hölderlins Hymnen "Der Ister"* (1942), both of which I will examine in this chapter. This "time-space" realm of the poem is not the transitoriness of natural memories — is not, therefore, to be understood as a verse on the finitude of "natural" life (GA 52, 35–36). Thus Heidegger must confront Hölderlin's philosophical essay on "Becoming in Dissolution" (ELT 96–100), which in fact treats of this transitoriness and how it can be thought poetically-idealistically. Hölderlin's essay, as we will see in the next chapter, could provide a clue as to how to read the course of the poem "Andenken" (for it treats of poetic recollection (*Erinnerung*) that then makes possible a grasp of the "whole" sense of nature or life despite its momentary transitoriness). Heidegger, recognizing the nearness of the themes of "Andenken" to the still "metaphysical" language of this essay, must find an essential connection between them without subscribing to the latter's metaphysical elements, its acknowledgment of subjectivity. In recognizing the connection between the language of the essay and that of Fichte, Schelling, and Hegel, Heidegger argues nevertheless that this language only "conceals" (*verbirgt*) what is essentially there, and so dismisses Hölderlin's theoretical articulations that might pertain to the poem. Of Hölderlin's essay, Heidegger writes, "In fact his conceptual language (*seine Begriffssprache*) is also not only an external husk, rather the formulation (*Fassung*) of his still metaphysical thinking. Hölderlin still thinks metaphysically. But he poetizes otherwise" (GA 52, 199–120). In the essay, the state between Being and non-Being is described by Hölderlin as a "divine dream" (*göttlicher Traum*) that can only be grasped in *Erinnerung* and thus only in "truly tragic language" (ELT 97). The image of the dream appears in "Andenken," too; just as subjective memory is intertwined with the landscape, here the dream is linked to the northeast wind with which the poem commences by here saturating the breezes:

> Und über langsamen Stegen,
> Von goldenen Träumen schwer,
> Einwiegende Lüfte ziehen.

> And slow over footpaths,
> Heavy with golden dreams,
> Drift lulling breezes.

Heidegger does not take up the problem of *Erinnerung,* which would link *Andenken* to a notion of subjectivity or the inwardness of feeling and memory. Rather, Heidegger interprets the poem as reconciliation and balance (GA 52, 85–86) according to the "divine dream" (GA 52, 120–122). The "dream" connects the poem and the essay, then read not as the transition between becoming and dissolution in nature, life, or spirit in *Erinnerung* but as that between the foreign of the other *(das Fremden des Anderen)* and the proper *(das Eigenes)* (GA 52, 86) — the German and the Greek[30] (GA 52, 121). Such a dream is perhaps imageless; but in the poem it is inextricable from the landscape painted by the speaker. Hölderlin has treated the theme in the Böhlendorff letters,[31] to which Heidegger turns in avoiding the metaphysics of "Becoming in Dissolution." In "Andenken," the poet's reference to springtime, in March, a transition between seasons — "Wenn gleich ist Nacht und Tag" (When day and night are equal) — is again not a factual recollection of a particular memory (though Hölderlin's stay in Bordeaux extended from his arrival in early winter until his return in summer) but as the transition from foreign to home. It is this transition that constitutes the *Schicksal* that, according to Heidegger, the poem poetizes (GA 52, 88–90).

Heidegger's interpretation of the poem must continually wrest the latter from the poet's experiences witnessed in the poem's images. If the wind of the northeast brings to Saying the *Schicksal* of *Andenken* as this homeward-bound journey, it does not for Heidegger concern the poet as an experiencing subject. If in the poem the wind blows "to me" *(mir),* Heidegger insists,

> in the "me" Hölderlin certainly means himself. But the I [*das Ich*] which speaks of itself is not the person Hölderlin. The ground for the penchant [*Vorliebe*] for the Northeast [wind] lies not in personal situations, needs, or biographical relations [*lebensgeschichtlichen Verhältnissen*] of the person Hölderlin. (GA52, 36)

The speaker writes of the wind — which blows from the direction of Hölderlin's home — not out of his personal homesickness or reflections on his own journey, far from his friends, his lover, his familiar and beloved landscape. Rather, the northeastern wind brings the seafarers[32] who presence: "Announcement, assurance, granting" *(Ankündigung, Zusicherung, Schenkung)* (GA 52, 175–178), as the historical *Schicksal.*

Hölderlin's line on the northeastern wind, for Heidegger, thus announces the poet's belongingness (*Zugehörigkeit*) to the poet's vocation (GA 52, 41–42) defined as the "open belongingness to Being" and the historical founding of destiny in the relation of gods and humans, itself "founded" in the festival or feast (GA 52, 41, 3, 88–90). While in "Andenken" there is no representation of feast (only a reference to the city's holidays recalled among other details of the poem's landscape), Heidegger turns to the poems "Wie wenn am Feiertage" (GA 52, 50) and "Brot und Wein" (GA 52, 75–76, 67–71) for description of the feast or festival, the site (*Ort*) of the historical founding. This allows Heidegger to insist that the poet's vocation is not a matter of the poet's personal well-being (*persönliches Wohlbefinden*) but rather a belongingness to this feastly founding of Being—stemming from and returning to its "open" (GA 52, 41). This belongingness is a belongingness to *Schicksal* as the past (*das Gewesenes*) and the arriving (*das Kommendes*), and as such is the "innermost essence of freedom" (GA 52, 41). The Northeast carries the poet into the essential direction of that which he must fulfill; the joy of the poet, which resounds in the first stanza— and therefore that of the feast from "Wie wenn am Feiertage"[33]—is not personal, not pertaining to poetic Dasein with its own specific *Befindlichkeit* and mood, the joy is only such that the poet may "stand in this essence" (GA 52, 41–42).

The greeting[34] referred to in the fifth line is, Heidegger argues, the letting-be (*Seinlassen*) of what is greeted (GA 52, 50), and yet it is also the transition to the proper of each essential thing (GA 52, 51). Such greeting is not understood to be essentially linked to the entities, the factical specificities, which are recalled in the poem, as when Hölderlin writes, "Geh aber nun und grüße / Die schöne Garonne, / Und die Gärten von Bordeaux." ("But go now and greet / The beautiful Garonne, / And the Bordeaux gardens.") If the poet claims that "this all now comes to mind" ("noch denket mir das wohl"), this is not the poet's longing for what is lost to him. In founding historically, the poetic word brings each thing into the destiny that it alone recalls and awaits. "Through the greeting first came the greeted into being [*seiend geworden*]" (GA 52, 53). As such, the poet discloses not merely beings but the origin, which gathers beings into an essential belongingness to the historical sending. If the poet founds "what remains," his remembrance is not merely the "unselfconstancy of a ruin [*Unselbständigkeit eines Restes*] which can no longer help itself and only atrophies [*verkümmert*]. Remaining behind is a greeting [*Grüssen*], and the greeting [*Gruss*] beams an inwardness [*Innigkeit*] which must come of its own source." This source is not the poet himself but the original source, that of the "homely" (*das Heimliche*) of the *Ereignis* itself (GA 52, 53–54). This *Ereignis*, homely and inceptive, is "strong enough" to draw out and preserve

Gedenken, "the indelible [*unauslöschliche*] of the having-been [*des Gewe-senen*]" (GA 52, 54). As such, the greeting is *Andenken*, and is then a *"Denken."* Thus in the greeting is found the "gathered unity" (*versam-melten Einheit*) of the greeted (GA 52, 56). The greeting is then linked to the festival, as "the ground and essence of history" (GA 52, 68). As we will see, this history is, as in "The Origin of the Work of Art," conceived in explicitly nationalist terms.

With reference to themes from the Böhlendorff letters and the poems "Wie wenn am Feiertage" and "Brot und Wein,"[35] Heidegger seems to have uncovered the "essential unity" of the poem: the greeting is the *Ereignis* in relation to origin, which then grants the relation of humans and gods as the historical sending; *Andenken* is the journeying from out of the foreign to home, the original source of *Ereignis;* the founding of history, of "what remains," is accomplished in uncovering "the concealed essence of history" (GA 52, 70), its awaited "gathering" (GA 52, 73). The festival is "the *Ereignis*" of the inceptive greeting (GA 52, 70); the poet, himself a seafarer, is set on a journey (*Meerfahrt*) that marks out the concealed source (*Quelle*) of history: the return to the proper German "Heimat" (GA 52, 168) from out of its (Greek, authentic) source (GA 52, 128–132)—a destination Heidegger again derives from the Böhlendorff letter. According to Heidegger, "Andenken" thus "thinks" the "holiness of the fatherland" (though the *Vaterland* or the national is nowhere mentioned in this poem) (GA 52, 132–136). Heidegger thus claims that "poetizing and thinking is the authentic searching (*Dichten und Denken ist das eigentliche Suchen*) for the highest (*das Höchste*), the *Vaterland*" (GA 52, 134).

With each facet of his interpretation, Heidegger silences the authentic poetic voice of the poem, which involves poetic receptivity announced in the repetition of the dative "me" (*mir*). The wind is referred to as most beloved "to me" (*mir*); by reference, commencing the second stanza, to the speaker's own memory: "Noch denket das mir wohl und wie" (Still these thoughts came to me and how); and with the longing for a fragrant chalice of "dark light" that would afford the speaker (indexed again with the genitive "mir") rest in the shade. If the poet asks in the third stanza for a dialogue (*Gespräch*) with friends to calm his loneliness, Heidegger claims that "only the poet, who knows the destinal" ("der das Schickliche weiss"), can commence the poetic conversation (*dichterisches Gespräch*) that is *Andenken* (GA 52, 165). When the poet, asking for his absent friends, longs to "speak the heart" (*des Herzens Meinung*) with his friends about "days of love and deeds," he is in fact asking only after the essence of his mission. The poet asks: "But where are the friends?" and recalls communion with them: "Doch gut / Ist ein Gespräch und zu sagen / Des Herzens Meinung, zu hören viel / Von Tagen der Lieb,' / Und Thaten, welche geschehen" (Yet conversing is good / And to say what's in the heart / And to hear much / About days of love / And deeds that have happened). Despite these references Heidegger understands the poet as an isolated figure who alone is essentially called to the origin, for the friends "shy from" the source (GA 52, 169–172). When the speaker in Hölderlin's poem asks for his friends, Heidegger thinks, he is asking after himself, poetizing what belongs to himself—not *as* a self but as the "supreme isolation of his mission" (EB 192), as the vessel of an essential destiny. Heidegger writes:

> The poet asks of and poeticizes the homely [*das Heimische*]. The poet alone asks poetically. The unveiling stepping-forth of the question is nonetheless a veiling. What is seemingly undetermined in the question is what is suspended in the veiling, which nonetheless intimates what it asks for. The poet asks for his company and for his friends and asks nonetheless, if not only, after himself. Certainly, he is not brooding over the "I" of his person, rather he asks away from this "I" toward the essential abode of the self, for what is proper to this self is alone the fulfillment of the essence of a poethood. (EHD 129)

The "essential abode of the self" is the historical-ontological sending that is founded in awaiting recollection; thus this "self" is given texture and dimension not as a self in the world (in the sense of Dasein's *in-der-Welt-sein*), explicitly not as one with a particular, factical history, feelings and experiences, relationships and moods, but rather in a wholly ontological-historical sense: as the reception, indeed the proximity to, Being. Thus the loneliness that Hölderlin expresses, the absence of friends, is the "essential" loneliness of being called forth for a destiny not unlike the solitude of resolute Dasein when Dasein, "exiled from the world,"[36] remembers itself "under the eyes of death" (BT 134/382). We might note, however, Hölderlin's warning in "Andenken" that "It is not good / To lose one's soul in / Thoughts of death" [Nicht ist es gut, / seellos von Sterblichen / Gedanken zu seyn]). In this context Heidegger claims again that when Hölderlin writes, in the poem "Die Titanen," "but I am alone" ("ich aber bin allein"), his "I" does not mean the poet himself but the difficulty (*die Schwere*) of being called to the between of the transition, of founding, on the journey, the coming of the holy to word (GA 52, 179, 193–194). Hölderlin's notion of

"*Innigkeit*" (inwardness, intimacy) is thus not the logic of an experiencing "I" or of a soul (GA 52, 153) but rather the *Schicksal* of founding history (GA 52, 91).

Yet Hölderlin's poem "Andenken" itself gives resources for competing interpretations, as I have suggested throughout this account of Heidegger's interpretation.[37] And while Heidegger rids the poem of its subjective dimensions—the "I" and "me" of the speaker, the speaker's "experience"—Hölderlin's own writings on the relation of poetic language to the "reflection" within the "I" or "self" render Heidegger's interpretation unlikely, if not also essentializing. This "still metaphysical" philosophical dimension of Hölderlin's thinking—that of subjectivity—is placed within Heidegger's formulation of the *Vollendung* of metaphysics and so ejected from the realm of essential thinking. Hölderlin's poetry as the recollection of an origin that is solely ontological-historical and wholly beyond the subject is rendered only by obscuring the nuances and texts of Hölderlin's own thought. If it is true that, as I shall argue in chapter 3, the poem "Andenken" is both a recollection of origin, to some extent compatible with Heidegger's interpretation, and nonetheless essentially involves the experiences of a subject, this subjectivity will have to be examined in detail.

The Event of Thinking: From Being to the *Ereignis*

Remembrance of origin as the destinal recollection of Being is given further articulation in Heidegger's thinking of *Ereignis*. Heidegger proceeds from the founding of truth in an essential-destinal sense to thinking the "primal phenomenon" that is beyond, but appears in the wake of, the crisis instituted by subjective-metaphysical thinking. This "primal" or primordial thinking becomes in Heidegger's thought the *Ereignis* treated at length in the 1962 essay "Time and Being," which in some sense provides the final reversal of *Being and Time*'s still too subjectivistic grounding of temporality in human Dasein.[38] *Ereignis* as the "event" of "appropriation" (*Ereignis*) is the name for the temporality of Being as a sending that is not grounded in Dasein and is not merely the ground of beings. Heidegger formulates the *Ereignis* in a treatment of poetry and of Hölderlin in the decades preceding this essay. The history of Being can be thought only in a thinking of *Ereignis*, and that depends on the essential word, as Heidegger writes in *Die Geschichte des Seyns* (1938–40): "The 'history of Being' is the name for the attempt to turn back the truth of Being as *Ereignis* to the word of thinking, and thus to entrust the word and its sayability to an essential ground of the historical human being" (GA 69, 5).

The "es gibt" and the Ereignis in "Time and Being" and On the Way to Language

Heidegger begins his lecture "Time and Being" by asking his listeners to suspend the expectation that his ruminations be immediately intelligible. Just as we do not expect a great painting, poem, or theory of physics—such as those given to us by Paul Klee, Georg Trakl, and Werner Heisenberg (an inclusion to which I will return shortly)—to be immediately intelligible, so too must we patiently follow the "movement of showing" ("dem Gang des Zeigen zu folgen") that a thinking might demand. This thinking is both inevitable (*Umumgängliches*) and preliminary (*Vorläufiges*) (ZSD 1/OTB 2). Heidegger must formulate his thinking here carefully, for the attempt here to speak about Being as such is more difficult even than in *Being and Time;* for there the meaning of Being was to be accessed through an analysis of Dasein's relationship to beings as the "place of disclosure of Being."[39] Now, Being is to be thought "without regard to its being grounded in terms of beings" ("ohne die Rücksicht auf eine Begründung des Seins aus dem Seienden") (ZSD 2/OTB 2). Thus the thinking of Being is more difficult and even requires a change of terminology. Heidegger thus employs the "it gives" (*es gibt*)—the German phrase for "there is," corresponding to the French *il y a*—and the "event of appropriation" (*Ereignis des Eignens*) in order to unhinge a thinking of Being from that of beings. Yet Heidegger had already accomplished a thinking of the *es gibt* and the *Ereignis* in his interpretations of Hölderlin's poetry. The essays of the 1950s in *On the Way to Language* examine a "poetizing thinking" of *Ereignis* and appropriation (*Ereignen*). In the essay "The Essence of Language," in which Heidegger interprets a line from Hölderlin's "Germanien" and Stefan George's poem "The Word," Heidegger writes,

> The word . . . conceals within itself that which gives Being. If our thinking does justice to the matter, then we may never say of the word that it is, but rather that it gives [*es gibt*]—not in the sense that words are given by an "it," but that the word itself gives. The word itself is the giver. What does it give? To go by the poetic experience and by the most ancient tradition of thinking, the word gives Being. Our thinking, then would have to seek the word, the giver which itself is never given, in this "there is that which gives." (OWL 88)

In "The Way to Language," Heidegger writes that the *"Ereignis* gathers [*versammelt*] the design [*Aufriß*] of Saying, and unfolds it into the structure [*zum Gefüge*] of manifold showing" (OWL 128/US 259). In order to approach a thinking of *Ereignis*, it must come "to light how astounding a power the word possesses" (OWL 88). The word "bestows being" to the thing (OWL 86), gives the fourfold in which things and human beings are "face-to-face with one another" (OWL 104). Words, Heidegger claims in reading the line from Hölderlin, rise from the earth as the "flower of the mouth," and the steps to think this arising "fuse into a concentration upon the selfsame thing, and wend their way back to it" (OWL 102). And yet the *Ereignis* is not a phenomenon, for it does not appear, but is rather the most inconspicuous (*das Unscheinbarste des Unscheinbaren*) (OWL 128/US 259). How is this thinking of the word's bestowing being to the thing compatible with a thinking that aims to bring to word what does not appear—or, as Heidegger writes only three years later in the "Time and Being" essay, for a thinking of Being not grounded in beings? In the *Ereignis* finite things have their stay or sojourn (*Aufenthalten*), and Hölderlin's language shows that the saying of *Ereignis* "brings to light all present beings in terms of their properties—it lauds, that is, allows them into their own essence" (OWL 135). In bestowing being to the thing, the "face-to-face with one another" of human beings and things of the world are brought to echo their "more distant origin" (OWL 104). This origin is called in Hölderlinian fashion the "fourfold," but it echoes *Ereignis*: "the time-space that gives free scope to all things" (OWL 106). In listening to poetic language, the thinker approaches the fact that time and space are the "Same" in the sense of a "face-to-face encounter" issuing as a movement of granting (OWL 104). Heidegger outlines this movement in "Time and Being" as the time-play-space (*Zeitspielraum*) opened out by the lingering-whiling presencing of *Ereignis*. Thus, despite the granting of Being to the thing in the poetic word, here we are removed from the realm of what occurs from the specificities of the poet's ontical experience in order to follow the "origin" of occurrence itself. In the lecture on "Andenken," this lingering-whiling is thought as the nearness to the origin or the source (*die Quelle*).

In *Being and Time* Being was not to be thought, as in metaphysical onto-theology, as a being grounding all other beings, but as the *"transcendens"*—the horizon of absence that makes presencing of beings possible, grounded in the *Zeitlichkeit* of Dasein. In "Time and Being" Being is no longer to be thought as the Being of beings on the basis of the ecstatic structure of the self of Dasein. Heidegger thus writes that "what this text contains, written three and a half decades later, can no longer be a continuation of the text *Being and Time*" (ZSD 91/OTB 83).[40] "Time and Being" cannot be simply the completion of *Being and Time* because between the two texts Heidegger's attempt to think Being is joined with a more extreme and more urgent critique of subjectivity; not only does Heidegger move away from the "anthropocentric" analysis of Dasein, but he also takes up the thinking of Being within the oblivion of the technological crisis that Heidegger analyses as the secret "essence" of subjective-metaphysical thinking (ZSD 7/OTB 7). Thus Heidegger claims that his thinking in "Time and Being" is necessary — that it is precisely needed by the oblivion of the forgetting of Being, "because otherwise, it seems to me, there is no longer any possibility of explicitly bringing into view the Being of what *is* today all over the earth" (ZSD 2/OTB 2). Thus Heidegger implies that a nontechnological account of beings — of language rising from the earth[41] in granting Being to the being, cannot be given at all if we do not first, as a preliminary step, wrest our thinking from beings and attempt to think Being "as the sole occurrence" (EP 79). Such a thinking is issued by Heidegger's discoveries about the essence of language, and yet in the readings of poetic language a tension arises between its role as the revealing of beings in their essence — that is, in relation to origin — and of the revealing-withholding of origin itself. This strain between the phenomenological and the ontological is perhaps a deeper source of Heidegger's difficulty in assessing the images in Hölderlin's poem, which, if not each read according to the Saying of origin, come close to presenting *Andenken* as a recollection of (subjective) experiences, or a mere tangling amid beings.

Similarly, Heidegger will argue that language refers not to beings but to itself. In "The Way to Language" Heidegger argues that the *Ereignis*, by way of language, appropriates (*ereignet*) mortals. Language is thus conceived as the response, as the "sounding" of answering to origin. Language is not merely the naming of beings, but yields "the way to language" as the saying of the *Ereignis*. Language thus speaks of and to itself,[42] and therefore such answering is language being brought back to its own (*eigenes*) historically. As in "The Origin of the Work of Art," response is linked with submission to destiny. "All true language, because assigned, sent, destined to the human being by the way-making movement of saying, is in the nature of destiny" (OWL 133). While we will discuss this in the last two chapters of this book, it might be pertinent here to wonder about the status of unessential language pertaining to the specific being or the specific speaker. What are we to make of occurrences about which it might be urgent to speak but that do not speak of the "origin" or are excluded from the "original?" This will become a problem, as mentioned earlier in terms of witness, when attempting to reach beyond Hölderlin toward poets who speak from standpoints excluded or alienated from the sources that would sustain them.

Heidegger begins his consideration of time and Being by indicating that Being has always, in the history of metaphysics, been accounted for in terms of time—that is, as enduring presence or as the Being of what is present—but only in precisely covering over this temporality of Being and in treating time as if it were a thing, that is, a being (ZSD 3/OTB 3). In such an account, as Heidegger writes in the Hölderlin-George essay, time is thought "in the succession of 'nows' one after the other as elements of parametric time" (OWL 104). Being is, however, not temporal like a thing is, and time *is* not in the way in which a thing is. Just as it can be said that Being is not a being, time is nothing temporal. In order to avoid determining Being according to time as (temporal) presence and time according to (existing) presence, we must think Being and time in their own elements (*nach ihr Eigenes*) (ASD 5/OTB 5); we take a step back from both Being and time in order to say "there is being" and "there is time," thus indicating the "there is" (*es gibt*), which also means "it gives." For this "a transformation of language is needed" (OWL 135).

It is the "it gives" that holds Being and time apart toward their own element and together "toward each other." But how can we think this "it gives"? Heidegger once again insists on the necessity to move away from thinking about beings.

To think Being itself explicitly requires disregarding Being to the extent that it is only grounded and interpreted in terms of beings and for beings as their ground. . . . To think Being explicitly requires us to relinquish Being as the ground of beings ["das Sein als Grund des Seienden fahren zu lassen"] in favor of the giving which prevails concealed in unconcealment, that is in favor of the It gives. (ZSD 6/ OTB 6)

But language, thought poetically, is "the relation of all relations" and thus of the relation between time and Being, time and space, space and Being. Language "relates, maintains, proffers, and enriches the face-to-face encounter of the world's regions, and holds them apart, in that it holds itself . . . in reserve" (OWL 107). Language is itself not about beings but a thinking of presencing in its spatial-temporal unity; and in "Andenken" poetic language prepares a thinking of the "distant origin." To think language is to think the *Ereignis* and the *es gibt*. The poetic notion of the fourfold allows the thinking that: "of time it may be said: time times. Of space it may be said: space spaces" (OWL 106). But this does not yet take into account the "encounter" of both (OWL 106).

In relinquishing Being as the clearing of beings' emergence into presence—in relinquishing a thinking of Being as "presencing" (*Anwesen*) of beings (ZSD 6/OTB 6)—we can remove our thinking from those beings in order to think the "it gives," which does not presence itself but withdraws in favor of what is presenced—a thinking of that which "hold itself . . . in reserve." Thus the jug—perhaps Heidegger's most favored example of a thing as site of the fourfold—*is* more essentially what it is "in the void that it holds" than in the "material of which consists" (PLT 169). If the word that brings the "it gives" to language is still awaited, this awaiting is in turn a recollecting *Andenken*, for the "giving which gives only its gift, but in the giving holds itself back and withdraws, such a giving we call sending [*Schicken*]." In the "Time and Being" essay, Being, now the *"es gibt"* or this "sending," is no longer the presencing of beings—the bestowing of Being onto things of the world—but the sending itself, which holds itself back in the sending. As in Heidegger's emphasis on concealment in "The Origin of the Work of Art," what is named here is then not the presencing but the *withdrawal* of Being that makes presencing possible, and that can no longer be experienced or heard at the level of what is presenced, or what "is." Each transformation (*Wandlungen*) of Being within history must be determined according to this "sending." This sending is a history of Being that thus thinks and recollects *withdrawal*—and not the "discernible" gift, or Being as the ground of beings within any epoch—as primary (ZSD 9/OTB 9).[43] The epochs themselves, sent in an incalculable and yet not accidental way, "overlap each other" such that the "original" sending of Being as presence is "more and more obscured" (*verdeckt wird*) and in "different ways" (*auf verschiedene Weise*) (ZSD 9/OTB 9). This sending and its recollecting retrieval is the task of *Andenken* Heidegger adopts from Hölderlin: if the subject is "without origin" (EP, 63), poetry brings the origin to thought in *Andenken*, which no longer concerns the subject. Freedom is again divorced from the specificity of a subject or a particular will: "thinking the freeing into freedom for the truth of Being" is beyond humanism—is *"un-menschlich"* (GA 69, 24). The history of Being as a thinking of *Ereignis* must take the human beings into account only in a limited sense: "The fact that the human being belongs to the history of Being only in the scope of his essence which is determined by the claim of Being, and not with regard to his existence, actions, and accomplishments within beings, signifies a restriction unique in its manner" (EP 182). Regarding the silenced subjective experiences and their images articulated in Hölderlin's poem "Andenken," one might connect this refusal of the subject to Heidegger's attempt to think beyond beings. Almost preempting this reading, Hölderlin concludes the first version of "Der Einzige" ("The Only One") with the claim that "The poets and the spiritual too / must be of the world" (Die Dicheter müssen auch / Die geistigen Weltlich seyn).

But Heidegger's retrieval of origin requires a still more radical consideration of the temporality of Being and of the Being of time. For Being's "presencing" is determined in fact by the dimensionality of "true time," which Heidegger calls "poetic time" (DI 8). In poetic time presencing itself (*Anwesen*) is what is "offered" in the "absence" (*Abwesen*) of what withdraws. In the future as coming-toward us (*Auf-uns-Zukommen*), approaching but "not yet present," absence offers presence; in being what is no longer present, what has been presence as such is granted. If the ecstatic self of Dasein temporally opened out of the space of a world in *Being and Time* (§70), here Being is opened out by the approaching-withholding character of the dimensions of time and by the play that is their unity, the unity of the event (*Ereignis*) itself. In "The Nature of Language" on Hölderlin and George, Heidegger writes:

> Time in its timing removes us into its threefold simultaneity, moves us thence while holding out to us the disclosure of what is in the same time, the concordant oneness of the has-been, presence, and the present waiting the encounter. In removing and bringing to us, and space's throwing open, admitting and releasing — they all belong together in the Same, the play of stillness. (OWL 106)

Within this presencing, "there opens up what we call time-space (*Zeit-Raum*), which we also call the open (*das Offene*) as the unity of the dimensions of time — the three dimensions of future, past, present accompanied by a fourth, the "playing in the very heart of time," which is the playing of each dimension toward the other. (ZSD 16/OTB 15). Heidegger adopts the notion of the "open" from Rilke, a notion that Heidegger reads according to the Hölderlinian danger-saving motif, and for whom the term designates "the whole draft to which all beings, as ventured beings, are given over" (PLT 106). The giving in "it gives time" is then the "extending, opening" that opens the four-dimensional realm in which Being presences (ZSD 17/OTB 17). This realm (*Bereich*) is the "it" that gives Being. Time and space can thus be thought together: the "open" is now the time-space of presencing: "room" is made by the mutual self-extending (*das im Einander-sich-reichen*) of the three dimensions of time; and this extending is "space" (*Raum*) given or en-spaced (*einräumen*) (ZSD 15/OTB 15). While Heidegger gives more thought here to time than to space, he refers to his essay "Building, Dwelling, Thinking" as a correlative showing of the spatial element of that relation (PLT 143–161). If temporality implies human historicality as the historicality of Being, this spatiality determines human "dwelling" (OTB 23).

The relation between Being and time is given particular attention here because it is this relation that can be first articulated as "appropriation" (*Ereignen*). In the relation of appropriation, time and Being are each given over into "that which is their own" (*ihr Eigenes*). But this relation is itself an "event" and thus this determining of their own is together called "*Ereignis*"—the event of appropriation. This does not indicate, however, a single or particular "event"—not the opening of Being for beings—but "that which makes any occurrence possible"— the sending that itself withdraws (ZSD 20/OTB 19). Appropriation is that which brings time and Being into their own, makes them stand together, and yet holds them apart in their own, and is itself "concealed in destiny and in the gift of opening out." Thus the *Ereignis*, although irreducible to the history of Being as the history of discernable epochs — and thus beyond history—is the historicality that makes this history possible. Being, thought as Appropriation (*Sein als das Ereignis*), must mean for us that Being belongs to Appropriating (*das Ereignen*)—not as a species of Being, but as the self-withdrawal itself. It is the "transformation of appropriation" (*Ereignen*) that "brings mortals into the path of thinking, poetizing building" (EP 110). If in "The Origin of the Work of Art" poetry was too closely aligned with history and the political, here poetic language recedes far out of the reach of any discernible decision that might be made with regard to beings.

In thinking the *Ereignis*, Heidegger has traced Being "to its own" (*in sein Eigenes*) through thinking "true time" (*eigentliche Zeit*). Here it is said that Heidegger's thinking "has arrived at its goal."[44] This goal is now not even the "overcoming" of metaphysics, which involves the uncovering of Being as the abyssal ground of beings, but to leave metaphysics—and its subjective "forgetting"—entirely behind (ZSD 25/OTB 24). At the end of his lecture, Heidegger thus repeats the claim he made at its commencement: "To think Being without beings means: to think Being without regard to metaphysics. Yet a regard for metaphysics still prevails event in the intention to overcome metaphysics. Therefore, our task is to cease all overcoming, and leave metaphysics to itself" (OTB 24).

Since Heidegger, two years after "Time and Being," returns to the history of Being in "The End of Philosophy and the Task of Thinking," in which he traces metaphysical determinations of Being from Plato to Hegel and Husserl, this cannot mean that Heidegger has stopped tracing the self-withdrawing of Being as a history—that the thinking of the *Ereignis* marks the end of the thinking of the *Seinsgeschichte*. But the "end of the history of Being" is the thinking of *Ereignis*, which itself heeds both the notion of origin—as the "first," unthought possibility of thinking—and "end" as the last, most extreme possibility (OTB 59). The *Ereignis* is an event that is sent in the "it gives" in which the sending withholds itself in favor of what is sent, and that what is sent is that which determines the noncalculable but also nonaccidental destiny of the epochs. The "end of the history of Being" means then the beginning of thinking this original "unthought" as the *Ereignis*. In this limited sense, then, Heidegger's thinking succeeds in the "reversal" of *Being and Time* itself announced therein: to think Being, which is "beyond beings." What is to be thought, then, is the task (*Aufgabe*) of thinking, which has been concealed in the history of philosophy, a task that, in the progress of scientific thinking and metaphysics, has withdrawn itself increasingly as that which is to be thought (OTB 59). If Heidegger has traced the *Ereignis* in "Time and Being," he pauses to note at the end of this lecture that the form of the lecture itself, which has "spoken merely in proposition," remains an obstacle to thinking the *Ereignis* genuinely. We know from the essays in *On the Way to Language*, and, further, from Heidegger's lecture courses on Hölderlin's "Der Ister," that there is, however, another kind of language that might yield an access to *Ereignis*.

Ereignis in the Lecture Course on "Der Ister" (1942)

Although Heidegger articulates *Ereignis* as an explicit rethinking of the relation between time and Being in the lecture "Time and Being," and elsewhere, he has set up the thinking of the *Ereignis* as appropriation (*Ereignen*) in an interpretation of Hölderlin and poetic language two decades earlier. Let us look at Heidegger's lecture course on "Der Ister" for a further illumination of the relation between poetic language and *Ereignis*. Like a thinking beyond metaphysics, poetizing is "to tell something . . . that has not yet been told." Thus "a properly unique beginning thus lies in whatever is said poetically" (DI 8). The *Ereignis* here is also informed by the *Ereignis*-origin that Heidegger had illuminated in the lecture course on "Andenken."[45]

Heidegger begins with a consideration of "poetic time" that differs from the mere presence of a "now." The beginning of Hölderlin's poem "Der Ister" is, "Now come, Fire!" ("Jetzt komme, Feuer!") But according to Heidegger, this beginning, the "now" that denotes the present, tells of something other than the presence decided in the history of metaphysics, and something other than the "now" of Hölderlin's own "historiographical" or subjective moment. The "now" refers to something already sent. "The 'now,' names, rather, an event of appropriation" (DI 9). Hölderlin's poem tells us of the "concealed fullness of poetic time and its truth," for Heidegger finds in the poem a directionality of time that cannot be reduced to mere chronology. The present in fact points to a future that in turn speaks from a past that has been "sent," that "has already been decided."

> The "Now come" appears to speak from a present into the future. And yet, in the first instance, it speaks into what has already happened. "Now"—this tells us: something has already been decided. And precisely the appropriation that has already "occurred" [*sich "ereignet"*] alone sustains all relation to whatever is coming. The "now" names an *Ereignis*. (DI 9)

In "Time and Being" the mutually drawing-forth and withholding character of the dimensions of time opens out space (*Raum*). Likewise, Heidegger immediately announces the "here" in Hölderlin's poem, which he claims is implicated in this temporal event. The "naming of a here" brings about the question of place, which in the poem itself is the river at which humans "wish to build." But the fact that Hölderlin chooses the river "Ister" (Roman) or "Istros" (Greek) is significant. For it is the upper course of the river ("Danubus") to which the lower half "returns," as if "back to its source."[46] The place established by "here" refers again, and is in fact opened out by, the temporality of the "event" of returning. In Hölderlin's poem "the Ister appears, almost, to go backwards." The river is "coming" and at the same time "vanishing," revealing a "concealed, unitary relation to what has been and what is of the future—thus to the temporal" (DI 12). The specific place of the poem—where the narrator stands—submerges into temporality.

The flow of the rivers does not simply run its course "in time" as if the latter were merely an indifferent framework extrinsic to the course of the rivers. The rivers intimate and vanish into time and do so in such a way that they themselves are thus of time and are time itself. (DI 12)

While the specificity of the river is important, Heidegger finds what is revealed in Hölderlin's river poems in general to be of significance.[47] For the river is this temporality, and yet also a "dwelling." Rivers are the place where human beings set down to dwell and what they also celebrate, and this dwelling and celebration is intimately connected with the relation between time and space, as that which opens up a world. Rivers are both a temporality and a locale of dwelling — time-space of "wandering" and "whiling." It is the relation between the "now" — the temporality that is not mere presence but the coming of arrival and the holding-back of what has been — and the "here" of locale as such that is the "essence" of rivers as "'bearers' of an as yet unveiled 'meaning'" (DI 15).

In order to access this "unveiled 'meaning'" Heidegger must first, as in the other lecture courses on Hölderlin, once again distinguish his reading from that of the metaphysical account of art, which relies upon the notion of symbol, metaphor, or allegory to connect an "image" of the river with a "nonsensuous meaning" (DI 16; PR 48; OWL 100). But the distinction between sensuous and nonsensuous, which Heidegger locates in Plato, first of all, and then in Kant and Hegel, belongs to a metaphysics that Heidegger has long called into question. I will turn to Heidegger's critique of this tradition in the next chapter; here I want to note only that Heidegger argues that Hölderlin's poetry "is not concerned with symbolic images at all." It cannot be, for what Hölderlin poeticizes is "mysterious" and belongs to the problem of "unveiling" of what metaphysical thought has concealed. This is, namely, that the place or space of "locale" is opened out by the temporality of the river's movement, which Hölderlin as poet unveils. It must be noted that Heidegger again grants an immediacy to the language of the poet,[48] one unobstructed by willing and representation, unobstructed by the mediation involved in the aesthetics of symbol and metaphor and image. The *Ereignis*, Heidegger has claimed, is "immediate" (*unmittelbar*) in the poetic word, occurs there "*unvermittelt*" (GA 52, 36, 24). While Hölderlin ends his poem with the lines "But what the river does / no one knows" (Was aber jener thuet der Strom / Weiss niemand), Heidegger claims that "the poet is the river" and vice versa (DI 165), just as he has claimed that the feast of which the poet writes is itself the "essence and ground of history," that it *is* the *Ereignis*. Heidegger argues that the word of the poet founds, and therefore even *is*, in turn, the "holiness" of the river, what Hölderlin calls the river's "spirit," and implicates something about the human being whose "abode" is there. Heidegger attempts to articulate this more clearly as "journeying" — the temporalizing that opens out place. The flowing of rivers follows what Heidegger names a "twofold direction. As vanishing, the river is underway into what has been. As full of imitation, it proceeds into what is coming. The river is a singular kind of journey, insofar as it simultaneously proceeds into what has been and what is to come" (DI 29). This imitation is a temporal one, and Heidegger calls it recollection or memory (*die Erinnerung*), which recalls as well Hölderlin's notion of *Innigkeit* Heidegger all but dismissed during his treatment of "Andenken." The river's vanishing appears to be going into the past, but can "also be an inconspicuous passing away into what is coming, into a decisive belonging to whatever is coming" (DI 39). Echoing his thesis on destiny, Heidegger similarly argues in the essay "Recollection [*Erinnerung*] in Metaphysics" (*Nietzsche*, I), "that which is original occurs in advance of all that comes. Although hidden, it thus comes toward the historical human being as pure coming. It never perishes, it is never something past" (EP, 75). Hölderlin's river poem shows that what is to come comes out of what has been, but simultaneously what has been passed into the future: into the destiny that is "given," that is "intimately entrusted with what has been from out of the fullness of its own proper essence, so that vanishing into what is coming has no need whatsoever of any belated turning toward what has been" (DI 30). The river is not merely a flow of past into future or future into past — both of which would conform to philosophical conceptions of time in Aristotle and Husserl — but a mutual granting of past (what has been decided) into future (what is coming). Thus what is coming has already been sent and is destinal.

This mutual relation between future and past is the holding open of presence — both temporally and as space or place — by virtue of vanishing, or withdrawal, anticipating the discussion of time-space we found in the essay on Hölderlin-George and in "Time and Being." Heidegger binds the relation between temporality and space or place yet more closely. For Hölderlin's journey corresponds to locality, and each gives the other: "We name the consummate essence of the journey [*Wanderung*] a journeying [*Wanderschaft*], corresponding to the locality [*Ortschaft*] of the locale [*Ort*]. The river is a journeying" (DI 30).

Heidegger seems to be addressing with poetry ontological problems that resound with those of modern physics. If the river is an "enigma," it is so in this belonging-together of space and time that metaphysics has not yet thought and, in its determination of Being as presence, cannot think. "Locale and journey belong together like 'space and time'" as an "originary unity" that "first lets that which is unitary spring forth, yet without it springing free from the ground of this unity" (DI 39). As in both aforementioned texts, Heidegger here distinguishes this unity from what is metaphysically calculable: here as the quantification of time and the ordering of space in technology, or as the Aristotelian notion of space as that which "counts and is counted in respect of motion" (*Physics* IV, xi, 219b 1). Kant, too, determines space and time metaphysically as "that which enables a manifold of appearance to be ordered in certain relations." Perhaps Heidegger also has in mind Werner Heisenberg's uncertainty principle of quantum mechanics, which prevents two quantities—location and momentum, "locale" and "journeying"—from being measured simultaneously with equal accuracy. These metaphysical determinations "prevent us" from thinking the original unity, cover that over (DI 48). Yet it could be argued that the cognitive withdrawal that occurs in accurately determining either position or momentum, the other then being subject to a describable uncertainty (describable with reference to Planck's constant, according to Heisenberg's theory, but an uncertainty all the same), announces a kind of presencing that withdraws, itself modeling an ontological clue toward thinking the *Ereignis* that Heidegger thinks poetically. Is their unity ironically announced in the very withdrawal of total determination, in the play of mutual obfuscation between position or location and time or movement in space? One wonders if there is not a closer relation between poetry and physics than Heidegger acknowledges. At least in this case Heisenberg's principle disallows a reduction of Being to absolute presence or certainty. Of course, rather than determine locale and journeying according to a theoretical-quantifying determination of space and time, we try to think here space and time according to Hölderlin's river, locale and journeying, and only then can we understand their primordial unity. It is in this sense that, unlike physics, "poetizing is a telling finding of Being" (DI 119).

Yet poetic language is shown to have the structure of *Ereignis:* in Saying, the unsaid is "left unspoken," withheld and thus concealed, but conditions the occurrence of showing. Language "does not bring itself to language but holds back." Both language (OWL 107) and the *Ereignis* (OWL 135) are thus called the "relation of all relations." It is the very holding back of language which is said in the poem, and thus Heidegger emphasizes the poet's silence as well as what he brings to word.[49] The origin of Saying, "which has never yet been spoken" is "given voice" in poetic language, and "everything depends upon whether language gives or withholds the appropriate word. Such is the case of the poet" who is "compelled" to bring into language its essence (OWL 60). In saying the *Ereignis*, "two kinds of utterance *par excellence*, poetry and thinking," have been brought into "their proper habitat, their neighborhood" (OWL 81). For "poetry moves in the element of saying, and so does thinking" (OWL 83). Saying is illuminated as the presencing-withholding region of Being, just as Heidegger had argued that the poet's greeting of what is recalled in the poem brings them into their relation to the "source." As such, in naming "the word appears as the mysterious wonder" of *Ereignis*; does this wonder not indicate that *Gelassenheit* with which the human being, as receptive to this occurrence, is then to dwell? Are we not brought back to dwelling—to "those ways that belong to the region"—from a thinking which had to remove itself from the sphere of beings (EP 79), or which was to think Being "without beings" (OTB 24)?

The *Ereignis* in the lecture course on Hölderlin is unveiled by the poetizing of rivers found in Hölderlin's hymns, and finds an expression here as well with regard to the human dwelling, which, as Heidegger claims in "Time and Being," was articulated correlatively in "Building Dwelling Thinking." Yet Heidegger still colors this dwelling with the "decisiveness" of the historical founding, as we saw in "The Origin of the Work of Art" and its nationalist tones. In "The Essence of Language" this thinking is given less a texture of destinal recollection than an attendance to *Ereignis* as the open region that unveils language as showing; in the lecture courses on Hölderlin the language of a gathered, decisive destiny is far more prevalent. In this lecture course on "Der Ister" Heidegger thinks the unity of time-space and history-dwelling according to the simplicity of the destiny demanded by historical dwelling[50] and demands from it a decision (a "decisive act") as to the "singular history of the Germans" and their "becoming homely [*heimlich*] . . . within the history of the West" (DI 133, 134, 124). Theoretical physics and Heisenberg himself say nothing of the source or origin because they speak neither to the unhomeliness of cognitive withdrawal nor to the unity of origin that withdrawing indirectly reveals. Moreover, physics speaks of time and space as such but not the specific locale of the German historical destiny. If in "Building Dwelling Thinking" Heidegger discusses this dwelling in terms of the relation of things to the fourfold, here it is thought in a theory of tragedy brought about by a meditation on Sophocles's *Antigone*, which Hölderlin translated into German, and about which Hölderlin theorized in "Remarks on Antigone."[51] For Heidegger tragedy illuminates the human being's "uncanniness" (*Unheimlichkeit*) in which the human being's unique relation to transcendence and the clearing of beings is a "strangeness" which is also a relation to Being's (self-revealing) withdrawal. In drawing out the problem of poetic subjectivity, we will return to the notion of uncanniness in chapter 6. Heidegger's meditation here is still characterized by the "abyssal" character of metaphysics, or rather of what makes metaphysical thinking possible, namely Being's withdrawal and the human capacity in the forgetting of Being to articulate "grounds" on the basis of an unthought groundlessness. *Das Ereignen* here is then thought on the level of human dwelling as the problem of "one's own," or the proper, and the "foreign"—which is, both in the "Der Ister" and "Andenken" lecture courses—and of the far more "decisive" treatment of the German in the lecture course on "Germanien" in the 1930s[52]— the exclusive property of the German-Greek destiny. Appropriation is the *Ereignen* of the *Eigentumlich*, and the problem of proximity to difference is taken up as the coming into the proper (*das Eigene*) through an encounter with the foreign. If the logic of "forgetting" belongs to the "entanglement in subjectivity" of a metaphysical humanism (DI 132, 165), in the "Der Ister" lecture course it is a forgetting of the "law of becoming homely," a law inseparable from the notion of poetic founding. This law, as well as the structure of *Andenken*, is still to be challenged by *Gelassenheit* dwelling that remains within the bounds of phenomenological disclosure.[53] An alternative engagement with Hölderlin in the next chapter and in the rest of this book will bring this problem to the fore, and suggest that the founding of this law, and the ambitions of founding in general, are strained by and give way in tension with the more humble, but also more radical, notion of poetic shelter, itself part and parcel of a fragile, indeed, analeptic, subjectivity.

3

Poetic Subjectivity and the Elusiveness of Being

If the meaning borne by poetic language seems elusive, that which it brings to words, when regarded ontologically, is the very elusiveness of Being—the impossibility of grasping Being as absolute presence. Since Being must be accessed as withdrawing-emerging presence—as a complex play of presence and absence—poetic language, in contrast to prose, admits a unique capacity to bring Being to language.[1] Poetic language, through an array of formal strategies of indirection, expresses this play by evoking relations to the world which are other than a straightforward signification. It is thought that in such language the elusiveness of Being itself can be brought to the fore, can, paradoxically, be brought to virtual appearance. In Heidegger's view this affords a historical founding or, in Heidegger's later alternative, a sheltering relation to earth.[2] A question that remains to be answered is whether this unique capacity of poetic language eschews all vestiges of subjectivity, as Heidegger claims in his account of the poet's role in the remembrance of Being, or whether there is not, as I argue in this chapter, an essential structure of subjectivity and selfhood at the heart of the poetic utterance. While I will here situate my arguments in reference to Hölderlin's poetology, I hope the analysis to initiate a more general theory of poetic subjectivity, or poetic Dasein, as such.

Heidegger's view is informed not only by Hölderlin but in the onto-logical account of poets Rilke, Trakl, George, Char, Hebbel, Silesus, and is, if in a "missed interlocution," relevant to the work of Paul Celan.[3] But it is Hölderlin who, as the primary model of the ontological poet, signifies the subjectless reception of Being or the divine, a view that, incidentally, reigns in some form in philosophical accounts of poetical inspiration since Plato, inaugurated by Homer's reference to the muses. Yet it is precisely as a poetic dialectic of the self that Being's elusive-ness can be approached through and expressed in language. This approach and expression, too, requires a philosophical attention to the conditions and strategies of poetic form, which constitutes not an imme-diate, but only a highly mediated and, indeed, creative receptivity.

Indeed, at first glance Hölderlin's poem "Wie wenn am Feiertage" ("As if on Holiday") presents, in two of its later stanzas, a model of the res-olute and pure poet as vessel of Being, in this instance in the symbolism of the gods. Heidegger has taken literally such presentation as inspira-tion for his model of the heroic poet who is messenger for the divine. Ear-lier in the poem the speaker had declared "Und was ich sah, das Heilige sei mein Wort [And what I saw, the holy, would be my word]." This prox-imity or immediacy seems to be confirmed when Hölderlin writes:

> Doch uns gebührt es, unter Gottes Gewittern,
> Ihr Dichter! Mit entblößtem Haupte zu stehen
> Des Vaters Strahl, ihn selbst, mit eigner Hand
> Zu fassen und dem Volk ins Lied
> Gehüllt die himmlische Gaabe zu reichen.

> Yet it behooves us to stand under godly thundering,
> You poets! With bared heads to stand
> In the father's ray and with one's own hands
> To grasp it itself and wrap it in song
> To extend to the people the heavenly gift.

A literalist reading of these lines renders a view of the poet as bear-ing a direct access to the holy or to Being. Such an access is uncompli-cated by worldly and selfly concerns of the poet as individual and does not reflect the complexities of poetic speech. As examined in chapter 2, Heidegger rejects any reduction of Hölderlin's poetry to a merely sub-jective expression — to psychological or personal circumstances, to a sub-jective language, to specific historical conditions — and this has been praised even by those who most harshly criticize Heidegger's interpre-tations.[4] Yet the strategies of his evasion of subjectivity in regard to

Hölderlin require a neglect of much evidence, in theory and poetic practice, that the latter configured the elusiveness of Being or the divine in relationship to a poetically reconfigured understanding of the subject and an inventive understanding of poetic form. Heidegger argues that Hölderlin's poetry is inexplicable on the basis of Hölderlin's literary biography or empirical existence. Yet the immediacy and proximity he grants to the poetic word in the figure of Hölderlin, an immediacy and proximity essential for the notion of poetic "founding" examined in chapter 1, literalizes certain aspects of the poetry while neglecting the complexity of Hölderlin's poetic individuality. In "Wie wenn am Feiertage," very shortly after the passage cited above, the speaker rescinds his certainty about the poetic vocation. In the penultimate stanza, which is divided from the last by two isolated fragmentary lines (thus breaking the poem's rhythm elliptically and indicating incompletion), the speaker refers to his own painful encounter with the divine. The fragments, difficult to render in English, nonetheless can be said to involve the personal suffering or shame of the speaker:

> Doch weh mir! Wenn von
> Weh mir!

> But still shame to me! If of
> Shame to me!

After these fragmentary breaks of rhythm, the speaker qualifies his view of the poet's role with reference to the "I" and the "me." The poem then ends again on an elliptical fragment.

> Und sag ich gleich,
> Ich sei genaht, die Himmlischen zu shauen,
> Sie selbst, sie werfen mich tief unter die Lebenden
> Den falschen Priester, ins Dunkel, daß ich
> Das warnende Lied den Gelehrigen singe.
> Dort

> I was to draw near, to gaze upon the heavenly,
> They themselves, they cast me down deep below the living.
> Me the false priest, into the dark, so that I
> Would sing the warning song to those who would hear.
> There

Here the poet is no longer illuminator of Being by conducting the heavenly rays, but is cast into a subterranean darkness, associated with falsehood. This demotion of the poet from bold grasper of the divine light to uncertain castaway is emphasized by the subjunctive mood and by the final fragmentary line, "dort," which renders the poem inconclusive. Where "there" might be is not altogether certain, nor is the poet's role vis-à-vis the gods and their message of warning. This uncertainty of place will be echoed by the speaker of T. S. Eliot's "Four Quartets": "I can only say, there we have been: but I cannot say where," an undecidability certainly at odds with resolute founding. In a similar vein Hölderlin's character Hyperion, who represents the poetic striving, will be forced to declare that "fate casts me adrift in uncertainty [das Schicksal stößt mich ins Ungewisse hinaus]" (H 97 / WB I, 400).Hölderlin is credited with having articulated the coming of the danger of Being's oblivion to a people beset by historical decision. Heidegger reads Hölderlin's poems according to this ontological founding, prophesying, and saying. Yet Heidegger misreads the signs of warning in Hölderlin, as when the speaker of "Wie wenn am Feiertage" is shamefully cast down. The problem of poetic receptivity in Hölderlin concerns a struggle to articulate the paradoxical nature of subjectivity and the precariousness of its grasp on what is to be poeticized. This is why Stanley Corngold has argued that "Hölderlin's poetry is unthinkable except as a dialectical poetry of the self." While at some moments in his poetry Hölderlin lyrically and hymnically declares a unity with life, the divine, or Being, this oneness is continually interrupted, as we can see in the poem cited above. Thus, in Corngold's terms, "Hölderlin's experience changes the mood or tonality of his struggle . . . experience shifts the weight of his concerns within the struggle, but the spring that keeps the tension, that lives the tension, is the dialectical subject, the mediating self."[5] I argue that, due to his refusal of this experiencing and mediating subject, Heidegger's inscription of Hölderlin's poetry into a history of Being exceeds phenomenological insight,[6] particularly when ascribing Hölderlin's poetry to Being's "single conversation."

According to Heidegger, with poetry we can approach the darkness of our times, the abyss of the end of metaphysics from which the old gods have fled and to where the new ones are yet to come—a situation that might well be described as a radical loss of meaningfulness in an age flatly determined by technological positivism. In this light poetic language, far from a distraction from philosophy, provides a new orientation for thinking, one that promises a heroic "saving" at the moment of danger. Yet Heidegger presents an incomplete picture, overlooking Hölderlin's critique of hubris and his repeated expressions of uncertainty. This uncertainty we find again, for instance, in the late hymn "Lebensalter" ("Ages of Life"):

Jezt aber siz' ich unter wolken, darin
Ein jedes eine Ruh' hat eigen, unter
Wohleingerichteten Eichen, auf
Der Heide des Rehs, und fremd
Erscheinen und gestorben mir
Der Seeligen Geister.

But now I sit under clouds, where
Each has his own quietude, under
Well-furnished oaks, on
The deer's heath, and foreign
And dead appear to me
The blessed souls.

That loss of a grasp of, and even an access to, the divine as expressed
in these lines is touched upon only in Heidegger's notion of the danger provoked by the penurious state of human understanding in a technological age; but Heidegger's notion obscures the specificity of the
distinctly individuated self—the quietude as "each . . . his own"—within
which this penurious circumstance unfolds. As we saw in the previous
chapter, Hölderlin is incorporated into Heidegger's "overcoming of
metaphysics," which has left the subject behind and promises, in belligerent or peaceful form, a nonsubjective reengagement with Being's
founding in the moment of this danger. The *Ereignis* or event that is
witnessed and instigated by poetic language is incompatible with a creativity that involves a subject, as in the "genius" of Kantian and Schil-
lerian aesthetics. Hölderlin's accomplishment cannot be properly called
his own in that it is not that of a subject or a self or a genius,[7] despite
his affirmation of the notion of genius and of other principles of aesthetics (H 130/ WB I, 436). Hölderlin, as the "poet of poets," is rather
the conduit or vessel of Being's sending; the poet becomes exclusively
tethered to the interstice of the ontological difference.

I argue that what Heidegger believes is the simple unity of the essential in poetic language obscures the thoroughly modern philosophical
problematic to which Hölderlin's work is inextricably tied. This problematic involves the unique paradoxes of subjectivity. Heidegger is no
doubt right that the subject of modern philosophy is an insufficient
basis for a theory of poetic language; yet the failures of the cognitive
subject to which the Romantics responded present for Hölderlin oppor-
tunities to recover the subject poetically. This recovery affords a challenge to Heidegger's constitution of Hölderlinian language as the founding of history, as we shall see below.

The Poet as Vessel of Being in the *Seinsgeschichte*

Before turning to Hölderlin's writings, let us examine Heidegger's ontological figuration of the poet. In his reading of Hölderlin's poetry, and
of the rivers and demigods, memories, celebrations, and landscapes
that appear there, Heidegger identifies the poet with the elements that
appear in the poems.[8] The demigod, the river, the "between" of uncanniness (DI 139; EB 288–289) *are* the poet himself, since the poet's word
is the "telling-naming" (DI 139), which has "decisive" power (DI
92) in the naming of the gods (DI 135). This does not anthropomor-
phize these elements, but, conversely, desubjectifies the poet. The poet
is himself a "sign" (DI 135), which is not a mere symbol; though the
interstice "between" humans and gods and thereby mediating between
them (GA 52, 123), the poet himself is not mere mediation,[9] but is
called to a unique and dangerous proximity to Being. Heidegger writes:
"the sign, the demigod, the river, the poet: all these name poetically the
one and singular ground of becoming homely of human beings as historical and the founding of this ground by the poet" (DI 154).

As founding, the poetic word is the occurrence of truth. In language
issuing the appearance of the lost gods (EB 263), poetic language is said
to institute history in its historical destiny. In the *Andenken* lecture course,
Heidegger is explicit about this proximity as the immediate (*unmittelbar*)
character of the poetic word: the *Ereignis* "lies and therefore is immediately in the word" (GA 52, 36). If the poet is mediator, the poet and the
poetic word are thus themselves unmediated (*unvermittelt*) (GA 52, 24).

Given this immediacy, the poet must be ready to prepare for inceptive thinking, ready to receive the sending-withdrawing call, as a vessel of remembrance or memorialization of that which both has and
has not yet fully entered into presence or thought. The nonsubjective character of the poet's reception of Being is thus characterized
by Heidegger in the following ways, some of which rely upon an interpretation of lines from Hölderlin's poems: (1) As the essential speaker
of a saying that originates not in himself[10] but in Being, the poet is
the one called (*der Angerufene*) to what overcomes him (GA 52, 7); (2)
the poet is *messenger*—of Being, of "the gods," and delivers a message
of that which is sent (*geschickt*) in the destiny (*Schicksal*) of the *Seinsgeschichte;* (3) as such, the poet is uncanny *venturer* into the abyss; (4)
the poet is *founder* of "what remains," of history (GA 52, 7), and pre-
server of things in their Being; (5) the poet is the *gatherer* of traces,
of the echoes of Being and the gods; (6) the poet is *interpreter*—of the
gods and of the people's voice.

If the poet is beyond subjectivity, the poet speaks, moreover, of a history removed from mere actuality, from "beings unthought in their essence." The poet is not merely a being among beings, but a structure and shelter of the interstice between Being and beings, and one who can wrest himself, or rather is wrested, from the domination of beings as mere actuality or mere presence — in order to utter the historical, essential word of remembrance and preparation. Beyond subjectivity, the poet's will is "even more daring" than the desire to own and conquer or, in rational concepts and technological thinking, define, measure, or reproduce. The poet is not the model for the post-metaphysical "everyman,"[11] though the poet's word makes possible a different, poetic kind of dwelling for human beings. For the poet receives his call in the "supreme isolation" of a "mission," as a unique, isolated instance of the reception of origin beyond subjective thinking. Yet the poet is not individuated as a subject whose cognitive, metaphysical, transcendental structures, individual personhood, feelings, memories, moods or experiences, provide the source of his expressions (GA 52, 22–24, 28–29, 36, 50, 54, 58, 61, 71, 170). The poet does not poetize (*dichten*) so much as he is overcome (*überdichtet*) by that which is to be poetized (GA 52, 5). Here Heidegger plays on the ambiguity of the word *dichten;* in German it can suggest the gathering thickening or condensation of the poeticized, for which the poet is a heroic vessel. The poet or artist is not a genius who creatively masters, even in "inspiration," a given art,[12] who gives expression to his aesthetic intellect or to his unique, heightened experience, as we might say of Walt Whitman or the poet-artist of Goethe's *Sorrows of Young Werther.* Nor is the remembrance of the poet governed by the poet's subjective memories, the poet's own life, real or imagined, as in Proust's *Remembrance of Things Past,* or even by a *mémoire involuntaire.* The poet represents neither the everyday human being nor the aesthetic genius; there is no existential solitude of a subject adrift in the world, as in Keats's odes. The poet serves, rather, as the highest source of thinking, for an obedient, pious questioning of our relation to Being, serves then also the possibility for our creative *Auseinandersetzung* with Being.[13] The poet is not, Heidegger writes, "entangled in subjectivity," but rather must "be struck and blinded in the face of the 'fire'" of a unique, heightened proximity to Being (DI 165). Thus poetic language, when it is essential, is not to be reduced to communication, nor to culture, both of which imply Enlightenment-humanist rather than historical-ontological concerns.

Heidegger argues that the poem "does not 'express' the experience of the poet, but rather takes the poet into the sphere of his essence which is opened in the poem" (EHD 51). This essence is articulated as an immediate proximity to Being. Language is not expression (OWL 34–36) but rather, essentially, the "Saying of Being." For this reason, according to Heidegger, "all essential poems say the Same." Language is not, contrary to theories ranging from Aristotle to Husserl to Kristeva (see chapter 6), the practice or expression of a subject of utterance. Because the poem "does not 'express' the experience of the poet," Heidegger claims in the midst of an interpretation, "Who the author is remains unimportant here, as with every other masterful poem. The mastery consists precisely in this, that the poem can deny the poet's person and name" (PLT 195). Yet Heidegger elsewhere refers to experience from a poetic point of view.[14] Despite Heidegger's uncompromising rejection of the poet's own experience (GA 52, 4–5), Heidegger now and then refers to a "poetic experience" (OWL 57, 69). In *On the Way to Language* (*Unterwegs zur Sprache*) he explains what he means by "poetic experience" since it is not the experience of a subject or self in any traditional sense:

> To undergo an experience with something — be it person, thing, or a god — means that this something befalls us, strikes us, and comes over us, overwhelms and transforms us. When we talk of "undergoing" an experience, we mean specifically that the experience is not of our own making; to undergo here means that we endure it, suffer it, receive it as it strikes us and submit to it. It is this something itself that comes about, comes to pass, happens. (OWL 57)

The poet "undergoes an experience with language," and that this experience is "given voice and put into language" in a poem (OWL 59). What Heidegger calls poetic experience is an experience exclusively of language and essence, and of the origin, and is to be thought beyond all humanist determination. For Heidegger, to undergo this experience "means to let ourselves be properly concerned by the claim of language by entering into it and submitting to it" (OWL 57). It is, essentially, in service to ontology.

In this representation of the poet's vocation (*Ruf, Beruf*), the poet as self, as subject, is rendered transparent such as to recede entirely; biography, the accounts of experiences and memories in his poems — and the "I" and "me" in the poem — disappear in favor of that to which he is called.[15] We have seen this in relation to Hölderlin's poems

"Andenken" and "Der Ister." Likewise, Trakl's poem "Wandering Stranger" is said to speak, just as does Hölderlin's translation of Sophocles's "Antigone," to the uncanniness of the human being as transcendence—not so much as a being, entangled in beings, but as the rift (*Riß*) between Being and beings, as the site (*Ort*) of this rift. The pain of which Trakl writes in his poem is the pain of this ontological rift, as is the suffering of Antigone who, cast from the polis, is the rift between Being and beings . Heidegger argues that the feeling (*Gefühl*) and experience (*Erlebnis*) of the poet do not belong to what is "essential" in poetic language, and that a subjectivistic aesthetics is to be displaced (GA 52, 4–5, 31; PLT 195; EHD 51, 129; DI 165). According to the nature of his interpretive access, Heidegger claims that his readings of Hölderlin have nothing at all to do with the historically "accurate" Hölderlin, with the "imagined world" (*Vorstellungswelt*) that Hölderlin himself experienced, with what Hölderlin meant (*meinte*) (GA 52, 6).[16] For, as Heidegger argues, the poeticized in the poem, as well as the poetic word itself, is not the property of the poet, and the notion of intention already obscures the complexities of poetic receptivity. Heidegger aims to free the word in Hölderlin's poems to its proximal relation to the "holy," for "the holy gives the word and itself comes in this word. The word is the event of the holy" (EHD 76).

Heidegger's rejection of self and subject, of humanism in general, is highly problematic for a Hölderlinian-inspired theory of poetic language. Language as it is given to the human being requires a transformation by the poet; it is, for Hölderlin, as he writes in "Der Rhein," "impoverished in tones, / just as beginners who learn from nightingales" ("sorglosarm an Töner, / Anfängern gleich, bei Nachtigallen zu lernen"). The poet's task is to devise formal means by which mere (ordinary) naming is transformed into an indirect reception of the feeling of life or the holy, which evades usual conceptual signification. Hölderlin's poetological writings on the experience of poetic language articulate the task of poetry as quite otherwise than the nonsubjectivistic founding that Heidegger in fact identifies with the "essence" of Hölderlin's poetic thought. Hölderlin's philosophical-poetological treatment of the poet as the figure who departs from rational subjectivity engages issues that are entrenched in the discourse of the modern Enlightenment. We can see this in the repetition, in Hölderlin's poetology, of terms associable with humanism: reflection and "poetic reflection," (ELT 47, 75, 68, 81); the "I" and the poetic "I," (ELT 71, 72, 75); the subject and subjective as the "foundation of the poem" (ELT 60, 61, 67, 75, 77); the "self" (ELT 132); "the various faculties of the human being," and the "soul" (ELT 101, 109); the "real life" and its relation to the "spiritual life" of the human being (ELT 91) and the "particular relations he [sic] bears to the world" (ELT 93); the "intellectual intuition" (ELT 67, 77, 86); "consciousness" (*Bewußtseyn*) (ELT 70, 71, 77, 79) and "cognition" (*Erkenntnis*) (ELT 72, 75, 79); feeling (*Gefühl, Empfindung*) (ELT 65, 67, 86); and experience (ELT 92). Hölderlin aims, philosophically and poetologically, to account for the relation between subject and object or "self and world" in a radically new way (ELT 37–38, 58–65; 75–78; 132). If in Hölderlin poetic experience is both tethered to the self and subject and transcends that self or subject[17] —wherein the subject "moves beyond himself" (ELT 52, 75–76) — in Heidegger that movement of transcendence is precluded by the submissive receptivity of the poet who, in essence, has no subjectivity. In Heidegger's account, the poetic self, such as there is one, has no history of experiences as a being among beings, but is subordinated to the essential movements of history, which, thought essentially, no longer concern the sphere in which a subject, or even Dasein, would find itself as a self.[18] Again in his uniquely philosophical reading, Heidegger can thus write of Hölderlin as poet that Hölderlin's historical moment is irrelevant to his poetry and poetic thought, that "Hölderlin's time is after all particularized singularly through his word" (EHD 76), and that "history is only then, when the essence of truth is inceptively decided" (EHD 76). For Hölderlin as for Heidegger,[19] the poetic word is not the poet's own nor is it his possession (GA 52, 7), and it is as such that poetic language has access to the elusiveness of Being. And yet I argue that the elusiveness of Being is discovered as the point of departure for a subjectivity not left behind but unraveled, not irrelevant to poetry but rather poeticized. The significance of this claim for Heidegger's thought and for the alternative theory of poetic language I put forth in the chapters that follow still remains to be examined.

Poetic Form: Proximity and Indirectness

The Simplicity and Purity of the Poetic Word as Proximity in Heidegger

Proximity to Being is articulated as a gathering simplicity of meaning. In order to be able to think the "essence" of the poetic word, Heidegger must lay out the inexhaustibleness (*Unerschöpflichkeit*) of the "genuine" (*echtes*) word (GA 52, 15). Yet while Heidegger defends the plurivocity (*Vieldeutigkeit*) of the poetic word against the superficiality (*Oberflächlichkeit*) and univocity (*Eindeutigkeit*) of the logical or technical word, Heidegger contracts the scope of poetic meaning such that it remain within the bounds of his thought; the inexhaustibleness of the poetic word is given a singular essence accessible to "thinking" (GA 52, 10–15). In the "preliminary remarks" to his winter semester 1941–42 lecture course *Hölderlins Hymne "Andenken,"* Heidegger writes:

> The wealth of each genuine word, which is precisely never a mere strewn-about plurality of meanings [bloß verstreutes Vielerlei von Bedeutungen], but rather the simple unity of the essential, is grounded in the fact that it names the inceptive [*Anfängliches*] and in that each inception [*Anfang*] is at once inexhaustible and singular. (GA 52, 15)

The inner unity of Hölderlin's poetry is this simple unity, the "poeticized" in the poem, which, not fully articulate, requires the thinker to bring its saying to completion. The thinker is needed, furthermore, to bring into dialogue these poems and the selected, essential lines from Hölderlin's other writings, such that the "poeticized," the essence of the poems, gets a hearing. This essence is reflexive, for poetic language is the laying out of its own task and role, which is why for Heidegger Hölderlin "poetizes the essence of poetry." In this lecture course, this role is the poet's waiting for the arrival (of Being), a "gathering" of each grasp into the "not yet homely" sphere of arrival (GA 52, 14). Hölderlin's poetry is then in need of thinking—or an *Auseinandersetzung*, a creative interpretation—which brings to full saying the "thought" that is already incipient in the poem. As we have seen, Heidegger names this thought *Andenken* (GA 52, 16).

But what *Andenken*—recollection or remembrance—means for Hölderlin is also complicated by poetic form, Hölderlin's theory of which, as we will see shortly, cannot be divorced from the problem of subjectivity as the form or structure of receptivity. In Heidegger's account, poetic saying, as "founding" the history of Being, possesses the clarity of pure reception and comes close to univocity. Poetic form, which Hölderlin treats in rigorous and difficult essays, and which has been executed with unique rigor in Hölderlin's poetry, is given no consideration in Heidegger's account. Yet Heidegger's own interpretive strategies determine that the poetic word, as essential and pure, and as belonging to the simplicity (*Einfachheit*) of *Schicksal,* is released from ambiguity, ambivalence, and equivocity, and from the intentional structures of form: verse, stanza, line, symbol, allegory, metaphor, and meter. Though the poet's mission is "dangerous," the "message" his word is to hold is uncomplicated by the vessel that is to contain it, and thus an account of poethood for Heidegger need not attend to what Hölderlin calls the "creative act" (ELT 99).

In contrast, for Hölderlin, "poetry is in need of especially certain and characteristic principles and limits" (ELT 101); poetry needs an account of the various "forms of poetic composition" (ELT 41–44); a "poetic logic" (ELT, 109); a "lawful calculation," (ELT 101), a complex "alteration of tones" (ELT, 63, 83–88). Hölderlin likewise treats symbol, allegory, metaphor, syntax, and tone as essential elements of poetical composition, without which poetry would be lifeless. It has been argued that Heidegger's attempt to find the simplicity of an essential message in Hölderlin's poetry "is contradictory insofar as he seeks the immediate that occurs in the discourse of the poem,"[20] and that Heidegger literalizes the poet's message, whereas Hölderlin's language contains discordant and even disruptive oppositions that render the assertion of such a "category of meaning" impossible.[21] It is curious that Heidegger makes little mention and gives no sustained reading of Hölderlin's theory of poetic form,[22] in that for Heidegger, Hölderlin belongs to a privileged moment in the *Seinsgeschichte* explicitly not as a thinker but as a poet—despite the references Heidegger makes to Hölderlin's essays. Yet the formal characteristics of the poems themselves are also of derivative importance in Heidegger's readings, because Heidegger's strategy requires a strictly ontological, not philological, approach. There are, however, philosophical consequences here that exceed any possible objections by strictly literary theorists or philologists. For Hölderlin the poet's vocation, as we will see in this and the next chapters, is defined according to the paradoxical nature and limits of subjectivity and a transcendence of the inwardness of a self. If Being is elusive and refuses to be defined by the word of its self-granting, the poetic word in Heidegger's account nevertheless offers a simplicity of essence, just as "poetic experience" is reduced to the simplicity of submission to historical happening as such. Poetic language "clears" the open, "institutes" a history (DI 164) in which the elusiveness of Being as a self-withdrawing sending is revealed. In poetic language, Being exposes itself precisely in its elusiveness. Yet this exposure in the word, according to Heidegger's view, requires a proximity that is pure; poetic language, as the pure, essential word, is a "simple saying" uninfected by the obscuring duplicity of Being—absent of ambiguity—and is uninfected by the complications of the poetic subjectivity that, in Hölderlin, must be transcended.

In contrast, in Hölderlin's theoretical accounts of poetic language he seems painfully aware of the limitation of human saying in its relation to the divine. Hölderlin accordingly writes in "On the Operations of the Poetic Spirit": "thus the human being, in a too subjective as well as in a too objective state, seeks in vain to reach his destiny which consists in that he recognize himself as a unity contained within the divine" (ELT 77). This is why the poetic dialectic of language can only indirectly rein-scribe that possible unity in "reflection" (ELT 79–81) which is a form of "differentiation" (ELT 77). The self thus contains an inner tension of striving to unify with Being and recognizing its own limitations. This differentiation is connected to the problem of hubris, warning against the poet's assumption of identity with or immediacy to that which is to be uttered; the self is, therefore, within itself "a divided identity and a perpetual beginning in language."[23] Though Heidegger, too, recognizes the situation of the human being as "uncanny," as "expelled" from the realm of beings in an interstitial, but for Heidegger nevertheless founding, relation to the holy, the poet's simple naming is taken to be the occurrence of the holy itself. It has thus been argued that the "difference between naming and being is . . . blurred in Heidegger's interpretations" of Hölderlin.[24] If Hölderlin's understanding of poetic form is to be understood in ways that diverge from Heidegger's theory, it is with reference to the problem of subjectivity that the difference between naming and Being, and thus of poetic form, becomes an issue. Contrary to Heidegger's theory of language, "Hölderlin avoids the confusion of saying and Being."[25] That the self admits alterity, that it is not transcendentally grounded in a simple unity, does not disqualify the self as individuated being which would provide a mediating receptivity for Being. The paradox of subjectivity in Hölderlin concerns the affirmation of the poet's experience, even when experience is of the self's momentary "obliteration."[26]

The Philosophical-Poetological Grounds of Hölderlin's Account of Poetic Form as Indirectness

Hölderlin argues that Being cannot be "received" except from what he calls, in "Remarks on Antigone," an "askew perspective" (ELT 116). Hölderlin's theory of poetic form is a response to this problem, for his view of poetic language is based on his transgression of the metaphysics of consciousness and the transcendental philosophies of Kant and Fichte (ELT 33–38, 72–73, 125, 131, 137). Being eludes articulation and conceptual grasp because language, or judgment, is a synthesis on the basis of a separation (ELT 37–38), one that invokes for the subject of ontological reflection an inescapable longing. This is why "the impetus to name and the impetus toward dissolution are both effective in Hölderlin's discourse."[27] While Hölderlin writes in a letter to Immanuel Niethammer of his aim to dissolve the oppositions "in which we think and exist . . . between subject and object, between our self and the world" (ELT 131–132), a dissolution that requires an "aesthetic sense," this "resolution of dissonances," as is promised again explicitly in a preface to *Hyperion*, is ultimately deferred in a dialectic with an elusive *telos*, the recognition of which requires some attention to form (WB I, 295).

In much of Hölderlin's work, particularly the intensely lyrical epistolary novel *Hyperion*, the human condition, even for the poet whom the title character represents, is conditioned by longing to be "one with all." It is worth quoting here from *Hyperion* at length to illustrate this problem. At the novel's commencement Hyperion writes to his friend Bellarmin in highly lyrical tones, repeating the principal phrase that sets the tenor of his longing:

> Eines zu sein mit Allem, das ist Leben der Gottheit, das ist der Himmel des Menschen.
>
> Eines zu sein mit Allem, was lebt, in seliger Selbstvergessenheit wiederzukehren ins All der Natur, das ist der Gipfel der Gedanken und Freuden, das ist die heilige Bergshöhe, der Ort der ewigen Ruhe, wo der Mittag seine Schwüle und der Donner seine Stimme verliert und das kochende Meer der Woge des Kornfelds gleicht.
>
> Eines zu sein mit Allem, was lebt! Mit diesem Worte legt die Tugend den zürnenden Harnisch, der Geist des Menschen den Zepter weg, und alle Gedanken schwinden vor dem Bilde der ewigeinigen Welt. . . .

> To be one with all—this is the life divine, this is man's heaven.
>
> To be one with all that lives, to return in blessed self-forgetfulness into the All of Nature—this is the pinnacle of thoughts and joys, this the sacred mountain peak, the place of the eternal rest, where the noonday loses its oppressive heat and the thunder its voice and the boiling sea is as the heaving field of grain.
>
> To be one with all that lives! At those words Virtue puts off her wrathful armor, the mind of man lays its scepter down, and all thoughts vanish before the image of the world in its eternal oneness. (H 4 / WB I, 297)

This *hen kai pan,* or unity of nature within its great diversity, is experienced by Hyperion in fleeting and cyclically repeated moments of bliss among the beauties of nature, in dreams, in friendship, and in love.[28] This unity, as well as its loss, is also addressed in many of the poems. In the poem "Rousseau," the speaker suggests that the human being will never grasp immediately the natural life to which Rousseau was uniquely sensitive. Out of his grasp is "the overflowing infinity of life / That glimmers around him [Des Lebens Überfluß, das Unendliche, / Das um ihn . . . dämmert]." In this poem the speaker indicates that we need not despair, for though it evades us, an understanding of life or nature is within as a seed within a fruit: "Yet it lives within him and present, / Warming and effecting [Doch lebts in ihm und gegenwärtig, / Wärmend und wirkend]." Despite its evasiveness, life's melody and rhythm, mirrored in that of the poem itself, might be known to one who longs for it poetically; it is known, the speaker tells us, in interpreting the language of strangers, "die Sprache der Fremdlinge." This is a language, perhaps, foreign to reason and philosophy, despite Rousseau's occupation; his insight is more akin to poetical reception. In such language, a hint about the workings of life can dawn upon the human being, if only sketched out in its promise, just as the first sign of something implies what is to come: "And wonderful, as if from the very beginning / The human spirit had experienced / The becoming and effecting of all the ways of life [Und wunderbar, als hätte von Anbeginn / Des Menschen Geist das Werden und Wirken all, / Des Lebens Weise schon erfahren]." The unity of life to which Hölderlin refers in *Hyperion* and "Rousseau" is a source of celebration, which puts in abeyance this cycle of endowment and loss in a moment of equilibrium. When "all the living ones celebrate," Hölderlin writes in "Der Rhein," "fate is leveled out for a while [Es feiern die Lebenden all, / Und ausgeglichen / Ist eine weile das Schicksal]."

But the moment of bliss is continually interrupted by both the limitations and finitude of human subjectivity: an "instant of reflection hurls me down," claims Hyperion, from the feeling of an immediate belonging to the unity of life.

Ich denke nach und finde mich, wie ich zuvor war, allein, mit allen Schmerzen der Sterblichkeit, und meines Herzens Asyl, die ewigeinige Welt, ist hin; die Natur verschließt die Arme, und ich stehe, wie ein Fremdling, vor ihr, und verstehe sie nicht.

I reflect, and find myself as I was before—alone, with all the griefs of mortality, and my heart's refuge, the world in its eternal oneness, is gone; Nature closes her arms, and I stand like an alien before her and do not understand her. (H 4 / WB I, 297–298).

This ejection from blissful oneness with nature is enacted formally in the novel, as I will discuss shortly. In the early poem "To the Young Poets" ("An die jungen Dichter") Hölderlin optimistically recommends that poets seek counsel in nature: "Fragt die große Natur um Rath." Yet Hölderlin's youthful view soon yields to a more nuanced, and darker, understanding of poetical reflection. In "Die Heimath" ("Home"), Hölderlin renders this according to the notion that the gods who have given have, as in "Wie wenn am Feiertage," also taken away a glimpse of life's unity: "Then they who loan us the heavenly fire / The gods give us holy suffering too / And it will remain so. A son of the earth / I seem to be; was made to love, to suffer [Denn sie, die uns das himmlische Feuer leihn, / Die Götter schenken heiliges Laid uns auch, / Drum bleibe diß. Ein Sohn der Erde / Schein' ich; zu lieben gemacht, zu leiden]." In "Die Heimath" Hölderlin relates this sorrow to images of the grief of love and to the loss of the forests of childhood and the embrace of family which could ease the suffering. The alterations of belonging and loss that pertain to love, as to the unity of life, nature, and the holy, are not described in this poem, for we find the speaker already in the aftermath of loss, longing for what has been lost. Yet Hyperion's consciousness in the novel is throughout structured by this alteration, as he describes in a letter to Bellarmin. The alteration is enacted formally in the organization of his lyrical utterance, in which two principal words, forgetting and hushing (*Vergessen* and *Verstummen*) change places in the two sentences which express opposing states of being or moods:

Es gibt ein Vergessen alles Daseins, ein Verstummen unsers Wesens, wo uns ist, als hätten wir alles gefunden.

Es gibt ein Verstummen, ein Vergessen des Daseins, wo uns ist, als hätten wir alles verloren, eine Nacht unsrer Seele, wo kein Schimmer eines Sterns, wo nicht einmal ein faules Holz uns leuchtet.

There is a forgetting of all existence, a hush of our being, in which we feel as if we had found everything.

There is a hush, a forgetting of all existence, in which we feel as if we had lost everything, a night of our soul, in which no glimmer of any star nor even the fire from a rotting log gives us light. (H 32 / WB I, 329).

In several works this problem of alteration is articulated as that of the self's reflection. In *Hyperion*, the "askew perspective" induced by the "difference" that Being indicates for the reflective subject is constituted by stages of reflection that in turn constitute a process of infinitized longing which is expressed most effectively through images — as in the citation above, images of lack (no star, not even a rotting log to give light). In *Hyperion* the longing is infinitized by the structure of repetition of the novel in which at the end the reader is left where Hyperion began — about to leave Germany for his native Greece from where, upon his arrival, the first letter was written. The consciousness of the speaker is characterized by a more complex, though also more anguished, understanding of nature's unity, a complexity demanded by the education of the soul from a state of simplicity to one of greater complexity (which the author, in a "Fragment" on *Hyperion*, calls "Bildung" [WB I, 440]). The novel ends with Hyperion's unfulfilled promise of "more soon."

This Hölderlin calls in his preface the "eccentric path" (*exzentrische Bahn*) which describes the manner by which Hyperion can articulate in his letters an alternative grasp of the divine or nature through his love for Diotima, his revolutionary friendship, and his blissful reception of the beauty of the natural landscape. But this bliss is punctuated by repeated occasions of bereftness. One such occasion is Diotima's death, about which Hyperion asks: "We were but one flower. . . . And yet, yet was she not torn from me like a crown usurped and laid in the dust? [Wir waren Eine Blume nur . . . Und doch, doch wurde sie, wie eine angemaßte Krone, von mir gerissen und in den Staub gelegt]" (H 49 / WB I, 347–348). But this bereftness is inevitable for the mortal being who nonetheless cannot but help to strive for eternity (H 31).

In contrast to rational reflection, characterized by concepts which only grasp "what has degenerated and been repaired [was einmal schlecht gewesen und wieder gut gemacht ist]" (H 4 / WB I, 298), and thus cannot grasp an original unity or innocence, poetic reflection is enacted to grasp the original unity eccentrically. Rather than articulating the essential matter directly, poetical language, including the lyrical novel, enacts the eccentric path in which the joining of nature and art follows a progressive, dialectical circularity in which no center can be located. This differs from Heidegger's own sense of "gathering" of the essence, for in Hölderlin it leads to poetical uncertainty as much as to momentary bliss of divine covenance or, as in Heidegger, in a courageous confrontation with the gods. In Hölderlin's *Empedocles*, the tragic verse drama in three unfinished versions, the difference becomes a tragic conflict that, when the poet is guilty of hubris, leads to his extinction. I would argue, then, that the poetic novel and the tragic drama are both aesthetic or literary responses to collapse of unity between the subject and Being, which Hölderlin analyzes in the essay "Judgment and Being,"[29] a collapse that is, according to Hölderlin, inevitable for the conscious being, for the one who has language.

Though not a philosophical system, this brief text, as Dieter Henrich argues,[30] represents an original critique of Kantian-Fichtean principles that was crucial to the initial development of German Idealism as laid out in the work of Hölderlin's classmates Schelling and Hegel.[31] Yet the text is to be seen, furthermore, as the foundation of Hölderlin's departure from philosophical systematicity and the ontological skepticism that grounds his poetology. Hölderlin's understanding of Being is approached in the context of the question of judgment or consciousness and of the identity of the subject in its relation to object. For according to Hölderlin, Being is that "necessary presupposition" of unity of which the conscious being must conceive as prior to consciousness and the divisions it entails.[32] And yet Being cannot be named, as in Fichte, as the identity of subject and object, for identity presupposes division. Any access to a unity preceding division is grasped only in an "infinite approximation"[33] of a poetic path Hölderlin will elsewhere outline, one that follows the articulation of harmoniously opposing alterations (*harmonische Entgegengesetzte*) (ELT 62) and aims to reinscribe, analeptically, the recollection (*Erinnerung*) (ELT 71) of that unity. In "Operations of the Poetic Spirit," Hölderlin aims to theorize this indirect, poetic possibility of a reconciliation for the conscious being divided from Being or the "unity of life." Poetic form reinscribes a lost unity, one irretrievable to the conscious being in concepts. Thus poetic language is characterized by oppositions that Hölderlin aims to unify harmoniously, but only indirectly. Despite the idealist tones in Hölderlin's theory, he nevertheless maintains the primacy of difference over synthesis. He writes:

> Between the expression [*Ausdrücke*] (the presentation [*Darstellung*]) and the free idealistic treatment, there lies the foundation and significance [*Bedeutung*] of the poem. This is what lends the poem its seriousness, its firmness, its truth . . . its expression . . . is characterized by being everywhere opposed to itself. (ELT 66)

This opposition is a "hyperbolic operation" and yet is "harmoniously opposed and connected," and constitutes the "life" to which poetry and art are to give expression (ELT 66–67). This poetic logic is, however, a logic of receptivity that expresses not the teleologic or dialectic of destiny but is interrupted by "accident" and is "founded by poetic reflection" (ELT 68) itself under the sway of "mere" fortune (*bloßes Glück*) (ELT 33). The poet's conditions of receptivity are not those of conceptual or even ontological-essential proximity to Being, but rather involve the limitations instituted by consciousness and the accidental, fortunate glimpse of the poet to the "unity of life" or the "holy."

While Heidegger claims that modern metaphysics, as a philosophy of subjectivity, has forgotten Being, Hölderlin's critique of Fichtean and transcendental subjectivity involves a Platonically inspired anamnesis or recollection of an ontological dimension preceding consciousness.[34] If, for Fichte, truth and knowledge can be based upon the fundamental ground of a self-identical consciousness, this view demands that the "I" is the "undivided unity of subject and object prior to knowledge itself."[35] The subjective and the objective are the "undivided unity" that Fichte calls the "intellectual intuition," the "act required of the philosopher: an act of intuiting himself while simultaneously performing the act by means of which the I originates for him."[36] This is for Fichte the basis for a system of laws that supplies "the basis or foundation of all experience."[37] Subject and object are for Fichte "immediately united within self-consciousness and are absolutely one and the same,"[38] and if this identity is rendered in Hegel as a dialectic of identity and difference, in Hölderlin the subject is denied foundationality even as a synthetic dialectic of self-consciousness. Rather, judgment is in Hölderlin the principle, not of synthesis, but of primordial separation, an *Ur-theil* (ELT 37). Hölderlin's brief treatise takes up this problem:

> *Judgment* [*Urtheil*]. In the highest and strictest sense, is the original separation of object and subject which are most deeply united in intellectual intuition, that separation through which alone object and subject become possible, the arche-separation. . . . "I am I" is the most fitting example of this concept of arche-separation.

> *Being* [*Seyn*] expresses the connection between subject and object. Where subject and object are united altogether and only in part, that is, united in such a manner that no separation can be performed without violating the essence of what is to be separated, there and nowhere else can be spoken of *Being proper*, as is the case

with intellectual intuition. Yet this Being must not be confused with identity. (ELT 37)

The argument of "Judgment and Being"[39] might be represented as follows: Hölderlin challenges the Fichtean distinction between consciousness (I) and self-consciousness (I = I) as the first principle of a philosophical system. Self-consciousness is that identity of subject and object in reflection, one that rests upon or is conditioned by the "spontaneity" of the unconditioned "I."[40] This distinction is for Hölderlin unintelligible, for both the fact of and our access to consciousness and self-consciousness are based on "something radically prior to all consciousness, something that makes intelligible, even conceivable, the thought 'I' and with it the fact of self-consciousness."[41] This radically prior something is Being, but as the "very precondition" of consciousness, Being yields subject in its relation to object, thus the division between them. The difference between subject and object is issued on the basis of an ungraspable and only presupposable unity. Being cannot be known, cannot be the first principle of philosophy, for it is what makes knowledge possible; Being, for Hölderlin, is that by virtue of which subject and object are there, and the positing of the absolutely primary could not then account for the elements separated out in judgment, that is, for consciousness that posits.[42] Philosophy thus has foundations neither in judgment nor in Being, for the subject cannot simply revert to a direct relationship to that primordial unity. Consciousness of Being is, paradoxically, also consciousness of the loss of a conceptual grasp of Being.

Thus Hölderlin's text involves a thoroughly modern philosophical problem: that the possibility of self-consciousness, the self's conceiving of itself, is the subject's subjection to a division in which the "I" becomes subject and object of a proposition. And yet, Hölderlin thinks, not only self-consciousness (I am I) but also consciousness per se (I) implies this division, for consciousness cannot be said to be consciousness without reflection. Hölderlin writes, "How can I say: 'I' without self-consciousness? Yet how is self-consciousness possible? In opposing myself to myself, separating myself from myself, yet in recognizing myself as the same in the opposed regardless of this separation" (ELT 38). The "I" is thus grounded in a unity it can only presuppose, and which becomes the "boundary concept" of the intellectual intuition.[43] If self-consciousness is the paradigm for an intellectual intuition, for a grasp of identity, Hölderlin argues that "identity is not = absolute Being" (ELT 38). Contrary to Fichte, the intellectual intuition for Hölderlin is impossible theoretically or cognitively, impossible to ground as the basis for a philosophical system; but it is promised as the withheld goal of the dialectic of harmonious oppositions inherent in poetic "expression" (*Ausdruck*). Tragic poetic language is then named as the "metaphor of an intellectual intuition." If the subject is characterized by consciousness, it is also enslaved to the impossibility of grasping the *hen kai pan*—the intellectual intuition of unity. For reflection in Hölderlin, as Manfred Frank argues, "divides, what was theretofore one."[44] But the unity was itself only presupposable; for Hölderlin, as for Heidegger, Being is difference. If for Heidegger its movements of self-withdrawal and self-granting can be "gathered," for Hölderlin, Being can only be poetically longed for, as lost to the subject of reflection. And yet reflection for Hölderlin also grounds the indirect, askew logic of poetic reinscription or recollection of that which is lost, which becomes apparent to the subject only in accidental fortune, in the "feeling of life" granted by a poetical receptivity to nature. Thus Hölderlin offers an account of "poetic reflection" in "Operations of the Poetic Spirit" as an outline of poetic formality which can indirectly articulate Being in its elusiveness. The latter can only be called "Being"[45] not in the reception or gathering of an historical essence but as the *paradox of subjectivity itself*. In the later writings Hölderlin's view shifts from the effort to ground the reinscription of unity according to a dialectic of harmoniously opposed differences to the "mourning" of loss, which withholds itself from reconciliation.

Yet Hölderlin's still metaphysical thought provides a critique of idealist philosophy that shares something in common with Heidegger's own. For if Heidegger the philosophy of subjectivity is characterized by the reduction of Being to actuality, subject to the "gaze" of cognition, Fichte indeed claims that "the nature of the intellect consists precisely in this immediate unity of being and seeing."[46] For Heidegger, Being is forgotten in this reduction to actuality, to what is present to cognition, and thus the receptivity of hearing[47] and listening is emphasized as an alternative to the "gaze" of metaphysical thinking. For Hölderlin, no immediate unity of Being and cognition is possible, and the "logic" of poetic language both promises an indirect grasp of the ungraspable, and gives expression to ineffability as such.

As I have hinted, the reconciliation between subject and object, issued in the wake of the loss of unity, takes changing forms throughout Hölderlin's poetological writings: in epic, lyric, and tragic form (ELT 41–44, 83–88); as the endless deferral of telos or as the forced, tragic union of subject and object (ELT 50–61); as mourning loss or the "unthinkable" (ELT 110), which is formulated in *Hyperion* as well as in the later poems written after Hölderlin gave up philosophical-poetological writing. If, for Fichte, idealism means that "we are the subject who thinks whatever it is that we may be thinking, and there-fore . . . we can never encounter anything independent of us,"[48] for Hölderlin it is precisely subjectivity that renders what we think estranged from us, that renders it the object of loss. The unity of nature or Being is thinkable only as difference, or as loss, as something recollected. This unity, the "godly language," is what the speaker hopes to recol-lect in the poem "Der Archipelagus" ("The Archipelago") despite the frenzied churning of time:

> Und die Göttersprache, das Wechseln
> Und das Werden versteh,' und wenn die reißende Zeit mir
> Zu gewaltig das Haupt ergrifft und die Noth und das Irrsaal
> Unter Sterblichen mir mein sterblich Leben erschüttert,
> Laß der stille mich dann in deiner Tiefe gedanken.

> And to understand the godly language, the change
> And the becoming, and if the impetuous time
> Seizes my head too forcefully and need and errancy
> Among the mortals shatters my mortal life
> Let me remember the stillness in your depths.

The distance or difference that is suggested here—the shattered mor-tal life of need and errancy—nonetheless preserves life from its reduc-tion to mere mechanism, because it indicates the finitude of the subject of understanding. When Hyperion claims that "there is a gap in my exis-tence [Es ist hier eine Lücke in meinem Dasein]" this punctuation with nothingness, this interruption of the self's unity, is the condition for bliss: "I died, and when I awoke I was lying against the heart of the heavenly maiden. [Ich starb, und wie ich erwachte, lag ich am Herzen des himm-lischen Mädchens]" (H 58 / WB I, 358). Thus, while it provokes the poet's loneliness, difference can also evoke joy, celebration, even a feel-ing of freedom; Hölderlin's political thought, to be discussed in the next two chapters, can be understood as a response to this feeling.

Hölderlin's critical appraisal of subjectivity is connected to the subjective foundations of poetry and the formal means by which they are both transcended and preserved in poetic language. Hölderlin's theory of tragic poetry supports his critique. The theory, articulated in his essay "The Ground for Empedocles," both contributes to an articulation of poetic form as a medium of transcendence beyond the limitations of a finite consciousness and, at the same time, invokes a warning against hubris, the assumption of too great a proximity to the holy or the "unthinkable." The function of poetic form is to provide a shelter for the experience of the poet as a living self within a world upon which it is dependent, recalling Hyperion's confession to Bellarmin that "I wanted to take with me what I could of all this fleeting life; everything outward to which I had become attached, I wanted to preserve within me [Ich wollte noch mit mir nehmen, was ich konnte, von all dem fliehenden Leben, alles, was ich draußen liebegewonnen hatte, wollt ich noch hineinretten in mich]" (H 17 / WB I, 312). One could argue that Hyperion's letters themselves enact this preservation. The terminology of preservation here is intrinsically evocative of the inner life: "hineinretten in mich." Yet Hyperion's capacity to preserve is tied to the indirectness of language and the indirect form of his utterances, here in letters (which Hölderlin had tried to write in verse) principally to a silent interlocutor, Bellarmin, who remains distant throughout the novel. The inner self is itself a structure of mediation, not, as Empedocles will attempt, a direct reception of the divine wherein the subject becomes objective. Hölderlin claims, opposed to a Fichtean synthesis, that "the poetic I remains in real contradiction with and for itself" (ELT 72). Symbol and allegory (and, indeed, for Hyperion, poetical image) function, in the "genius" of form, to articulate the subject's "experience" and "reflection," such that the "inwardness" (*Innigkeit*) of a poem is no longer only subjective but articulates "spirit," which joins subject and object, self and world. This is possible only through poetic transcendence, wherein, in sharp contrast to Heidegger's interpretations, the "subjective foundation of the poem" is the poem's "point of departure and return" (ELT 69).

If, as Heidegger claims, the poet's word is the "event" of the holy (EHD 76), there is no confusing the sacred itself for the poetic announcement thereof, for the poet's own attempt to "mediate" the sacred and the human. Hölderlin is not a mystical or mythological poet in any immediate sense. As Adorno points out, this "critique of synthesis with which Hölderlin repudiates idealism also distances him from the mythic sphere."[49] Even the mythological elements of Hölderlin's poetry, Lawrence Ryan argues, must be understood according to the problem of the subject.[50] Hölderlin proposes, as an alternative to the Fichtean "act," a "new state" where the individual is not canceled by its differentiation from others; this involves freedom granted in reflection, the ability to abstract from oneself as a kind of knowledge of self. The individual "must strive to recognize himself" and yet his own self-identity "as something recognized is also an illusion" (ELT 77). When one lives too intensely in the objective or universal sphere (for example, in Empedocles's identification with the gods), one can no longer recognize oneself. Thus the poet ought to be neither "too selfless . . . too self-forgetful," as in Platonic contemplation (or the Heideggerian reception of destiny), nor "too selfish" in an identification with a poetic object, as in Fichte or Empedocles. Hölderlin writes: "The great poet is never abandoned by himself" — in contradistinction to Empedocles, knows his boundaries (ELT 45).

While Heidegger rejects the notion of "symbol" or "allegory" as belonging to a subjectivistic "aesthetics" (OWA; DI 16–17), these elements of form play a significant role in Hölderlin's theory, facilitating the simultaneous preservation and transcendence of the self's experiences within the formal structure of a poem. Symbol and allegory function to both transcend and preserve the intimacy of the self's experience. With these poetic measures, Hölderlin can avoid both self-forgetfulness and solipsism, even when he claims that "life is determined and founded by the poetic reflection" (ELT 68). Although "it is the most profound inwardness which is expressed in the tragic dramatic poem" it is "no longer the poet and his own experiences which appear" therein (ELT 51). For "nothing whatsoever can be understood and animated, if we cannot translate our mood and experience into a foreign analogical subject matter" (ELT 51). Thus Hölderlin has chosen the ancient Greek figure Empedocles as a foreign "analogy" to the modern poetic subject.

Entirely at odds with Heidegger's interpretations of "Andenken" and "Der Ister," among other poems, Hölderlin's poetic theory is, while intensely formal, also irreducibly personal. The symbolic formality of the poem, its structural analogue, allows the poem's "subject matter" to reflect the poet's own "life and world," "our own mood and experience" and the "divine which the poet senses and experiences in his world" (ELT 51). For the poet, the "image of life which is and was present to him in his life" is taken up in a symbol of "intrinsic kinship" with that life, and allows the latter to appear as the receptivity of "life in general." For Hölderlin "every poem, thus also the tragic one, must have emerged from poetic life and reality, from the poet's own world and soul — because otherwise the veritable truth will be missing" (ELT 51). This holds even for an experience of the "holy," which, in Heidegger's reading, the poet selflessly announces. Hölderlin writes, "thus the divine which the poet senses and experiences in his world is also expressed in the tragic-dramatic poem; for him the tragic-dramatic poem, too, is an image of life which is and was present to him in his life" (ELT 51). The divine for Hölderlin as given analogy in the tragic drama *Empedocles* is the divine "as felt by the poet in his world" (ELT 52), and symbol and allegory serve to both preserve and transcend the limitations of this world's particularity. Foreshadowing Eliot's notion of the "objective correlative," wherein inner feeling is to be preserved in an objective poetic image, the more foreign the allegory of the visible subject matter of the poem to its original matter of the poet's experience, the less the poet's experience may be denied (ELT 51–52). The subject matter of a poem, though expressed in symbol and allegory (ELT 51), "underlies the mood and world of the poet" (ELT 52), which are preserved all the more intimately as the "founding sensation" of a poem the more foreign the analogy the poet uses. The poet's experience is accordingly preserved "all the safer" (ELT 52). Only thus does the "lyric law" preserve "the most intimate sensation." Hölderlin writes that in a poem "the most intimate sensation is exposed to transitoriness precisely to that degree to which it does not deny the true temporal and sensuous relations" (ELT 52).

This preservation of the concrete relations and sensations of the poet's experience is a protest against the transitoriness of this experience;[51] this does not lead to the subsumption of the finite by the universal, as in a Hegelian dialectic, but to the preservation of the finite as finite into a "foreign" element where it is kept "safe." It is "precisely because he expresses the deepest inwardness, the tragic poet denies altogether his individuality, his subjectivity" (ELT 52). And yet for Hölderlin's character Empedocles,[52] *Innigkeit* is in "excess" (ELT 51), and the capacity of Empedocles to deny the limits of his subjectivity in preserving it objectively leads to the evolution of Empedocles to a god. Empedocles appears to have grasped the secrets of nature, as he declares:

> Was Eines ist, zerbricht,
> Die Liebe stirbt in ihrer Knospe nicht
> Und überall in freier Freude theilt
> Des Lebens luftiger Baum sich auseinander.

> What is one breaks apart,
> Love does not die in its budding
> And everywhere in unbounded joy
> The airy tree of life divides.

This only "seeming resolution" (ELT 59) is a provisional synthesis of the divisions of natural life within the poet's utterance; here the situation "appears to be resolved," since Empedocles "had assumed the objective form of the object itself" (ELT 58). In this delusion, Empedocles loses both his grasp on the object and his subjectivity, his selfhood. In the third version of the drama this is expressed by virtue of Empedocles's loss of his song:

> Zerschlagen ist das zarte Saitenspiel.
> O Melodien über mir! Es war ein Schertz!
> Und kindisch waft' ich sonst euch nachzuahmen,
> Ein fühllos leichtes Echo tönt' in mir,
> Und unverständlich nach

> The tender lyre is shattered.
> Oh melodies above me! It was in jest!
> And I childishly wagered to imitate you,
> A soft numb echo rang in me
> And resounded without being understood

He loses, then, as a first moment of alienation, the feeling of life granted to him by nature, a feeling that was the "subjective foundation" of his poetizing. In the case of Empedocles, the particular universalizes itself, a situation that, as Plato describes in the *Republic*, constitutes tyranny. Nature, which gives itself as a gift to the receptive poet, fails to respond to the tyrant. Empedocles finds himself alone and bereft; this is the result of Empedocles's "loss of subjectivity." As a second moment of alienation, Empedocles's lost subjectivity takes form elsewhere, in the dynamic with his enemies, who force him into exile. The people "turn cold against him" when the "delusion" ceases (ELT 61). Empedocles's tragic error, his hubris, is that he had "given himself away" (ELT 60). The completed union of subject and object can only end in the "death of the individual"; particularity "discards its subjectivity," and Empedocles is expelled from life (ELT 60). In *Hyperion* arrogant striving to conquer turns deadly for the aggressor, depicted here, after the looting and plundering of the Greek revolutionaries for whom Hyperion had once fought, in the mutual burning of Turkish and Russian fleets: "thus one poison wreaks vengeance upon the other [so straft ein Gift das andre]" and "thus do tyrants exterminate themselves [so rotten die Tyrannen sich selbst aus]" (H 103 / WB I, 406).

If for Heidegger the poet transcends the *aporia*, and enters into the abyss to achieve a dangerous proximity to Being, for Hölderlin this *aporia* is the inherently human predicament. Thus, according to de Man, *Empedocles* is a warning against the temptation of hubris for the poet who transgresses his limitations and aims for too great a proximity to Being.[53] Empedocles will be one who transgresses the boundaries of natural and divine granting. As he proclaims before his downfall:

> Und ich! O Erd und Himmel! Siehe! Noch
> Noch bist du nah, indeß die Stunde flieht,
> Und blühet mir, du Freude meiner Augen
> Als wärest du mein

> And I! O earth and heaven! See, still
> Still you are near, though the hour is fleeting,
> And you bloom for me, you joy of my eyes
> As if you were mine

Poetic language requires a "lawlike calculus" of form because language itself, as in the case of judgment, points to the failure of subjectivity—which can only and must attempt to think or articulate Being—to ground its thought or articulation of that from which it is separate. It is this separation that Empedocles denies in feeling nature as if it were his own. This separation appears not only in Hölderlin but also in Heidegger and Rilke. As we have seen, Heidegger recognizes a removal from Being as the "uncanniness" of the human being, in a lecture course on Hölderlin's Hymn "Der Ister" in the summer of 1942:

> For it belongs to this kind of uncanniness, that is, unhomeliness, that whatever is of this essence knows of beings themselves and knows of them as beings, addressing them and enunciating them. This is something of which no thing of nature and no other living being is capable. Human beings alone stand in the midst of beings in such a way as to comport themselves toward beings as such. (DI 76)

For Rilke, too, consciousness is the "parting" of the human being against the Open; Heidegger both takes up Rilke's notion here of "uncanniness" and distances himself from its metaphysical elements (its reference to consciousness), whereas Hölderlin, as a more "essential" poet, is entered into the "gathering" of *seinsgeschichtliche Andenken.* Heidegger understands this "uncanniness" as the source of human beings' forgetting of Being: "as a consequence of this state of forgetting, the human being is in a certain manner outside of that wherein all beings are beings, namely, outside of Being" (DI 76). That we can address and enunciate beings, for Hölderlin, provokes a form of "forgetting" as a fallacious grounding of the unity of beings in the theoretical efforts of philosophy (or the hubris of poetry), which Heidegger also implicates in a critique of the forgetting of Being. But for Hölderlin, this cannot be reconciled by the poet's "founding" of truth or Being, nor by his immediate, nonsubjectivistic reception thereof.[54] Rather, only poetic form, and a poetological account of subjectivity's limitations, offer an access to Being—and at that only an indirect, deferred access. As he writes in the poem "Brod und Wein" ("Bread and Wine"): "Aber Freund! Wir kommen zu spät. Zwar leben die Götter, Aber über dem Haupt droben in anderer Welt" ("But friend, we come too late. The gods do live, / but above our heads, up there in another world"). While Heidegger enlists this absence of gods to bolster the poet's proximity to Being (by virtue of poet as venturer), Hölderlin's position is one of a radical skepticism, both epistemologically and ontologically.[55] It is this skepticism that makes room for poetic language and renders its radical significance. Heidegger takes the poet's naming of the gods and of the lost origin literally,[56] whereas I will formulate it according to an ambiguity that is correlate to Hölderlin's skeptical position.

In Hölderlin, remembrance is tethered to the accident of being granted a rationally inconceivable glimpse of Being; and the lack of ontological foundations sets the subject "wandering." Hyperion, whose very name suggests a hyper-wandering, experiences "more presently than anything else the majesty of a fateless soul [die Majestät der schicksallosen Seele]" (WB I, 403). This sharply contradicts Heidegger's notion of the founding of a *Heimat*. In *The Space of Literature*, Blanchot gives a counter-reading of Hölderlin according to the notion of "exile" that attends this wandering. This is relevant for Heidegger's discussion of the abode or home, which the poet is said to found in founding historical Being (and to which we will turn at length in chapter 6). Yet Empedocles is sacrificed; Hyperion is alienated from his native Greece and is wholly estranged from the ways of the German north, which he harshly criticizes. Heidegger's Hölderlinian question "What are poets for?" is answered by Blanchot according to a skepticism more true to Hölderlin's views than to a theory of poetic founding. Indeed the phrase from which Heidegger borrows the question in "Brod und Wein" begins with " . . . and what to say/ I don't know": "weiß ich nicht." Though Hölderlin articulates a rigorous poetic form as a reconciliation of the aforementioned loss, Blanchot remarks that "the wanderer's country"—the space of the Hölderlinian question of Being—"is not truth but exile."[57] This is corroborated by Hans-Jost Frey's argument that in Hölderlin's utterance of the sacred "the event is not expressed as a contemporary event but as a desire. By expressing the event as something that should be, Hölderlin contrasts his current discourse . . . with the word that would be the occurrence of the sacred."[58] Hölderlin's poetry would be then a subjunctive form of expression, not a direct conduit of Being. Blanchot interprets this radically. To the question "Wozu Dichter?" Blanchot thus claims that "there can be no response. The poem is the answer's absence. The poet is the one who, through his sacrifice, keeps the question open in his work."[59] If for Blanchot the "poem is exile," then "the poet who belongs to it belongs to the dissatisfaction of exile. He is always lost to himself, outside, far from home; he belongs to the foreign, to the outside which knows no intimacy or limit. . . . The poem, then, makes the poet a wanderer, the one always astray . . . the one who is deprived of a true abode."[60]

Blanchot's reading is offered in response to Heidegger's neglect of the radically uncertain nature of the poet's journeying. Repeatedly Heidegger tethers the wandering—of the river, of Antigone—to the revealing of the homely (*das Heimliche*), the national abode. Perhaps this is why Heidegger neglects *Hyperion* in his readings. It is, to quote one scholar, "paradoxical that the philosopher of *Unheimlichkeit*, of anxiety as well as of estranged joy, the thinker of the abyss of being as the wholly other than beings . . . has so fully privileged the poetic question for the Homeland and for the proper, familiar, domestic abode."[61] Heidegger's notion of the poet as the founder of truth—admittedly Hölderlinian in origin—nonetheless overlooks the very complex criticism Hölderlin offers of the hubris of poetical proximity to Being, the divine, or truth, and the devastating implications this would have for any resolute nationalism.

Yet Blanchot's emphasis exclusively on lostness and alienation misses the other side of the poetic experience–that of affirmation and creation. According to Blanchot, the poet "does not belong to truth because the work is itself what escapes the movement of the true." This absolute skepticism undermines the gathering of a Heideggerian event as one whose essence speaks of an historical destiny. Yet I will argue, against the finality of Blanchot's notion of absolute exile, that the terminology of truth, albeit radically qualified, must be retained. This implies as well a retention of some structure of the subject or self despite its complexities. As Stanley Corngold argues of Hölderlin, the impossibility of being a self is coupled with the necessity of the self. 'Obliteration' and exile must be understood in the context of reaffirmation, of what I have called the self's analeptic or restorative nature. And it is in a similar way that the impossibility of truth (as absolute rational cognition of the whole of life) is also what makes truth (as poetical utterance) possible. Taken as a whole, the unending cycle of belonging and exile, or having and losing a grasp of life, speaks to an affirmative process of restoring what was previously divided. In this context, phenomenological revealing is due equally to receptivity and to a poetical creativity in the productive sense. Even the experience of loss is affirmed and creatively projected as experience, as the substrate and informing structure of poetical life. As I will discuss further in the final chapter, poetry does not only inscribe the already existing reality within the textures of appearance but projectively evokes and preserves possibility. For within poetic language we find what Corngold calls an "aspiration to new images"[62] through which new stances toward the world, life, Being are always possible.

Most importantly for the present concern is that Hölderlin's diagnosis of the elusiveness of Being—its conceptual ineffability—complicates not only Heidegger's attempt to leave out a consideration of subjectivity from his theory of the poet, but also the deep simplicity Heidegger grants to the poetic word in its founding relation to Being. Language is for Hölderlin the "paradox" (ELT 89) of saying what we realize cannot be said; judgment or language, which enables us to think in unities, always disturbs unity in admitting upon inspection a rift between saying and said, subject and object. This would also disturb the "essential unity" of the "single conversation" of Being discovered, or founded, in the "simplicity" of the poetic word. Thus Hölderlin has been compared to Keats of the odes, for whom "self-encounter and self-transcendence occur in one single, destructive moment that puts the entire strategy of the work into question."[63] Hölderlin's theory as well as his poetry indeed point to the darkness of Being's withdrawal, which Heidegger names the "oblivion." But this is inextricable from what Dieter Henrich has called "the bewilderment and disorientation of conscious life," indeed not exclusively the shelter of Being but the "anguish of an unsheltered subject."[64]

Poetic Subjectivity: Transgression of the Philosophical Subject

The Subject's "Constitutive Failure"

In claiming that Hölderlin poetizes the "essence" of poetry and of language, Heidegger aligns Hölderlin's oeuvre and task with a "simple" ontological saying and the "dignity" of that saying. Heidegger writes: "Hölderlin poetizes purely from out of that which, in itself, essentially prevails as that which is to be poetized. When Hölderlin poetizes the essence of the poet, he poetizes relations that do not have their ground in the 'subjectivity' of human beings" (DI 165). Yet in Hölderlin the question of Being concerns not the poet who straightforwardly recalls, says simply, clarifies by interpreting, receives as a univocal vessel—a poet who yields a proselike message. If Hölderlin's theory of the poet is thus not beyond subjectivity but poeticizes the latter in the transcendence of the self, it involves what Heidegger of *Being and Time* would call the factical encounter with the world. This includes feeling and experience that recall *Befindlichkeit* and *Stimmungen* ("state of mind" and "moods") in Being and Time. Hölderlin sees "correspondences between ideas and particular existents everywhere,"[65] which accounts for the abstract character of his language and yet the specificity of "content." While for Heidegger poetry is historical because it attends to and opens up the withdrawing-sending of Being in a "founding" of historical essence, for Hölderlin poetry is tethered to the specificity of historical moments, which both articulate the movements of a *Geist*[66] and also remain at the level of the merely particular. Poetry is historical because it is an enacting of the movements of spirit, one that, in the harmonious opposition of alternating tones, opens moments within which freedom, love, and community appear possible; and yet Hölderlin escapes a "geschichtsphilosophisch" narrative that subordinates these elements to a (Hegelian) teleological or (Heideggerian) *seinsgeschichtliche* structure. In Hölderlin the "concrete particulars of experience" cannot be tethered to the "deep structure of a narrative signification."[67] Poetry is the longing for and mourning of the unattainable; but at the same time it is the accidental and analeptic glimpse into what is withheld, a glimpse that is inextricable from the nontotalizable singularity of life, a singularity recalling again Heidegger's category of facticity from the 1920s and repeated, according to Agamben, in the notion of "dwelling" of this period.

As such Hölderlin's poetry can be said to provide a utopian and political function, one that, at the same time, is addressed to one's own historical moment and its particularity. According to Adorno, Hölderlin's poetry "expresses, better than any maxims could and to an extent that Hegel would not have approved, that life is not an idea, that the quintessence of existing entities is not essence."[68] Poetry retrieves us from the one possibility Heidegger located (in GA 60) in "factical life"—namely its "falling tendency" (*abfallende Tendenz*) toward a subjectivizing "logic of objects," in order to grant the "turning around" also motivated out of factical life's possibilities. But the deeply personal character of this other factical motivation—read in early lectures in terms of Paul and Augustine, for example, and involving the notion of an intimate "self-world"—has been lost in the critique of subjectivity that follows *Being and Time*, which still maintained an examination of a self and its experiences. It is clear that Heidegger's critique of subjectivity loses sight of this earlier intimacy of a self encountering the world. What for Hölderlin is the transformation and transcendence of intimate conditions of a specific poetical consciousness becomes absorbed into a wholly impersonal *Seingeschichte*.

We remember that subjectivity, Heidegger thinks, is not only a forgetting of Being but a violent objectification of the "earth," a "will to power" that consumes and destroys. Reflection, as the ground of modern conceptions of subjectivity since Descartes, is a self-representation that grounds all representation, wherein the subject presents to itself, and according to its own conditions, its object, builds up a world of objects over and against, and measured by, itself. For Heidegger "reflection is transcendental in its true essence," which means that reflection guarantees the objectivity of objects according to the conditions of the representing subject (EP 62). Yet, as we have seen, Hölderlin undermines this transcendental character of the modern subject not in abandoning it but in rendering it "unsheltered": "poetic reflection" invokes the difference that the subject is from what it attempts to utter. Thus Hölderlin develops a theory of "aesthetic reception" which cannot be exhausted by "conceptual determination."[69]

Derrida also criticizes Heidegger's categorical "disqualification" of subjectivity in a discussion regarding Hölderlin, in that the very failure of the subject can be seen to be a "constitutive" one, relevant to an account of a nonidentical self.[70] Although Heidegger's accounts of mourning in Hölderlin are "very powerful and very beautiful," Derrida argues for a "re-elaboration, rather than a simple disqualification of the concept of the 'subject.'"[71] Yet a poetic self that expresses a complex of renunciation and affirmation at once, both receptivity and productive spontaneity, has until the present project yet to be articulated in the wake of Heideggerian poetics. Such a reelaboration amounts to an articulation of a post-metaphysical subject which deconstruction has not yet offered. Poetically, we can say that language would be understood as a paradoxical capacity to conjure what is lost, is indirect or "impossible" in ordinary cognition.[72] Beyond Hölderlin, modern works of art in general might be suggestive of this paradox. They are, it has been argued, representative more of the subject's failure than of the mastery and egoism that Heidegger associates with the modern aesthetic genius. One scholar claims that "modern art works, works of genius, thrive on their own inessential impossibility, on their failure to be works of great art, to disclose world. . . . Hence through them we come to experience the sense of periphery as a periphery, and thus the meaning of the sway of the center."[73] I take this to mean that modern works of art establish the partiality of their revealing; rather than grand narratives, they tell of a very singular and elusive perspective on what evades straightforward signification, even as they declare (an aspect of the) world luminously.

To speak deconstructively of the poetic subject's "failure" is perhaps misleading in terms of my argument here, unless that be in the sense of a reflection that "never closes on itself" — in the way it can be said that "*we* are never *ourselves* . . . a 'self' is never in itself or identical to itself." But this can be articulated phenomenologically, for instance, in Sartre's argument that the ego or the reflecting "I" can never catch up with itself, that it is "by nature fugitive."[74] A unified ego is not the source of the self; rather the unity of sense of self is itself an accomplishment of consciousness and always a tentative or provisional one. In this sense, it must be said that Hölderlin's aim to develop a poetic logic that reinscribes the loss of unity with Being or "life" within poetical consciousness fails to reach its telos; and yet it is this failure that engenders Hölderlin's formal discoveries. *Hyperion* perhaps best illustrates the deferral of telos, for the poet-figure experiences the bliss of belonging and isolation of loss in an apparently endless cycle. As aforementioned, the narrative structure refuses closure — for the novel ends at its beginning, and proceeds not in progress but in stages of reflection that do not arrive at a conclusion. Yet in *Hyperion,* the unraveling of center, and the poet-self adrift in that centerless cycle, grant the moments of bliss, glimpses of unity and life in the feeling of the poet. If the subject's lack of absolute identity to nature or life (and thus to itself) issues mourning, it also yields joy. Hölderlin's poetology thus relies both on the rigorous logic of "calculation," which can be practiced in poetic form, and on the "mere fortune" (*bloßes Glück*) of attunement — for the logic does not guarantee a glimpse of that which is lost. Only in failure to ground itself does the self receive a glimpse of Being, which resounds with Heidegger's claim that *Gelassenheit* thinking requires a difficult and challenging releasement of representational thinking grounded in the conditions of subject (DT 58–90).

Transcendence of the Kantian Transcendental Subject

For Heidegger, the transcendental-philosophical "system, thought as the unity and order of knowledge" not only appears as "the paradigm of portrayal for everything knowable in its structure" but "is the essential structure of the reality of what is real" (EP 49). This is the representation of systematic philosophy as the organization of beings and is thus inadequate to a thinking of Being. Hölderlin, too, counters the systematicity of philosophy and its attempt to exhaust Being in an a priori representational structure. Poetry is not, as Hegel formulates, one stage in a dialectical system along the way to a cognitive grasp of the Absolute, nor does it, as in Kant, bridge a "system" of transcendental reason via "aesthetic ideas." According to Hölderlin's claim that the subject is unified only a posteriori, the contingent, the "real" itself— that is, phenomenal, specific experience in the realm of beings—challenges the a priori and systematic claims of transcendental philosophy. Thus Hyperion claims that "poetry . . . is the beginning and end of philosophical knowledge" (H 6). It is the subject's experience of the "real" that opens the caesura and illuminates the (contingent) subject's glimpse into the elusiveness, the caesura, of Being.

A further delineation of poetic subjectivity as I have sketched it out in reference to Hölderlin's poetology must take into account Hölderlin's relationship to Kantian philosophy, which lays the groundwork for an aesthetic subjectivity.[75] Since we will take up Kant and Hölderlin's critique of Kant in the next two chapters, I will discuss here only briefly two short texts in which Hölderlin criticizes the transcendental systematicity of the Kantian subject. Hölderlin is informed by Kant's insistence that a unification of the realms of pure and practical reason—an access to the "feeling of life"—cannot be fashioned by rational concepts, but rather only by an experience of the beautiful. For Kant, the union of the incompatible realms must be performed symbolically; in the analogy of hypotyposis, the beautiful is to be a symbol of the morally good, thus unifying the distinct realms of moral freedom and phenomenal nature. Hölderlin articulates what will become a tragic account of this problem when he undermines the Kantian system in favor of an a posteriori and accidental union.[76] From Hölderlin's point of view—which valorizes the union of freedom and nature and the "feeling of life" over the systematicity of reason that was Kant's concern—the symbol is insufficient; for in hypotyposis the conceptual and the aesthetic are left separated by the very analogy that joins them. In asserting a "moral

instinct" as an experience of this union, an accidental and phenomenal feeling of the moral law, Hölderlin situates the union within
the experience of the creative subject who is dependent on the creative imagination and, therefore subject to contingency.

Hölderlin's critique of Kant is issued in his essay "On the Law of
Freedom" (ELT 33–34), among other writings. The "law of freedom" is Hölderlin's attempt to join the sensible and the sacred, freedom and necessity in an intellectual intuition, rather than by way of
Kant's merely analogous symbol, an attempt that, despite his critique of Fichte, betrays Hölderlin's Fichtean influence. The intuition of the moral law is, according to Hölderlin, possible in the
"moral instinct" of the subject's "creative imagination," but, as such,
it is possible only "accidentally." Despite Kant's attempt to ground
their unity a priori, freedom and necessity cannot be unified, Hölderlin thinks, in necessity. Dependent upon an experience of transgression and punishment, the intellectual intuition that Kant—by insist-
ing on a merely analogous joining of phenomenal beauty and the
concept of freedom—ruled out appears only analeptically, as a restoration of a prior rift. The synthesis does, Hölderlin thinks, take place
in the subject's feeling. But given the analeptic and contingent character of this synthesis it is, Hölderlin writes, "mere fortune to be
thus attuned" ("bloßes Glück so gestimmt zu sein") (ELT 33).

The epistemological skepticism regarding the subject's access to
Being is articulated again in "On the Concept of Punishment," wherein
Hölderlin considers the recognizability of the moral law, which, he
claims, announces itself only negatively. The immediate voice of the
Kantian "ought" (which Hölderlin calls the "moral instinct") discloses
itself only by default, as response to our having willed against the moral
law. Punishment is therefore not only the infliction of suffering upon
the transgressor but, as in Hegel, contains the law within itself. One
can find here Hölderlin's epistemological-ethical basis for longing, in
which what is lost is elicited through its opposite, as in the poet's procla-
mation of the fled gods. Punishment is the contingent evidence for the
existence of the moral law within oneself. It belongs, not to reason, but
to instinct. The unity of the moral subject, and the subject itself, is
therefore again challenged, for it is to be grasped only a posteriori in
the punished, transgressive (and, according to "On the Law of Freedom," creative) subject, as in the logic of tragic poetry. With the a posteriori character of the subject's unity, an *aporia* is introduced into consciousness; the moral law is always a contingent response and can never
be united with a pre-transgressive subject. Again the ideal—here the

moral law—appears in relation to its transgression or loss of immediacy. Hölderlin's view that the intellectual intuition is possible (contra Kant), but only analeptically and contingently (contra Fichte) and only in poetic language, divorces Hölderlin from the idealism of his contemporaries and steers him in a decidedly poetological direction.

Hölderlin's critique of philosophy in favor of a poetological access to Being issues, as in Heidegger, from an attempt to undermine the subject-object distinction of metaphysics that renders the subject divorced from the object for which it longs or, in Heidegger, exhausts the object in the consumption of the technological will (EP 104–106). Yet for Hölderlin, the human being, as conscious, is limited by subjectivity, even if these very limitations promise a deferred reconciliation—in longing, mourning, remembrance, or joy. Thus we find the evasive conclusion in the penultimate stanza of "Germanien": if the law of nature, the truth that separates day and night, should be made apparent, it seems to remain unsaid: "Dreifach umschreibe du es, / Doch ungesprochen auch, wie es da ist, / Unschuldige, muß es bleiben [Thrice you circumscribe it. / Yet unsaid also, as it exists, / Innocent, it must remain]." The aesthetic-poetic alternative to a transcendental and epistemological subject is, in Hölderlin, grounded in the "unsaid." The subject's experience is no longer mediated by conditions of representation; this is not because the poet is able to escape a metaphysical or representational encounter with the world, but because these conditions are themselves not unifiable, in the *aporia*—between subject and object, language and world, within the subject itself in reflection—for which philosophies of consciousness cannot account.

Andenken and the Poetic Subject

Hölderlin's poetology is grounded in subjectivity as its rupture, its transgression, as well as its analeptic and provisional-poetic recovery. The remembering of Being—as mourning or *Andenken*—is, as Michel Haar writes, a displacement of subjectivity, its poetic "decentering."[77] Yet Hölderlin's poetry is grounded in "poetical reflection," which suggests not the autonomy and rationality of an Enlightenment subject, nor a freedom grounded in autonomy. In poetic reflection, the poet experiences "the world" and "life" from an aesthetic rather than rationalistic perspective.

Yet poetic utterance is always-already tainted by the subject's fragility, by what Kant called, in reference to aesthetic judgment, the sacrifice of the subject's "legislative" role. The poetic subject is a subject turned inside out, where its conditions do not guarantee the unity of experience, but might reflect the disjointure and distress that belongs to being a self, being a self that is indeed theoretically ungraspable, but factically and politically "real." This, of course, recalls Heidegger's insights into the *Gewor-fenheit* of Dasein, which renders Dasein powerless, *ohnmächtig,* and subject to the situation in which it finds itself. *Befindlichkeit* or Dasein's attunement is thus concordant with that of Hölderlin's poetic subject; both are not self-grounded, but radically without center, and it is only as lacking center—as ecstatic or eccentric—that they exist as facticity, as relationship to beings in their Being. Thus Hölderlin's poetic self might be illuminated by Heidegger's Dasein, whose *Sorge* as the unity of ecstases Heidegger calls a "self." In the final chapter I will indeed outline a "new poetics of Dasein" as an alternative theory of poetic subjectivity and language, and Heidegger's early work will yield structural scaffolding by which to outline a poetically reconceived self.

Heidegger's reading of Hölderlin's poem "Andenken," as discussed in the last chapter, relies largely upon the *seinsgeschichtliche* significance of the last line: "was bleibet aber stiften die Dichter" ("what remains is founded by the poets"). I have attempted here to mark out a stark differentiation between what Heidegger means by the poet's role as "founder" of Being and what Hölderlin's theoretical writings might bear out by illuminating the elusiveness of Being in its relation to poetical expression and to the subject conceived poetically. I turn, in concluding this chapter, to philosophical arguments surrounding the kind of subjectivity in question in poems such as "Andenken," in order to mark out within the debates my claims that what is gleaned from Hölderlin's poem must be understood according to his theoretical insights about the nature and limits of subjectivity, its estrangement from Being, and the role of poetic language in reconciling this estrangement.

Dieter Henrich argues that the poem is to be understood as a "course" of remembrance that follows the structure of the poem as a whole, what Paul de Man calls the poem's "totality." While the poem is not merely an illustration of Hölderlin's theoretical views or a transcription of Hölderlin's personal experiences (though Henrich documents Hölderlin's journey to Bordeaux in detail), it in some sense enacts and furthers the view of poetic language I have set forth in this chapter. Although the poem transcends the poet's particularity, there is, nonetheless, a "devotion to the reality he experienced"[78] in Hölderlin's poem "Andenken." Yet Henrich's view, while illuminating, invokes a more idealist view of poetic unification than the one upon which I ultimately settle; and the compelling argument about Hölderlin's late poetry by

Anselm Haverkamp, who argues instead for a shattered subjectivity, is not yet affirmative enough of the (analeptic) self for the poetics I would like to articulate here. Even so, both arguments present important differences from Heidegger's claims, which can be enlisted in a new theory of the subject of poetic language.

An alternative to Heidegger's account of "Andenken," which Heidegger claims is both divorced from Hölderlin as "thinker" or philosopher and from Hölderlin's "actual" experiences, is given in Henrich's *Course of Remembrance*, which follows a lengthy and significant study, *Der Grund im Bewußtsein*, of Hölderlin's early thought.[79] For Henrich, the unity of the poem's modulating images, both with reference to their counterparts in experience and to the "poetic logic" of their recollection, is to be thought with regard to the indirect reconciliation of varying dimensions of life as experienced by a conscious subject. In order to contextualize Henrich's claims, we turn briefly to Hölderlin for evidence that remembrance might be located as the jointure between the experienced life of the poet, which includes both the feeling of life and an awareness of the loss thereof, and the logic of reinscription in the "creative reflection" that "is language" (ELT 81). In "Becoming in Dissolution" (to which Heidegger refers in GA 52, 119–120), Hölderlin indeed gives an idealist-oriented account of the path of remembrance by which the finite dissolves into the passage of becoming, is preserved as loss, and makes way for the new. This involves both the problem of transition (*Übergang*) and that of the relation between actuality and possibility. Transition is made possible only by dissolution as the "state between being and nonbeing" ("im Zustande zwischen Seyn und Nichtseyn"). Hölderlin writes: "the *possible* which enters into *reality* [in die Wirklichkeit] as that *reality itself dissolves* [sich auflöst] is operative and effects the sense of dissolution as well as the remembrance [*Erinnerung*] of that which has been dissolved" (ELT 97). And further that:

> there emerges by way of recollection (due to the necessity of the object in the most finite state) a complete feeling of life [*Lebensgefühl*], the initially dissolved; and after this recollection of the dissolved, individual matter has been united with the infinite feeling of life through the recollecting of the dissolution, and after the gap between the aforesaid has been closed, there emerges from this union and adequation of the particular of the past and the infinite of the present the actual new state, the next step that shall follow the past one. (ELT 98)

Recollection (here as in many of Hölderlin's poems, the term is *Erinnerung*, which connotes a sense of inner intimacy) is the path to what Hölderlin, following Kant, calls the feeling of life (*das Lebensgefühl*). Henrich argues that for Hölderlin "poetry is the consummation of what is only begun in philosophy, in as much as it allows an ultimate and genuinely synthetic insight to emerge in pure expression from out of the experience of conscious life."[80] Yet Hölderlin's poem is the unification of transitory, oppositional differences that Hölderlin claims is possible only in poetic language, not in philosophical discourse.[81] Poetry is not only philosophy's end but also its beginning. In "Becoming in Dissolution" Hölderlin claims that poetic, or "truly tragic language" enacts the recollection that expresses relations between possibility and actuality, the finite and the infinite, becoming and dissolution (ELT 97).

This view of *Erinnerung* is repeated in "Operations of the Poetic Spirit," wherein "language remembers cognition" of the feeling of life (ELT 79) and in "On Religion" (ELT 92). While Hölderlin claims that one does not encounter the experience of the poet in a poem directly, it is taken up in a course of expression, for "every poem . . . must have emerged from poetic life and reality, from the poet's own world and soul—because otherwise the veritable truth will be missing" (ELT 51). Recollection, taken up in the poem itself as *Andenken*, is the course of integration of loss of both differentiated finite moments—of concrete "particular relations" (ELT 92) of the subject to its world—and the unity that is presumed to have issued them, into a whole course of "poetic reflection." In this course the finite and the infinite are both preserved and lost at once. *Andenken*, read in light of this *Erinnerung*, is not mere repetition "in thought nor merely in memory" (ELT 91), but in poetic inscription. Read tragically, "Andenken" issues the "paradox" (ELT 89) of loss that makes remembrance possible, of remembrance that recaptures the loss as ungraspable. "Andenken" is thus tragic (as the "metaphor of an intellectual intuition") and lyric (as "the continuous metaphor of a feeling") recollection at once, and refers to the epic (the heroic "metaphor of great aspirations") (ELT 83) only at a distance, in the figure of the seafarers greeted and recalled by the speaker.[82]

Henrich's reading attempts to reconstruct a "connection between poetry and experience," which, Anselm Haverkamp counters, "is not to be denied . . . yet . . . lies not in the field of literary studies."[83] Henrich's attempt to give specified content to a reading of the poem yields a profit not so much in literary or literal explanation of the poem's "content" but by way of a philosophical account of its form in relation to Hölderlin's theory of poetic language and its enactment in and through such language. For the transition from experienced life, in its transitoriness and dissolution, to the "feeling of life" — what Hölderlin also calls the individual's "real" and "spiritual" life — concerns both Hölderlin's poetology as such, and the significance of the notions of "founding" and "remaining," which appear as the stronghold of Heidegger's interpretations.

In this chapter, I presented an interpretation of Hölderlin's essay "Judgment and Being" in order to account for the skepticism underlying Hölderlin's turn from philosophical to poetic language. Philosophical reflection, as in the aforementioned essay, illuminates the self-refuting character of theoretical language in grounding Being in consciousness. If Hölderlin's later poetry can be understood, in the words of contemporary theorists, as a "poetry of shards,"[84] in Haverkamp's terms of "cryptic subjectivity,"[85] as "solitude's poverty,"[86] all of this is related to Hölderlin's view of the impossibility of grounding theoretically the diversity and transitoriness of life's elements. The latter issue from the difference that Being's "unity" turns out to be for the subject who can only grasp unity as a "necessary presupposition." We have seen that "The Ground for Empedocles" is one source for Hölderlin's theory of poetic form, which involves the objective preservation of subjective experience within the limitations prescribed by the warning against hubris. The symbol in poetic language is both the joining of subject and object as well as the making-apparent of the impossibility of such unity in judgment. Henrich's interpretation shows that *Andenken* is both more than remembrance of a particular landscape, and indeed just that, according to a logic of reflection in language. Yet Henrich remains perhaps too optimistic regarding the promise of unification in poetic language, overlooking the skepticism that issued such promise. Henrich's Hölderlin remains too much an idealist, Henrich claiming that "even in the very concept of *Andenken* Hölderlin remained a student of Fichte."[87] With this assertion Henrich falls prey to Heidegger's critique of subordinating Hölderlin's poetry to the idealist philosophy of his day. For Henrich the poet's "founding" would be the unification of division and lost finite moments within consciousness, a unification aiming at clarity. Eric Santner has recently argued that this very clarity is a turn to the discrete elements of experience in which both remaining and founding must be understood more modestly than as an historical institution.[88] The view I have articulated thus far is also concordant with those of Adorno and Hans-Jost Frey, for whom the character of Hölderlin's poetic language prevents the fulfillment of the promise of unification or foundation — for Adorno it is a wish, a subjunctive claim, a "critical and utopian" aim.[89]

In Blanchot's terms this founding is wholly overridden by an irreversible "exile" from unity or wholeness, an exile that, contrary to Heidegger's reading, knows no return home—to a destiny, a people, or an historical truth.[90] In "Andenken" the speaker asks: "But where are the friends?" and refers to Bellarmin, a nomination that links this poem to *Hyperion*, which I have engaged earlier in this chapter as a cycle without center. The poet finds himself only "under the heavens," as Hölderlin writes in "Abend-phanasie" ("Evening Fantasy"): "Dunkel wirds und einsam / Unter den Himmel, wie immer, bin ich [Darkness falls and lonely / Under the heavens I am, as always]." Yet contrary to Blanchot, it is my view that the affirmative nature of the poetical self—the possibility of genuine creation— is deeply inscribed within Hölderlin's radical skepticism.

Henrich claims that, "*Andenken* is insight, and hence, departure, ascent, and transcendence, all in one,"[91] and that in Hölderlin's poem this notion "enters into the philosophical domain Hölderlin worked out years before," a domain that "puts in perspective those dimensions of life that all human existence knows as its own essential possibilities."[92] But such possibilities encounter separation and difference, transitoriness,[93] and a truth that arises only in acknowledgment of its loss. Heidegger's reading of the "uncanniness" inherent in poetic language speaks to this acknowledgment insofar as the poet seeks the homely and does not yet find it.

Henrich's reading coincides with Heidegger's in that both acknowledge *Andenken* as "a form of *Denken.*"[94] *Andenken* is not merely a content for "literary" exposition but the process or "course" of Hölderlin's poetic address to thought. The difference between these readings involves the "inwardness" or intimacy (*Innigkeit*) in Hölderlin, which Hölderlin grants his tragic character Empedocles in "excess." *Innigkeit* is not absorption of the external into the internal, but rather the indirect intimacy that, within limits, allows the poet a glimpse into life and grants the poet the joy of that glimpse, as well as the mourning of its loss. I would want to bring Heidegger's notion of *Gelassenheit* into the realm not so much of historical saying but of a poetic self and of *Innigkeit*. For *Gelassenheit* should suggest an intimacy with things of the (personal) world, the sheltering-unsheltered space of a self among beings in their "livingness," their elusive emergence and passing away. According to Hölderlin's incipient theory of the poetic subject, this intimacy would be tempered with an awareness of distance and elusiveness. If *Andenken* is, in Heidegger's reading, a matter for a *Seinsgeschichte* beyond the subject, in Henrich's reading, *Andenken*, as a course and process of recollecting *Innigkeit*, "guides conscious life . . . through a series of moods in which it collects itself."[95] Following my reading of the tragic and skeptical elements in Hölderlin, I would qualify Henrich's formulation with a greater sense of the provisionality or tentativeness of this self-collection. This self-collection could be considered, to quote Haverkamp's reading of Hölderlin's late work, "the structure of a crypt through which . . . a loss is preserved" and one for whom language is a process of displacement, of a "discourse canceled and crossed out."[96] That is, poetic language, insofar as it utters truth, implies the radical provisionality of such utterance. Most importantly, the poetic self must be related to truth in some other way than founding, though it ought not be, I will argue, altogether "deprived" of truth,[97] as Blanchot claims and Haverkamp implies, since as a "crypt" the preservation of loss is absent of the joy of what has been lost. For poetic language is, beyond, or even in and through loss, a showing, disclosing, and nonarresting illumination of emergence—of "becoming" and "dissolution" both.

Haverkamp, in his more "deconstructive" reading, finds Henrich's account, as well as Heidegger's, still too philosophical and phenomenological.[98] Haverkamp is right that Henrich's account involves "the idealist preoccupation with the reflection of reflection,"[99] but it does so in respect to Hölderlin's theoretical writings and the incessant topic of reflection that emerges in his poetology. Haverkamp does away with a Romantic "melancholy" (à la Keats and Kierkegaard) in Hölderlin in order to make room for a deconstructive, post-Freudian account of mourning. When looking at Hölderlin's late work, Haverkamp's view is convincing, and recalls the experience of Blanchot's "exiled" self. But I would argue that, when taken in the context of his larger oeuvre, including the theoretical writings I have discussed them here, the unraveling of the philosophical subject occurs within the same complex of operations where begins the weaving of a poetic one, characterized both by mourning and by the affirmatively creative. When so read, Hölderlin's work thus engages the "re-elaboration of the concept of 'subject'" for which Derrida asks and to which de Man refers when he defends the notion of a "self" in Hölderlin.[100] If Hölderlin's late poetry "thinks structure as the impossibility of that which it inaugurates,"[101] Hölderlin's poetology is the incipience and necessity of that thought as a point of departure for poetic thinking; thus Hölderlin here enacts, in his own post-transcendental way, what Heidegger calls "inceptive thinking," a thinking of a new beginning for post-metaphysical thought. This inceptive thinking departs from, but does not leave behind, the relation of an analeptic subject to his world. The subject is not, as Haverkamp and Blanchot seem to suggest, wholly barred from truth; rather poetic language, as creative, enacts truth as a process of withholding emergence, a process whose element of withholding is due not principally to the self-concealment of Being, but to the limitations and finitude of the poetic self and of poetic subjectivity.

In Adorno's account of Hölderlin, the poet cannot deliver a message because language is tainted with the subject's transgression. "Without externalizing itself in language, subjective intention would not exist at all. The subject becomes a subject only in and through language."[102] If the subject's legislation is "sacrificed" in language, according to Adorno, "Hölderlin's procedure takes into account the fact that the subject, which mistakes itself for something immediate and ultimate, is utterly something mediated." This mediation is accomplished in poetic form as a response to the elusiveness of Being—or of the divine, the beautiful, nature, or life—which the poet longs to grasp. In chapter 6 I will analyze the notion, drawn from Kristeva's poetics, of a subject "in process/on trial," which revolutionizes the notion that, to use Kant's term, the aesthetic subject is "nonlegislative." But while both Adorno and Kristeva tether poetic language to a revolutionary politics of negation, I will emphasize, again, the imaginative creation of the subject of poetic language, which I will outline in the final chapter in light of its always provisional nature.[103]

In contrast to Heidegger, Paul de Man defends the notion of a self in Hölderlin's poetry that is decidedly nonheroic. De Man claims that "because his own medium, language, has a mediate relationship of a self-conscious, reflective type toward actions and deeds, the poet never achieves the same proximity to being" as the historical hero.[105] The poet in "Wie Wenn am Feiertage" whom Heidegger associates with the historical founding of truth in the lightning-moment of destiny, emerges, according to de Man's reading, only after the storm, in contrast to the historical hero.[106] The poet's sacrifice beyond subjectivity "fails to hear the tone of this critique" of the "sacrificial urge," a critique that comprises the warning against hubris we have seen in Hölderlin's *Empedocles*.[107] For de Man, the Hölderlinian poet (and this means both Hölderlin as poet and the poet-figure who appears in his poems) can be the founder neither of Being nor of history, because the poet's standpoint "can only be that of a consciousness that is ontologically . . . oriented but that nevertheless remains a consciousness, rooted in the language of the subject and not in being."[108] My reading of "Wie wenn am Feiertage," as I discussed it briefly at the beginning of this chapter, takes note of the formal disjunctiveness of the last sections of the poem and the corresponding qualification of the poet's role. The heavenly gift the poet is to give the people becomes, by the poem's end, a "warning song" issued at the expense of the poet's own pain, ejection from the divine realm, and ultimately uncertain location among and even below the living. This uncertainty cannot be ascribed simply to the ontological rift, for it is a personal uncertainty, and is echoed in other poems as well, for instance in the second of two stanzas which make up "Hälfte des Lebens." Again we find the phrase "weh mir" (of which there is, admittedly, no English equivalent despite my translation here) initiating the last reflections which compromise an earlier ease of the poet's relation to the divine or, in this case, nature. While the first stanza resounds with summer's luscious comforts, we find in the second stanza a poet saturated with anxiety and doubt. He is not the vessel of a message but a questioner who has no one in particular to address:

> Weh mir, wo nehm' ich, wenn
> Es Winter ist, die Blumen, und wo
> Den Sonnenschein,
> Und Schatten der Erde?

> Oh shame, where will I take, when
> It is winter, the flowers, and where
> The sunshine
> And shade of earth?

The poem ends here no longer in warning, as in "Wie Wenn am Feiertage," but in declaration of bereftness clearly tied to the speaker's inner loneliness, his own loss of certainty projected onto the blank, "speechless" walls:

> Die Mauern stehn
> Sprachlos und kalt, im Winde
> Klirren die Fahnen.

> The walls stand
> Speechless and cold, in the wind
> Clatter the weathervanes.

Heidegger's theory of language, when not overwhelmed by the destiny of the *Seinsgeschichte*'s sending, offers a new orientation for thinking in the collapse of epistemological, transcendental truth claims, and in the failure of Enlightenment thought to secure, alongside the notions of human rights and autonomous freedom, a reconciliation with nature or earth against which it posits the human. Such a poetic thinking is in Heidegger, as we have seen, explored both in terms of *Gelassenheit* and its form of dwelling, as well as in terms of the *Streit* of founding. My account, along with the indications of de Man, Corngold, and Henrich, supplies this poetic thinking with a retrieved self of that experience, one whose own particular, finite, even discrete memories and experiences, feelings and concrete engagements, can be accounted for. Haverkamp's and Blanchot's emphasis on the shattering of the subject in Hölderlin, while perhaps disallowing an account of poetical truth for which I would like to make room, assist in deheroizing the poet-figure as is needed in the wake of Heidegger's interpretations. Hölderlin's humanist concerns, which appear in his essays and letters, as well as *Hyperion* and the poetry, are given shelter in the self of "poetic experience," a self afforded not submissive or resolute reception of destiny but intensely personal concerns. Hölderlin accomplishes this without tethering that humanism to the principles of rationalism and transcendentalism.

My examination of poetic subjectivity in Hölderlin will engage in dialogue with Heidegger's notion of *Gelassenheit* and, further, with the self (*Selbst*) Heidegger outlined in *Being and Time*. This self might be rehabilitated according to Heidegger's later poetic insights, and in the wake of Heidegger's critique of the violence of rational-technological subjectivity and will. If Heidegger in his critique of subjectivity "has only partially accounted for what would take the place of the destroyed categories of substance and subject," an account of the poetical alternative must be a thinking "from the world." As Werner Marx writes:

> The thinking that comes "from the world" will have to reach far back so that it can do justice to the fact that man [sic] not only "stands out in Being" and is "open to the world" but that he is in many respects a "self," an individual, that he — thus understood — is a "subject" . . . This non-Cartesian and non-idealistic "kind" of "subjectivity" should be determined in detail.[109]

This determination is precisely what I hope to accomplish in this analysis of poetic theory and the poetic subject. If *Andenken* "is devoted in *Innigkeit* to what it reflects upon,"[110] it should be able to be thought as the *Gelassenheit* of a poetic subject or self. Thus poetic thinking is both the thinking of a self "entangled" in the realm of beings and in subjectivity, and rendered poetically responsive to Being's elusiveness. Poetic thinking would emerge in the way Heidegger describes thought emerging, in the slow reflection of an "awakening," an increasing wakefulness after a contemplative preparation, and yet one that is "beyond reflective comprehension." Such an awakening "frees thinking" — and the poetic self — "for its own ultimate possibilities,"[111] and for the world into which it finds itself "thrown."

4

The Critique of Technology and the Poetics of "Life"

One of the principal aims of Heidegger's poetics is to counter the technological attitude toward an objectified nature or earth by offering the poetic as an alternative configuration of human dwelling. In this chapter, I first present Heidegger's critique of technology in the context of its fundamental rejection of subjectivity and then question whether the alternative offered by the poetic requires this outright rejection. I argue that a radical revision, but not eschewing, of subjectivity can be articulated in light of the idealist-romantic notion of "life" initiated by Kant's *Critique of Judgment.* This demands some analysis of Kant's notion of reflective aesthetic judgment; in his dependence on this Kantian notion, I will argue, Hölderlin is able to maintain for the subject of poetic language, on the one hand, an epistemological relevance, and, on the other, a challenge to the subject as legislator of its object. This engenders Hölderlin's conception of a radically receptive subject, for whom nature is a source of what Kant calls the "feeling of life." Such feeling provokes a uniquely sheltering experience of nature and, at once, indicates radically the subject's limits. In Hölderlin's poetics and practice of poetry, this aligns aesthetic judgment with an unraveling of the subject's transcendental unity, indicating both a most precarious hold on its relation to the world and alternative possibilities of dwelling commensurate with Heidegger's critique of metaphysics.

Technology as Fractured Poiesis

First I would like to outline in brief the ontological cast of Heidegger's critique of modern technology in its relation to poetic language. Heidegger's essay "The Question Concerning Technology" addresses two interwoven themes: the destruction of the earth by technology, and our failure to ask about the philosophical origins of this destruction. Both contribute to what Heidegger calls the "extreme danger" of our times (QT 33). Heidegger argues that technology cannot be understood as a tool of human manipulation; technology belongs, rather, to a mode of revealing that obscures our essential relation to Being: namely, that we are, as bearers of language, the horizon by which Being is revealed. Therefore, the question of technology is not whether technology enhances or degrades our quality of life, whether we can master it, whether we use it according to proper aims. Heidegger's question is not whether to embrace technology or to reject it, but rather whether the questioning itself of technology is still possible—for at the end of metaphysics, Heidegger argues, our capacity to think about our relation to technology, and likewise about our relation to nature and earth, is endangered.

Yet it is the earth and its energies that are, as Heidegger writes, enframed, harnessed, processed and reproduced, and regulated by technology, which "sets upon nature" (QT 15). What is lost is the earth as the site of what Heidegger, after Hölderlin, calls "poetic dwelling"; the river is seen as the source for a hydroelectric plant and not the "locality of human abode" that serves, as we saw in chapter 2, as a model for meandering, ecstatic time, or as the site of wonder and meditative reflection. The earth is compromised as the site of what Heidegger calls "the possible," a site for which we are responsible, one that must be sheltered and "watched over" (EP 109). It is undeniable that the threat of nuclear annihilation, the progressive destruction of the environment, the extinction of significant numbers of the world's animal and plant species are alarming evidences of this endangering of possibility, even if they are not the essence of the problem itself.

Yet the human being is privy, as the bearer of language and particularly poetic language, to another possible relation to the earth, a relation that modern philosophy precludes in its attempt to ground scientific truth-claims in the rational independence of the cognitive subject from nature. According to Heidegger, in the completion of metaphysics, the technological danger itself is to reveal a saving power. This saving power is the recognition of a "turn homeward" toward the earth and Being, one that effects a "renunciation of self-will," and a revisitation of the question of thinking (QT 41, 47). At issue is our relation to what is other to rational cognition, what is to be released from the domination of quantifying, "enframing" means; once again, for Heidegger this thinking requires a thoughtful engagement with poetic language; for Heidegger "*physis* is indeed *poiesis* in the highest sense" (QT 10).

Heidegger's thesis is not, however, reliant upon a simplistic opposition of *poiesis* and *techné*. Poetic language is the proper source for thinking the essence of technology because poetry and technology share the process of revealing, which determines their essence. *Poiesis*, understood as a bringing-forth, is the essence of *physis*, as the "highest sense" of bringing-forth. But *poiesis* involves a range of meanings, both as the essence of poetic language as we know it from Hölderlin and the essence of technology, and thus both poetic language and technology have a relation to nature as *physis*. *Poiesis* is, as Heidegger cites Plato's *Symposium*, "every occasion for whatever passes over and goes forward into presencing from that which is not presencing" (QT 10). Poetic language is a bringing-forth of beings into emergence. This is made perhaps most explicit in Heidegger's essay on George's poem "Das Wort"("The Word") (OWL), as mentioned in chapter 2. There Heidegger argues that the poetic word, gives Being to, and shelters, what it names.

Like poetic language, *techné* is, too, such a bringing-forth. In its early Greek sense "*techné* is the name not only for the activities and skills of the craftsman, but also for the arts of the mind and the fine arts. *Techné* belongs to bringing-forth, to poiesis; it is something poietic" (QT 13). Heidegger points out that in Greek philosophy, *techné* was linked with "knowing in the widest sense," *episteme* (QT 13). Such "knowing provides an opening-up," for it is too a revealing. Aristotle then distinguishes between *episteme* and *techné* according to what is revealed and how. *Techné* is linked with *alétheuein*, and it reveals whatever does not bring itself forth and does not yet lie here before us, whatever can look and turn out now one way and now another. . . . Thus what is decisive in *techné* does not lie at all in making and manipulating or in the use of means, but rather in the aforementioned revealing" (QT 13). It is in this sense that *techné* is linked to both craftwork and artwork. As such *techné* belongs to revealing, to *aletheia*, and thus to the happening of truth.

Yet modern technology, as a mode of revealing, is a fractured poiesis: for it reveals, but hides its process of revealing, and no longer brings-forth what is, but sets upon (*stellt*) it. Thus modern technology "does not unfold into a bringing-forth in the sense of *poiesis*," but is rather a challenging (*Herausfordern*) of what is (QT 14). As setting-upon and challenging, modern technology is also an enframing (*Ge-stell*). The danger of technology is that it conceals itself as revealing, and, more problematically, "conceals revealing itself" (QT 27). Thus enframing "blocks *poiesis*" (QT 30), and thereby opposes revealing as such. Technology, setting-upon static presence and actuality, is thus opposed to the phenomenological truth of poetic language as revealing disclosure, and is alienated from nature, or *physis*, in its own process of self-disclosure. Poetic language is needed to uncover the concealed essence of technology as revealing, and is thus the source for a redirection of thinking as it takes up again the question of nature or earth.

In this demand for a redirection of thinking, Heidegger follows in the wake of a tradition articulated most radically in the romanticism of Schlegel, Novalis, and Hölderlin—initiated by Kant's aesthetic theory—wherein poetic language is to give voice to what escapes the realm of the legislative concept. Nature, not as mere mechanism but as the source of "life," lends itself to expression more in the indirectness of poetic language than in the transparency of rational truth-claims. From the point of view of rethinking nature, it is thus immanent that we must "learn that the making of poetry, too, is a matter of thinking" (PLT, 100), a claim foreshadowed in the "Earliest-System Program of German Idealism," wherein the young Hegel, Schelling, and Hölderlin (the text is attributed to all three, in Hegel's hand) announced that if philosophy was to become poetry, that it needed an "aesthetic sense."

Hölderlin serves as the leitmotiv of Heidegger's notion of poetic dwelling—poetic language's illumination of the "turn homeward." That philosophy has exhausted its capacity to pose our question concerning technology is a claim already anticipated by Hölderlin's poetology and by his devastating criticisms in *Hyperion* of the lifelessness of modern Germany and its estrangement from nature. The interpretations of Hölderlin withstand over three decades of transitions in Heidegger's thinking, from the eschatological-political aesthetics of the 1930s to the thinking of *Gelassenheit* as a quiet sheltering of possibility in the 1950s and 1960s. It is from Hölderlin that nature is retrieved as the abode of human dwelling, for it is nature not scientifically, but poetically and aesthetically, understood that infuses the poet with what Heidegger calls "the blessing" of the possible (EP 109) and what Hölderlin calls the "holy" or "divine." *Physis* as poiesis is illuminated by Heidegger as a "Hölderlinian" problem of Being[1]—that of earth and the turn, the reversal (*Umkehr*) of human understanding, and even of poetic thinking, "homeward" to earth, which is, for Heidegger, that of the turn from a thinking of beings to that of Being. In Hölderlin this is a reversal of *"the striving from this world to the other* into a striving *from another world to this one"* (ELT 112)—or from the attempt in Greek antiquity to grasp the "fire from the heavens" into the modern return to the earth (*Erde*).[2]

In Heidegger's reading of Hölderlin, the response to a loss of a more poetic relation to earth is a response to the forgetting of Being, which I discussed in chapter 1, a forgetting that corresponds to an historical destining on the part of Being itself—the silent shadow of Being's self-withdrawal. Like poetry, technology is the gathering sending (*versammelnde Schicken*) of the human being upon "a way of revealing, destining [*Geschick*]." Moreover, "it is from out of this destining that the essence of all history [*Geschichte*] is determined" (QT 24). The subjectivity and humanism that characterize metaphysics are for Heidegger the emblem of *Seinsvergessenheit*—both our forgetting of Being, and its own withdrawing—which comes to its apogee in modern technology. Thus fashioned, the *Seinsgeschichte*, and Hölderlin's place therein as a reversal of thinking, are to be thought for Heidegger beyond humanism. The task of "overcoming metaphysics" is then to think Being outside the auspices of beings. For "the history of Being is neither the history of the human being and of humanity, nor the history of the human relation to beings and to Being. The history of Being is Being itself, and only Being" (EP 82).

For Heidegger technology, as the expression of Being's withdrawal— as the human being's fixation upon beings, the ontic, and what is present, rather than upon ek-sistence (QT 27), as such—is itself the "coming to presence of Being"; and the "turning of the danger," the possibility of another, poetic mode of revealing, belongs to Being as well. Thus the task of the poet, then, in "destitute times," is the recollection, remembrance (*Andenken*) of Being—turning thinking from forgetfulness to remembrance without recourse to subjectivity, thus allowing the *Seinsgeschichte* to emerge, for the thinker, as the history of forgetfulness, but also as the remembering-awaiting of an arrival. Poetry, for Heidegger, thus overcomes the history of the subject in favor of the thinking of Being, and as such is to afford human beings a vastly different dwelling upon earth and within nature.

For Hölderlin, nature is illuminating and dark, revealed and concealing, peaceful and wild, sensuous and sacred; but it is also the source of what Hölderlin, after Kant, calls the "feeling of life" (*das Lebensgefühl*). Nature is harmonious or unified, but also singular: a singular tulip or birdsong serves as the occasion of Kant's reflective judgment, as does for Hölderlin the river, which, he insists, "no one knows." Regarded aesthetically, nature endows the poetically receptive subject with an experience of the feeling of freedom and the utopian promise of a community that expresses this freedom —what Kant calls in the *Critique of Judgment* the "*sensus communis*" and Hölderlin names "peace" (*der Frieden*). The subjectivity of will with which Heidegger diagnoses modern rational or scientific consciousness is displaced by Hölderlin in a skepticism of unique order, by a subject accounted for poetologically rather than epistemologically or transcendentally. Nature is, for Hölderlin, unknowable in its wholeness and conceptually ungraspable in its singularity.[3] What is left in the ruins of Enlightenment epistemological optimism —one challenged by current ecological disasters —becomes in Hölderlin's theoretical writings a subject reconceived aesthetically, a subject that no longer demands, as Heidegger claims of the rational animal of metaphysics, to be lord of the earth, and is no longer opposed as rational to nature as irrational.

Thus read, Hölderlin poses a problem for Heidegger's critique of subjectivity at the very same juncture at which Hölderlin is rightfully Heidegger's inspiration for the overcoming of technological thinking. Heidegger rejects the metaphysics of subjectivity altogether as the philosophy of the will and of representation according to which the earth is an object. The subject is for Heidegger the essence of technological, anthropocentric thinking. Yet Hölderlin's writings, which initiate in a unique way to the Romantic, poetic displacement of the subject, promise a nondominating, poetic account of subjectivity that Heidegger's view of the subject as will precludes. In Hölderlin's writings we find —in his struggle to articulate a "living" poetry that, as he writes in a letter to Schelling, "emerges simultaneously from genius, experience, and reflection" (ELT 145) —the sketches of this theory, the incipient articulation of this poetic subject. While for Heidegger, subjectivity means anthropocentrism, individualism, the rationalism of the *ego cogito*, Hölderlin, lifted out of Heidegger's ontology, opens up an alternative criticism of the modern philosophical subject. For Hölderlin, in the wake of Kant's *Critique of Judgment*, the subject is to be conceived aesthetically, and, beyond Kant, it is to be disabused of its a priori pretensions. This is a subject for whom nature is accessed only in an "eccentric path" (*ekzentrische Bahn*) of belonging and loss, only "from an askew perspective."

I argue, then, that the loss of a harmonious relation to nature is for Hölderlin characterized not primarily by the forgetting of Being, but by the loss of the "feeling of life" —and, with it, of the promise of freedom and of community—that nature, aesthetically experienced, grants us. Nature, for Hölderlin, poses questions pertaining to our tarrying within the realm of beings—how, among beings, we are subject to a feeling of life that is irreducible to a scientific, technological, or anthropocentric explanation, a feeling characterized both by joy and mourning. For Hölderlin, the feeling of life points to a tragic conflict within the subject between its rational powers and its aesthetic sensibilities, which become wedded in an epistemological, even ontological skepticism.[4] What Hölderlin might provide—reduced neither to Kant (for whom aesthetic experience services a transcendentally secure system of subjectivity) nor to Heidegger (who rejects the subject altogether)—is a sketch of subjectivity that escapes what Heidegger calls "technological thinking." This underlies Hölderlin's poetic account of nature, which unhinges such thinking from its epistemological—Heidegger would say metaphysical—conditions.

Nature and Reflective Judgment in Kant's Aesthetic Philosophy

In his account of poetry and art as the sheltering of a "saving power" in a technological age, Heidegger rejects Kantian aesthetics—and aesthetics as such (QT 34; PLT, 39)—as belonging to the philosophy of the subject that characterizes metaphysics. His critique of aesthetics rightly applies to Kant insofar as Kant's aesthetic judgment conforms to the structures Heidegger outlines and rejects as metaphysical in "The Origin of the Work of Art": the categories of beauty and genius, the notions of symbol and allegory, and the distinctions between matter and form, rational and irrational and, most broadly, subject and object—all of which Heidegger understands as a "violent" account of the work of art and "unsuitable" for an understanding of art as the "founding of truth" (PLT 27, 30, 77). Yet what Hölderlin finds in Kant's notion of reflective judgment is a philosophy of freedom grounded in a reflective, that is, nonlegislative, account of nature. What Heidegger considers the violence of metaphysics is displaced by this nonlegislative character of judgment. Hölderlin finds in aesthetic judgment—released from its subservience to the transcendental system—the point of departure for a radically different, poetic understanding of subjectivity, in which the stability, self-certainty, and autonomy of the rational subject is displaced in favor of a stance to some extent akin what Heidegger calls *Gelassenheit*.

A brief review of the principles of Kantian aesthetic judgment prepares the way for considering Hölderlin's appropriation. In the

Critique of Judgment Kant presents an account of nature that obviates its subordination to the causal mechanisms of the human subject's conditions of phenomenal experience. Here Kant develops a theory of reflective judgment — that is, judgment that does not subsume objects under concepts, as in determinative judgments, but rather provides a concept that "does not cognize anything but which only serves as a rule for the power of judgment itself" (CJ 169). Reflective judgments are either aesthetic or teleological; in both judgments, the concept of purposivity is deprived of its determinative function. In aesthetic judgments, the purposivity of the beautiful in nature is presumed to be "without purpose"; that is, no possible concept of a purpose or interest can be given, and the object judged remains singular (no generalization about the beauty of roses can be made upon the judgment of a particular rose). If aesthetically experienced, even "a mere blade of grass" outdoes our attempts to think it; the reason for this will become clear shortly, when we discuss the purposivity without purpose that Kant ascribes to nature.

In reflective judgment, the human subject experiences nature not as an object of the determination of the faculties of reason (a manifold of sense governed by the concepts of the understanding, which are in turn synthesized according to higher principles of reason) but as an occasion for the subject's own "quickening" (*Beleben*) (CJ 315, 238, 245). One experiences the "feeling of life" (*das Lebensgefühl*)[5] in reflective judgment, for the harmonious play of the imagination and the understanding is given without rule and without the domination of the manifold of intuition by the concepts of the understanding. If elsewhere Kant defines "life" rather narrowly, here the feeling of life is connected not only with freedom but also with nature experienced as beautiful.[6] Aesthetic experience — judgments of the beautiful in nature or art — exceeds conceptual determination; objects are indeed cognized as objects, but the imagination's subordination to the understanding is a lawfulness only in play. According to Kant, concepts remain, in this "cognition without concepts," suspended in their determinative capacities, and the subject feels the play of the faculties, then, as a "free play" (CJ 217). Aesthetic ideas, to which the genius gives form, likewise exceed conceptual determination; and the communicability of the pleasure taken in beautiful judgments is not reducible to concepts and, therefore, is a "communication without concepts," an irreducible subjective feeling. Because they are irreducible to the determination of the understanding's concepts, judgments of the beautiful give the subject an experience of the freedom that, in turn, belongs to the "supersensible" and is analogically given, through hypotyposis, in the beautiful.[7] Though subjective, aesthetic judgments issue the *sensus communis:* the objective certainty that this subjective pleasure, this freedom, is universal, holds "for everyone," has a "universal voice." Aesthetic judgments, Kant writes, "must involve a claim to a subjective universality" (CJ 215, 212).

In order for judgment to operate in such a prodigious function, its power must be a priori. That determinative judgments are a priori finds its legitimation in the subsumption of particulars under universals according to conditions outlined in the *Critique of Pure Reason* (CPR a131–136 / b170–175). But reflective judgment "gives a law only to itself, and not to nature" (CJ 180). The unity of nature's empirical laws, that is, nature's unity in diversity, we understand according to a principle of the "purposiveness of nature" that "has its origin solely in reflective judgment" (CJ 181). That we understand nature as a unity that supersedes the diversity of its particular empirical laws has its grounding not in theoretical reason but in reflective judgment. Kant writes: "Hence judgment also possesses an a priori principle for the possibility of nature, but one that holds only for the subject, a principle by which judgment prescribes, not to nature (which would be autonomy) but to itself (which is heautonomy), a law for its reflection on nature" (CJ 185–186).

The law of judgment is prescribed not to nature but to the subject itself. Thus we can say that in aesthetic judgment indirectly, the subject receives law from nature. In teleological judgment, we judge the harmony of nature as "contingent, yet also indispensable for the needs of our understanding" (CJ 186); from the point of view of judgment, the harmony is subjective, but transcendentally a priori (CJ 185). The concept of nature's purposiveness is felt by the reflective subject as the "attainment of an aim" (*Absicht*) that is "always connected with the feeling of pleasure" (CJ 187). Nature is presumed by judgment to be in harmony with the subject's own faculties, and the pleasure taken in this harmoniousness is assumed "a priori and valid for everyone . . . merely because we refer the object to the cognitive power" and not to an interest in the object itself (CJ 187).

Yet Kant's grounding of the a priori validity of reflective judgment requires a stronger connection between the purposiveness of nature and the subject's feeling of pleasure. In "On the Aesthetic Presentation of the Purposiveness of Nature," Kant claims that "we call the object purposive only because its presentation is directly connected with the feeling of pleasure, and this presentation itself is an aesthetic presentation of purposiveness" (CJ 189). The purposivity of nature, a principle that originates only in judgment, is aesthetic because it refers the subject only to itself; and this self-reference on the part of the subject, the subjective presumption of the harmony of nature with our own faculties, a "harmony only in reflection" (CJ 190), is a pleasure that is "not based on any concept" (CJ 190). This is because the pleasure is initiated by the lawful play between the understanding and the imagination, which is "recognized through a perception upon which we reflect" (CJ 191). The pleasure is connected not with the concept of the object, but with its perception, and, despite being confined to particular, nonuniversalizable perceptions, it "is always possible for such a judgment to be valid for everyone despite its intrinsic contingency" (CJ 191). Kant writes, "What is strange and different about a judgment of taste is only this: that what is to be connected with the presentation of the object is not an empirical concept but a feeling of pleasure (hence no concept at all), though, just as if it were a predicate connected with the cognition of an object, this feeling is nevertheless to be required of everyone" (CJ 191).

The pleasure in aesthetic judgments is found in its subjective though universal conditions. This universality Kant calls the *sensus communis*, a presumption of community that can never be actualized (can never belong to the phenomenal, rule-governed world) but does not remain merely noumenal. If we call an object, in nature or art, beautiful, "we believe we have a universal voice" (CJ 216) and lay claim to everyone's agreement despite that it is based on sensation (aesthetic = *aesthei*, sense). To be more precise, the pleasure felt in the observation (*Beobachtung*) of the beautiful is the harmony of the faculties of the imagination and understanding in a free relation of lawfulness, a nonconceptualizable harmony that provides the basis for the principle of nature's purposivity. Since nature is not merely a set of empirical laws, but rather laws unified by a purpose that we cannot determine (that does not come from us or our concepts and that we cannot ascribe to nature's intentions) (CJ 360), the presumption of its harmony is issued in our experience of the freedom felt when the imagination and the understanding harmonize in free play—a freedom we cannot ascribe to the object but, rather, to ourselves and, as a priori, to everyone else. The conditions of the a priori character of judgments of taste are outlined in the deduction.

Contemplation of the beautiful joins the nonconceptual, reflective presumption of nature's unity (purposivity) with the sensation of a harmonious, free unity of cognitive faculties on the part of the subject.[8]

The "inner causality" of the harmonious play of the faculties mirrors the nonconceptual, nonmechanistic causality underlying nature's harmony, which we presume in reflective judgment. Although from the point of view of intellectual cognition or determinate judgment, nature is driven by mechanistic causality, the purposivity we presume in reflective judgment is without determinate purpose. The subject then experiences the contemplation of the beautiful in nature (or art, which is given rule by nature) as a "feeling of life." The inner causality of the free play takes on characteristics we presume—from the point of view of reflective judgment—nature to have: self-reproduction according to no determinate purpose. The "inner causality" is a paradoxical causality of freedom. It is not theoretical, for it determines no object but contains a "mere form of the subjective purposiveness of a presentation." It is, likewise, not practical, for it does not engage desire either on the basis of agreeableness or on the conceived good; this causality is a mere lingering. With a description of this lingering Kant provides a compelling articulation of aesthetic-poetical experience:

> Yet it does have a causality in it, namely, to *keep* [us in] the state of [having] the presentation itself, and [to keep] the cognitive powers engaged [in their occupation] without any further aim. We *linger* in our contemplation of the beautiful, because this contemplation reinforces and reproduces itself. (CJ 222)

The relation between the subject and object in aesthetic experience is, from the point of view of the understanding, merely "contingent"; nevertheless, this experience is assumed to be a priori by the faculty of judgment and therefore finds its place within the reconciled transcendental architecture. Aesthetic experience is to be the "mediating link" that bridges the "great gulf" that yawns between pure and practical reason—a mediation that cannot be accomplished by concepts (CJ 177, 195). Thus reflective judgment, in particular aesthetic judgment, unifies the transcendental subject. Kant's analysis of the "moments" of judgments of taste provides the a priori basis for the jointure of freedom and necessity that structures the feeling of life. Not based on interest, charm, emotion, or the concept of perfection, but only on the undetermined form of purposiveness, the experience of the beautiful "quickens," gives life to the subject by virtue of the subject's experience of the necessary, free, and at least in principle communally shared character of its pleasure. As such, Kant calls the feeling of life a "very special power of discriminating and judging" (CJ 204). Hölderlin, in his poetic rendering of subjectivity, will liken this power to a form of "cognition" (*Erkenntnis*) (ELT 79). In the last chapter I will argue for a notion of poetical cognition that recalls these Kantian principles.

Kant's analysis of aesthetic judgment turns from considering the observation of the beautiful to its production in art, which, however, does not leave the realm of the beautiful in nature. The ability to present aesthetic ideas belongs to the genius, who is, Kant claims, "given rule by nature." For Hölderlin, aesthetic ideas were to be the subject of an aesthetic treatise, and, as Friedrich Strack has shown, were furthermore transformed into his formal procedures for poetic practice.[9] An aesthetic idea, as a counterpart to a rational idea, is a presentation of the imagination; it "prompts much thought, but to which no determinate thought whatsoever, i.e., no *concept*, can be adequate, so that no language can express it completely and allow us to grasp it" (CJ 314). Whereas a rational idea is one that exceeds the capacities of intuition, an aesthetic idea is one that exceeds the capacities of conceptual thought. Again we encounter a demand for a form of expression and expressability that exceeds the capacities of conceptual language. For Kant "symbols could stand also for pure concepts of reason as for freedom; and that is in fact what an artwork accomplishes when it is more than a [mere] allegory."[10] This demand inaugurates the romantic movement. For early romanticism, the Absolute, the "soul of the world," the unity of freedom and necessity, can find their expression not in philosophical concepts but in art and poetic language—an orientation that leads, as in Hölderlin, to radical reformulations of the philosophical task. Thus for Novalis the world must be romanticized through poetry,[11] and in Schlegel's *Athenaeum*,[12] we find that philosophy is itself treated as an aesthetic task. While Kant chooses poetry as the highest form of genius precisely because, he claims, poetry expresses most adequately an aesthetic idea, it belongs to the form of poetry's efforts to proceed in what Keats names the "uncertainties, mysteries, and doubts" that its own awareness of language as medium brings about. Poetry is a "negative capability" of expressing or, as Paul Klee expressed of painting, making apparent the world precisely because it recognizes the limits of language as the form of its own attempt to utter the ineffable. The difference between poetry and abstract thought, as Paul Valéry argues, is not in that poetry is accidental, fragile, fortuitous, and irregular—for abstract thought is, too, and if this fortuitousness is denied, repressed, ignored by abstract thought, it is poetry's guide and motive. Poetry makes words linger, repeat themselves, acquire a value divorced from practical concern; poetry enters a dream of its own order, a "language within a language."[13] For Hölderlin, poetic endeavor—as a "lawlike calculus," an "alteration of tones," a "paradox"—expresses in form the impossibility of its own utterance, of a direct or conceptual expression of "life." It forms "a world within the world" (ELT 70).

Kant, too, sees that the aesthetic idea, when presented particularly through poetry, is to "arouse more thought than can be expressed in a concept determined by words." The "proper function" of the aesthetic idea "is to quicken [*beleben*] the mind by opening up for it a view into an immense realm of kindred presentations." Fine art and particularly poetry take

> the spirit that animates [*beleben*] their works solely from the aesthetic attributes of the objects, attributes that accompany the logical ones and that give the imagination a momentum which makes it think more in response to these objects, though in an undeveloped way, than can be comprehended within one concept and hence in one determinate linguistic expression. (CJ 315)

Kant recognizes that the art of poetry has the power to express what cannot be expressed in ordinary language, in the "determinate linguistic expression." Poetic language can express "the thoughts of much that is ineffable" (CJ 316). In "On the Division of the Fine Arts," Kant defines poetry as "the art of conducting a free play of the imagination as if it were a task of the understanding" (CJ 321), for in poetry words are employed as if they belonged only to the realm of concepts; but also exceed the logic of concepts. That poetry's expression of aesthetic ideas "makes us think more" than we could think only in terms of concepts "quickens our cognitive powers." Poetry enlivens the subject by expanding the realm of cognition beyond the realm of determinate concepts and "beyond the bounds of experience." It grants the poet and, presumably, the reader of poetry, the spirit that Kant defines as the "animating principle of the mind" (CJ 313). It presents "the feeling of which quickens our cognitive powers and connects language, which otherwise would be mere letters, with spirit" (CJ 316).

The Feeling of Life in Hölderlin's Poetology

In a fragmentary "Reflection,"[14] following Schiller's adoption of Kantian aesthetics,[15] Hölderlin writes that "all cognition must begin with the study of the beautiful" (ELT 77). One must understand living beings, human and otherwise, and the relations among them, not mechanistically but according to a living intuition (*die lebendige Anschauung*) that issues from a principle of what Hölderlin calls "joy," which, as he makes clear in *Hyperion,* concerns the wholeness and organic-ity of nature, its lack of merely arbitrary or fractious opposition. The "living intuition emerges," he claims, "objectively from thought, from joy" (ELT 47). It is the study of the beautiful in nature that aids the poet in the living intuition, wherein the poet "feels and intuits the whole," the unity of life's disparate strivings. Kant's aesthetic theory, among other influences,[16] provides the philosophical problem of aes-thetic judgment to which Hölderlin's articulation of the poet's task responds.[17] The opposition of joy and necessity reflects the freedom and necessity that mingle in Kant's notion of free play of the facul-ties when lingering before the beautiful; for Hölderlin, love, like joy, is the aesthetic grasp of freedom and necessity together, which allows the lover, or poet, an access to "life." This is why one of the poetical unities in *Hyperion* is expressed in the title character's love for Dio-tima. As in *Hyperion,* Hölderlin's task was to "discover poetically a living concept of life."[18]

Hölderlin, like his Romantic contemporaries, learns from Kant that it is the aesthetic genius who is, in Kant's words, endowed with the capacity to communicate, without conceptual determination, the feel-ing of life.[19] If Kant insists that it is poetry that is best able to exhibit aesthetic ideas — to articulate this feeling — then Hölderlin takes up this project in deed.[20] The notion of "life" then comes to form a major con-cern of Hölderlin's poetics. In a letter to his friend Ludwig Neuffer in November 1798, Hölderlin asserts: "Livingness in poetry is what now most preoccupies my mind and senses." In its engagement with the feeling of life, "poetry creates an entirely new possibility of thinking."[21] Hölderlin here claims that "through the idea of life ["durch die Idee des Lebens überhaupt"] . . . the poet gives the ideal a beginning, a direc-tion, a significance." It is only through "poetical reflection," Hölderlin continues, "that the idea of life is possible at all" (ELT 67).

For Hölderlin, "life" is constituted by the contradictory and like-wise harmonious tendencies that underlie nature and all living beings — particularly those of "freedom and necessity . . . the sensuous and the sacred" (ELT 67). These tendencies "must, despite their opposition, be conceived as issuing from the same origin if they are to truly be unifiable."[22] For Hölderlin, as for Kant, this unification in the sub-ject is conceptually impossible; but Kant's *hypotyposis,* in which the beautiful is the sensuous symbol of the supersensible, does not sat-isfy Hölderlin as a reconciliation of two conceptual realms, for the divi-sion that the symbol is to reconcile analogically must be accounted for, and not merely "bridged," aesthetically.[23] Some aspects of Hölderlin's critique of Kant were presented in chapter 3. The division of life into the realms of necessity and freedom, rather than joined by the subject, rend it asunder and render it thus inaccessible. Romanticism then follows, as Philippe Lacoue-Labarthe and Jean-Luc Nancy have argued, the "crisis of the question of the subject" inaugurated by Kant's divisions.[24] Philosophy had failed to grasp what Nietzsche would call nature's "mysterious primordial unity,"[25] what Hölderlin calls "the soul of the world" (ELT 121). In order to understand the aesthetic as a mediation, Hölderlin develops the notion of an "ex-centric path" (*die exzentrische Bahn*) in which language allows an indirect unification, a "resolution of dissonances" (*die Auflösung der Dissonanzen*).[26] In love and joy (but not only as such) the poet experiences nature as beautiful, irreducible to determinative concepts of purposivity—that is, to the "one-sidedness" of necessity (ELT 47). This is to say that Hölderlin's "nature" is not without mechanistic laws; but nature can be exhausted neither by these laws nor by a science of them. For this reason, inspired by Kant's aesthetics and by Neoplatonism, it is words of feeling— joy, love, suffering, despair—that Hölderlin employs to express the poet's task, and he claims, as if in challenge to Heidegger's appropriation, that it is the poet's "inner life and experience" that are essential to poetic expression.

Yet the poet's task is not simply a matter of some nonconceptual, emotive content that is removed from epistemic claims. If Kant locates the transcendental unification of the cognitive subject in feeling (the pleasure or displeasure that is effected in judgment), Hölderlin dismantles the rationalist opposition between feeling and thought. In this poetology, feeling is not relegated to a bodily, emotional, and secondary property that complicates a primarily rational being—as Kant, even in his aesthetic theory, argues when he attempts to purify pleasure from mere "charm" or emotion, and from physical desire, in order to preserve judgment's a priori disinterestedness. For Hölderlin, feeling is, as the source of the "living intuition," what makes thought possible. The "living intuition" issues, he claims, more objectively from thought and joy than from necessity; for when nature is experienced as beautiful, necessity must mingle with freedom: Kant insists that the tulip's lack of objective purposiveness initiates a freedom felt by the subject of pleasure. The poet's task is indeed one of feeling; it is, however, not merely the articulation of this feeling in poetry, but the feeling itself as taken up into language, that conforms to the rigorous laws of the "operations of poetic spirit." Feeling is thought, thought in its aesthetic, that is, self-reflective and nondeterminative, grasp of nature that, Hölderlin claims, "remembers" the cognition of life only in language. Feeling, then, in poetry follows a "lawlike calculus" so that what Hölderlin calls spirit, life, and the individual engage in a "continuously relating and unifying" balance, which Hölderlin sketches out in a poetic theory of the alteration of tones (ELT 82).

For although Kant describes in detail the feeling of the "free play" of the faculties when confronted with the beautiful, he does not describe the experience of the genius's reception of the law from nature, or the "free play" of the genius in the act of producing aesthetic ideas. In "Operations of the Poetic Spirit" (ELT 62–82/TS 39–62), Hölderlin gives a description of this very process, which becomes, then, his most sustained treatment of the poetic "logic," or poetology. Whereas for Kant there were no "rules" for genius, Hölderlin gives a rather strict "calculus" of poetic form and its relation to the "feeling of life." For Hölderlin, cognition (*Erkenntnis*) and language show a special relationship, the articulation of which also outlines, from Hölderlin's point of view, how the genius is to express aesthetic ideas.

In the "Suggestions for Presentation [*Darstellung*] and Language [*Sprache*]," a subsection of the same essay, Hölderlin claims, "Just as cognition intuits language, so does language remember cognition" ("So wie die Erkenntnis ahndet die Sprache, so erinnert sich die Sprache der Erkenntnis") (ELT 79/TS 58).[27] Cognition is, before it intuits language, an as yet "unreflected pure sentiment of life" (*Empfindung des Lebens*) that repeats itself "in the dissonances of the internal reflecting, striving and poeticizing" of a silent intuition. This "silent intuition" is a "primordial, living sensation" that, after exhausting all internal attempts to "master and internalize its complete outer and inner life," "moves beyond itself" to a "higher divine receptivity" (ELT 79). Here, it is a "pure mood" (this latter word often repeated in Hölderlin's theory of poetic form) "that is receptive to something infinite." Hölderlin writes:

At precisely this moment when the primordial, living sensation which has been purified into the pure mood that is receptive to something infinite, exists as infinite within the infinite, as an intellectual whole within a living whole, it is at this moment that one can say that language is intuited. (ELT 79)

Language in the poetic process is, for Hölderlin, a product of this creative reflection (ELT 81). And yet it is, paradoxically, also the condition of "remembering" the cognition of life that first instigates the reflection. If aesthetic judgment is for Kant reflective, this reflection is rendered by Hölderlin in poetic form. The expression of the poet depends first upon a prelinguistic cognition of "life" in nature that is internally reflected and followed by the reflection of the moment of the birth of language. This reflection now "restores to the heart everything" that the original reflective moment "took away from it" (ELT 79). The birth of poetic language is now an enlivening (*belebende*) art; it renders form to the feeling of life, as if "with one stroke of magic." It invokes the lost life all the more beautifully until it feels once again entirely as it used to feel originally (ELT 79). It is worth citing Hölderlin's essay here at length:

> So the poet intuits, at that level where he, too, out of a primor-dial sensation, has struggled in opposed efforts to the tone, to the highest, pure form of the same sensation and where he conceives of himself as altogether comprehended in his inner and outer life by that tone; on that level he intuits his language and along with it the actual perfection for the present and thus for all poesy.

> It has already been said that on that level there enters a reflec-tion which restores everything to the heart that had been taken from it, which is enlivening art for the spirit of the poet and his future poem, just as it had been intellectualizing art for the pri-mordial sensation of the poet and his poem. The product of this creative reflection is language. (ELT 81)

The process of expression (*Äußerung*) as Hölderlin describes it, looks very much like Kant's reflective judgment in reference to the exhibi-tion of aesthetic ideas by genius. Language, for Hölderlin, is the prod-uct of a "poetic reflection," and its creation follows the form of such reflection. We can here define four moments of this reflection and, in parentheses, their Kantian parallels: (1) cognition as a pure, unreflected sentiment of life (as freedom mingling with necessity); (2) the inter-nal, form-giving reflection of this sentiment, in its dissonances and self-reproduction (much like Kant's self-reproduction of the free play in aesthetic experience); (3) the purification of the sentiment as a pure mood, thus receptive to life as not only particular but infinite (the supersensible or sacred); (4) and in the latter, the birth of language as intuited in remembrance (communication without concepts). Expression gives form to what Hölderlin now calls "primordial life in its highest form," which, Hölderlin insists, "is accomplished work and creation, and which is only found in expression" (ELT 80). Hölderlin, unlike Kant, will understand this process not as governed exclusively by a priori laws, but as occurring within an experience dependent upon chance, as discussed in the previous chapter.

It can then be shown that, Heidegger's rejection of the notion of "genius" notwithstanding, the notion is a part of Hölderlin's attempt to reformulate the receptivity of nature aesthetically. Paul de Man thus argues that Hölderlin's poetology involves a "failed interiority" (failed, I would argue, in its inability to be rendered according to the "lawful calculus" insofar as that excludes "accident"), that his "poetry partakes of the interiority as well as the reflection: it is an act of the mind which allows it to turn from one to the other."[28] Language is a kind of *Erkenntnis* for Hölderlin, which he argues explicitly in the "Operations of the Poetic Spirit" essay (ELT 78). Yet insofar as this view appropriates Kant's genius, it disqualifies Heidegger's outright rejection of aesthetics insofar as the genius is taken the originary site of art's creation; for the genius in Kant, like Heidegger's own poet of *Gelassenheit*, is granted inspiration from nature only according to a poetic attunement, not as a legislative subject. In Hölderlin, the poet's language is "intuited" (*ahndet*) or remembered, which points to the Platonic notion of *anamnesis* that also subtends his essay. The genius is, in Kant's terms, the "mouthpiece of nature"; Hölderlin's poet remains a genius in the Kantian sense because nature, in its nondetermined purposivity, "gives law" to the poet. The poetic novel *Hyperion* gives a still more explicit articulation of Hölderlin's understanding of this "attunement." But attunement is not a subjective accomplishment. It is—and the title character, Hyperion, experiences this in a cycle of blissful belonging to nature and a loss of this belonging—a "mere fortune to be thus attuned." If in Kant's understanding of the experience of the beautiful the sensible and the supersensible are joined symbolically, in this "natural state" of Hölderlinian attunement "necessity and freedom, the restricted and the unrestricted, the sensuous and the sacred seem to unite" (ELT 33).

As we have mentioned, for Hölderlin this state is precarious, tethered to the "gentle shyness of the accidental," to "accident." Here Hölderlin again criticizes Kant's transcendental project: the subject cannot be thought in exclusively a priori terms, for the conditions of the subject's unification are contingent. The moral law is felt not a priori but after the fact of transgression, as Hölderlin argues in the essay fragment "On the Law of Freedom." This "natural state," Hölderlin claims, is not only "dependent upon natural causes" but also, as a feeling of life, belongs to the poet's "particular relations to the world" (ELT 33, 93). The observation of "freedom in nature" is situated within the poet's precarious position in the natural, phenomenal world. Kant's argument for the disinterestedness of aesthetic judgments (free from sensual charm and worldly interest) and the "safe place" from which the subject is to observe the sublime suggest that Kant's subject is, though aesthetic and characterized by feeling, not the subject of a life-world but a rational one in which the subject is conceived according to a priori structures. In this reading, Hölderlin's critique[29] amounts to the dismantling of the subject's transcendental unity; dependent upon accident within experience, the subject is interrupted in its self-sufficiency; a posteriori, chance belongs to nature as aesthetically experienced and is granted to a subject who is denied a constitutive role. For Hölderlin, the aesthetic subject cannot be sheltered from nature nor secured from its charms, and it is in its own precariousness that it becomes the bearer of *Gelassenheit*.

For Hölderlin, poetic articulation is, because it is receptive in the Kantian aesthetic sense, a process of reflection, a process that we have followed according to "Operations of the Poetic Spirit"; for Hölderlin it is not immediate but rather a nuanced reflection on the part of the subject "within a living whole." If the first reflection loses an intimacy in severing the subject from immediate feeling, the second, in which the poetic utterance is born as language, "reissues it." This double-reflection indicates, however, that the "living intuition" is not an immediate cognition of nature or life at all, but is rather grounded, for Hölderlin, in a rupture within the subject itself. The feeling of life is achieved only as a recovery from a lost unity. This again articulates the subject as analeptic. Thus cognition as the immediate feeling of life is "remembered" in language the way Platonic love remembers the "blessed vision" from which the human being has fallen (*Phaedrus*). Poetic language, in grasping the unity of life, can do so only as a reflection of its loss.

For in Hölderlin, the process of the articulation of the feeling of life on the part of the poet reveals the primordial division underlying judgment, which I outlined in the preceding chapter. Although Kant intends aesthetic judgment to unify the transcendental system as a "bridge" between pure and practical reason, Hölderlin ultimately rejects the possibility of this unification. Poetic expression, therefore, is possible only as recovery from a loss; it is analeptic, always a dual expression of belonging and estrangement. It can never be a direct expression of the feeling of life, never a translation of an "inner" feeling into "outer" language, according to the classical theory of expression. Poetic expression articulates the feeling of life as an alternation of belonging to and loss of nature. This points to the philosophical underpinning of Hölderlin's theory of poetry as mourning and remembrance. It is in this way that Hölderlin "shows that life and poetry become one in remembrance."[30] The aesthetic subject that Kant introduces—the reflective, nondeterminative subject of feeling—compromises the subject of epistemology. Because only the aesthetic undertaking can acknowledge loss as the ground of its operations, "the aesthetic can no longer be considered as a mere function of a theoretical, rationalist system."[31] The aesthetic is, rather, the point of departure for philosophy. Thus, as Dieter Henrich writes, "Hölderlin was the first in the successors to Kant's philosophy of freedom to dispute that the highest point of departure for philosophy is the unity of consciousness in the "I" as the subject of thinking."[32] Hölderlin's notion of the "poetic I," the formulation of "poetic reflection" (ELT 72, 68), sketches out the refuge of this departure.

If cognition and language are, as we have seen, divided by a twofold process of reflection, judgment is, too, at heart not a unification but a division of the subject. It is, Hölderlin claims, "the original separation of subject and object . . . the arche-separation" (ELT 37). The realm of the theoretical is for Hölderlin "an activity which can only gloss over or acknowledge the lack of its proper foundations."[33] Hölderlin claims that the reunification of the separation that judgment implies is always-already one that must acknowledge a loss. Here Hölderlin anticipates Nietzsche's theory of tragedy, wherein the Dionysian longs for a fusion into nature that the Apollonian, as the principle of division, perpetually interrupts. For Hölderlin, "the goal of human striving is to reconcile this split, reattune the poles of self and other." But, Hölderlin adds, "any ultimate reconciliation is infinitely deferred."[34] This division finds its reparation, the reissue of its unity, in poetic expression; and still the poet's attunement to life is precarious and analeptic. This introduces the structure of Hölderlinian mourning, which in Heidegger's reception serves an eschatological vision.

Judgment and the Grounds of Mourning

If the task of the poet is the articulation of the "feeling of life" that joins a community in freedom, it is also the expression of the fragility of this freedom, the fragility of the community joined ideally in the *sensus communis*. Hölderlin's view of judgment constitutes an epistemological skepticism, a transcendental skepticism, in which judgment, cognition, and epistemology itself are to be handed over to a philosophy thoroughly, and from the inside out, aestheticized. Hölderlin's writings (and particularly "Judgment and Being," which we outlined in chapter 3) suggest that the

Cartesian, Kantian, and Fichtean "I" — in which modern philosophy is to be grounded — is based on reflection that admits a radical separation within. As such, the theoretical enterprise is gainsaid by Hölderlin. This is the basis for Hölderlin's argument that consciousness makes nature and "life" theoretically inaccessible. Nature, therefore, cannot be grasped theoretically, for the separation that is intrinsic to it cannot be known.[35] This separation, this gulf, this aporia can be formulated in concepts, but only as indicating the vanity and self-refutation of the transcendental-theoretical effort as such. In poetic language, this separation is acknowledged in form. Read, in Adorno's terms, as a paratactical disjunction, Hölderlin's "language manifests remoteness, the separation of subject and object for the one who stands looking in wonder."[36]

If modern philosophy demands that the conceivable unity of nature (as mechanism, force, or *telos*) is grounded in human cognition — a demand Heidegger challenges in his critique of metaphysics — then Hölderlin's aesthetic displacement of philosophy calls this relation into question. This is, for Hölderlin, not so much because metaphysics constitutes a "forgetting of Being," but because the transcendental unification of the subject is in principle impossible, for the subject's unity is never secured and is based upon the contingent, accidental world of experience, factors denied by a philosophy that claims the subject to be the source of nature's unity. For Hölderlin, poetic language and a "poetic logic" disclose that it is not the rational subject, which renders nature unified, but nature, which provides a reconciliation for the subject who suffers, in consciousness itself, a primordial division. In joy, in the experience of nature as beautiful, in what Hölderlin, as the young Hegel, names "love," in the harmony of friendship, the subject encounters nature as a promise of reconciliation, a feeling of life that promises, too, the subject's freedom. This joy, what Kant likens to aesthetic pleasure is the feeling of a "higher purpose" to human existence above necessity, and is the source of religious feeling and myth, which Hölderlin treats in the essay "On Religion." This joy is, most of all, a feeling of freedom that the aesthetic relation to nature nourishes, and this is a reversal of the Enlightenment association of freedom with rational subjectivity and science, which Hölderlin, like Heidegger, understands as reductive.

This has political implications. For Hölderlin, democracy and peaceful political dwelling cannot be based on the assumption that freedom is identical to rationality and objectivity, nor is "human harmony" to be a dissolving of differences. And yet Hölderlin claims that only a harmonious relation to nature makes peaceful dwelling possible. It is the lack of this harmonious relation that Hölderlin identifies as the discontent of modernity in the foreword to the penultimate version of *Hyperion:* "We've become estranged from nature, and what, as one can believe, was once unified, now stands in discord with itself and lordship and bondage alternate by exchanging places."[37]

For Hölderlin, the recklessness of the human being over and against nature is the result of a rational arrogance of one who, privy to the concept of the infinite, fears nature, which renders him finite. As Hölderlin writes in "Der Mensch,"

> Und Waffen wider alle, die atmen, trägt
> In ewigbangem Stolze der Mensch; im Zwist
> Verzehrt er sich und seines Friedens
> Blume, die zärtliche, blüht nicht lange.
>
> And weapons against all that breathes,
> In an incessant pride, the human being carries;
> In torment he consumes himself
> And the flower of his peace,
> The tender one, does not bloom long.

It is in this arrogance and fear that the philosopher mistakes the unity he finds in nature as originating from himself. Yet Hölderlin insists that nature, as unity, is never theoretically graspable as such. As he writes in "Am Quell der Donau" ("At the Source of the Danube"): "Kommt eine Fremdlingin sie / zu uns, die Erwekerin, / Die menschenbildende Stimme" ("She comes a stranger / to us, the awakener, / the voice that forms out what is human"). Nature must be received not in rationality as divorced from feeling, but in a reason "of the heart." Without such feeling we "almost walk like orphans" ("gehn wir fast, wie die Waisen"). Heidegger argues, too, for such a turn to "the work of the heart" (PLT 138) and to feeling, as in his discussion of the "thing" in the "Origin of the Work of Art":

> Occasionally we still have the feeling that violence has long been done to the thingly element of things and that thought has played a part in this violence. . . . [But] perhaps what we call feeling . . . is more reasonable—that is, more intelligently perceptive. (OWA 25)

It need not be argued at length that Heidegger, in his rejection of the subject, does not make much room for an articulation of such feeling, as he immediately tethers it to the intellect. Alternatively, the aesthetic-poetic subject is, for Hölderlin as for Kant, a subject of feeling; but the pleasure and displeasure of Kant's theory of the "feeling of life" do not go far enough to express the extremes to which Hölderlin's subject—one of the primordial separation—gives voice. In the unraveling of the subject's transcendental unity, feeling cannot be restricted, as in Kant, to pleasure and displeasure, not even to joy and love, but will also include suffering and pain, which—along with the body, nature, the emotions, the "feminine"—is for the Enlightenment subject, as for Kant, irrational and, as such, excluded from philosophical thinking, an exclusion that forms one basis of Nietzsche's critique. Hölderlin's aesthetic reformulation of philosophy does not exclude reason, but it contextualizes reason within a subjectivity that is, in its foundations, precarious, for which suffering follows division. If for Novalis "thinking is a dream of feeling," for Hölderlin feeling grounds thinking, at least thinking aesthetically reformulated. Suffering, then, belongs to the poetic subject as much as pleasure and displeasure belong to Kantian aesthetic judgment. If, as is well known, "we find confessions of anxiety and personal suffering in Hölderlin's works,"[38] we are not to reduce this to an exclusively personal pain, though it may be that, too. What Georg Lukács calls Hölderlin's "grievance over a solitude, a cry of distress" is not to be reduced, as in Lukács, reading to Hölderlin's political disappointments, though it belongs to the latter as well. Nor is pain to be celebrated, as in Nietzsche, as the tragic bliss. For Hölderlin's account of suffering belongs to his thinking of the problem of philosophy as such—which is, then, the problem of poetry—and constitutes the form of his aesthetic response to this problem; mourning has a poetological function as the presencing of what is impossible to grasp. That Kant's third *Critique* validates feeling grants to aesthetic experience a transcendental role in the unification of the subject; but for Hölderlin, feeling is the expression of the precarious, paradoxical character of this unification, which is founded on loss and is issued only as a recognition of this fact. The relevance of feeling for Hölderlin's poetic theory includes, then, an acknowledgment of pain and loss as keys to understanding the relation of the human being to nature. This is, for Hölderlin, the structure of mourning, wherein "we almost make our way like orphans."

The epistemological skepticism of Hölderlin's theory, then, not only initiates the aesthetic as the point of departure for the understanding the cognition of nature, but also introduces the question of its loss. Although Kant inaugurates an account of a nonlegislative relation to nature, he cannot, within the limitations of the notion of pleasure and displeasure and the insistence on the disinterestedness of the subject with regard to the object, address our estrangement from nature; it is this estrangement that is indicated in Heidegger's "technological crisis" and the "extreme danger" of our times, which we "must hold always before our eyes" (QT 33).

The Darkness of Earth

The dangerousness that Heidegger associates with Being's withdrawal might be read in Hölderlin as in the human being's inevitable "crossing over into the world of *Ur-teilungen*," or divisions, that belongs to subjects from whom the unity of life withdraws. Hölderlin sometimes depicts the world as "pervaded by darkness" in which "insight and catastrophe" can "occur simultaneously."[39] For Hölderlin the earth is not only, as nature, the source of "life," but comes to be understood, as in Heidegger, as an obscuring darkness. At the turn of the nineteenth century, "the concealing, secret, preserving, covering becomes emphasized" in Hölderlin's poetry, and Hölderlin soon gives up writing theoretical-philosophical treatments of poetic language as a promise for the enactment of spirit.[40] The "feeling of life" is also the acknowledgment of the finitude of life—of its "intimate brevity"—of human limitation (ELT 143). This does not suggest the resolute "being-towards-death" of the Dasein of *Being and Time,* but rather the singularity of what we encounter, the fragility and finitude of self, the loss of harmonious dwelling. In the wake of Hölderlin's ultimate departure from Kant and transcendental philosophy, nature is accessible only in its own self-giving granting, and the precariousness of this relation for the human being or the poetic subject can be celebrated only as the "danger" to which the "saving power" of poetry is an aesthetic counterpart. If the poet claims, as in "In Lovely Blue," "Ein heiteres Leben seh' ich in den Gestalten mich umblühen der Schöpfung" (I see a gay life blossom about me in the forms of creation), the poet also recognizes this as fragile, for the sun that shines also burns: "But this is also suffering." Nature is the source, then, of anxiety and fear, as we find in the poem "Die Kurze" ("Brevity"): "hinweg ists! Und die Erd' ist kalt, / Und der Vogel der Nacht schwirrt / Unbequem vor das Auge dir" (Vanished, the earth is cold / And the bird of night whirls/ uneasily before your eyes).[41]

The "saving power grows" where the danger is because it is from this precariousness, this rupture of the subject in its loss of epistemological autonomy and transcendental stability, that poetry as an aesthetic undertaking provides a reconciling salvation. If for Heidegger the message of Being rendered by the poet heals the oblivion of its forgetting in what he calls, after Hölderlin, "destitute times," for Hölderlin this threat belongs to our condition as precarious, the precariousness of freedom and harmonious community with and within nature. Hölderlinian mourning orients us toward a refusal of autonomy from and over nature, refuses violence and aggression in favor of "dwelling poetically," which for Hölderlin is peaceful and even pacifist, a point that, as Fred Dallmayr points out, Heidegger mocks in his pre-*Gelassenheit* writings.[42] To identify nature with Being in Hölderlin as closely as Heidegger identifies *physis* and Being[43] neglects, both philosophically and politically, the complexity of Hölderlin's encounter with modernity and with the violence of reason. If Heidegger thinks nature "according to the traits of being,"[44] for Hölderlin, nature is indeed an ontological question, but one exhausted and explained neither by the ontological difference nor by the destinal sending of Being. Hölderlin's embrace of nature is not "unchained to the heaviness of an ontic reality" even if, as Adorno points out, Hölderlin's poetry is populated with abstractions.[45] The distinction and sometimes even opposition between ontic and ontological is a Heideggerian motif that I discussed in chapter 1; for Heidegger it guides a reigning distinction between the "essential" and the "inessential" that is not characteristic of Hölderlin. The absence of this distinction, Adorno claims, "protects Hölderlin from the curse of idealization, which always gilds what is singular."[46] For Hölderlin, as for Kant's aesthetics, nature as aesthetic is not sublimated to an ideal; it is rather the source of access to ideality in the "celebration of life as such." Yet if for Heidegger *Andenken* of Being is "gathered" (GA 52, 1), for Hölderlin, as in Adorno's reading, "the experience that what was lost, and what clothed itself in the aura of absolute meaning—cannot be restored becomes the sole indicator of what is true and reconciled."[47]

Hölderlin's poetic subject is, further, not that of the Goethean lyrical "I" that still anchors its legitimation within an Enlightenment optimism about the possibility, if incompleteness, of grounded knowledge. Hölderlin's view of poetry is as much a critique of the transcendentally unified subject of Kant as of "the type of subjective lyric that had become the norm since Goethe's early work."[48] In Hölderlin, as in Keats, the subjective reflection is negated by the "fallibility and finitude of the individual, which accompanies the poetic 'I.'" The subject does not celebrate itself as objective, but rather gives itself over to its object, thus dissolving its legislative function. The poetic "I" is, as Adorno writes, "neither the absolute nor the ultimate," and it is, furthermore, no proper beginning for philosophy.[49] The poetic subject is always a subject recovered—from its inability to secure the self-grounded self-certainty of

Descartes, Kant, and Fichte, as well as from the dangers of hubris or self-deification. If Hölderlin suggests nature's darkness and ungraspability as a danger, this danger belongs to the conditions of thought and the ever-impending threat of hubris on the part of the human subject. It is the challenge of maintaining an aesthetic access to nature in the face of a scientific-technological one, which implies the exclusivity of its truth-claims and explains nature according to its exclusive vision, and thus, as Heidegger argues, obscures the truth of other ways of revealing. But the poet's task is to articulate this danger in a way that calls even its own legitimacy as utterance into question.

Poetic language, then, for Hölderlin, articulates the feeling of life endowed by nature as pointing to the subject's own precariousness. The poetic subject both celebrates nature and mourns it as a loss, thus recognizing that the threat of estrangement from nature is part and parcel of the subject's own conditions, and that therefore the subject itself, dependent upon rather than constitutive of the phenomenal world, is likewise precarious. For Hölderlin it is not the loss of rationality as an autonomous basis for subjectivity but the loss of the feeling of life, of a harmonious relation to nature and aesthetic receptivity, that threatens the subject's feeling as a free being. Hölderlin prefigures Heidegger's assertion in "The Question Concerning Technology": that "the essence of freedom is originally not connected with the will or even with the causality of human willing" (QT 25). In the autonomy presupposed by the subject as rational, Hölderlin thinks that the freedom is supposed but not felt and is based on spurious foundations. The ideal of freedom in community is likewise endangered by a loss of harmony with nature, and it is therefore a freedom that cannot be rescued by epistemological or moral certainty. Yet in Hölderlin the notion of freedom is not essentially determined by the articulation of historical destiny, as in Heidegger (see chapter 1). Hölderlin's ideal is utopian, which in no way means irrelevant to, but rather precisely needed by, the now. The precariousness of the subject's relation to nature suggests also the precariousness of our capacities to imagine a free and peaceful community of dwelling. Which is to say that for Hölderlin a non-anthropocentric humanism is not an oxymoron; for Hölderlin, the "saving" depends on this.

If the question concerning technology is, as Heidegger writes, a question of our estrangement from nature and earth as a shelter and home for harmonious, receptive dwelling, a concern for the threat that the human being will, "always and everywhere, encounter only himself" (QT 27), then we ask, with Heidegger, if the poetic cannot aid us in "dwelling" otherwise. If we are, as Heidegger argues, to turn to poetic language in the crisis of technology for direction for a new way of thinking, what is to be learned from Hölderlin is not the "disqualification" of the subject but its fragility, an alternative to what is for Heidegger its technological will to power. An aesthetic approach to nature from a Hölderlinian point of view is a nondetermining, nonexploitive, nontechnological, nonviolent, even pacifist dwelling that houses the "living intuition" of freedom of self and other, and is understood according to an aesthetic, rather than irrationalized, account of nature. If the question of technology can be revealed only in other means of disclosure in which other possibilities of dwelling and thinking are preserved as possible, in Hölderlin, I would argue, we find such a possibility. And we find, too, an account of our own precariousness, an account that is left, for Hölderlin, in the interstice between philosophy and poetic language—which is to say, in the folds of reflection that slip through the grasp of concepts, in the lap and shelter of the possible. A critical alternative to technological thinking begins to appear in the subject of poetic language, without abandoning the specificities and tribulations of that subject as a self in the world.

5

The Politics of Sacrifice
The Sublime and the Caesura

Heidegger's views of poetic dwelling—his alternative to modern metaphysics and its reduction of the lifeworld to mere objectivity and static presence—vacillate between reference to factical life and a striving toward pure ontology, such as when he articulates the event or occurrence, *Ereignis*, apart from the specificity of what occurs. This duality perhaps mirrors a deeper division within Heidegger's post–*Being and Time* thought, when Heidegger describes dwelling alternatively in *Gelassenheit* terms and in terms of an original violence. As we will see in this chapter, both terminologies of dwelling are rooted in Heidegger's arguments for the ontological significance of the artwork, and in his Hölderlin interpretations. The aspect of art's "original violence" and the violent dwelling it evokes recall not only a Nietzschean notion of overpowering, but, as I will argue in this chapter, also the Kantian sublime. What is for Heidegger an overwhelming power in tension with the "constant concealment" of Being, is in Kant associated with a violent sacrifice of the imagination. Not only in *An Introduction to Metaphysics* and "The Origin of the Work of Art," but also in his readings of Hölderlin's "Der Ister" poems, Heidegger reinscribes a Kantian division between art as evocation of the beautiful and the aesthetics of sublimity, a reinscription that becomes most problematic in light of Heidegger's politics. But it is Hölderlin's own relationship to Kant and to the whole project of the Enlightenment, which marks the difference between Heidegger's Hölderlinian thought and Hölderlin's own incipient poetics. In contrast to Heidegger's readings, Hölderlin's critique of the German and the "national" must be viewed with regard not only to an imagined Greek past, but also to the promises of the contemporaneous humanistic philosophies. Hölderlin's view of Germany is actually criticized by Heidegger as "untimely for our hard times," for it provides a decidedly unheroic figuration of the poet's role in human destiny incompatible with Heidegger's renderings. In my interpretation of Hölderlin's notion of the poetic caesura, and in readings of the caesuric moment in Hölderlin's poetry, I aim to establish an alternative to both the Kantian sublime and the violent origins of dwelling. Poetry will be excluded both from transcendental systematicity and the resoluteness of historical founding; poetic language is for Hölderlin a warning against transcendental hubris, which, when heeded, remains phenomenologically disclosive.

Learning to Dwell

In these first two sections, we begin by drawing out the twofold notion of dwelling Heidegger articulates as Hölderlinian poetic theory, in order to pose this twofoldness later as the reinscription of a Kantian paradigmatic division. The poetics of dwelling, first of all, is drawn from Hölderlin's poem "In Lovely Blue," which is interpreted in an essay entitled, "Poetically Man Dwells" or "Dichterisch wohnet der Mensch" (PLT). This poetics belongs to Heidegger's interpretations of the crisis of the technological age; Heidegger aims for an alternative to modernity (and postmodernity), one that would evade the domination, manipulation, and exhaustion of nature by the ordering of the *Gestell;* Heidegger articulates a poetic-philosophical reverence for the things of the earth. Poetry beckons us to a quiet listening, a listening for the echo of a lost, more essential engagement with the world, with the possibility of nature's sacredness, for the sense of the holy that Hölderlin finds in the "architectonics of the skies" (PLT 227). Poetry thus teaches us how to dwell. Yet for Heidegger, the human being is capable of poetry "only to the degree to which his Being is appropriate to that which itself has a liking for the human being and therefore needs his presence. Poetry is authentic or inauthentic according to the degree of this appropriation" (PLT 228). Thus authentic poetic language comes to light as such only when the human being is prepared for poetic dwelling. This preparation has been described by Heidegger as the preparation, again, for the sending (*das Geschick*), or fate (*das Schicksal*). For this preparation and its appropriation, *Ereignen*, associated with *Ereignis*, the human being "must ever learn to dwell" (PLT 161). Dwelling must be learned because ontological sensitivity does not come to the human being immediately, and is obscured by other modes of revealing Being, such as in *techné* as discussed in chapter 4.

Here we are to learn dwelling as Heidegger's *Gelassenheit*, which I described briefly in chapter 1 as Heidegger's account of "peaceful" dwelling; such dwelling is that of "care and cultivation," of quiet reverence and listening. This receptive account of poetic dwelling is perhaps the most compelling dimension of Heidegger's rejection of metaphysical subjectivity; here poetic language is granted a role of "taking measure" beyond quantification and objectification. Poetry illuminates another "way," another access to the world in which the human being is not reduced to cycles of production and consumption, the tasks of enframing and calculating (QT 19–21). The human being is rather the "safekeeping of the coming to presence of truth" (QT 33).

Yet Heidegger's writings on poetic language and his overcoming of subjectivity involve a second, more contentious dimension of poetic dwelling. This kind of dwelling is purely ontological. In "Poetically Man Dwells," Heidegger argues that poetic dwelling is not to be confused with the "dwelling conditions" of the human being, of the homelessness[1] pervading postwar Germany, of the "dwelling" of an everyday human collective.[2] In the "Letter on Humanism," Heidegger claims that we live in a "homelessness," to which poetry is our essential access; but this "homelessness," is, too, not to be confused with ontic homelessness, with the suffering of human beings within an unjust society, oppressed, in the aftermath of war, with a homelessness that evidences our "appalling and scarcely conceivable bodily kinship with the beast" (LH, 206). Thus the question arises as to the factical or ontical content of Heidegger's "original ethics," as promised in the "Letter on Humanism."[3] For the task of thinking Being as the sending that withdraws, concerns the human being "only in the scope of his essence which is determined by the claim of Being, and not with regard to his existence, actions, and accomplishments within beings." Heidegger asks:

> What happens in the history of Being? We cannot ask in this manner, because there would then be an occurrence and something which occurs. But occurrence itself is the sole happening. (EP 79)

For Heidegger such thinking is preparation for a return "home"—that, if we are to dwell among beings in a nontechnological, nonsubjectivistic fashion, we must first clear thinking in order to think the withdrawal. As such, the tendency of factical life, or human Dasein, to become ensnared in static presence, will be "overcome."

The Violent Origins of Art

In the essay "The Origin of the Work of Art," preceding the "Letter on Humanism" by more than a decade, we find the beginnings of a violent account of dwelling that is issued in the turn to Hölderlin's poetry.[4] Here, poetry is divorced from subjectivity—it does not issue, Heidegger claims, from the artist as subject, but from the concealing-revealing nature of truth, from the destiny of Being itself. Poetry is placed outside the subject and—contrary to the later receptivity of *Gelassenheit*—into the strife (*der Streit*) between "world" and "earth"[5]—or the "destiny of a people" and its "sheltering foundation." The relationship between world and earth is a violent one, "belligerent by nature," and is instigated, Heidegger claims, by the work of art, of which poetry is the essence (OWA 55). In Heidegger's account world and earth as the counterpoles of revealing are "understood as a primeval strife."[6] The work of art "fights the battle between world and earth"; the unity of the work "comes about in the fighting of the battle." Poetry is the "continually self-overreaching gathering of the world's agitation." Art, as "truth setting itself to work" (OWA 39), is a matter of countering "world withdrawal and world decay," which "can never be undone" (OWA 41). A glance at some of Heidegger's terminology makes clear the ontological and political significance of his view of art. The artwork "opens up a world" (OWA 40) in which the earth, as a "sheltering agent" (OWA 42), subsists as its countering element. The work accomplishes both "the setting up of a world," which is "erecting in the sense of dedication and praise" (OWA 43), and the "setting forth of the earth." World and earth are then related as the "destiny of the people" and the "shelter of that destiny" (OWA 48), which are "different from one another and yet are never separated." The relation between world and earth is an "essential striving" in which "the opponents raise each other into the self-assertion of their natures." Yet this self-assertion is the "surrender to the concealed originality of the source of one's own being." Thus "the striving becomes ever more intense as striving, and more authentically what it is." In this "agitation" world needs its opponent earth if, "as the governing breadth and path of all essential destiny, it is to ground itself on a resolute foundation" (OWA 49). The clearing must be "wrested" from concealment, and thus world and earth are seen to be "always intrinsically and essentially in conflict, belligerent by nature. Only as such do they enter into the conflict of clearing and concealing" (OWA 55).

This "agitation" recalls Kant's notion of the sublime, wherein what Heidegger now names the "intimacy" of striving (OWA 50), which is attributed to Being as historical concealing-revealing, can be likened to a battle among the faculties.[7] The work of art, and in particular poetry, instigates the "primal conflict" (*das Gegeneinander des ursprunglichen Streites*) in which the "open" of the unconcealedness of Being must be won (OWA 55). The work constitutes, to use Werner Marx's terms, a "violent co-creating."[8] If the "earth" strives to shelter and conceal, the destiny of "world" must be, in a violent struggle, revealed, and opens its space of revelation in the battle won by, first and foremost, the historical character of poetic — that is, essential — language. This striving is a "veiled destiny between the godly and the countergodly" (OWA 53). Although this striving recalls the Kantian sublime, Heidegger links it to the "appearance of the beautiful": "this shining, joined in the work, is the beautiful. Beauty is one way in which truth occurs as unconcealedness" (OWA 56). Yet Heidegger insists that the creation of this battling strife does not issue from a subject, from Kant's "genius,"[9] but rather from the "historical being of man itself," from the sending-withdrawing of Being. "Earth, nature . . . and language equally belong to the overpower of Being."[10] Heidegger writes, "This Being must therefore contain within itself the essential traits of conflict. . . . As a world opens itself, it submits to the decision of an historical humanity the question of victory and defeat, blessing and curse, mastery and slavery" (OWA 63). Poetry is for Heidegger the essence of this founding act:

> The linguistic work, originating in the speech of the people,[11] does not refer to this battle, it transforms the people's saying *so that now every living word fights the battle* and puts up for decision what is holy and what is unholy, what is great and what small, what brave and what cowardly, what lofty and what flighty, what master and what slave. (OWA 43; italics mine)

Here Heidegger's analysis of world and earth and the role of language in their strife is given clearly Nietzschean overtones[12]; as Michel Haar comments, here the "proximity to Nietzsche is very great: art as a harnessing, as conquest, implies in both thinkers a struggle, *an act of power.*"[13]

Heidegger joins this striving of poetry to other modes of revealing; one is, most problematically in early 1930s Germany, the "act of founding a political state." Another is "essential sacrifice (OWA 62).

Despite Heidegger's rejection of subjectivity, this battle places the human being "in decision," requires "resoluteness." This resoluteness is not the deliberate action of a subject, but the opening up of human being, out of its captivation by beings, to the openness of Being (OWA 67). Rather than *Gelassenheit*, here the poetic is a violent founding of truth. In Heidegger's theory, here "poetry and art as well as political institutions are the founders of history, but they are also understood as wrenching being from its veiled state by sheer struggle."[14] Given the preparations of the German nation for a fascist-driven war of invasive and murderous appropriations, the terminology and tone here are disturbing, to say the least.

Despite the Nietzschean elements, it is Hölderlin, "whose work," according to Heidegger, "still confronts the Germans as a test to be stood," who is chosen as the model for Heidegger's "belligerent" poetry.[15] Hölderlin is the poet who speaks to the Germans as an "essentially historical people" and "confronts" them with the "decision" whether or not to yield to this violent founding of truth. Heidegger writes:

> The poetic projection of truth that sets itself into work as figure is also never carried out in the direction of an indeterminate void. Rather, in the work, truth is thrown toward the coming preservers, that is, toward an historical humanity. . . . Genuinely poetic projection is the opening up or disclosure of that into which the human being as historical is already cast. (OWA 75)

"The disclosure of that into which the human being as historical is already cast"—a disclosure that, Heidegger thinks, is opened in Hölderlin's poetry—resounds with what in "Poetically Man Dwells" is named the "letting come of what has been dealt out"; but here we find not a "letting-come" as a phenomenological shelter of beings but an aggressive founding of Being. History, in this view, is the matter of the struggle for disclosure of the site of the founding—that is, co-creating—of truth. As the "confrontation," "Hölderlin's work still confronts the Germans as a test to be stood" (OWA 78).

The concealing-revealing character of truth, in the terms of *Gelassenheit* dwelling which characterizes the writings of the 1950s, is the resistance of things and of the world, and perhaps even of other human beings to the violence that, as Heidegger argues in *The Principle of Reason*, renders all things objects of appropriative cognition. In "The Origin of the Work of Art," however, this resistance is given violent overtones, even if Heidegger here attempts to salvage things from the "violence" imposed upon them by metaphysical thinking.[16] If in *Being and Time* "uncanniness" was the "call of conscience" that pursues Dasein to remind Dasein of its finitude, the artwork similarly reveals that the "immediate circle of beings" in which we dwell, in which we "believe we are at home," conceals the uncanniness of things. Our "immediate circle" is "that which is, is familiar, reliable, ordinary. Nevertheless, the clearing is pervaded by a constant concealment in the double form of refusal and dissembling. At bottom, the ordinary is not ordinary; it is extraordinary, uncanny" (OWA 54).

In chapter 1, I argued that this pervasion of "constant concealment," and not only the strife associated with its disclosure, becomes abstracted from the phenomenological origins of Heidegger's argument regarding the thing and the work of art, the work's belonging to a world and to earth. Phenomenologically, poetry "makes the very occurrence of the division between the apparent and the non-apparent appear."[17] And yet here this is issued in the struggle between revealing and concealment, for Heidegger claims that "the nature of truth is dominated throughout by a denial" (OWA 54). This denial is not merely a *Verfallenheit*, necessary to the "Being-there" of factical life even after Dasein's moment of *Entschlossenheit*. Here, this "concealing denial" of truth is the "opposition of the primal conflict," between the revealing of world and the concealing of earth (OWA 55). Here the *aletheia*-character of truth is itself understood as violence. In "Introduction to Metaphysics," Heidegger understands this violence as belonging to the revealing of *physis*, in an account linked to Sophoclean tragedy: "violence against the preponderant power of Being *must* shatter against Being, if Being rules in its essence, as *physis*, as emerging power" (IM 136). The shattering that belongs to the revealing of Being, issues the "necessity of disaster":

> The human being is forced into such a being there, hurled into the affliction [*Not*] of such Being, because the overpowering as such, in order to appear in its power, *requires* a place, a scene of disclosure. The essence of being-human opens up to us only when understood through this need compelled by Being itself. The being-there of the historical human being means: to be posited as the breach into which the preponderant power of Being bursts in its appearing, in order that this breach itself should shatter against Being. (IM 137)

This "overpowering" is linked to "The Origin of the Work of Art" in Heidegger's discussion of the "violent, creative human being," who is given the task of "accomplishing" being, just as the task of the artist is, through the work, the "founding of truth" by opening the "scene of disclosure." Heidegger writes:

Being hurls the human being into this breaking-away, which drives him beyond himself to venture forth toward Being, to accomplish Being, to stabilize it in the work, and to hold open the being as a whole. . . . In all this the violent, creative human being sees only the semblance of fulfillment, and this he despises. . . . To him disaster is the deepest and broadest affirmation of the overpowering. But all this not in the form of "psychic experiences" in which the soul of the creative human being wallows . . . but wholly in terms of the accomplishment itself, the putting-into-work. As *history* the overpowering, Being, is confirmed in works. (IM 137)

Here subjectivity (conceived as psychic experience or that of the "soul") is again displaced in favor of the putting-into-work, for subjectivity is here differentiated from history. If subjectivity is irrelevant to, or a distraction from, essential historicality, the work, conceived without the subject as its source, is history's accomplishment. Thus creative activity has not merely a phenomenological function, but an ontological-historical one; it not merely discloses Being in the realm of beings but, moreover, "accomplishes" Being. This is the relation between disclosure and the (sometimes violent) founding of truth we saw in chapter one. In *Introduction to Metaphysics*, this violence is explicitly linked to poetry:

The violence of poetic speech, of thinking projection, of building configuration, of the action that creates states is not a function of faculties that the human being has, but a taming and ordering of powers by virtues of which the being opens up as such when the human being moves into it. This disclosure of the being is the power that the human being must master in order to become himself . . . i.e., in order to be historical. (IM 137)

As disclosive in the original sense, poetry is then a kind of "original violence":[18]

Only if we understand that the use of power in language . . . helps to create, (i.e., always, to bring forth) the violent act [*Gewalttat*] of laying out paths into the environing power of the being, only then shall we understand the strangeness, the uncanniness of all violence. (IM 132)

Uncanniness appears again in the lectures on *Hölderlins Hymne "Der Ister"* in 1942, wherein Heidegger takes up Sophocles's *Antigone* as relevant to understanding Hölderlin's poetry, for Hölderlin himself had translated the drama and wrote the essay "Remarks on Antigone" upon which Heidegger comments (DI 115–118; GA 52, 72–73). Hölderlin's essay concerns the problems of representation and consciousness as taken up in the temporality of tragic poetry, what he calls the "tragic-moderate weariness of time" (ELT 110). Heidegger argues that the uncanniness, the "strangeness," of the human being is the human being's strange, primordial proximity to Being. In Hölderlin's essay, uncanniness is grasped by the difficulty of depicting "human understanding as wandering below the unthinkable" (ELT 110). For Heidegger, this uncanniness is the "unthought." It is

> an extreme derivative and essential consequence of the concealed uncanniness that is grounded in unhomeliness, an unhomeliness that in turn has its concealed ground in the counterturning relation of Being to human beings. (DI 90)

Here it seems that violence is the result of the failure of human beings to "dwell," of the "unhomeliness" of modern consciousness and representation to which poetic dwelling offers an alternative. Poetic dwelling, and its institution, is nonetheless thought to require violence (DI 90); the "risk" of the poet's dangerous mission is still a matter of struggle and mastery (DI 89). The polis is thought in terms of the "counterturning possibilities" that "thrust one into excess . . . and tear one into downfall" (DI 86). It is most distressing that Heidegger, in this context, refers here without criticism and without explanation to the "historical uniqueness of National Socialism" (DI 86, 80), a view he had also articulated in 1953 in *Introduction to Metaphysics* (referring to the "inner truth and greatness of this movement" [IM 166/EM 152]), even if it has been argued that Heidegger's turn to Hölderlin marks his turn away from that engagement,[19] and even if Heidegger had long been critical of National Socialist theories of literature.[20]

Uncanniness, and the polis itself, are linked to violent activity, and the link between uncanniness and the polis, too, "the poet says clearly enough" (DI 87). Here, we are to think the polis according not only to the gods, festivals, and celebration, but also "out of the relationship between master and slave, out of a relation to sacrifice and battle, out of a relationship to honor and glory, [for] out of the relationship between these relationships and from out of the grounds of their unity, there prevails what is called the *polis*" (DI 82). The "seeking homely" of the poetic law "shies at no danger and no risk" (DI 74).

Yet the concealing of Being, which for the human being takes the form of representational "turning against the open"—as Heidegger argues in his readings of Rilke[21]—opens itself to human beings as uncanniness, as the exile from Being then linked to the destinal (*das*

Schicksalhaft). Uncanniness "in general has opened itself to humans and is this very open" (DI 91). This uncanniness constitutes not a "turning away" from Being on the part of the human being but the "expulsion" of the human being from this "abode" (DI 93). Here the twofoldedness of forgetting—our forgetting of Being as subjects and Being's own self-concealment—seems to fold into one dimension, namely the fate of historical sending that Antigone undergoes as expulsion. As the "poem itself," Antigone's expulsion is the fate of the poet who, in being cast out into the foreign, must be called home as a "vessel" of Being's sending (DI 79). This links Antigone to Hölderlin's Böhlendorff letter, which contemplates the differences between Greek and German poetry and "spirit," which Heidegger considers here, as in the lecture course on *"Andenken,"* in detail. If Antigone is the poem, she is also the emblem of the *polis*, which is, Heidegger insists, "nothing political." The *polis* is, rather, the sending of destiny that determines history: "for whatever is fitting [*Das Schickliche*] determines destiny [*das Geschick*], and such destiny determines history [*die Geschichte*]" (DI 81). The *polis* is then to be thought as the "becoming homely" that involves, in the wandering, a return home, for which classical Greece and contemporary Germany are tied together in destiny. But human beings, as the "most uncanny beings," are the ones who involve "risk" in being "cast out" from Being, and those who, "in accordance with their essence, seek to become homely within a particular site" (DI 90). Such site is the "homely," which for Heidegger means to think "more German than all Germans hitherto" (DI 81). Despite Heidegger's insistence that it is not political, his reading of Hölderlin and Sophocles is ripe with the heroism of nationalist ideology.

But this obscures Hölderlin's understanding of the Greek of antiquity and the German,[22] which avoids collapsing the German destiny with an immediate retrieval of an imagined Greek heroism. For in his text Hölderlin makes a distinction between the "specifically Greek art form" and "the patriotic form of our poets, when there are such, [who] are still to be preferred" (ELT 115–116). This is because "for us," in modernity, "the infinite, like the spirit of the states and of the world, cannot be grasped other than from an askew perspective" (ELT 116). If the "fire" of Greek tragic time has a "wild origin," in that it is "considered a firm notion engendered by divine destiny," for the modern poet—for whom consciousness allows only an "askew" access to the divine—the problem is precisely the "lack of destiny" (ELT 114). Therefore the "seeking one's own" through the foreign—or the German through the Greek—cannot collapse the two; for it is in their very difference that the foreign can illuminate what is true of "one's own."[23] In "Remarks on Antigone," Hölderlin contrasts the poetic procedures of Sophocles, in depicting the "political" conflict between Creon and Antigone, to the *"vaterländisch"* or modern-German:

> For us such a form is relevant precisely because the infinite, like the spirit of the states and of the world, cannot be grasped other than from an askew perspective [*aus linkischem Gesichtspunct*]. The *vaterländische* forms of our poets, where there are such, are still to be preferred, for such do not merely exist in order to comprehend the spirit of the age but in order to grasp and feel it once it has been understood and learned. (ELT 116)

Thus Hölderlin claims that "it is also so dangerous to deduce the rules of art for oneself exclusively from Greek excellence" (ELT 150). Greek tragedy is useful for the modern poet not because the modern poet can return to this origin, but because the juxtaposition of the Greek and the German—which Hölderlin calls a "reverse" relation of the foreign and the proper—might teach the German poet to "freely use" what is proper to his own.[24]

Heidegger defines Hölderlin's hymnal poetry as "river poetry" in its essence, not because Hölderlin poeticizes actual rivers and landscapes but because he poeticizes the "becoming homely of unhomeliness," the need of Germans to experience the foreign—the fire of the gods—and is thus a "journeying," a "whiling" and "locale," which the river instances. Here Heidegger again employs the Böhlendorff letter as the expression of the encounter between the "foreign" and the "national." Here Heidegger acknowledges that the "relation to the foreign is never a mere taking over of the other" (DI 143). And yet Heidegger explicitly restricts the foreign to Greece and Greek (neglecting, for instance, Hölderlin's references to Asia); the foreign must already be "proper." While Hölderlin's river in the poem *"Der Ister,"* "appears . . . almost to go backwards / and I presume he must come / From the East," Heidegger presses: "Yet he did not go in the direction he was driven, toward the East." The river is, rather, a return to origin. "Here, in this almost going backwards, there is yet another not being able to forget the origin" (DI 146).

Heidegger argues that the notion of sacrifice is related to this "origin." Heidegger includes the notion of sacrifice in thinking Hölderlin's "intimacy" to the ancient Greek world as the "foreign with respect to the historical humankind of the Germans" (DI 54). Insofar as the contrast between the German and the Greek—and not their essential, destinal *Wiederholung*[25]—is found in Hölderlin's Böhlendorff letter and the "Remarks on Antigone," Heidegger remains within Hölderlin's own frame of reference. The notion of sacrifice enters for Hölderlin in the tragedy, particularly his own tragedy "Empedocles" and his essay "The Ground for Empedocles." Yet Heidegger's thematization of Hölderlin here tends to overemphasize the danger, the tragic element—for though Hölderlin aims to think tragedy philosophically, as the "metaphor of an intellectual intuition" (ELT 83), lyric and epic forms are integral to his theory of poetic forms, and the "tone" of each form is involved in each other form (ELT 88). (In fact, for Hölderlin *Antigone*, though a tragedy, has a "lyrical" style, "more subjective" [ELT 86].) More obviously pressing is that the political and historical context of Hölderlin's thinking of the "*vaterländisch*" or "national" or the proper is also obscured.[26] In the "Remarks on Antigone," the problem of the *Vaterland* is explicitly political (rather than, as Heidegger argues in the "Der Ister" lecture course, "beyond" the political), in the conflict between (human) law and order and the (divine) "infinite," or the "formal and the counter-formal" expressed by Creon and Antigone (ELT 115–116). This is also the relation between art (associated with the organic, finite, following the law of succession—*Gesetz der Succession*) and nature (called aorgic, infinite, suggestive of unity)—and it is this relation that defines Hölderlin's notion of *Schicksal* in tragedy.[27] While Hölderlin's understanding of the "national" and the "German" is tethered to his democratic and revolutionary views, and, as we shall discuss below, is, further, intertwined with his hopes for the success of the French Revolution, Heidegger lifts the "national" out of Hölderlin's own context, which yields, as Fred Dallmayr argues, a "blurring of Hölderlin's democratic-anarchistic elements."[28] Hölderlin's understanding of the "German" is an attempt to foster a democratic movement in a land under rule by locally despotic means, where freedom of thought, speech, and self-determination are lacking; and his affections for ancient Greek poetry involve an idealized "harmony"—for it is a world in which poetry is granted significance. It is worth quoting at length a letter to his brother of 1799 in which Hölderlin writes of the political benefits of poetry and, in the same breath, of Kantian Enlightenment philosophy (ELT 137). Such letters, it is assumed, were to be part of Hölderlin's never-completed "New Letters on the Aesthetic Education of Man" which he had announced to his friend Immanuel Niethammer three years earlier (ELT 132), shortly following the publication of Schiller's "Letters on the Aesthetic Education of Man." Hölderlin writes:

Much has already been said about the influence of the arts on the education of humanity, yet it was always expressed as though nobody were serious about it, and that was natural, for they did not consider what art, and particularly poetry, are in their essence. They only referred to its unassuming exterior appearance, which of course is separable from its essence, yet which forms nothing less than the character of art; one took it as play because it appears in the unassuming figure of the play, and hence it logically could not produce a different effect than that of the play, namely distraction, almost the opposite of what it effects where it is present in its true nature. For then the human being collects himself within it, it affords him a repose, not the empty, but the living repose where all forces are active and are not recognized as active ones only because of their intimate harmony. It nourishes people, and unites them, not like the play where they are united only insofar as everyone forgets himself and no one's particularity appears. (ELT 138)

It is in this context that Hölderlin juxtaposes again the Greek, with its "geniality and piety," to the German, which is in need of more than merely political-philosophical, but also poetic, "higher enlightenment" (ELT 92) in order to achieve harmony and democratic, tolerant freedom. Again, Hölderlin writes:

I said that poetry unites humanity not like the play; it unites people if it is authentic and works authentically. . . . Is it not true. . . . The Germans could well use such a panacea, even after the politico-philosophical cure; for, regardless of everything else, the philosophico-political education already contains in itself the inconvenience that it knits together the people in the essential, inevitably necessary relations, in duty and law; yet how much is left, then, for human harmony? (ELT 139–140)

In "On Religion" this harmony is expressed as a free community in which life is celebrated poetically.[29] Religion is then a celebration of representations in which

it must not be forgotten here, that the human being can also put himself into the position of another, that he can make the sphere of the other his own, hence that it can naturally not be so difficult for one to accept the mode of feeling and representation of the divine which emerges from the particular relations that he bears to the world. (ELT 93)

Religion is thus "poetic in its essence" (ELT 94) because it is to "give freedom to the limitation that each individual representation has" of the divine. This limitation each representation

> must have in that it is now comprehended in a harmonic whole of representational modes and—precisely because in each representation there also lies the significance of the particular way of life which everyone possesses—to simultaneously accord the necessary limitedness of this mode of life its freedom in that it is comprehended within a harmonic whole of modes of life. (ELT 93)

Because this "common sphere" of celebration is poetic and not only a philosophical-political matter, it "expresses the character of the specific life which everyone can live and lives infinitely in his own way" (ELT 93). Such promise for community in diversity recalls Hölderlin's aim in the aforementioned letter for simultaneous "truthfulness against ourselves" and "tolerance against the world" (ELT 140).

Heidegger neglects this Enlightenment context when employing Hölderlin's use of the "national" and the "German" and the "homely," when he argues Hölderlin is to be read outside its merely "'historiographical' 'influences' or dependencies, which one can demonstrate in all poetry." Such contextualizations are for Heidegger merely "the illusion of historiographical observation" (DI 50), and does not approach Hölderlin's poetry in the Heideggerian form of *Auseinandersetzung*. While Heidegger interprets the Böhlendorff letter as a comparison (rather than a contrast) of Greek and German historicality (rather than of poetic form) and reads Hölderlin's "river poetry" as a meditation on the "historical humankind of the Germans within the history of the West" (DI 124), Heidegger abstracts from Hölderlin's decidedly modern Enlightenment influences in Kant, Goethe, Schiller, and Rousseau (DI 50, 130) in favor of the terms of his creative-philosophical interpretation.[30] If the Böhlendorff letter becomes in Heidegger's treatment a treatise on Greek-German destiny, this destiny is thought to demand the poet's "obedience" (DI 124). In Heidegger's discussion, Hölderlin's harsh criticism of Germany at the end of *Hyperion* appears only briefly (DI 136).

Hölderlin's criticisms of Germany in *Hyperion* are read, moreover, according to Heidegger's interpretation of the Böhlendorff letter, to which he has already assigned, in the *"Andenken"* lecture course, a logic of wandering home through the foreign. Heidegger writes (possibly criticizing a biologically or racially defined notion of the "German" in favor of a culturally-historically defined one):

What is thus "inborn" cannot properly become what is their own for the Germans so long as this ability to grasp has not been made to confront the necessity of grasping the ungraspable and of grasping themselves in the face of what is ungraspable. It is from out of such knowledge of the historicality of the Germans, and only from out of such knowledge, that Hölderlin's harsh words at the end of *Hyperion* are to be thought. (DI 186)

Hölderlin's novel, however, takes up a far more humanist (though not anthropocentric) criticism than Heidegger's mode of interpretation admits. In *Hyperion* the title character writes (in letters to his friend Bellarmin that comprise most of the novel) that the "Germans are insensitive to what is beautiful in life," are overtaken by science and industry, are without feeling for "the beautiful," are insensitive to nature, and live in unfree relations of mastery and slavery. Hölderlin argues that the Germans are "silent and cold" and lacking "life" because they lack a relationship to nature that brings "love and brotherhood to towns and houses." The Germans live upon a soil where no "blade of grass" grows — perhaps a reference to Kant's example of the ungraspability of nature, in a single blade of grass, by concepts, and as such a symbol of freedom. Hyperion hopes not for a resolute, violent German people, nor for an essential, grounded one, but a "people full of love and spirit and hope" (H, 130).

Hölderlin's attempts to foster a feeling of freedom and democracy in his homeland are then blurred with Heidegger's own notions of the essential destiny of "this historical people." While Heidegger argues that the great poet, beyond subjective feeling or experience, gives sway to "another origin" (DI 51) than mere "originality" of genius, the poet, according to Heidegger's nonhistoriological reading, likewise has the capacity to choose his influences. This is Heidegger's justification for reading the French Revolution, the figure of Rousseau, and the political events of Hölderlin's time out of Hölderlin's poems. For Heidegger, Hölderlin is influenced only by Sophocles and Heraclitus; it is not contradictory to claim that, though the poet is receptive and beyond subjective "will," "it is the prerogative of great poets, thinkers, and artists, that they alone are capable of letting themselves be influenced" (DI 50).

This view is questionable according to Heidegger's own view of the poet is *Gelassenheit* receptivity; the poet would be not so much "resolute" as "thrown" (*geworfen*) into a world and a history; it would not be the poet's willful prerogative to decide what is essential and what is inessential, to choose his influences or to determine that precarious constellation of horizons into which he has been "thrown." In the receptive account, the poet would be chosen by what encounters him. Yet Heidegger's reading is intended to draw Hölderlin into the discourse of the *"eigen"* — one's own, of the logic of sacrifice. The "law of becoming homely" (DI 125) of the Germans to which Hölderlin is seen to give voice is for Heidegger is a destinal "waiting" that requires "sacrifice":

> We stand at the beginning of historicality proper, that is, of action in the realm of the essential, only when we are able to wait for what is to be destined of one's own. [*die Zu-schickung des Eignen*]. Yet being able to wait . . . is a standing that has already leapt ahead, a standing within what is indestructible, to whose neighborhood desolation belongs like a valley to a mountain. Yet could such a thing ever happen without, *through the notion of sacrifice*, the historical humankind of this commencement first becoming ripe for whatever is of the commencement as its own? (DI 51)

The "mystery" of that "coming to be at home of human beings as historical is the poetic care of the poet of the river hymns," Hölderlin. For Heidegger we thus "experience everywhere in Hölderlin's hymnal poetizing the countering of resonance of a poetic work that poetizes the essence of human beings" (DI 55). In "Recollection in Metaphysics," the notion of the historical is again joined to the notion of sacrifice:

> There sometimes arises from the claim of Being the attempt at a response in which humankind must sacrifice the individuals addressed who recollect Being, and thus think its history from the essential past. (EP 77)

In *What Is Metaphysics?* necessity is "consummated in the freedom of sacrifice" (EB 358), even if this "sacrifice is the expense of our human being for the presentation of the truth of Being" (EB 358).

> Sacrifice is a valediction to everything that "is" on the road to the preservation of the favor of Being. Sacrifice can be made ready and can be served by doing and working in the midst of what-is, but is never consummated there. . . . Sacrifice is rooted in the nature of the event through which Being claims the human being for the truth of Being. (EB 359)

Repeating this link with sacrifice, Heidegger ends his reflections in "The Origin of the Work of Art" with a quote from Hölderlin, and hearkens to Hölderlin in the notion of "sacrifice." Hölderlin does have his own account of sacrifice; sacrifice happens in the caesura, the "tragic transport" in which the subject is sacrificed to the object for which it longs—namely, divine nature. When Heidegger thus writes that "when art happens a thrust enters history as the transporting of a people to its appointed task" (OWL 77), we are reminded of Hölderlin's "tragic transport," after which "only the conditions of time and space remain," and of the fact that Hölderlin chose the figure Empedocles, who was "doomed to sacrifice," fated by his epoch (ELT 56). Hölderlin, then, has been associated with not only the receptive account of dwelling in Heidegger, but also the violent one. Lacoue-Labarthe, to whose arguments we will return in concluding this chapter, understands the caesura to be an expression of the tragedy of our times, identifies the caesura and the *Ereignis*, and likens Hölderlin's notion of the caesura to Auschwitz, which is "beyond tragedy," and after which "nothing remains."[31] Yet for Hölderlin, something else happens when "art happens"—not a thrust entering a history of Being, but the unraveling of the subject, one which does not call for "resoluteness," as in "The Origin of the Work of Art," does not require an essential "decision," but leaves the subject vulnerable, ruptured, precarious, and indebted to the realm of the inessential—in Hölderlin's words, to the *"gentle shyness of the accidental"* (ELT 142). This belongs to poetic language as much as does the fate of tragedy; here we must address beings and what occurs to them, rather than only the *Ereignis*, the site of pure occurrence itself.

Although I want to avoid posing it in terms of a simple dichotomy, a twofold story of poetic dwelling does become apparent, an articulation of dwelling that has taken on significantly different, and yet somehow intertwining, dimensions in Heidegger's thinking, as I set forth in the introduction. The first dimension is that of *Gelassenheit;* here, dwelling is a dimension of the beautiful, of nature's irreducibility to rational concepts and its nurturing of quiet meditation. The second dimension is the violence of the sublime, and requires "battle," "essential sacrifice," "victory," "strife," "resoluteness," "fighting," "law," "decision," and the "thrust that enters history." In this second story of poetic dwelling, poetic language is itself linked to the violence of truth.

These competing stories of the beautiful and the sublime reappear in Heidegger's reflections on Hölderlin and poetic dwelling, and I have in previous chapters attempted to unravel them not merely as two philosophies of Heidegger,[32] but rather as competing tendencies along Heidegger's path of thinking which sometimes imply each other even as they seem most divorced. In this chapter I argue that Heidegger, despite his rejection of Kantian aesthetics in "The Origin of the Work of Art," reinscribes a Kantian division: that of the beautiful and the sublime as the freedom of the imagination and its sacrifice. Even though Heidegger explicitly rejects the subjectivism of Kantian aesthetics and, in fact, the concept of "aesthetics" altogether, Hölderlin as I interpret him here remains within the context of Kantian theory. For in Hölderlin, sacrifice attends the unraveling of the self-certainty and autonomy of subjectivity; poetry "occurs" between the joy of the beautiful and the violence of the sublime.[33] The "tragic transport" is a movement through the subject, one that the subject undergoes in its longing for the divine. In Hölderlin, the subject will achieve only an askew access to the sacredness of nature, a partial vision of the "totality" of what is; but in so doing the subject will be disabused of its legislative, what Heidegger would call technological, function. In Hölderlin's account of the caesura—the "counterrhythmic rupture"—violence turns upon the subject itself, contrary to the rhythms of the Kantian sublime, and perhaps otherwise than Heidegger's founding of truth, which yields not only the "setting up of world" but also historicality as such. The "counterrhythmic rupture" is turned, in Hölderlin, against the subject's own autonomy; and it is thus in Hölderlin, between Heidegger and Kant, that sacrifice establishes the precariousness of receptivity and the exposure of the subject to the "accidental" in the realm of beings, where the subject is to encounter divine nature.

Hölderlin's "Unheroic" Worldview

For Hölderlin, poetry is to unite a community in the "feeling of life" inspired by nature, and to nurture the sense of freedom that Enlightenment reason alone failed to vouchsafe. Pierre Bertaux's study *Hölderlin und die französische Revolution* shows Hölderlin's ideals of freedom to be linked not only to the Rousseau who appears in his poems, but also to the aesthetics of religion practiced by the early French revolutionaries.[34] Bertaux documents evidence of Hölderlin's awareness of the details of the revolution via the pages of a *Tagebuch* sent to him by van Posselt; that he read with Hegel and others newspapers reporting the events; received firsthand accounts from friends and acquaintances; wrote supportively about it to his mother, sister, brother, and his friend Neuffer; celebrated its early victories; mourned its bloody outcomes; and was not merely a distanced observer but took part intellectually. Bertaux's study confirms Georg Lukács's argument that Hölderlin remains faithful to the "spring" of the revolution, whereas he could not support its violent outcomes.[35] One might argue on the basis of these studies that Hölderlin's point of view on the revolution remains utopian, insofar as the freedom, equality, and brotherhood the revolution promised was not fulfilled, or was at least violently compromised. In Hölderlin's novel *Hyperion,* the title character applauds revolutionary striving but is presented, then, with the failure of violence to secure the ideal for which the revolutionary longs. Thus Hyperion fights to liberate Greece from Turkish domination, only to find his own comrades looting and plundering, compromising the ideal of freedom that was their aim. It is Diotima, symbolizing the beautiful, nature, and freedom, who urges Hyperion to pursue peaceful means of change, primarily through education of the people. In a letter to Hegel, Hölderlin expresses his own "ideal of a public education" (ELT 126); according to such an ideal, poetry is employed to teach tolerance, diversity within harmony, and a nonmechanistic relation to nature. Poetry is to be the "teacher of humanity" (ELT 155). For Hölderlin—and this is a point Heidegger mocks—was a pacifist, which, according to Lukács, made Hölderlin's politics utopian.

Heidegger's reading of Hölderlin's poem "Germanien" reveals his conscious discord with Hölderlin's own political views.[36] In this lecture course, Heidegger reads "Germanien" "at the beginning, in order to indicate a beginning. With this is said: this poem refers to the origin, the farthest and most difficult, of what encounters us at last under the name Hölderlin" (GA 39, 4). Nevertheless, Heidegger argues that the poem has to be read "poetically" and explicitly not according to "Hölderlin's worldview [*Weltanschauung*]." For in Hölderlin's image (*Bild*) of Germania, she is "a dreaming girl 'hidden in the forest with blooming poppies'" (GA 39, 17). For Heidegger this image is too "romantic," (*romantisch*), too "feminine," (*feminin*) too "unheroic" (*unheroisch*). Heidegger lends the poem, then, a more fitting image, that of the strong and terrible Germania on the Niederwald monument, a *Mordsweib* "with flying hair and a gigantic sword [*einem Riesenschwert*]" (GA 39, 17). As we have seen in previous chapters, Heidegger's view of the poem's unity does not rely upon a reading of its images, and thus this replacement does not conspicuously discord with the principles of his method of "listening."[37]

It is no wonder, Heidegger continues, that Hölderlin employs this "feminine" image, for it is apparently in harmony with the "world view" and even "character" of the poet himself (GA 39, 17):

Hölderlin is thus openly a "pacifist," who apparently favors the defenselessness of Germany and still more, for a one-sided disarmament. This borders on treason [*Landesverrat*]. But that fits well with the person of the poet: he was incompetent in life, could compete nowhere, was tossed from one house-tutor position to another, never once became an instructor in philosophy as he attempted in Jena. (GA 39, 17)[38]

Therefore it would seem that Hölderlin's "Germanien" is "untimely for our hard times," though Heidegger's role as thinker promises to uncover what is more "essential" to the poem than the poet's worldview and the images he employs. In order to counter this pacifist image of Hölderlin, Heidegger refers to two letters that Hölderlin wrote, one to his friend Ludwig Neuffer, another to his brother Karl (GA 39, 18–19). In both letters, Hölderlin refers to the difficulty of the times and the duty that might call a poet to action, to "go . . . where the need is greatest and where we are most needed." But here Hölderlin is referring to democratic yearnings in the wake of the French Revolution, in order to "see with all clarity and tenderness how we arrange everything human within ourselves and others in an increasingly free and intimate relation" (ELT 140). In neither letter is violence defended nor is taking up arms mentioned.

For it is not Heidegger's "founding of a political state" to which the act of poetry is to be tethered, as in "The Origin of the Work of Art," but rather to the freedom of the human being, a freedom that, as Hölderlin writes with the young Hegel and Schelling in the "Oldest System-Program of German Idealism," is "beyond the state" (ELT 154). The revolutionary politics of poetry are not to be found in the founding of a people's destiny, but rather in awakening a people to the possibility of freedom that a "feeling of life"—inspired by nature—endows. Poetry is to be the expression of this communal freedom, even if it is a utopian one. Thus, although Heidegger claims that Hölderlin's poetry and relation to the Greeks is "essentially other than humanism" (LH, 219), in a letter to his brother Hölderlin remains clearly within humanist concerns. He writes:

> My love is the human race. . . . I love the race of the coming centuries. Thus this is my most blissful hope, the belief, which keeps me strong and active, that our descendants will be better than we, that freedom must once come, and that virtues will thrive better in the holy warming light of freedom than in the ice-cold zone of despotism. We live in times when everything aims at better days. (WB II, 813)[39]

It is the thriving in the "warming light of freedom" that Hölderlin hopes for as his own version of "Enlightenment," that informed for Hölderlin "each aim—education, the betterment of the human race, that we in our lifetimes will perhaps achieve only imperfectly" (WB II, 813). That poetry is to "unite people . . . in a living, thousand times divided, inward whole" (ELT 139) is Hölderlin's aim. This togetherness is a community of differing individuals who are united not "insofar as everyone forgets himself and no one's particularity appears" (ELT 138), but in a unity of varying representations of life (ELT 90–95). It is in sharing these varying representations in community, in "peace and freedom," that they attain their holiness, the expression of "joy" above the needs of mere necessity. Thus peace and harmony are "advanced through the notion of the widespread human society" (ELT 138). If for Hölderlin "the peace of all peace is irretrievably lost . . . we would not even seek after it if that infinite unification, that being in the only sense of the word, were not present to us. It is present—as beauty."[40]

Kantian Sublime Sacrifice

As we have seen in previous chapters, Hölderlin—and this is a point that Heidegger's interpretations do not address—is inspired by Kant's *Critique of Judgment,* and by Kant's attempt there to bridge the "immense gulf" between pure and practical reason in reflective, that is, nonlegislative, judgments of the beautiful. What is known to us as "aesthetics" is undertaken in order to unite the transcendental subject and its pure and practical reason. The unification of the subject, further, is to solve another problem: the presentation of freedom in the world of sense, which had hitherto been impossible and had left the subject divided between two incommensurable worlds. Hölderlin writes that Kant "is the Moses of our nation," and he claims that the education of culture should include, along with poetry and "political literature," Kantian philosophy. For although Kant "keeps too one-sidedly to the great autonomy of human nature" his is, "as the philosophy of the epoch, the only possible one" (ELT 137).

We have discussed in the previous chapter in greater detail the philosophical concepts that Hölderlin adopts from Kant. But we might focus on another dimension in Kant's aesthetic theory, that of the sublime, which, like Heidegger's story of poetic dwelling in "The Origin of the Work of Art," is a violent one. In a proposed (not extant) essay on Kant's notion of the aesthetic idea, the problem of the beautiful and the sublime in the *Critique of Judgment*—and thus Kant's overcoming of epistemological restrictions of the *Critique of Pure Reason*[41]—was to be taken up, a project that Hölderlin describes in a letter to Neuffer in 1794 (WB II, 550–551). The treatment of the Kantian aesthetic idea would involve a more radical and, at the same time, more radically skeptical account of poetic language. And yet the aesthetic idea, as that of the beautiful, must be accompanied by an account of the sublime. For Hölderlin "the presentation of the tragic rests primarily on the monstrous" (*das Ungeheure*), understood as the boundless separation and boundless unification of the finite and infinite (ELT 107; TS 100). Hölderlin's notion of the tragic caesura, which he links to the "calculation" of the faculties (ELT 101), must then be linked to Kant's sublime—for both involve a rhythm and a rupture (ELT 102) within the realm of the knowable, such that the understanding is faced with a wandering "below the unthinkable." (ELT 110). Hölderlin, as we will see, reverses the rhythm of Kant's sublime sacrifice—for it is in Hölderlin a "counterrhythmic rupture"—rendering the subject precarious, contingent, and subject to the divine in nature (ELT 102). This is how Hölderlin begins to challenge the "great autonomy of human nature," to which Kant adheres despite the nonlegislative relation to nature achieved by reflective judgment. For whereas in the philosophy of the beautiful, Kant asserts, even a "blade of grass" infinitely defeats the mind (CJ 378, 400), in the analytic of the sublime, reason triumphs as superior even to nature's magnitude and force.

Kant defines the sublime (*das Erhabene*) as the "absolutely large" (*schlechthin groß*), that which is "beyond all comparison" (CJ 248). It is a "magnitude that is equal only to itself," or that "in comparison with which everything else is small" (CJ 250). It is to be sought in "crude nature," but refers us to our own ideas, and the incapacity of the imagination to represent what exceeds it, namely, the infinite. The greatness of nature's forces, and the "infinity" of the "immense whole" that belongs to nature (CJ 257), exceed the imagination's capacity to present them in sense. The sublime is to be seen in the natural elements, for example, in "bold, overhanging, and, as it were, threatening rocks, thunderclouds piling up in the sky and moving about accompanied by lightning and thunderclaps, volcanoes with all their destructive power" (CJ 261).

The sublime, though threatening, must be seen from what Kant calls the "safe place," for though the intimidation of these elements is great, what the sublime, paradoxically, provides, is the feeling of the human being's independence from nature. The "sublime does violence to an inner sense . . . and yet this same violence . . . is still judged purposive *for the whole vocation* of the mind" (CJ 250). For although we feel the "agitation" of the sublime's "resistance to the interest of our senses" (CJ 267), this agitation is followed—as in Aristotle's "tragic catharsis"—by a release; this time it entails a "respect" for rational authority, in that reason's concepts overwhelm the capacity of the imagination to present the magnitude in sense. The imagination is, Kant argues, "sacrificed" (CJ 271) to reason, and thus the subject feels the superiority of its "rational vocation" to even the most immense of nature's presentations. Kant writes:

> For although we found our own limitation when we considered the immensity of nature and the inadequacy of our ability to adopt a standard proportionate to estimating aesthetically the magnitude of nature's domain, yet we also found, in our power of reason, a different and nonsensible standard that has this infinity itself under it . . . and since in contrast to this standard everything in nature is small, we found in our mind a superiority over nature itself in its immensity. (CJ 261–262)

The sublime, ultimately, affords us "an ability to judge ourselves independent of nature," and "keeps the humanity in our person from being degraded" by nature. The human being thus "holds the title of the lord of nature," as Kant writes in the "Analytic of Teleological Judgment" (CJ 431).

The "agitation" effected in the sublime is that of the incapacity of the imagination, a damning result for poetic theory. While the beautiful affords us a "restful contemplation," the sublime in nature provokes a "rapid alteration of repulsion from, and attraction to, one and the same object." The repulsion is that of the imagination's fear of the thing it is to apprehend in intuition and cannot: for the thing is an "abyss in which the imagination is afraid to lose itself" (CJ 258). Yet reason's own "idea of the supersensible" comes to the rescue, providing a feeling of freedom above the inapprehensible nature. As Lyotard argues in his treatment of the sublime economy, here we find a pleasure in displeasure, a masochism, for it is only at the cost of sacrificing the imagination that reason wins its triumph, and the feeling of freedom on the part of the subject is no longer in accord with the beautiful object, but is rather opposed to, and then above it.[42] Kant writes that a "liking for the sublime is only negative," for "the imagination *feels* the sacrifice or deprivation and at the same time the cause to which it is being subjugated" (CJ 268). Imagination is "sacrificed" in favor of reason so that reason feels itself free in its superiority. The "idea of the supersensible," the moral vocation of free subjects, is now won in the conflict between reason and nature. Despite that "any spectator who beholds massive mountains climbing skyward, deep gorges with raging streams in them, wastelands lying in deep shadow and inviting melancholy meditation . . . is seized by amazement bordering on terror, by horror and a sacred thrill," the sublime is posited only in the subject's own moral "vocation" (CJ 268).

That Kant denies the sublime an access to the *sensus communis*, then, is to be seen in the light of the opposition between reason and nature (CJ 264). The sublime does not provide the a priori promise of universal agreement, does not provoke feeling of life to which freedom is given over in communal belonging. It is, rather, the autonomy of the rational subject that is heralded. Although the sublime relates us to our moral feeling (CJ 265), we have no a priori validity in assuming this moral feeling in everyone. The failure of the sublime to promote the feeling of community is grounded in the inherent violence with which one faculty dominates another. The sublime sacrifice constitutes a "sacrilege" against nature.[43] Because the divinity of nature is violated, it ceases to offer the "feeling of life" — of freedom — that Hölderlin associates with nature. While in the beautiful, the "free play" of the faculties is an experience of the freedom symbolically presented, in the sublime, this freedom is won in conflict.

Though beyond the scope of these reflections here, it might also be asked how the sacrifice of the freedom of the imagination here relates to other elements of Kant's championing of reason. In the "Critique of Teleological Judgment," the tender reverence for nature found in the analytic of the beautiful gives way to the hierarchy of the human being, as rational, over nature, and to other kinds of violence. Human progress is a matter of "making ever more headway against the crudeness and vehemence of animality," but this entails as well a defense of war as necessary for the cultivation of the human species. Kant argues that "though war is an unintentional human endeavor (incited by our unbridled passions), yet it is also a deeply hidden and perhaps intentional endeavor of the supreme wisdom." War has "something sublime about it" in providing "one more incentive for us to develop to the utmost all the talents that serve culture" (CJ 433). Almost foreshadowing Heidegger, Kant thinks the fact that a people has carried on in the face of danger and has stood its ground promotes its "way of thinking." On this view, war is beneficial to humankind[44] because it elevates the thinking of a people and raises them from the merely "commercial spirit" that a "prolonged peace tends to make prevalent" (CJ 263). In this way, we can see an alliance between the Kantian theory of the sublime and belligerent founding of truth as set forth by the poet.

The Caesura

It is possible to read Hölderlin's brief essays on Kant and Fichte as his attempt to undo the systematic nature of the transcendental subject; for Hölderlin, the imagination is not to be dominated by reason but issues, instead, the undoing of the subject's autonomy. The imagination is the locus of the feeling of freedom that an aesthetic experience of nature provokes, and it is this experience, this "accidental," merely fortunate, glimpse into the union of freedom and nature, which denies the rational subject its a priori validity. In the essay-fragment "On the Law of Freedom," "the imagination implicitly threatens the alleged systematicity of the theoretical as such."[45] For Hölderlin, the imagination opens the subject to nature in a way for which transcendental philosophy is incapable of accounting. If it is through the imagination that the accidental, the a posteriori, enters and thus undoes the transcendental system, the gap that results takes the form, in the writing on tragic poetry, of the caesura. Whereas the imagination in "the development of Kant's system involves the eventual relegation of the imagination to a merely reproductive and hence derivative function,"[46] and then is sacrificed to the sublime, in Hölderlin the imagination begins to unravel the transcendental system, an account that reaches its climax in the tragic sacrifice of *Empedocles*, "The Ground for Empedocles," and "Remarks on Oedipus." Hölderlin's notion of the caesura, the "counterrhythmic rupture" in which, as Adorno argues, the subject's legislative faculty is sacrificed, provides a counterpoint to Kant's understanding of the sublime, and one that, contra Kant, refuses the ultimate domination of nature by reason. Not legislation, but eccentricity is demanded by consciousness.[47] The imagination, I argue in the final chapter, must therefore be retrieved in a new poetics grounded in Hölderlin's thought.

What Hölderlin calls the "tragic law" is the form in which the sacrifice of subjective autonomy occurs. In *Empedocles* nature is sung in a word that is about to collapse, "in a twilight word" ("im finstern Wort"). In "Remarks on Oedipus," Hölderlin claims that tragic poetry requires the caesura, "the counterrhythmic rupture."[48] The caesura is the form of poetry—following the sublime's "rapid alteration"—in which the rhythm of representations follows an "eccentric rapidity" so that it ends in rupture,

> in the rhythmic sequence of the representations wherein transport presents itself, there becomes necessary what in poetic meter is called caesura, the pure word, the counterrhythmic rupture;

namely, in order to meet the onrushing change of representations at its highest point in such a manner that very soon there does not appear the change of representation but the representation itself. (ELT 102)

Hölderlin, like Kant, argues for a tripartite account of subjective faculties (representation, sensation [imagination], and reason) that enter into relation. For Hölderlin, the elements of the conscious subject exist in a "calculation," exist "more as a state of balance" than, as in Kant, as competition (ELT 102). Here we find neither Kant's violent sublime sacrifice nor the "essential sacrifice" of Heidegger's historical founding. The rupture that follows this state of balance, this "lawful calculation" (*gesetzliche Kalkul*) (ELT 101/ TS 94) ends in the death, or self-sacrifice, of the tragic character, which we have read as Hölderlin's own warning against the hubris of unbounded consciousness. The ideal is granted only in its absence, in the "askew access." Read as the rupture of the subject's balance of faculties, the caesura denies the possibility of reason's domination over the imagination, and thus denies the subject's domination over nature. The "agitation" of the Kantian sublime becomes, in this reading, the counterrhythmic moment in which the subject submits to nature by admitting the "gap" in (theoretical) consciousness, wherein "representation itself" appears rather than what is represented. This gap is the apogee of the caesura, and here the poetic word is transformed into silence, what Hölderlin calls the "pure word," which, lacking now the tension of the play among representation, reason, and sense, cannot represent anything, but presents only itself, as empty representation itself, *"unbedeutend,"* in silence. This is why Hölderlin claims that at the point of the paradox in the tragic poem, the "Sign = 0" (ELT 89). Silence is not, as in Heidegger, the "unsayable" ground of poetic saying, but is the moment in which the subject, through poetic language, unravels, wherein "knowledge — after it has broken through its barriers . . . is spurred by itself to know more than it can bear or contain" (ELT 104).

While Hölderlin defines the caesura as a moment in the tragic poem, Adorno finds the caesura in the poem "Celebration of Peace" ("Friedensfeier"), a copy of which was first discovered in France in 1951.[49] In Adorno's account, the caesura is referenced in this poem with the lines: "this is a law of fate, that all learn / that when silence turns, there is also a language [Schicksalgesetz ist dies, daß Alle sich erfahren, / Daß, wenn die Stille kehrt, auch eine Sprache sei]."[50] Heidegger resists this particular formulation of silence or caesura. Heidegger treats the same line in *On the Way to Language,* though as a law of song not the "opposite of a discourse, but rather the most intimate kinship with it" (OWL 78). For Heidegger "the song remains discourse" even if the "word passes into darkness" (OWL 78–79). Yet Adorno claims that the poem contains a real caesura, which silences the word, one found earlier in the poem, in the lines that also mention "fate":

> Und kommen muß zum heilgen Ort das Wilde
> Von Enden fern, übt rauhbetastend den Wahn,
> Und trifft daran ein Schicksal, aber Dank,
> Nie folgt der gleich hernach dem gottgebnen Geschenken.

> And to the holy place the savage must come,
> Ignorant of ends, and crudely feeling it, proves
> His delusion and thereby strikes a fate,
> but never at once does gratitude follow such gifts

The word "but" (*aber*) "establishes a caesura in the poem; the linguistic confrontation defines gratitude as the antithesis of fate." This is the "qualitative leap that in responding to fate leads out of it."[51] Adorno thus means to show that in Hölderlin's poems the form is at odds with the content; that is, structure is a "totality of moments" that at the same time "transcend this structure." For this reason, Hölderlin's poems cannot be read literally, as prose, as Adorno argues Heidegger reads them when the latter claims that the poet is the "messenger" of Being. It is, rather, the "dialectical disjunction of form and truth content,"[52] which makes Hölderlin's poems critical and utopian, or irreducible to prose. It is for this reason that Hölderlin as poet cannot be "confused" "with the founder who intervenes in Being itself."[53]

If one is to read Hölderlin's theory of poetic calculation as a metaphor (ELT 83) of the faculties of the subject (ELT 109), then the caesura, where the limitations of human understanding are exposed by the infinite (ELT 108), complicates their unification. Yet the absence—in the empty word of paradox—of any signifying grasp of that infinite, returns the human being, as Lacoue-Labarthe claims, "back toward the earth."[54] If aesthetic experience was for Kant to close the gap of the system, bridge what is considered the "immense gulf" between the phenomenal and noumenal worlds, between pure and practical reason, the caesura in Hölderlin guarantees the abyssal character of this gap, inserting loss into a theory of the subject's experience. Accordingly, Lacoue-Labarthe and Nancy claim that Kant's aesthetics, rather than closing a bridge, opens the space that makes romanticism possible.[55] In longing to be one with nature, in grasping after the "unity of all that lives"—a unity denied to the conscious subject as the condition of consciousness—the human subject must sacrifice its legislative character, must be returned to its own "inwardness" that it has denied in attempting to legislate the object of knowledge or of poetic naming. Hölderlin's "eccentric path" (*die exzentrische Bahn*) thus returns mortals to the finite realm of beings, just at the moment when its striving for the infinite is greatest. For Hölderlin nature is sacred; but this sacredness is comprised of particular, historical, yet ontical moments no longer guaranteed to be "original" in Heidegger's sense. Hölderlin and Heidegger both leave behind the autonomous, rational subject; Hölderlin's theory admits, however, a dependence upon the contingent world of beings and the "gentle shyness of the accidental" that complicates the *Schicksal* defined as Heidegger's sending. Despite poetry's "lawlike calculus"—or, perhaps, because of it—the human, poetic subject is excluded from transcendental systematicity; but it is also excluded from the obedient "resoluteness" of historical founding, which, in Heidegger's 1930s and 1940s account, takes the place of subjective-metaphysical will.

For these reasons, it is possible to assign to Hölderlin, as Adorno does, the "critical and utopian function of art." Adorno argues that Hölderlin's utopian longing is not, as in Heidegger's notion of the destinal sending of Being, divorced from the particularly historical moment of the life of the poet, nor tethered primarily to Being's revealing-concealing play. If poetry overcomes subjectivity, it does so in the "sacrifice of the legislative subject."[56] Hölderlinian community is utopian, and issues from the ruptured subject, in loss; on this basis, I have argued that the community of Hölderlin stands outside the rhetoric of "resoluteness" and "decision" that accompanies Heidegger's "founding of truth."

Despite the resonances with them, Hölderlin's notion of the caesura must be to a significant extent distinguished from the dimensions of violent sacrifice in both Heidegger and Kant. If Heidegger rejects Kantian aesthetics, he nevertheless reproduces the violence found as a component to Kant's philosophy of the beautiful, one that finds its way into Hölderlin's caesura. I have situated the "sacrifice" of Hölderlin's caesura between the first and second, that is, the receptive and violent, of Heidegger's stories of poetic dwelling, and, at the same time, between the beautiful and sublime of Kant. Kant's notion of the beautiful reflects harmonious receptivity, and is yet in tension with sublime violence, conflict, and domination; and Hölderlin's poetic theory requires both. However, if the violence of the sublime is, in Kant, that of the subject's own rational vocation turned against nature, the sublime figures, in

Hölderlin, as the subjective epistemic will turn against itself. The divinity of nature—along with the ideal, utopian freedom its feeling of life engenders, the joy of sharing in community, the particularity and tolerance such community requires—is preserved, to use Kant's term, in the "abyss" (*Abgrund*) the subject's own self-undoing provides. In Hölderlin, sacrifice puts the subject, to use Kristeva's term, "in process/on trial"; the subject, as Heidegger admits of Trakl's "wandering stranger," is seen to lose itself—a loss that means "to loosen one's bonds" from resoluteness and decision, perhaps even from fate (OWL 171).

Yet in concluding this chapter we must return to the notion of sacrifice and the political reading it has been given. In *Heidegger, Art, and Politics*, Lacoue-Labarthe associates the Heideggerian-Hölderlinian motif of sacrifice with the Holocaust. In concluding this discussion of the violent sublime, I want to address critically Lacoue-Labarthe's attempt to identify the Holocaust, which he calls the "tragedy of our times," as a caesura in the Hölderlinian sense. Following a Heideggerian association of the caesura with *Ereignis*, Lacoue-Labarthe writes: "I propose to term such an event a caesura in the sense Hölderlin accorded this term."[57] The caesura is the "scansion of the tragedy" as that which opens up an "irreversible and discordant" temporality, in which "what follows the caesura will never be the same as what went before: the end will never again resemble the beginning."[58]

I will not attempt in these concluding observations to discuss the Holocaust or Auschwitz as such; for if Auschwitz can be called, as Lacoue-Labarthe calls it in this context, a "pure event"[59]—an *Ereignis*—at all, a discussion of its eventhood cannot be encompassed by what could be said about poetry, tragedy, or Hölderlin's understanding of either. Yet it seems that the conflation of Heidegger's *Ereignis* and Hölderlin's caesura must be addressed if one is to disentangle Hölderlin's political views from those of Heidegger, the distinction between which I have laid out in this chapter, and if one is to render more cautious and discerning the attempts to locate moments in the history of German ideas that seem, at least on a mimetic or foreshadowing level, to be implicated along with the heinous moments of actual German history in the twentieth century. Heidegger's involvement with National Socialism, his suppression of Hölderlin's own political views, as we have seen in this chapter, and Heidegger's failure to respond, or at least to respond in an adequate way, to the historical burden of the Holocaust,[60] open up Heidegger's thought to Lacoue-Labarthe's critique. The notion of *Ereignis* upon which Lacoue-Labarthe focuses, in the context of Hölderlin's caesura, is what is to be implicated in what

Lyotard calls the "politics of forgetting": for in Heidegger the "sole occurrence" is to be thought beyond that "which occurs" (EP 79). Although it is true that "what follows the caesura will never be the same as what went before" surely belongs to the definition of Hölderlin's caesura,[61] this does not span the bridge between a discourse on literary practice and the events of history. Lacoue-Labarthe's move replicates Heidegger's own attempts to render Hölderlin exclusively historical and destinal without challenging this dominating facet of Heidegger's reading. This definition of the caesura, by which Lacoue-Labarthe implicates Hölderlin along with Heidegger, furthermore does not hold for the Heidegger's *Ereignis* — a notion that indicates more than a radical break or rupture in Being (as in the *Beiträge zur Philosophie*) but also a circular, elusive withdrawing that presences (as in the later essay "Time and Being"), one that inscribes that "which occurs" into the logic — and history — of the *Schicksal* of occurrence and withdrawal per se. As for Hölderlin, the caesura is a moment in poetic meter wherein the impossibility of saying asserts itself, and is, even in its index to sacrifice, involved less in a poetic inscription of history than an account of transcendental hubris.[62] Hölderlin's theory of tragedy, as located in the problem of hubris rather than catharsis, is thus not easily mapped onto a pathology of the "pure" that might be charged against Heidegger, and certainly against German fascism. What Blanchot calls the "disaster"[63] might resonate with the catastrophe as represented in the tragic poem; but if the caesura, as the moment in a tragedy, is for Hölderlin tethered to an implicit and sometimes explicit account of the limits of subjectivity, it is not a "thrust that enters history" nor the "deciding of what is holy and what is unholy." The caesura is an incomprehensibility of which, unlike the *Ereignis* of Heidegger, it cannot be hoped to be brought to essential representation, and thus does not belong to the realm of historical action. The caesura is for Hölderlin the apogee of paradox; it is the subject's silence; it is where poetry breaks off. It is not only beyond thematization by concepts, even those of an "event," it is also the limit of a theory of poetry, and where poetry becomes in fact what Adorno calls the subject's incapacity to "speak for itself."

If Heidegger's notion of the *Ereignis* is nevertheless to be understood as the "pure event" of "sacrifice," the *Ereignis*, in its ontological-historical dimensionality beyond the metaphysics of subjects, is thus to be distinguished from Hölderlin's notion of the caesura. I have attempted here, by reference to Hölderlin's writings, to differentiate Hölderlin's notion of the caesura, of the "tragic sacrifice," from Heidegger's notion of sacrifice and even of the *Ereignis*, in order that a more cautious examination replace this kind of conflation of Heidegger and Hölderlin in

Lacoue-Labarthe's text. Not only an implication of his theory of violent founding, but also a retrieval of Heidegger's *Gelassenheit*, might too usurp a "politics of forgetting" according to which subjects of history are eclipsed by the history of Being and its withdrawal. The submission in Hölderlin's caesura of the "acceptance of mediateness, or, in other words, of finitude"[64] is not the submission to an "essential" sacrifice, nor to a destiny as essential. What we are to learn from the tragic is a mode of dwelling that avoids, rather than celebrates, disaster.

Lacoue-Labarthe nevertheless raises challenging questions regarding Heidegger's philosophy and interpretations of Hölderlin, and he is right that the *Ereignis* has not yet been adequately "measured" against the "risk" and "shock" that Heidegger knows is involved in overcoming humanism (LH 225). *Ereignis* must be examined not only according to its "purity" but also according to the logic of sacrifice that anticipates its thinking; here we have accomplished only the indication of the urgency of such consideration. Poetic language, despite its relation to sacrifice, dismantles destiny and resoluteness just as it upsets the victory of reason over the imagination. It challenges Heidegger's association of poetic language, and therefore dwelling, with violence and with the violence of "purity." The violent ontological founding of truth is, for the reasons I have shown, unacceptable as an account of Hölderlin, and misses a radical, postmetaphysical humanism in Hölderlin's writings. Such violence is, furthermore, untrue to the phenomenologically disclosive, and therefore explicitly finite and sheltering, character of poetic language into which Heidegger showed significant insight in his later works.

6

Revolutionary Poetics and
the Subject-in-Process

A new account of the relationship among poetic language, existence, and truth might be achieved by a new poetics of Dasein. As we have seen, Heidegger's philosophy disqualifies the modern subject, and, after *Being and Time,* the anthropocentrism and humanism of an existential self. His poetics eschews all traces of subjectivism, particularly in elucidating the notion of *Andenken.* If Heidegger in his interpretations refers to an "essential abode of the self" (EHD 129), this is to be understood in a qualified sense; Heidegger eliminates the self we have outlined in the previous chapters as nonetheless essential for Hölderlin's poetological procedure. If the self's abode has little to do with a speaking subject, this is confirmed by the deconstruction of the self since Foucault's notion of the "death of the author." But it is at odds with Continental approaches in Kristeva, Blanchot, and Valéry, which suggest that every utterance, and thus every account of language, implies a subject, albeit one radically conditioned or "shattered." (I discuss the use of the terms "subject" and "self" in the introduction.) In this context, poetic language in particular reveals the processes of subjective life as its undercurrent; yet poetic language also involves rather a complex tentativeness with regard to meaning and truth. Heidegger's *Gelassenheit,* understood as a releasement of appropriative knowledge that confines its object, could be located at the site of such a subject.

A new poetics of Dasein, which I formally initiate in the following chapter but prepare for in the present one, claims that poetry is
a mode of "formal indication" of factical existence seen in the self's
sheltering imaginative relation to world. My view then departs from
postmodernism's refusal of an author or its total shattering of the
subject, but also from modernism's uncritical positing of the artistic
genius and Heidegger's view of the poet as the messenger of Being.
In contrast to Heidegger's rejection of the subject, I here employ the
notion of poetic subjectivity, configured throughout this book according to Heidegger's critique of metaphysics and Hölderlin's poetology. Poetic subjectivity, which I will call as well the poetic Dasein,
has neither the character of resoluteness nor an ontological purity;
it affords then not the nobility or dignity of a decision (DI 146, 147,
150) but a precarious procedure of exposure to and involvement
in the world through poetic language.

Some account of poetic Dasein's transcendence, by virtue of what
Heidegger had called projection (*Entwerfen*), must also be included in
a theory of the poetic subject. In my theory, transcendence signifies a
kind of transformation through language, in which what is preserved
in poetry is not merely the utterance of the personal self, but a strate-
gic and formalized engagement of the self's experience of encounter
with what is other to the self. Transcendence allows the poet to articulate not merely unmediated personal experiences, but rather a kind
of knowledge about experience of the world through its formal transformation. Transformation or transcendence thus allows the poet to
poeticize that which is beyond the grasp of rational cognition. Such
transformation is a transformation of the given, grounded in the factical lifeworld, even as it reaches toward the unsayable. This transformation, moreover, is made possible by virtue of initiative creation in
language. This, as I will argue in this chapter, exceeds a reapportion-
ment of relationships accounted for in, for instance, Kristeva's notion
of the revolutionary character of poetic language, which remains primarily negative. Nonetheless, her theory demands some attention insofar as it aids an advancement of Hölderlinian poetological themes; but
I will also critically outline the limitations of her view, which a new
poetics of Dasein must overcome. This new poetics will also reconsider Heidegger's rejection of the imagination as belonging to metaphysical aesthetics of the representing subject. A new existential phenomenology of the imagination is proposed in the next chapter, in order
to articulate the structural and experiential possibilities for transcendence or transformation as described above.

In this chapter I prepare for a new theory of poetic subjectivity through a critical engagement with the themes of self and otherness or alterity as they are interwoven throughout modern and postmodern poetics. Most principally what needs to be uncovered is the thread of continuity within poetics, despite radical differences, regarding the revolutionary nature of poetical language through which language makes accessible the unsaid underlying ordinary speech or cognition. Beyond this revolutionary nature, we should be positioned so as to be able to pose the following questions properly: If there is, as I have argued, indeed a subject of poetic language, how does this subject come to be known in poetry? How does it involve aspects of the self, for instance, the psyche and the embodied life, largely absent from Heidegger's theory? How is subjectivity, poetically understood, ultimately different from the metaphysical model of the subject — not only structurally, as we have discussed in previous chapters, but in its experience of uncanniness and alterity so crucial for the Heideggerian figuration of the poet? If the otherness of the world is not appropriated but preserved in poetry which attends it, and if this attendance can be addressed in terms of poetic Dasein, we might also venture that Dasein is a subject of *Gelassenheit,* exposing the incapacity of poetic language for an absolute founding of truth. This incapacity signifies poetry's critical function, configured in various poetic theories as "revolutionary." We begin by outlining this revolutionary nature of poetic language; but I will critically intervene throughout with claims for the positive value of the compositional, spontaneous, and creative nature of poetic language that is underserved in revolutionary poetics, and to which I will ultimately offer an alternative in the final chapter of this book.

Revolutionary Language

The notion that poetic language is revolutionary continually appears throughout the history of modern poetics, which we will outline from its origins in early German Idealism. The revolutionary character of poetic language is declared no more directly in the history of philosophy than in a text that emerged out of the circle of friends of Hegel, Schelling, and Hölderlin; this text anticipates, however, not its proposed "system program of German Idealism" but the departure from systematic philosophy altogether — a departure taken up by Hölderlin, instigated by Kant's "aesthetic ideas," which promise to unify a subject divided between the natural realm and that of freedom. Hölderlin attempts both in poetry and theoretical investigations of poetic language to overcome this division, thereby realizing the promise for an "aesthetic sense" (ELT 154–156) that Hegelian dialectics ultimately leaves behind. If poetry alone is to "survive" philosophy, for Hölderlin it alone can "dissolve the oppositions in which we think and exist." Philosophy's entrance into poetic language is for Hölderlin a path of no mere happenstance; we have seen that for Hölderlin philosophy's oppositions — which reflect those of political and communal life — cannot be harmoniously joined in the language of rational concepts.

As we have seen, Hölderlin aims for an indirect unification of the subject with its world, thereby undoing what he regards as the tyranny of the rational subject over nature, and thereby dismantling the unity of a transcendental subject whose freedom is grounded in opposition to its object. Poetry's revolutionary character for Hölderlin depends upon a radical skepticism; Kristeva calls for a rendering "impossible the transcendental bounding that supports the discourse of knowledge" (DL 145). I will dispute, however, the expulsion of poetic discourse from the realms of knowledge and truth, the latter necessarily considerably qualified. The unification of the subject with its other — what Hölderlin names "peace" (*der Frieden*) — cannot be grounded conceptually in a subject of legislative judgment, but only in an "askew perspective," preserving the alterity or otherness of the object. As such the subject is a receptive one, aligned with Hölderlin's deferred ideal for political liberation, which, as we saw in the previous chapter, involves a tolerance for differences based in the limitedness of any one representation of life or of religious feeling (ELT 90–95). This ideal involves Hölderlin's enthusiasm for the promises of the French Revolution and his disappointment in its brutal outcome; for Hölderlin, this utopian promise for political liberation remains grounded in the language of the poet.

In Kristeva's post-psychoanalytical poetics, the practice of poetry, in its opposition to ordinary speech, is inherently revolutionary in that it challenges the primacy of the rational ego — of the paternal law discovered theoretically by Freud — and engenders a "thetic rupture," which refuses the domination of the semiotic by the symbolic, terms that I will outline shortly. The self-enclosure of the symbolic subject from its intersubjective, social, bodily origins in the semiotic is torn asunder by practices that challenge the symbolic's exclusive possession of the sphere of meaning. The undermining of the symbolic is also a challenge to the privileges of theoretical reason in defining reality (DL 88, 146–147). Hölderlin's own theory, insofar as it is aligned with German romanticism in general, anticipates the overturning of what Kristeva links together as "science and monotheism" as the exclusive ground of truth-claims, and, like Kristeva, formulates the roots of poetic practice as intersubjective communal experience.[1] For Kristeva, the transgression of autonomous subjectivity returns the subject to the intersubjective roots of the emergence of language, and releases alterity into the sphere of meaning. Thus she claims that "the text is a practice that could be compared to political revolution" (RPL 17). Kristeva's account, in the wake of psychoanalysis, radicalizes this revolution by locating the challenge posed by poetic language in the sphere of specifically gendered, bodily, and socially legislating relations.[2]

A reading of Hölderlin's theoretical writings, in noting his unique departure from idealist dialectic,[3] engenders some comparison to this kind of semiotic analysis. For Kristeva shows that poetry compromises the fixing of a transcendental signified—because poetry illuminates language, and therefore the subject who posits, as a never complete process. Hölderlin's "askew perspective" and "eccentric path" are subjective strategies that likewise signify the resistance of the object of knowledge to the subject who formulates, identifies, and stabilizes it. Thus Hölderlin's poetic practice is at odds with ontological "naming" in any sense other than a subjunctive, utopian, profoundly disrupted and displaced longing.[4] Kristeva, likewise, suggests that "literary discourse enunciates through its formal decentering" (DL 145). Whereas in Hölderlin skepticism is transformed into poetic longing, in Kristeva poetry points to the "infinitizing" possibilities of language: not to usurp meaning altogether, but to prevent its closure. Poetic language "pluralizes denotation" and thereby "undermines meaning" (RPL 59). Kristeva's semiotics, thus, breaks with ideology, dialectic, and system (RPL 69) by illuminating in analysis that which resists closure. Both Kristeva and Hölderlin, then, show that poetry is a revolutionary practice, and that this—and not founding (*Stiften*) in a literal-ontological sense— is the function of its "truth content." Kristeva, too, recognizes in Hölderlin's poetry a "practice of language whose stakes" challenge the "legitimacy of theoretical discourse" and the transcendental grounds of epistemology (DL 145). She writes, "Since . . . Hölderlin, we could not avoid wondering about the possibility, or simultaneously, the legitimacy of a theoretical discourse on this practice of language whose stakes are precisely to render impossible the transcendental bounding that supports the discourse of knowledge" (DL 145).

With Hölderlin, Kristeva claims, we are "faced with this poetic language which defies knowledge" (DL 145). My position involves a subtle but significant differentiation from Kristeva's theory. We have seen in previous chapters that Hölderlin challenges theoretical knowledge not only in poetic language but philosophically, insofar as the imagination will not be sacrificed to legislative reason. Thus I have argued that knowledge is rendered provisional rather than absolute. While Kristeva focuses largely on the deconstructive aspects of poetic language, which then weaken its utopian function, I emphasize that poetry is also compositional and creative beyond its mimicry of the semiotic body and its drives. It is essential to note that the poetic imagination is not merely reproductive of the semiotic undercurrents of language, but also uniquely projective, and that means transformative and productive, features Kristeva reserves for language of the symbolic sphere. While I do not deny poetry's relevance for the non- or pre-rational stages of the subject's formation, the spontaneity of the poetic subject is denied if its utterances are determined by undercurrents of the unconscious, even if those escape rational determination. Though not able to institute truth, poetry enacts a projection and preservation that resound with Heidegger's *Gelassenheit* theory. Poetry's "negative capability," to use Keats's term, is an ability to abide in doubt and mystery, but it is also the capacity to press forth in creative projection upon an uncertain horizon. Negative capability is not, despite its nomination, merely negative, but also productively a traversing, perhaps a sheltering, of the unknown that lies beyond the bounds of the definitive or the verifiable. Like Foucault, Kristeva aligns knowledge with power and opposes poetry to the power of knowledge as a counterforce; but she does not—and here my poetics will diverge from her account—reformulate the boundaries of knowledge in order to include poetical truths within its sphere of reverberation. This requires, more than an account of the revolutionary nature of poetic language, a phenomenology of poetical knowledge. Such can only be initiated here, as I will attempt to do in the next chapter. Yet Kristeva's theory is worth examining in detail, for it will offer a method of investigating the relation between poetic language and alterity, which must be described in a new poetics of Dasein.

The Subject-in-Process and Poetic Spontaneity

Some review of Kristevian linguistics is in order so that we may outline in further detail the relation between the revolutionary character of poetic language, its relation to alterity, and that of the subject. For these purposes I draw upon Kristeva's major work on poetic language, *Revolution in Poetic Language,* and the essay "From One Identity to Another," as a truncated model for this theory. Here Kristeva argues that "every language theory is predicated upon a conception of the subject that it explicitly posits, implies, or tries to deny" (DL 124). Her premise is a critique of structural linguistics, in that the latter ignores the subject that "is present as soon as there is consciousness of signification" (DL 124). Kristeva's subject of enunciation is indeed not Husserl's transcendental ego, but rather a subject of drives, which exists "across and through the constitutive and insurmountable frontier of *meaning*" (DL 146). Kristeva draws upon the post-Freudian exploration of the relation between signifier/signified and replaces its supposed arbitrariness with "articulation"—which, though undecidable, represents signifying systems as motivated.

Kristeva's theory marks its ground, in the wake of Freud and Lacan, between structuralist and Husserlian theories of language. She credits Husserl with both maintaining a subject and locating judgment within language via the act of expression (DL 130). We must "first acknowledge, with Husserl," that "it is impossible to treat problems of signification seriously . . . without including in these considerations *the subject thus formulated as operating consciousness*" (DL 131). Structural linguistics—and in fact "all modern linguistic theories [that] consider language a strictly 'formal' object"—takes its cue from Saussure's discovery (postdating Husserl's writings) of division within the sign (signifier/signified); this opens up "play" within the signifying system just as much as it allows the latter to be understood according to mathematical models. But at the same time, these theories "eliminate the speaking subject," ignore that a "subject of enunciation takes shape within [that] gap that admits both structure and interplay . . . structural linguistics ignores such a subject" (DL 127–128; RPL 21–22). Yet if Kristeva maintains Husserl's speaking subject, Husserl's account is problematic, too; for this subject is always an "act of expressing meaning, constituted by a judgment on something" (DL 129). Husserl supposes the ego and its capacity to express meanings—its "thetic" capacities to articulate categorically (RPL 23)—without accounting for the construction of that ego; Kristeva argues that we must "search for that which produces, shapes, and exceeds the operating consciousness," and that "this will be our purpose when confronting poetic language" (DL 131).

This view diverges considerably from Heidegger's ontological account of language, and yet admits to some degree of resonance. Heidegger has shown that in order to understand language we must "be careful not to regard utterance, let alone expression, as the decisive element of human speech" (PLT 209). For Heidegger language is not "expression," as in Husserl, of an "internal" sense that, when given over to a sign, raises sense (*Sinn*) to meaning (*Bedeutung*) in communication from one subject (or *ego*) to another. Language cannot be reduced to expression because expression does not account for the physical character of language—to which Kristeva also attends—and for the fact of its "Showing," or its relation to Being. Heidegger argues that if we "listen" properly to language as saying (rather than as the speaking of a subject or what is thereby 'meant'), language is disclosed as self-revealing.[5] For Heidegger, language is defined by its role in ontological disclosure (OWL 63), irreducible to speaking subjects. While Kristeva shows that language is not merely the expression of self-possessed subjects and their intended meanings, for Heidegger "language . . . is not a mere human faculty" (OWL 107). The capacity "to sound and ring and vibrate, to hover and tremble" is just as much a property of language—and one that does not belong to the speaker—"as it is for spoken words of language to carry a meaning" (OWL 98). And in words—in their sensuous element, their vibrations in the organ of the mouth—"the landscape, and that means the earth, speaks in them, differently each time" (OWL 98). What the classical theory of expression neglects, according to Heidegger, is that the sensuality of language is our connection to "earth"—Kristeva would say the "maternal" or semiotic; thus Heidegger breaks up the immanence of subjectivistic theories of language.

Yet Heidegger claims further that poetry, which makes this relation of words to earth and to Being apparent, is "essential" language, and that the language of speaking subjects is actually derivative of a prior "Saying" on the part of Being, a Saying in which the poet, who "listens" to Being, engages. Heidegger claims that "language speaks" (OWL 124).[6] "Language" thus, for Heidegger, refers to the revealing and concealing that belongs to the Being of things as their relation to presence and absence; language, as the name for this process that precedes predication or postulation, is indeed not *directed* by speaking subjects even if it is related to human speaking. As Heidegger puts it, "speaking must have speakers, but not merely in the same way as an effect must have a cause" (OWL 120). We might engage in revealing things by virtue of our speaking, but the fact of revealing itself—that things can be revealed and also concealed in and by language, does not belong to us (OWL 125). In this sense, poetry is more "essential" simply in that it makes obvious its own process of revealing, and its own relation to the sensual—or to the emerging-into-appearance of nature—whereas other kinds of speaking or discourse do not. The word "essentially" does not exhaust or possess the thing to which it refers, that which it "reveals," but brings it to presence or "nearness" (OWL 86). Thus "the essential Being of language is Saying as Showing" (OWL 123).

Kristeva's theory follows Heidegger in criticizing language as the expression of meaning on the part of a self-possessed, intentional subject, and she lingers on the fact that poetry does indeed illuminate the musicality and sensuality of language, which exceeds—or in Kristeva's case precedes—categories of "meaning" and the "contents" of a subjective intention. Poetry contains within it a "heterogeneousness" to meaning and signification, which characterize the "disposition" of other kinds of language (DL 133). While Heidegger grants primacy and primordiality to the fact that language has an ontological function—as he argues, that it founds things in their Being (OWL 86–87), that "the word alone gives Being to the thing" (OWL 62)—Kristeva emphasizes the relation of language to social structures, and thus the subject must be understood in a social context.

Thus Kristeva's analysis diverges from the ontological account; the "unsayable," which for Kristeva, like Heidegger, underlies all saying, is tied up with the bodily and social grounds of speaking. Kristeva must explain why discourse is not only the "play" of signification, nor the logical/mathematical structures hidden in language (as in theories of generative grammar), nor even the process of disclosure that Heidegger has shown language to be, but an act that legislates and structures social relations, and thus the political, cultural, and symbolic sphere at large. Language is, for Kristeva, a practice. To exclude the "thetic" or thesis/judgment-positing character of the subject of language—even in favor of the ontological "unsaid"—is also to ignore the "constraining, legislative, and socializing elements" of language (DL 131). Following Husserl, Kristeva wants to maintain a subject who utters; following structuralism and Heidegger, she does not want to reduce utterance—in a text or a language—to a "single" meaning, a singular "thesis" that could be "meant" (DL 127). But what comes before the subject to condition it—bodily, social, and familial factors, psychological drives—indeed what also breaks down its thetic autonomy, is illuminated in poetic language. If Heidegger's *Gelassenheit* is issued as ontological rejection of the subject, Kristeva's analysis proceeds through the subject toward what exceeds, forms, and destabilizes it.

The reasons for Kristeva's turn to poetic language become clear as soon as we define poetic language as Kristeva understands it. In contrast to Heidegger, for whom poetic language is not a subjective practice[7] but an ontological "saying," Kristeva calls poetic language "a particular signifying practice" (DL 124). This practice is, "through the particularity of its signifying operations, an unsettling process — when not an outright destruction — of the identity of [a] meaning and speaking subject" (DL 125). Poetic language is distinct from ordinary language in that it is, though socially communicative, not exclusively an attempt at communication, which aims at conveying a meaning; poetic language involves, rather, a heterogeneity to meaning. This is not to claim that poetic language is meaningless, but that it is plurisignificant, resisting a singular and fixed meaning that would correspond to a subject's discrete intention. In poetic signifying, a thetic rupture is introduced into signification, one that compromises the exclusivity of meaning from what is other to it.

The difference between poetic and other signifying practices is seen in their relation to what Kristeva, in the wake of Lacanian psychoanalysis, calls the semiotic and symbolic elements of language. While for traditional psychoanalysis language begins in the transfer (via the Oedipal stage) to the paternal realm of the symbolic (or law/ discourse), Kristeva argues that language contains both symbolic — post-Oedipal — and semiotic — pre-Oedipal — elements. For her the semiotic is "obviously inseparable from a theory of the subject that takes into account the Freudian positing of the unconscious" (RPL 30). But the relation between the semiotic and the symbolic is already an effect of the pre-linguistic relation, of self-other within the family, biological processes, and sexuality: it both generates and negates the subject at once (RPL 30). Kristeva undermines traditional psychoanalysis by arguing that the maternal phase — according to Freud/Lacan, pre-linguistic — already contains symbolic elements; and that the symbolic, paternal phase, is interrupted in particular practices (such as poetic ones) by the semiotic.[8] In all language practices, the semiotic — drives and the articulation of drives in rhythm, condensation, and disruption — and symbolic — proposition, judgment — are "inseparable" from one another.

Kristeva's definitions might be useful here. For Kristeva "the symbolic [le symbolique], as opposed to the semiotic, is [the] inevitable attribute of meaning, sign, and the signified object for the consciousness of Husserl's transcendental ego" (DL 134). The symbolic is comprehensible within traditional theories of language as expression. The semiotic, contrarily,

is not that of meaning or signification . . . We shall call this disposition semiotic [le sémiotique], meaning, according to the Greek sémeion, a distinctive mark, trace, index, the premonitory sign, the proof, engraved mark, imprint—in short, a *distinctiveness* admitting of an uncertain and indeterminate articulation because it does not yet refer . . . or no longer refers . . . to a signified object for a thetic consciousness. . . . [This is] a disposition that is definitely heterogeneous to meaning but always in sight of it either in a negative or surplus relationship to it. (DL 133)

Because, according to Kristeva, all language presupposes these two "dispositions," different kinds of language are distinguished in their combining "in different ways to constitute *types of discourse*, types of signifying practices" (DL 134). The thetic phase is the break between the semiotic and the symbolic: the point wherein the symbolic, in order to posit a transcendental signified—a universal, a law, a univocal proposition—suppresses the semiotic element. The thetic is the "threshold of language" because it suppresses the surplus to judgment or meaning (RPL 45).

The difference between kinds of signifying practices is a matter of disposition, the relation between the semiotic and symbolic with regard to the thetic break that secures their separation. The "possibilities of truth specific to language" are conditioned by the thetic; true and false, and the boundary between them, are guaranteed by the thetic posture (RPL 58). Like Valéry in "Poetry and Abstract Thought,"[9] Kristeva contrasts kinds of discourse—scientific and poetic. The former "tends to reduce as much as possible the semiotic component," in "aspiring to the status of a metalanguage" (DL 134), just as everyday speech ignores, in Valéry's terms, the " strange resistance" of words to the transparent function of meanings.[10] Valéry, like Heidegger, suggests that in poetry, in the word's loss of communicative clarity, its nature becomes apparent. If in everyday speaking, or in abstract discourse of logic and science, the word "was only a means," in poetry the word is pronounced as an end in itself. For Valéry, the word is "an end, the object of a terrible philosophical desire. It turns into an enigma, an abyss, a torment of thought."[11] It is this torment with which Heidegger's ontological insights about poetic language contend, for in Heidegger the word's capacity to name or reveal (*entbergen*)—that it slips out of our alleged possession—points to the resistance of language to metaphysics. What for Valéry is the "true nature" of words revealed in poetry—their capacity to name, carry meanings, but also slide in and out of ambiguity, adjust themselves to new contexts and to each other—belongs for Heidegger to the essence of language as "showing." Does not this showing—to which the poet or dweller or thinker, listening to poetry, answers with *Gelassenheit*—precisely a putting the subject of utterance into question? All the same, Valéry's point of view does not leave the subject behind as Heidegger would prefer. Valéry's understanding of poetic creation is issued in an almost Cartesian phenomenology of how poetry and abstract thoughts each come into being.

Yet for Valéry and for Heidegger, it is the materiality (Heidegger says the "earthiness") that lets language be experienced properly, which unties it from a fixed meaning and thereby makes apparent how meaning comes to occur. In the expression theory of language and in our quotidian experience of language we pass through the word "without weighing on it"; the word seems to disappear into the world of a speaker so that language, as Valéry claims, seems to be "the negation of itself."[12] As Heidegger writes, "only because in everyday speaking language does not bring itself to language but holds back, are we able to simply go ahead and speak a language, and so to deal with something and negotiate something by speaking" (OWL 59). Yet in poetry the "physical element of language, its vocal and written character, is more adequately expressed" (OWL 98). The materiality of language comes to the fore only when our speaking as expression is called into question. Language, for Valéry, thus "gives itself as language . . . by way of contrast, or countering, that is, in and through the difference between modes of speaking."[13] In this difference the materiality of language becomes apparent. For Heidegger the "kinship between song and speech" (OWL 98) is its relation to earth, which again becomes apparent especially when language becomes "foreign." Translation of poetry, too—a philosophical topic considered by Hölderlin and Heidegger, as well as Kristeva and Benjamin—highlights an experience of this materiality, for instance when the phonic substrate and its rhythms offers resistance to absolute transparency in another language. In a semiotic account, this materiality is associated with "the archaisms of the semiotic body" (DL 136). In Kristeva's economy, the semiotic "tends to gain the upper hand at the expense of the thetic and predicative constraints of the ego's judging consciousness" (DL 134). Kristeva describes this gaining "the upper hand" as a return to the (maternal) sensuous, rhythmic elements of language in a break with, and a breaking up of, the thetic postulation of meaning that belongs to Husserl's transcendental ego. This is the rupture that "makes the meaning of the utterance undecidable" (DL 134). In that poetic language nevertheless retains, though compromised, a symbolic function, it is spared from being mere nonsense, psychosis, or worse.

For Kristeva, the semiotic processes—the ringing, hovering, trembling, tracing of language and the drives of the psychic-social body—are released in poetic language and its "unsettled and questionable subject." The semiotic processes in poetic language do not trail off into nonsense, are "far from being set adrift" (DL 134–135). Rather, they are the "never-finished undefined production of a new space of significance. Husserl's 'thetic function' of the signifying act is thus reassumed, but in different form." Poetry "unsettles" the signifying ego, unsettles the signified; but it "nevertheless posits a thesis, not of a particular being or meaning, but . . . [of] its own process as an undecidable process between sense and nonsense, between *language* and *rhythm*, between the semiotic and the symbolic" (DL 135). It is as this undecidability, this showing process as process—as Heidegger would say, language revealing itself, but for Kristeva not reducible to Being's narrative or history—that poetry gains a revolutionary character. Poetry transgresses the thetic in "crossing the boundary between true and false." It tends, as Kristeva puts it, "to prevent the thetic from becoming theological," which means that it prevents the law, the universal, the transcendental signified in its fixation and stasis, from "hiding" its origins in the fluctuating semiotic that produces them. Poetry thus bars the thetic "from inducing the subject . . . to function solely within the systems of science and monotheistic religion," (RPL 58–59) escaping the metaphysics of "onto-theology" that Heidegger has deconstructed. If Being cannot be formulated as the content of a "said," poetry illuminates Being's ineffability by disclosing what language is for the one who speaks.

With the exception of the possibilities afforded by the maternal semiotic, Kristeva's analysis of poetry's revolutionary character and its materiality remains primarily negative, having a critical but not also utopian character. By excluding poetry from the realm of knowledge, Kristeva manages to secure poetry a radical and even primordial position, but leaves as its positive substrate only the Freudian drives and their relation to the semiotic body, the reproduction or reconfiguration of the maternal realm wherein alterity rests within immanence (I will discuss the problem of alterity later in this chapter). Poetry's transcendence, its capacity to engender and create, to preserve and indeed to tenuously encircle truth, is eclipsed by its negativity and its releasement of the already given relationship between the body and law. Poetry is relegated to the passage between realms of rhythm and symbol, breaking and shattering, remainder of the already posited drives. Any further level of significance, a meaning different in kind from singular thetic postulation, is lost in the negative dimension of poetic utterance or is reduced to pre-given drives mapped upon the body politic and its unconscious. Prominently lacking here, I argue, is the nature of the spontaneity within poetic creation. For, exceeding the release of drives and the rhythms of the body, a new level of significance comes into being when a work of art, in our case a poem, is composed. This creation, related to transcendence or transformation as I described at the beginning of this chapter, indicates poetry's phenomenological and ontological relevance.

This relevance has two dimensions: first, creation signifies both a new, initiated (previously nonexistent) level of meaning—the world of its "truth"—and a shelter for the world and the factical life that it transforms in the language of images. Second, the poetic imaginary is paradoxically self-referential even as it borrows from the world, indicating its own provisionality. The poem both services the recognizable world that shimmers within it by virtue of the image and creates a new "world" to which those elements now belong, adjusted to wholly different measures of truth and falsity, reality and illusion. Both of these elements need to be thought in their relation to spontaneity of the poetic subject. I will visit this theme in the next chapter in suggesting a notion of freedom within a new poetics of Dasein.

Despite these limitations, Kristeva's view of language assists our consideration of the relation between the poet and alterity. In this regard, let us take a closer look at her theory in connection with Hölderlin's poetics. In *Revolution in Poetic Language,* Kristeva outlines several features of poetic language (and here she includes also myth and art) that function to call into question the stability of the thetic—and thus of postulation. Four are of importance here in indicating alterity:

1. The semiotic disposition of poetic language releases a "remainder" to postulation, one that, in rhythm, recalls the drives that produce and infect the subject of speaking, drives that are repressed in the symbolic disposition (RPL 51).

2. Poetry's relation to *mimesis* calls into question the stability of the transcendental signified; it produces a repetition that no longer refers to an "object identifiable outside language," but rather one produced within it. More than "classical mimesis," poetic language in modernity, Kristeva argues, "not only attacks denotation (the positing of the object) but meaning (the positing of the enunciating subject) as well" (RPL 57–58) because it "pluralizes denotation" and at the same time challenges the one who signifies (RPL 59). Mimesis "dissolves" (RPL 57) denotative function by pluralizing it. (This suggests another way to address Hölderlin's proliferation of names for Being and the gods.)

3. Poetry uses syntax but involves a noncompletion or ellipsis of syntax; it "involves both shattering and maintaining position within the heterogeneous process." (Is the eccentric path not such a shattering and maintenance at once?) This prevents the "other" from being posited as an identifiable syntactic term; "alterity is maintained," for the other "will not remain fixed in place." (Being is for Hölderlin difference in this sense, as resistant to the gathering of meaning except in longing after its dispersion). This noncompletion of syntax does not make the forming of sentences impossible,[14] but the sentence is "infinitized" (RPL 56).

4. Intertextuality, the "passage" from one system of signs into another, suggests alterity by refusing the stabilization of genre (RPL 59). (In Hölderlin one finds the interweaving of translation and poetizing, philosophical essay and poetic discourse, drama and poetry, letter and narrative.) This, Kristeva argues, functions to undermine the function of discourse as dominated by the concern for knowledge, because it continually alters the thetic position, shifting it from one economy to another. The denoted "object" of enunciation is prevented from identity and completion, and is rather "always plural, shattered" (RPL 59). Thus particularly revolutionary is modern literature (RPL 57), which is seen to cross boundaries between narrative, poetry, and scholarly discourse — as in romanticism's concern for a prose become poetic, for a philosophy become poetry, articulated explicitly in Schlegel's fragments. The narrative of Hölderlin's *Hyperion* (which Hölderlin also attempted in verse) shifts among epistle, novel, and philosophical dialogue.[15] Poetic practice is not in Kristeva's theory confined to verse; though for Hölderlin it should follow rigorous laws (a "lawlike calculus"), this is defined not classically but according to the movements of tracing an unnamable ideal in an "alteration of tones."

Although, as I indicate, connections can be traced between these features of poetic language and the practices of Hölderlin, a difference must nevertheless be asserted: the latter preserves, in formal calculus, the significance of utopian creation, even if that postulation is always indirect in nature, always tentative. Mimetic dissolution, remainder, noncompletion of syntax and refusal of singular genre indeed denote some characteristics of poetic language in its surplus beyond the absolutely defined, but they do not yet afford it an ontological role. While I have argued against Heidegger's notion of ontological poetic "founding," the tenuous and analeptic poetic subject maintains a nonetheless initiating and preserving ontological intervention, even if that relationship is itself subject to destabilization at the moment of utterance and is thus characterizable as receptive. Moreover, the multiplicity of genre in Hölderlin does not resist knowledge but reconfigures its form and purpose according to poetic subjectivity.

Nonetheless, it is worth attending to the aforementioned features of poetic language, among others, insofar as they destabilize univocal truth-claims and *introduce alterity into categorical meaning.* For Kristeva, poetry is a dialectic within the symbolic; it maintains meaning but introduces its pluralization. It takes place not within the chora of the semiotic but enacts a dialectic between semiotic and symbolic dimensions of language; the thetic is neither negated nor rendered absolute but involved in this paradoxical dialectic, revealing and reenacting the heterogeneous contradiction within the subject itself (RPL 82). It is literature, specifically modern literature, that for Kristeva illuminates this contradiction (RPL 82), which moved beyond both "madness and realism in a leap that maintains both 'delirium' and 'logic.'" Kristeva names Joyce and Bataille as "emblems" of the "test of the subject's dialectic," but she names Hölderlin, as does Adorno, at the incipience of this dimension of modernity (RPL 82). The entrance of *jouissance* into language is also the pluralization of any *telos* within the logical or even social order. For Hölderlin this is not the destruction of dialectic but its infinitization, the inscription of *telos* as infinitely deferred; loss, as Adorno argues, "has migrated into the concept" with Hölderlin. Yet loss is conditioned by the always striven-for utopian possibility; for most of his poetry, the deferral of *telos* is not its abandonment but its paradoxically impossible inscription. The poetic subject, as I have argued in earlier chapters, is not characterized by shattering but by analepsis.

Nevertheless, we accept to a certain extent this revolutionary character—insofar as it undermines the seeming givenness of institutionality—as occurring at its ground within the subject of utterance or the practice of enunciation itself.[16] Poetry puts the "subject in process/on trial" (*en procès*). The subject is no longer conceivable as the transcendental ego, postulating categorical articulations as the "objectivity" of a rational or structural-transcendental divorce from the empirical, bodily, social grounds of its existence. The transcendental ego is, in poetic language, decentered (RPL 30). Illuminated by poetic practices, the subject can no longer maintain its stability and identity vis-à-vis a likewise stable and identified transcendent "object" of reference—for example, mathematical or logical truth, God or Being. Because, as Husserl shows, judgment is dependent upon language, and, as Kristeva shows, language issues from the semiotic economy as well as from the symbolic, the knowledge of the speaking subject is itself guaranteed no autonomy from elements of alterity that precede and haunt it. Poetic language also opens us to the world of beings to which the poet inexhaustively attends and that it can never finally or univocally encapsulate. Poetic Dasein is an existence exposed to the otherness of that with which it tarries. One might call this a strange *Gelassenheit*, related to Blanchot's notion of "exile"(without, however, the absolute nature of that exile, as I have argued earlier in this book), related, then, to what Heidegger has named the "uncanny" or "being-not-at-home." At the time of *Revolution in Poetic Language*, Kristeva links this revolution in the speaking subject to political revolution: it is a release of the Other, of difference and differences, from the domination of the same. "Revolutionary subjects" are produced by revolutionary texts; the "law" within the symbolic is "renovated" by poetic language which makes apparent the (non-Hegelian)[17] "dialectical movement of the generating of significance" (RPL 164). But for Hölderlin the negating character of poetic language communes with its positive significance: a sheltering and preserving access to the "feeling of life." What Hölderlin denotes by "life," again, exceeds Kristeva's account of semiotic drives and their material substrate. Nor does life merely denote "nature" or the natural basis of subjectivity. "Life" is both immanent and transcendent, if that immanence is understood provisionally and that transcendence precarious; "life" involves spontaneity and freedom, for which a theory of drives and the law and its rupture is, I think, inadequate to account.

Hölderlin's Revolution: "Wandering" and Accident

In his letters and essays, Hölderlin grants poetic language a revolutionary role. Philosophy to become poetry, he declares with the young Hegel and Schelling, who along with Hölderlin observe from a close distance the events of the French Revolution and attempt to articulate an idea of freedom that would counter the absolutism with which the then local territories of Germany were ruled. Hölderlin's disappointment with the outcome of that revolution is documented in both Pierre Bertaux's study *Hölderlin und die französische Revolution* and in Georg Lukács's essay on *Hyperion;* both maintain, with Adorno, that Hölderlin's revolutionary ideals are "utopian." If freedom had to be established in thought, it must also be for Hölderlin a harmonious one. Hölderlin aims at a revolution in thinking and feeling, one that affords a nonlegislative relation to nature and a reverence for the "feeling of life." Like the French revolutionaries who invented their own religion, Hölderlin articulates a poetic one, as he writes in the essay "On Religion"—and in fact argues that any "religion" that refuses totalitarian sameness, that maintains plurality, maintains its roots in the "concrete and particular," diverse relations in which people live and exist. Religion, as the "varying representations" of these relations, is thus to be "poetic in its essence" (ELT 94).

Hölderlin's revolution is then a revolution in language, and even this revolutionary religion is built upon various representations of the feelings that exceed the mechanistic order—or systematic ordering—of things. That philosophy is to become poetry is articulated in Hölderlin's turn from philosophical studies—particularly those of Kant and Fichte—to the writing of poetry, and to writing essays, letters, and aphorisms on the form, task, and significance of poetry. If the Enlightenment, brought to Germany with Kant, had failed to offer political liberation, it furthermore did not yet question relations of domination between the subject and its other, specifically nature, nor did it grasp the very ungroundability of freedom. If the transcendental subject is to be unified, as Kant demands, this unification sets up a legislative totality vis-à-vis the object, the subject's "other"—or, in subjective idealism, wholly absorbs it. Hölderlin argues, instead, that we need to dissolve this opposition between "subject and object, self and world." The subject must become "receptive" (ELT 69).

In previous chapters I have discussed Hölderlin's poetological claims, which we might review here in brief. In two essay fragments, "On the Law of Freedom" and "On the Concept of Punishment," Hölderlin attempts to show that the transcendental subject cannot be unified a priori but is dependent upon "accident," and that the moral subject of reason is, furthermore, dependent not upon reason but what he refers to as "instinct"—which admits a radical dependence of the subject upon its "world." (Instinct is not to be interpreted as in evolutionary theory, but rather as a kind of intuitive receptivity that is not subject to the laws of cognition). In the fragment "Judgment and Being" it seems that Hölderlin argues that the identity of the transcendental subject admits difference within itself, that synthesis, on which the transcendental-rational subject is based, admits a gap for which theory cannot account. Judgment, like language, is not the "synthesis" of subject and object but its division, an original separation (*Urtheil*), one that leaves Being—their unity—ungraspable by philosophy. This is Hölderlin's epistemological, but also his ontological, skepticism. In admitting the gap between subject and world—indeed within the subject itself—Hölderlin shelters the "world," or nature, from the tyranny of the subject—one symbolized by the attempt of Empedocles to exhaust and divulge nature's secrets. While Hölderlin challenges the sovereignty of reason, his poetics is not principally negative: "revolution" aims at democratic "human harmony," peaceful diversity in a utopian "celebration of life as such" rather than catharsis of violent social drives. Hölderlin, unlike Kristeva, does not abandon transcendence as the ultimate goal of poetry in favor of the earthly material origins of language; rather, he reconfigures transcendence within poetical, rather than cognitive, terms.

Hölderlin's attendance to the "aesthetic idea" is important here: the only possible reconciliation of oppositions cannot be a dialectical, progressive synthesis aiming at a strictly defined, conceptually accessible *telos*, but rather the indirect *Gelassenheit* of poetic reception. This reconciliation takes several forms in Hölderlin's writings. Yet in each dimension thereof, it is poetic language as such that promises a liberation of the subject from its legislative role and the object from this legislation. For poetic language acknowledges explicitly that the "soul of the world" cannot be fastened onto by rational means, which "names" a transcendent signified (as in Kant's regulative ideals, themselves objects of a *focus imaginarius*), nor by a singular ideology or a monotheistic religion, but can be expressed only indirectly, in what Hölderlin calls an "askew perspective," an "eccentric path," a "paradox." Hölderlin thus employs many names for what Heidegger calls "Being" or the *Ereignis* or the *es gibt*, and this grounds Heidegger's discovery in Hölderlin that Being resists being said or formulated, that it is always-already *elusive*. But for Hölderlin, poetic language furthermore admits and emerges out of the gap in the subject—the subject's failure to be unified—and finds therein the indirect, and infinitely deferred, promise of reconciliation in the paradoxical acknowledgment of loss. Hölderlin argues that poetic language admits of a "lawlike calculus" that nevertheless cannot grasp what is to be said directly. What Kristeva calls "law" is infused with accident or contingency, and in the poetic context this signifies a placeholder for spontaneity and freedom.

So while Kristeva's notion of poetry wholly repudiates "knowledge," Hölderlin's skepticism poeticizes it. Where necessity ought be found, we find accident, and thus the knowledge/power collaboration is broken up. In addition to accident, there is in Hölderlin a persistent insinuation of loss. If the poetic subject is structured by the jointures of knowledge and accident, knowledge and loss, here is the site of *Gelassenheit* receptivity. Poetry, Kristeva writes, is a departure from knowledge and certainty, and it is this departure that, she claims in a single concluding remark of her essay "From One Identity to Another," was discovered in Hölderlin (DL 145). Yet knowledge for Hölderlin is always-already uncertain, since judgment is founded upon the "original separation." Knowledge is already poetical, proceeding, much like Kierkegaard's "indirect discourse," in an indirect access to what transcends the subject. Knowledge does not refuse alterity but is conditioned by it.

Hölderlin gives his most complete treatment of the form of poetic language in the essays "Operations in the Poetic Spirit" and "Ground for Empedocles." The former takes the aesthetic idea as its departure and argues that poetic reflection—a receptivity (ELT 69) to the "feeling of life" (in nature) on the part of the subject, and not the subject's legislative cognition—is the ground of language (ELT 81). For Hölderlin, poetic language admits the radical interdependence of self upon its other that grounds all language. Poetry, rather than suppressing this dependence, brings it into language in form. If Hölderlin calls this form the "lawlike calculus," it is, as "askew," not identical to law but the inversion of law. This is why Adorno finds in Hölderlin the "sacrifice of the legislative subject." While Adorno locates this in what he thinks is the form of Hölderlin's "paratactical" late poems, Hölderlin's own essays lay theoretical groundwork toward the same conclusion. The problem of opposition between self and other, subject and object, is treated in tragedy, wherein Hölderlin finds that the hubris of identification with the "other" in the realm of language provokes the downfall of the subject.

For Kristeva, the self must acknowledge, or at very least, undergo, the fact that it is already inhabited by its "other," a theme she investigates in *Strangers to Ourselves*. The problem of self-other concerns Hölderlin, who, as Kristeva writes of the semiotic activity, "introduces wandering . . . into language"; in his view, articulated to some extent in the Böhlendorff letter of 1801, only in an encounter with the foreign could one properly understand, or come to terms with, the familiar—and even this homecoming is not guaranteed. As we will see, this is not the appropriation of the other by the same, but an opening of self to alterity such that the self becomes "a sign" without static referent. (In "Mnemosyne," Hölderlin writes: "A sign we are, meaningless / . . . and we have almost / lost our language in a foreign land.")[18] It has been argued that Hölderlin's poems treat more of exile than they do of the return home—of homeless wandering and the "displacement of system" vis-à-vis the idealist dialectic, which aims at arrival.[19] One can see this thematized explicitly in the broken-up narrative of *Hyperion*, whose title character wanders from Germany to Greece to Germany without ever arriving, without final destination.

Hölderlin's writings examine the traumatic nature of proximity to otherness. Hölderlin, whose subject is condemned to distance by virtue of judgment and language, attempts to show the dangers of presuming a direct, graspable access to what is other. This assumption of distance occurs in self-consciousness, and the breach thereof is in the poem the caesura, which Hölderlin defines as a "counterrhythmic rupture." Repression of the lost, precognitive, harmonious and interdependent relation to what he refers to repeatedly as "mother earth" is rescinded. Yet direct access of consciousness to what is other — nature, the foreign, the sacred — is a dangerous matter. For if one does not accept the paradox of proximity within distance, one commits the tragic error of not knowing one's limits; one becomes a tyrant when one fails to recognize alterity as such, as unsayable. The caesura is manifested by Sophocles in *Oedipus the King* with the speech of Tiresias, who indicates the convergence of sameness and otherness with the announcement that the murderer (of Laius) is native, "lives with us," and is here, heretofore unknown, "as stranger" (ELT 104). Oedipus, of course, is both father and brother, son and husband, pursuer of a murderer and murderer at once. But Hölderlin defines the caesura not only according to a sequence of events, but also to the function of the word: it is the "pure word" which brings to light the violence that consciousness, as an "all-knowing, all-interpreting drive," ends up wielding not only against nature but also against itself in a calamitous proximity. The pure word recalls Valéry's "torment." Hölderlin links the caesuric rupture to the "insane questioning for a consciousness" (ELT 105).

Rupture: Effraction and Caesura

We turn again to the notion of the thetic rupture that is issued in poetic signifying acts. The thetic rupture in Kristeva is the breach of the boundary between semiotic and symbolic, maternal body and paternal law, that occurs in poetic language and instigates a "sacrifice" of meaning. But we ask now about the dangers of this rupture. If poetry is for Kristeva and Hölderlin the release of otherness, of alterity, into language, how are psychosis, suicide, and violent drives to be related to poetry as is suggested in both accounts?[20] What are we to make of the fact that Kristeva associates the semiotic and its "tendency to dissolve the logical order" (RPL 97) with violence? This is problematic particularly in light of the ambiguity of Heidegger's reception of Hölderlin, a discussion of which introduced this book and the political implications of which were treated in chapter 5. In the latter I argued against Lacoue-Labarthe's association of the tragic caesura and the *Ereignis* with the heinous violence of recent German history. Even so, this ambiguity is characterized by, on one hand, a proposal for poetic dwelling in *Gelassenheit* and, on the other, an "originary violence" and a violent founding of truth. A new poetics of Dasein takes root within a solution to this difficulty.

Although I have suggested that Hölderlin's poetics is incompatible with violent founding, the notion of revolution, and Hölderlin's insistence on the radical rupture of the caesura, justify a further scrutiny of the problem. Is there, as Kristeva suggests, an inherent relationship between poetic language — its revolutionary character — and violence? First we distinguish Kristeva's revolutionary, poetic language from her notion of "abject literature," which appears in *Powers of Horror* (1980) six years after the publication of *Revolution in Poetic Language*. "Abject literature" is that which releases the repressed "maternal" or semiotic into language — instinctual, Dionysian drives that Kristeva understands as violent and that she links to fascism. Abject literature, like poetic language, "calls into question language itself, along with the authority of the subject," and its function is to provide an aesthetic catharsis of these drives by releasing them into, rather than repressing them in, language.[21] Kristeva has been criticized for celebrating abject literature — for example the anti-Semitic writings of Louis-Ferdinand Céline (DL 145) — which, she argues, provides a "defense," by virtue of cathartic release, against "negative drives." Kristeva seems to locate the source of "violent impulses," of fascist drives,[22] in the maternal semiotic rather than in the postulation and repression of the paternal symbolic's power, thereby reinscribing an interpretation of fascism as cultural hysteria (rather than in terms of grossly misdirected, but still "masculine," calculation; in my view it is no doubt both). This understanding of fascism as hysteria attempts to make sense of the irrational nature of its violence, but ignores the very concrete advantages (such as economic ones) that are calculated and enjoyed by direct or indirect perpetrators. It remains to be articulated in what ways rationality itself can be complicit in mass violence. For even Kant, despite his strict ethics and his humanitarian view of freedom as autonomy, defends forms of violence, such as war and social inequity, on the basis of a teleological view of natural purpose, as I discussed in chapter 5. An articulation of this problem is beyond the scope of my project here, but it is relevant in what way Kristeva ascribes violence to the semiotic realm. Abject literature provides an aesthetic catharsis of semiotic violence that supposedly prevents actual violence. Not only Nietzsche, on whom Kristeva draws, but also Aristotle wondered about the pleasure associated with witnessing gruesome events in mimetic representation (though not in actuality) — the "wounding, maiming, and the like" that define calamity or catastrophe in tragic poetry. But Kristeva's view here is problematic in that her understanding of catharsis is again one-sidedly negative; we note that Aristotle defined *catharsis* according to the tragic emotions of both fear, *phobos*, and pity, *eleos*. Catharsis involves pleasure in not only mimetic suffering but also in sympathy the spectator feels for the character with whom he or she identifies. In tragic poetry, according to Aristotle, one has a special insight into possibility — what could happen — from which the spectator receives a special benefit. Hölderlin's poetics, furthermore, it is not the (semiotic) challenge to truth-claims but the (symbolic) demand for universal truth that invokes violence. Upsetting the paternal law (as does Antigone) perhaps releases the violence of that law from its symbolic containment, but the violence issued not from what is other to this law but from the law itself. Mass violence is often linked to the hysterical "feminine." Yet I would argue that the psychology of fascism involves perhaps rather obsessive and fixed identification with the paternal figure rather than the release of the maternal "irrational" underlying the symbolic. Release of the semiotic drives, in Kristeva's own theory, is a release of differences, and not, like fascism, a sober, constructed, highly calculated, and, as it was historically enacted in Europe, materially advantageous hegemony of the "same" which violently expels, and exterminates, the "other."[23]

Moreover, *catharsis* does not figure as the leitmotiv of Hölderlin's theory of tragedy, which involves, rather, a warning against hubris on the part of the poet who is tempted to take up where transcendental knowledge left off.[24] Hölderlinian tragedy, while catastrophic, is in this sense incomparable to Dionysian fusion and its overcoming of Apollonian division, which for Nietzsche celebrates both pain and joy at once — dream, ecstasy, intoxication, and terror.[25] What Hölderlin calls "life" is decidedly not Dionysian, not "abject," for it does not celebrate what Nietzsche calls "contradiction, the bliss born of pain, that spoke out from the very heart of nature."[26] Tragedy has nothing to do with the resignation of Schopenhauer; it is linked not only to what Nietzsche calls "an abysmal and terrifying view of the world"[27] but also to "joy" and loss of joy — utter destitution — when the human being transgresses the boundaries of knowing and understanding. For Hölderlin "life" comprises opposing differences, yet ones that originate from — and are aesthetically to be directed back to — the primordial unity that any conscious being must presuppose. "Spirit," as the movement that issues from this unity, is not identical to a synthesis of opposites, for it is also always-already deferred and glimpsed only in "from an askew perspective" (ELT 116). As Hölderlin writes in the essay "Becoming in Dissolution," the "idealistic" dissolution of opposites appears "not as . . . death, but as a reviving, as growth . . . not as annihilating violence, but as love" (ELT 99).

I leave aside here Kristeva's notion of abject literature by noting finally that abject literature is in Kristeva's view not revolutionary, but rather, as catharsis, apolitical. Another emblem of the violence of poetic language in her theory, however, involves a poetic anthropology of sacrifice; sacrifice, in a semiotic reading, functions in the theologization of the thetic as the positing of violence (though not its celebration) — a positing that ensures the symbolic order, though precariously, by positing its boundary. Sacrifice in culture as examined by social anthropology is seen to be linked to poetry as an accompanying practice, as in the Dionysian festivals of ancient Greece. Here the representation preceding sacrifice in dance, art, and song is the "expenditure" (*dépense*) of semiotic drives that mimes the "sacrificial slaying" to come. This recalls our discussion, in the previous chapter, of the notion of sublime sacrifice. Kristeva thinks that the fact of mimicry or mimesis, and not what is mimed, is decisive, for this in some sense diffuses the delirium or fusion with nature (RPL 80) which precedes the setting-up of symbolic order. "Anthropology has shown that the social order is sacrificial, but sacrifice orders violence, tames it" (WT 204). Poetic practice, which precedes sacrifice, is a mimesis "of the movement of the symbolic economy." "By reproducing signifiers—vocal, gestural, verbal— the subject crosses the border of the symbolic and reaches the semiotic chora which is the other side of the social frontier" (RPL 79). This "other side" is released before the setting up of the symbolic limit. In Hölderlin's poetology, sacrifice appears as the consequence of hubris; and as a warning against hubris, sacrifice prevents the very "theologization" to which Kristeva refers. The poet is to name the gods, but only in an indirect, askew, subjunctive mode of longing, a naming that is to be understood neither literally nor with unchecked ontological license. Kristeva thinks that modern poetic language, though related to such ancient festival practices (song, dance, images), itself accepts to some degree the thetic posture that maintains the symbolic distinction that binds drives, fusion, and delirium against meaning, law, and order. Thus such language, insofar as it is mimetic—in representations of fusion—is no longer purely Dionysian in its opposition to the Apollonian principle. Hölderlin's discussion of sacrifice illuminates the violence involved in the rational-transcendental order as this same, prohibited, fusion relegated in Nietzsche to the realm of the Dionysian. Whereas Kristeva understands religion as an accomplice to the symbolic order (RPL 80), Hölderlin argues for attunement to a different, nontheological, religious "feeling of life" that cannot be expressed in symbolic-transcendental concepts, but at the same time requires poetic presentation (*Darstellung*) (ELT 90–95). Belonging to life and representation thereof are not for Hölderlin at odds—as in the Apollonian-Dionysian opposition—if the representations are poetic rather than principally rational.

In Hölderlin, sacrifice is represented in the realm of language as the implosion of the "word"—thus of the speaking subject—when it attempts union with its object. The subject disposes of itself at the apogee of this fusion; Hölderlin's notion of "sacrifice" is in this sense no release of violent drives, no catharsis, but the end of drives in the death of the subject who transgressed—a danger involved as much in the poet's proximity to the feeling of life as in the presumptions of the transcendental philosopher's violent, all-consuming rationality. If suicide is a violent end to violence, poetry is to teach the indirect, "eccentric path" to the "joy" of unity, the creative preservation of harmonious communal relations and the harmonious stance of the self vis-à-vis nature. Hölderlin nonetheless articulates the economy, that of tragedy, within which this violence is enacted, for violence is clearly one danger of consciousness when it forgets its limitations, when it attempts in concepts or heroic action the "intellectual intuition" that Fichte defined as the unity of subject and object. Hölderlin articulates the paradox as a matter of proximity and distance at once. In "Remarks on Antigone," Hölderlin thus relates poetry to death and madness; tragedy is, he insists, not merely the depiction of "suffering and wrath" but, as aforementioned, of "understanding as wandering below the unthinkable" (ELT 110). Thus Hölderlin praises the character Antigone for confronting the universal (and we add, paternal) law with the relativity of the moral law—just as, he writes, the sun's relation to earth is for us relative. This evasion of the universal Hölderlin calls "sacred madness" and claims that it is the "highest human manifestation." But it is "more soul than language," cannot take place fully in language because it is "consciousness which cancels consciousness": to make the god—or any higher law—present is not only commit blasphemy, but to deny the limitations of human consciousness, which always involves distance (ELT 111, 113). Thus "the god is present in the figure of death"

(ELT 113). Yet death itself is for Hölderlin beyond poetry; which is why Empedocles's protosuicidal striving "to be all things" ruins his poetic access to nature and robs the sign of its content. Nature, the ground of poetic inspiration, no longer speaks to him, and his suicide occurs in the wake of that loss; in the caesura, "the sign = 0." The intellectual intuition, of which the tragedy is a "metaphor," is impossible. As poet, within language and its "poetic logic," Hölderlin cannot celebrate "sacrifice" even if this is the ultimate end of the tragic rhythm (ELT 109). Eccentricity is demanded in Hölderlin as the consequence of the finitude engendered not principally by death, as in Heidegger (DI 28),[28] but by consciousness itself. While Heidegger rejects a principle of "life," along with idealism in general, to what degree Hölderlin is informed by this principle is not to be overlooked, even in its poetic reformulation. Hölderlin turns after *Empedocles* from tragic to hymnal poetry, which conjures the lost unity between soul and world in a mourning recollection; only as such is the ideal possible. Recollection or *Andenken* employs a mimetic indirectness that calls into question the postulating, thetic subject by multiplying the longed-for transcendent object. If this compromise of the thetic is associated with the unreason of madness, it is not the madness of an "original violence" but of the giving up of (thetic) positing altogether. However, and despite Hölderlin's own biography, the descent into madness is not the *telos* of his poetics, unless infinite deferral is judged by reason as that kind of irrationality. A new poetics, I argue, must sketch out a poetic subjectivity that does not circumscribe and predefine, within a drive theory, its immanent alterity, and thus entangle it within the conflicting drives of the repressed unconscious and their releasement into violence or madness. That which is "heterogeneous to meaning" for Hölderlin is not the equivalent of the instinctual economies of which Kristeva writes, but rather includes a receptivity to harmony, joy, freedom; even loss and mourning, since they are invested with accident, serve as the locus for spontaneity, evading conceptual predetermination.

Yet we can say that if poetic language is revolutionary, if it puts the subject on trial, into crisis, it reveals the loss of any fixed identity, individual or collective. If the self has no inalienable essence — if Dasein wins no "totality" in resoluteness — neither does a cultural *Volk*. The common thread of consequence of the views of Kristeva and Hölderlin is that we cannot, as speaking subjects, rightfully presume a stable, static essence or identity, possession of that identity, or demand a truth founded by the poet's saying. Kristeva argues that poetic language discovers, opens out upon a "different subject" (DL 97), a "particular subject," "shattered," and nevertheless "coherent." Poetic language, Kristeva argues, might "condense the shattering of the subject, as well as that of society, into a new apportionment of relationships between the symbolic and the real, the subjective and the objective" (DL 93). Yet these new relationships ought to be examined in terms of the preserving-creative spontaneity of poetic freedom that is unaccounted for in Kristeva's acceptance of the Freudian drive theory; for the latter there can be no "feeling of life" that is not submerged in the semiotic morass of drives that prefigure and prearticulate the formation of law. Kristeva's poetics, despite its limitations, provides the model for a politics of difference, and, for the subject, "a productive but always only provisional identity, an identity whose constant companions are alterity, negation, and difference."[29] Yet Kristeva's account is limited in that poetry's production must be conceived as the liberated repressed; it is already foreseen, in being excluded from it, by the law of the symbolic. Beyond Kristeva, a new poetics of Dasein must unify the provisional identity of the poetic subject with the possibility of positive spontaneous creation, with truths that are provisional within the poetic imaginary, with preservation that does not equal institution.

The Foreign and the Proper: Alterity and Poetic Language

The new poetics for which I aim in this book relies on the notion of a provisional identity for the subject of poetic language: an identity that admits loss, mourning, rupture, and incompleteness even as it aims for or is receptive of joy, harmony, and the feeling of life. There is always something "other," something transcendent, something that is neither of the subject nor absorbable by the subject, to which the subject is receptive, and which the subject finds within its own sphere of immanence. This alterity signifies the loss of absolute foundation, since it cannot be positively identified, cannot be appropriated, though it can be fostered, preserved, and sheltered. This alterity is of the order of the mysteries, uncertainties, and doubts to which Keats referred, and of the correlative reenchantment of the world that poetry promises. Contrary to Hegel, the world does not yield entirely to the gaze of rational cognition but remains mysterious. In what way is this otherness a necessary correlative to the subject's abandonment of legislative power, vis-à-vis a world received or a meaning uttered? Is alterity an accomplice to *Gelassenheit?* Heidegger illuminates a dimension of poetic language upon which Kristeva centers her analysis—the problem raised in Hölderlin's Böhlendorff letter and in his interpretations of Antigone. In Heidegger it appears again and again, but particularly in his articulation of the "between" (*Zwischen*) the human being inhabits and of the uncanniness (*Unheimlichkeit*) which belongs to the human being endowed with language. For Heidegger, alterity issues in the interstice that unfolds between Being and beings, defined as the ontological difference. We will thus take a final look at Heidegger's poetics in the context of our reflections on alterity.

A discussion of alterity that does not confine it to the semiotic drives identified by psychoanalysis requires a new effort of imagining. Such an imagining begins with the discovery of what happens in poetic language as opposed to ordinary communication. This imagining, as a break from the prosaic attitude, is what the author has aimed for in her own poetic locutions, a discourse in which it is hoped that "the unsayable is suggested, encircled and, finally, magically uttered into existence."[30] Poetic imagining suggests that the world comprises both the actual and verifiable and the possible that reverberates beyond it. The poetical image thus shelters, in projective transformation, both the experienceable world and the receding other sides of things that render that experience negotiable, open to a formalized, thus not necessarily unbounded, multiplicity of possible or potential meanings.

In terms that recall Heidegger, Kristeva claims that poetic language opens our capacity to "listen," to recognize the "unspoken in all discourse" (ACW 156). Artistic-poetic practices are attempts "to break the code, to shatter language, to find a specific discourse closer to the body and emotions, to the unnamable repressed by the social contract" (WT 200). But again, in Kristeva's account, poetry's initiative is eclipsed by the notion of repression. Literature has the capacity to expose "the unsaid, the uncanny" (WT 207) below the social order, but the unsaid is wholly politically defined. It is not discussed in what way literature might transcend the social order by its deferred utopian creativity, nor what that unsaid might be outside the discourse of the semiotic drives. Even so, there is something compelling in her description of an identity that includes otherness, a "separation and coexistence of the self and of an other, of nature and consciousness" that can serve as "apprenticeship" in a gentle kind of self-forgetting (WT 206). The point is to acknowledge the flux of identity and difference as mutually challenging, shifting, and subverting; the subject does not appropriate and dismantle the alterity of the other but finds alterity within itself (SO 38). Kristeva suggests that such a subject would involve interiorization of the separations upon which the symbolic order is based (WT 210). Recalling Blanchot, again we find the notion of *exile* from subjectivity conventionally conceived, an exile associated with "excesses of the languages whose very multitude is the only sign of life, [where] one can attempt to bring out the multiple sublations of the unnamable, the unrepresentable, the void" (NTI 300).

In Heidegger, this "unnamable" is ontological and governs for the human being the "law of uncanniness." The unsaid, the uncanny, and the foreign of course all resound with the insights of Heidegger's theory of poetic language as articulated in his reading of Hölderlin, particularly in the "Der Ister" lecture course, which I have analyzed in previous chapters. Hölderlin's hymn and its "river" comprise a model for ecstatic, meandering time; they are likened by Heidegger to the "uncanniness" of Antigone, who wanders "outside" the polis, but who, Heidegger claims, also represents the polis. Uncanniness as Heidegger conceives it is the "essence" of the polis itself, and I analyzed in the previous chapter the problematic elements of Heidegger's treatment thereof as linked with violence. But Heidegger also treats the river poem and Antigone as models of "uncanniness" in the context of the relation between the "foreign" (∂aↄ Frem∂e) and the "proper" (∂aↄ Eigene) — both of which Heidegger reads according to his interpretation of the letter Hölderlin wrote, on the eve of his departure to France, to Casmir Böhlendorff in 1801 (ELT 149–151).[31] Given the relevance for a new poetics of the notion of alterity, we might elucidate further what Heidegger means by "the law of becoming unhomely."

This law is for Heidegger the uncanniness of the human being, but particularly of the poet, whose relation to Being, as we saw in chapter 3, is one of heightened proximity. Granted language, human beings are capable of disclosing beings, and thus of witnessing Being's own self-disclosure; the poet participates, according to the theory, in the "founding" (ↄtiften) of Being, just as the "technological" human being participates, by "forgetting" (vergeↄↄen), in its withdrawal. The poet is regarded as cast out into the "in between" of founding and forgetting, disclosure and withdrawal. Alienation from Being is also issued by the (groundless) ground of being able to say "Being," that is, to have a relation to Being. To have a relation to Being by virtue of language is itself paradoxical, for Being is the unsayable and the "unsaid" underlying all saying; yet Heidegger finds the "unsaid in what is said" in the case of essential poetry (DI 105). We have seen that for Hölderlin Being is not "arrived at" except as indicated indirectly, in endless deferral; it is "named" therefore in a self-refuting, subjunctive, and by his own account "paradoxical" sense. Heidegger allows the poet an access to Being via the naming-saying of the delivery of a "message" sent in the *Geschick*, as the retrieval of a trace, an echo, which must be communicated to a people. Here, we have seen, a difference is marked between Heidegger and Hölderlin on the function and task of the poetic word. While Hölderlin's understanding of the "unsayable" is indeed ontological, the poet's intervention is far more provisional and shot through with accident. But we have yet to examine in detail the problem of uncanniness itself, which saturates both theories of Heidegger and Hölderlin and dominates the "dialogue" (*Zwiesprache*) Heidegger establishes between them.

The human being's relation to language as a relation to Being cannot be extricated from finitude, which is one thread of uncanniness that separates human beings from all other beings. Finitude, which for Heidegger also conditions human freedom, is that uncanniness as a relation to Being—a theme which Heidegger establishes in *Being and Time* in the notion of being-towards-death, and which is reiterated during the next two decades in *Introduction to Metaphysics* and in the "Der Ister" lectures (DI 128). Yet whereas Hölderlin deals with the problem of death in his theory of tragedy, it is for Hölderlin, as aforementioned, not singularly death and the finitude of mortality but also, and perhaps even more significantly insofar as Hölderlin belongs to modernity, the finitude of consciousness and, in hubris, the "insane questioning for a consciousness" (ELT 105) which is the source of the human being's exile from the unity of life, the *hen kai pan*.[32] Consciousness pursued beyond its limits—toward the infinite, or the god—is associated with death.[33] Hölderlin links the two essays on Sophoclean tragedy in the "Remarks on Antigone" according to this motif:

> As has been hinted at in the remarks on "Oedipus," the tragic representation has as its premise that the immediate god is all at one with the human being . . . that the infinite enthusiasm conceives of itself infinitely, that is, in consciousness which cancels consciousness, separating itself in sacred manner, and that the god is present in the figure of death. (ELT 113)

The direct grasp of the divine is, then, "consciousness which cancels consciousness," or death.

Heidegger and Hölderlin both name this rift which is the human being—as mortal or conscious—an uncanny wandering; for both it is a matter of the relation between familiarity and unfamiliarity, between nearness and distance. But for Heidegger the *Ereignis* "gathers" the familiar and strange into a proper relation. For Heidegger the relation of the *Ereignis* and the mortal "occurs in and through language."[34] In language, we are cast out into the "foreign" as well as find the way to the "proper." Heidegger writes, "That which is unhomely [*das Unheimische*] is not merely the non-homely [*das Nicht-Heimische*], but rather that homely [*das Heimische*] that seeks and does not yet find itself, because it seeks by way of a distancing and alienation from itself" (DI 84).

Language is the seeking alienation, which recalls the *"exzentrische Bahn"* of Hölderlin's poet-figure, the "endless wanderer" Hyperion, and recalls the "askew perspective" of which Hölderlin writes in "Remarks on Antigone." In *Being and Time*, Dasein undergoes such a wandering, which is "lost" or "resolute" as *Verfallen* or in the state of *Entschlossenheit*. While Dasein is thrown, flees from itself (from its ownmost possibility in death), anticipatory resoluteness (*vorlaufende Entschlossenheit*) allows a "finding." Dasein "finds itself in the very depths of its uncanniness" by acknowledging its own finitude in death. Dasein, thrown into the world, recognizes itself not in the particularity of any given project but as "not-at-home" in the "nothing of the world" (BT 321/277). If the anticipatory resoluteness of death is Dasein's mode of coming home to itself, in Heidegger's reading of Antigone "dying is her becoming homely" (DI 104). Antigone is most uncanny in being expelled, and in reaching that limit, which is itself the limit of sayability. We recall that for Hölderlin death silences the tragic poem. For Heidegger, "Antigone is the supreme uncanny" (DI 104).

For Heidegger, the law of uncanniness is the "becoming homely within and out of such being unhomely." Home is, then, death, or the freedom of the "not" between Being and beings, to which the human being is alone privy. But it is also the proper relation to "earth" as the abode, or "hearth" (DI 105–106), as the "essential abode of the self" (EHD 129). Uncanniness is "an essential trait of Being itself" (DI 78). Yet Being, as we have seen in Heidegger's reading of the river poems, "returns to the source," involves the "inwardly counter-turning essence" away from unhomeliness—as Dasein is afforded the possibility of turning toward (*Ankehr*) itself, into its own thrownness, the "nothing of the world."

In Heidegger's reading, the poet finds the proper (*das Eigene*) through the foreign as the appropriation of the event, the *Eignen des Ereignis*. We cannot become homely merely in the realm of beings, an attempt that always "turns in itself . . . counter to what humans are fundamentally seeking from it" (DI 84). In order to become "homely" amidst beings we must relinquish the familiar, or beings, to embrace uncanniness itself. Only as such can we effect a return home. But becoming homely requires the appropriation of the proper through the appropriation of the foreign. The law of being unhomely, itself a "counteressence"

(DI 84), is the path of this return. Heidegger claims that this must be humans' appropriation of "the essential site of their history" (DI 87), just as in *Being and Time* Dasein is to retrieve itself authentically by a repetition (*Wiederholung*) of that which it has been (*das Gewe-sene*). This repetition is authentic historicity. The resoluteness of Dasein in the *Augenblick* is repeated or grasped again (*wieder-holt*) as the essence of a people's "becoming historical," countering the "unrootedness" of inauthentically being "everywhere and nowhere" (BT 221/177). If in *Being and Time* Dasein must "pass under the eyes of death," in the "Der Ister" lectures only a "relation of risk . . . places human beings and them alone in the open site in the midst of beings" (DI 89). The resoluteness of Dasein's repetition of its *Volk*-belonging, its participatory belonging to history, is the conclusion of its tarrying with uncanniness: it is Dasein's coming home to itself and to its people—most distressing in light of Heidegger's later association with National Socialism, as I mentioned in the previous chapter.

Risk for Heidegger is "no blind recklessness" but a risking of the human being in its essence (DI 95).[35] Such risk involves another kind of "knowing that belongs to those who are expelled."[36] In this other kind of knowing, "becoming homely, being unhomely"—or having a relationship to Being as *Ereignis*—"is first accomplished" (DI 115). *Andenken* is here again named as the "becoming homely" in contrast to "forgottenness of home." *Andenken* is that which "can rupture such forgottenness" (*Vergessenheit*). Thus Antigone, the one expelled, is unhomely only in an "ambiguous" sense (DI 115)—"to be sheltered within and to become homely in what is thus unconcealed" is Antigone's wandering journey which, through death, arrives home. Only in tragedy is the "decision" made about the "proper" kind—or path—of unhomeliness (DI 117). Heidegger links this to "belonging to death and blood" (as in the blood relation of Antigone to her brother) (DI 118).

Antigone, Heidegger reminds us, serves as the model for the poet: "Antigone, and that also means the poet" (DI 117). Heidegger explicitly links this reading to his Hölderlin as poet-vessel, citing three words from Hölderlin's "Remarks on Antigone"—which he nevertheless dismisses Hölderlin's account as an "explanation" of Antigone's actions (DI 115)—the notion of *Andenken,* and a line on life and death from Hölderlin's poem "In Lovely Blue . . ." ("In lieblicher Blaue . . .") (DI 118). Antigone, Heidegger argues, "names Being itself" and is "the purest poem itself." In other words, she is Sophocles, is Hölderlin, when both are accounted for as "essential" poets. She is "the singular thing" that is to be poeticized: "becoming homely in being unhomely" (DI 121). Absent from

Heidegger's discussion is the social context in which Antigone finds herself, the opposition of characters, and what Hölderlin names the "relativity of the moral law." Antigone's tragic situation is the subversion of avuncular-paternal law for the higher law of particularity—again, the problem of wholeness and separation, which is for Hölderlin explicitly "religious, political, and moral" (ELT 115). For Hölderlin, the principle of Antigone's distress is the problem of consciousness, for when it transcends human law in favor of the divine, it confronts the caesuric moment of "reversal" of human, finite, "modes and forms of representation." It is this reversal (*Umkehr*) of representations that Hölderlin names the *vaterländische Umkehr*—according to Beda Allemann's reading, the turn to the finite realm of art, which strives, in ancient Greek poetry, to grasp (*fassen*), in modern German to reach (*treffen*) the divine, and yet itself must follow not the divine law of infinite time but that of finite succession (ELT 109, 111, 115).[37] Heidegger's uncanniness as a "poetic knowing" would be the knowing of limits in this sense, which is, then, exiled from the realm of beings who do not suffer the limitations of consciousness, and yet also from Being as the unknowable. And yet, Hölderlin claims,

> An absolute reversal [*gänzliche Umkehr*] of these, as indeed an absolute reversal altogether without any pause [*ohne allen Halt*], is forbidden [*unerlaubt*] for the human being as a knowing being [*als erkennenden Wesen*]. (ELT 114–115)

The situations of both Antigone and Oedipus involve the attempt to know more than consciousness can bear, and in both cases a point of reversal is accomplished. Hölderlin describes this move: "It is a great resource of the secretly working soul that at the highest state of consciousness it evades consciousness and that, before the present god actually seizes it, the soul confronts him with the bold, frequently even blasphemous word" (ELT 111). Although, as for Hölderlin's own character Empedocles, this blasphemy is tempting for human understanding, even for the poet, such "high state of consciousness" is not allowed to the human being, and the consequences of hubris follow. Thus Hölderlin compares this state to "land that has become a desert, which in originally abundant fertility increases the effects of sunlight too much and therefore dries out" (ELT 111–112).

For Heidegger, Antigone is resoluteness; she is not described as caught between the domination of human law (Creon) and duty or care (her brother's burial) for the infinite—nor as pressing against the limits of human knowing. Her uncanniness is to face death: "she will not flinch in her resolve" (DI 102). In concluding his discussion of Antigone,

Heidegger returns to the Böhlendorff letter and argues that "the law of becoming homely" involves what Hölderlin named as the German and the Greek (DI 125, 123). Here exile has found for Heidegger its locale of return, and it is thought of as a meditation on German destiny (DI 124). While Hölderlin's letter, as well as the "Remarks on Antigone," concern a contrast of Greek and German poetry, for Heidegger

> Hölderlin's discussions in the Böhlendorff letters are not contributions to some future aesthetics of German 'literature' but rather a meditation on that which is essentially to be poeticized. And that is: the becoming homely of the historical humankind of the Germans within the history of the West. (DI 124)

> Heidegger's interpretation relies on Hölderlin's suggestion to Böhlendorff (upon whose play *Fernando*, sent to him, Hölderlin is commenting) that "what is familiar must be learned as well as what is foreign." Hölderlin argues that Greek and German poetry, rather than sharing common traits, have "reverse" strengths (ELT 150). The occasion of Hölderlin's letter is then also disclosed as Hölderlin's departure from Germany, "perhaps forever" (ELT 151). There is no explicit mention of history in Hölderlin's letter, while for Heidegger history is "nothing other than such a return to hearth." The hearth is Being (DI 108–109).

> Whether or not, in determining the historical interrelation between Greek and German historicality, Hölderlin has already hit upon what belongs to the commencement, is something we may ask only at that time when Hölderlin's word has truly been heard and when, as the poetizing that it is, it has awakened an appropriate obedience to it. (DI 124)

For Heidegger, the "law of encounter [*Auseinandersetzung*] between the foreign and one's own is the fundamental truth of the law of history to which the German *Volk* is to yield in obedience as if to its own essential nature."[38]

Heidegger's understanding of the foreign seems then to be guided, as Derrida suggests,[39] by the return home, in a way that belies a paradoxical anxiety[40] about the plurisignificance of uncanniness (DI 104, 166). Uncanniness must be seen to follow a law (DI 125) that does not get lost, as Hyperion does, in wandering; thus uncanniness is perhaps never truly characterized as a state of exile. Thus Heidegger demands that "Hölderlin's dialogue with foreign poets is removed from any arbitrariness" (DI 49.) While Heidegger expresses insight about translation and Hölderlin's experience of translation, Heidegger demands that

Hölderlin's experience has "a univocal character" (DI 49). The "foreign" must be carefully chosen; Hölderlin chose the Greek poets not as influenced by the "pagan" classicism of Goethe and Schiller[41] (DI 77); nor because Hölderlin had studied Greek literature and aesthetics at the *Tübingen Stift* (on which he wrote his *Magisterarbeiten*—"On the History of Fine Art in the Greeks" and on Hesiod's *Works and Days*, and on which he attempted to promote for a professorship in Jena); nor as a genius's admiration of philosophical and aesthetic elements therein. According to Heidegger, "the foreign and the foreign poets" are "not simply arbitrarily there" (DI 49) for Hölderlin—and that means not simply on the basis of Hölderlin's historical-cultural situation and influences; their presence is anchored in Hölderlin's proximity to the *Geschick*. Again, Hölderlin, not merely "thrown" into a sea of contemporaneous cultural-philosophical concerns, "had the privilege of possessing the intrinsic ability to be influenced by Pindar and Sophocles—and that now means, to listen in an originary and obedient manner to whatever is originary in the foreign from out of his own origin" (DI 50).

According to Heidegger's reading, if Hölderlin had an intrinsic obedience to the "Greek," a historical people must have reference to another, foreign language—but they must also recognize the "essential danger" in knowing just any foreign language, such as "the Anglo-American language" (DI 65). Even translation gets read as the appropriation of one's own language: "Thought in terms of historical reflection, translation is an encounter with the foreign for the sake of appropriating one's own" (DI 66).[42] Germans, Heidegger argues, "may learn Greek only when we must learn it out of an historical necessity for the sake of our own German language" (DI 66). This radically differs from Kristeva's reading of Hölderlin's translations, which involves exile in a much more radical sense, and to which she relates his line on the foreign (*das Fremde*): "we have almost lost our language" ("wir haben fast . . . unsere Sprache verloren"). This diverges as well from the poetological concerns we have found in Hölderlin's poetic critique of philosophy, which is perhaps "set adrift" in longing rather than return. Heidegger's attention to the problem of alterity, then, is anchored in an ontological account of historical destiny from which a new poetics of Dasein is to be released. I sketch out this new poetics in the next and final chapter of this book. The revolutionary nature of poetic language, and the provisional nature of the poetic subject, set this new poetics apart from Heidegger's alliance to homeland and the proper; the spontaneity and preservation of which poetic language is capable promises poetry's relevance for human dwelling and factical life without the logic of necessary return.

7

A New Poetics of Dasein

In letters discussing poetic strategy, the French poet Arthur Rimbaud repeatedly uses the following phrase: "je est un autre," or "I is someone else."[1] This formulation might suggest, at first glance, an ecstatic abandonment of self, confirmed perhaps in the multiple viewpoints the poet assumes in "Enfance," a poem from his *Illuminations,* when he proclaims:

> Je suis le saint, en prière sur la terrasse comme
> les bêtes pacifiques . . .
> Je suis le savant au fauteuil sombre . . .
> Je suis le piéton de la grand'route . . .
> Je serais bien l'enfant abandonné sur la jetée . . .
> le petit valet
> suivant l'allée dont le front touche le ciel.

> I am the saint at prayer on the terrace like the
> peaceful beasts . . .
> I am the scholar of the dark armchair . . .
> I am the pedestrian of the highroad . . .
> I might well be the child abandoned on the jetty . . .
> the little farm boy
> following the lane, its forehead touching the sky.[2]

One surely cannot anchor Rimbaud's poetry, its symbolism of shimmering images, to a singular biography of self. Yet when Rimbaud describes his poetic procedure in his letters, involving the upsetting of ordinary perceptions, even the disorientation of the senses that accompanied and afforded his early eruptions of genius, what is implied is a self or subject "in process." Explaining his method, he writes,

> The poet makes himself a visionary through a long, a prodigious and rational disordering of all the senses. Every form of love, of suffering, of madness; he searches *himself*, he consumes all the poisons in him, keeping only their quintessences. Ineffable torture in which he will need all his faith. . . . For he arrives at the unknown! Since he has cultivated his soul—richer to begin with than any other! He arrives at the unknown: and even if, half crazed, in the end, he loses an understanding of his visions, he has seen them![3]

The disorientation that Rimbaud describes need not be aimed exclusively at the fantastical or the sublime, as we find it in Rimbaud's work, in Charles Baudelaire, in Guillaume Apollinaire, and in the writings of Franz Kafka. For us it can signify any rupture of a prosaically practical or epistemologically appropriative horizon through which the world appears, disenchantedly, within the framework (Heidegger would say *Gestell*) of the subject's own production, its exhaustive knowledge, or as there for its utilization. Contrary to Kristeva, in my view it is not knowledge as such but rather the *exhaustiveness* of an appropriative, prosaic attitude toward the world that poetic subjectivity challenges. Rimbaud clarifies further that although in some instances of visionary seeing the understanding may be lost, there will be other poets who "will begin at the horizons where he has succumbed," so that work toward foraging into the unknown will have nonetheless been accomplished.[4] Attendance to the unknown or ineffable suggests that, flickering through the quotidian real, another, more elusive aspect of things is glimpsed. We could describe an examination of such in somewhat phenomenological terms. This attendance invokes the defixation of a prominently foregrounded familiarity; a release of the previously receding background; an alteration of focus illuminating the background itself; the bridging of logically disparate images and sensations which brings forth into imagined actuality what was heretofore merely receding into potentiality; and a resultant but contemporaneous state of stepping outside one's own ordinary mode of seeing. These are some possible nuanced stages of a poetical suspension of the natural attitude. This is clearly what Rimbaud has accomplished through language by way of a disorienting but strangely luminous assemblage of images, to quote from one of his poems, through an "unlooked-for logic" ("de logique bien imprévue").[5] The point is not to revel in disorder, but to "arrive at the unknown through the disordering."[6] Beyond revolutionary poetics, the break with the prosaic is, from the poetical point of view, an accomplishment of what Rilke thought to be "the right kind of seeing"; it can serve, as in Rilke and Hölderlin, new forms of clarity and structures of attunement.[7] This break with the prosaic points to the ecstatic nature of the self, the being-drawn beyond the sphere of immanence by the discovery of the otherness, the mysteriousness, of what is.[8] A poetical mode of experience is engendered by this rupture; it is indicated in and also brought about through poetical language. This ambiguous experience—of disorientation and clarity—is the real subject matter, for instance, of Rilke's novel *Die Aufzeichnungen des Malte Laurids Brigge* (*The Notebooks of Malte Laurids Brigge*), but also of much of modern poetry such as announced by Rimbaud. As Valéry writes in "Poetry and Abstract Thought," an essay I discussed in the previous chapter, "I discover naive impulses and images, raw products of my needs and of my personal experiences. *It is my life itself that is surprised.*"[9] The poetic indicates not a renunciation of knowledge—Rimbaud retains the terms "rational" and "understanding"—so much as a revision of cognitive boundaries and a putting into question of the categories of Platonist and modern metaphysics. Poetry thus aims to comprehend, in the sense of grasping, or at least pointing to in a "formal indication," that aspect of the real that is unknowable by other, exclusively cognitive means. Here rationality is not unraveled but allowed to join forces with what Keats termed "negative capability": the ability to abide in uncertainties, mysteries, and doubts, without renouncing claims to the real. This ability, I will suggest later in this chapter, is an aspect of the imagination, the retrieval of which is a necessary element of the poetics of Dasein.

Despite the grammatical and semantic challenge to the self in "je est," a challenge to the "I am" (*je suis*) of Descartes's *cogito ergo sum*, Rimbaud's formulation does not erase the "I"—does not render the "I," as did Nietzsche, a "fiction of grammar"—but formulates a subjectivity endowed with an unusual capacity for what we might call, borrowing a term from Emmanuel Levinas, "excendence," my use of which will become clear, I hope, in this final chapter. The new poetics of Dasein I set forth accounts for the subtle tones of giving and yielding and undergoing that belong to the poetic subject's experiences of creation. Such an account implies a radical form of receptivity and ecstasis—stepping outside the self—but does not obliterate the subject's creative initiation or the phenomenologically disclosable features of the subject of poetic experience. My account, I believe, is not only inspired by the reading of Hölderlin's poetics I have offered in this book but is also further to be corroborated by a spectrum of poetological stances that I would like to work out here in brief outline.

Turning from Hölderlin to a broader inclusion of modern poetry, we might mark out a continuum of poetical modes of experience over a wide, but of course not all-inclusive, range, the continuity of which is sustained by a maintenance of the "self" in and through experiences of ecstasis necessary, but not sufficient, for the advent of poetical creation. On this continuum, were we to engage in close interpretations of the works of many poets here, we might be able to situate—in differing ways, of course—the poetic language of writers as diverse as, for example, John Keats, Walt Whitman, Friedrich Hölderlin, Anna Akhmatova, Osip Mandelstam, Miklós Radnóti, Paul Celan, Franz Kafka, Charles Baudelaire, Paul Verlaine, René Char, Robert Frost, Theodore Roethke, Wallace Stevens, and perhaps even the fragments of Sappho.

On the two ultimate poles of the spectrum we find Rimbaud and Rilke. The spectrum ranges from the disordering-visionary poetics of Rimbaud, as discussed earlier, to the clarifying poetics of Rilke, my view of which I will briefly describe. For Rilke, "intimate" or "inner" space (*vertrauter Raum, innenraum*) is the experiential structure through which things are known to us poetically; such experience is an achievement issuing from the breakdown of ordinary familiarity with the real. Not by renouncing the self, but rather by intuiting the ecstatic nature of the "inner" self and the intimate nature of external reality, the poet is brought into a heightened intimacy with the receding features of the real, unknown structures or the ineffable background, what he often calls the "other side of things." Such things are approached through an ecstatic self, but the self is also intuited and experienced through a poetic glimpse of external things.[10] Interiority becomes known to us not by an egological meditation but by intuiting the hidden intimacy of "external" things, since external things model for Rilke a form of inwardness or an inner landscape. This is why Rilke's poems often are centered on things: the panther, the bowl of roses, an orange, the statue of Apollo, a tree. Likewise, things Cartesian metaphysics considers "out there," reflected only in representations of the mind, are known in their mysterious elusiveness by grasping how they, like the self, are full of intimate spaces analogous to (and such analogy is perhaps necessary for the discovery of) our own.[11] The spectrum of excendence

or ecstasis—of escaping the immanence of a self-contained ego—
that is involved in poetry as I am describing it here is thus a spectrum ranging from disorientation of the senses as an access to the
unknown to the accomplishment of a pristine, poetic "clarity" about
the true nature of the real aside from the reductive dichotomies of traditional metaphysics. It is my view that Hölderlin's poetry, when taking into account the full range of his work, from early dialectical-ide-
alist poems to his later "paratactic" works, can be located on various
points of the continuum from disorientation to clarity. Certainly his
Hyperion and *Empedocles* trace in differing ways courses of an aim toward
the clarity Rilke will describe, as well as its loss, while the sparser late
poems (such as "Hälfte des Lebens") and those written in madness
suggest at times an almost Rimbaudian disorientation through which,
the reader supposes, Hölderlin tarries with the unknown. But unlike
Levinas's engagement of the term, *excendence* here does not indicate the
goal of an abandonment of self in subordination to that alterity, that
otherness, approached by poetical seeing. The poetics of Dasein is a
poetics of existence as known and experienced and thus as phenomenologically accessible through the self, however altered or compromised; if the self is too radically compromised, as in some of Hölderlin's last, and least accessible poems, the phenomenological thread is
lost and there is no trail through the forest by which to trace the ineffable or the unknown.

In offering this alternative to the Heideggerian models of the resolute and the selfless poet, I by no means wish to imply that all poetry,
or even good poetry, is principally *about* the self. The mirroring in Verlaine's lines "Combien, o voyageur, ce paysage blême / Te mira blême
toi-même" ("how much this pale landscape, o traveler / mirrors your
pale self there"), suggests not a poetry about the self but an engagement of the world that takes up the self poetically rendered.[12] The
image of the pale landscape operates in contradistinction to a metaphysical separation of interiority and exteriority. Thus it is precisely
the experience of excendence, defined as a provisional escape of self
engendering a poetical experience of the world, interpretively still
anchorable to a self thrown into question, that much of the poetry I
am thinking about here concerns. I aim to read through poetic language the residues of subjective experience through which, in alterations of ordinary language and ordinary ways of seeing, new layers
of meaning are created. If poetic meaning is rare, it is because, in Valéry's
words, "all the exigencies of life are against it."[13] This means that the
prosaic, practical, or metaphysical understanding of the world in its

dominant mode, the natural attitude, does not, in the main, foster excendence or a notion of self in provisional exile from its ordinary station.

Of course, my poetics of Dasein cannot account for the geological "layer" of self in all forms of poetry, nor even all forms of modern poetry, but it does structurally formulate the experiential element discernible in the poetical address to the world that is evident in much of modern poetical language since Hölderlin. My account corrects what Levinas called the "disappearance of phenomenology properly speaking" from Heidegger's later thought,[14] which I addressed in the first chapter of this book as being in tension with Heidegger's poetic theory of ontological-historical founding. A new poetics of Dasein marks the subject's departure from absolute immanence or self-sufficiency, and from the kind of transcendence that is still tethered to an absolute guaranteed by theoretical knowledge, but it attempts to trace out the relationship of that departure to the self transformed through it. The subject of poetic language, which I can now term the poetic Dasein, has been characterized in this book as analeptic, or restorative, its immanence exposed to interventions of alterity. Here I have used language of the ineffable or the unknown to stand in for an experience of what is "other" to rational cognition; we must ask what this implies for our understanding of the relation of poetic language to truth. As I have hinted throughout this book, my view of poetic language does not sanction an abandonment of the notion of truth, as I find in Haverkamp's and Blanchot's readings of Hölderlin (see chapter 3) and in Kristeva's revolutionary poetics (see chapter 6). Yet the notion of poetical truth will require qualification, as I begin to articulate in this final chapter.

I want first to articulate some theses that initiate a new poetics of Dasein. These theses, woven together, present a model of poetic Dasein and thus a new poetic theory, still incipient here. This theory serves to account for what I have argued are modes of poetical "cognition" and truth neglected in contemporary and postmodern poetics. We will return to several of these theses in the description of Dasein's structure below. The nine theses are as follows:

1. A phenomenological attendance to poetic experience, such as I have indicated in the account of Hölderlin's poetics presented in this book, reveals a far more radical sense of what Heidegger calls "thrownness" (*Geworfenheit*) than he admits in his attempts to reign in the experience of alterity so that it serve the purpose of gathering and founding history. The "essential abode of the self" with which Heidegger once associates the poet is in part structured by this *Geworfenheit*. Such is the atmosphere of the factical life of Dasein that poetry serves—in

its reflecting and sheltering of world, as well as its loss of a grasp of its unity—as a unique complex of formal indications. Here the "abode of the self" recalls elements of the existential analytic of Dasein's self and its radical being "not-at-home" in the "nothing of the world" (BT 321/277). But it also affords the disordering or decentering necessary for a visionary alternative to prosaic metaphysics, a disordering to which Rimbaud attests, one that is not unrelated to the ecstatic nature of the experience of poetic clarity. The "thrownness" of the poet on both ends of the spectrum described earlier indicates an excendence incompatible with the absolute aims of founding history. In both situations *the unknown approached and discovered can never be recovered with the certainty of a founded historical destiny.*

2. The situation of poetic Dasein *precludes anticipatory resoluteness,* which Heidegger claims solidifies the identity of Dasein's self as the one who possesses a singular relation to Being. Certainly, the recognition of one's own finitude might yield entrance into an altered understanding of the world; death figures, for instance, in Rilke's *Notebooks* and his *Sonnets to Orpheus* as illuminating another "side" of reality, and finitude certainly figures in Hölderlin's poems. Yet authenticity is achieved not in being-towards-death, or in the recognition of one's own singularity before the finality of death. Poetically rendered, authenticity is a nonpossessive attunement to alternative horizons of meaning which render the world, poetically, plurisignificant. For an account of authenticity, we might draw upon Heidegger's later notion of *Gelassenheit.* We note that is not his own death but that of the other, the loss of Eurydice that presses Orpheus into new modes of song. Not heroism but poetical intuition is the texture of the poet's indirect access to Being.

3. Poetic language involves excendence. As revolutionary to some extent, it *prevents the closure of identity of self* suggested by resoluteness. Poetic Dasein is never rid of alterity—in this sense "I is someone else"—and so the return home is never completed. The very grammar of Rimbaud's phrase demands a recognition of the mutual indebtedness of "I" and other. As a subject-in-process, poetic Dasein is prohibited closure in any other than a poetical, and that means provisional, sense. This also applies to the retrieval of a *Volk* or national identity, despite the common use or abuse of art for nationalist ideologies. Some evidence as to this resistance to singular identity is rendered by the breadth of totalitarian efforts to curtail or repress the work of poets who, even if nationalist, render doubtful such singular closure. What we have said in this book about the provisionality of poetical truths renders ambiguous any role it might play in "setting-forth" such ideologies.

4. While poetic subjectivity breaks with the everyday, it remains *ever engaged in a lifeworld of beings*. For poetic Dasein, fallenness, the inauthentic state of mind, is described not as absorption with quotidian beings (for it is among other things an intense relationship to those beings) in distraction from Being and the singularity of death. Rather, fallenness is a fixation within cognitive and scientific, as well as prosaic, horizons through which things would be exclusively interpreted. Heidegger's description of equipmentality, while opening out the hermeneutic nexus for his ontological grasp of the world, remains prosaic in its description of our relation to beings as predominantly practical. From a poetical point of view, Heidegger's description of world as equipmentally disclosed remains in the natural or prosaic attitude. As Henri Bergson suggests, an "actual contact with reality" requires an emancipation "from the ways of perception engendered by action" in the non-majesculated sense of the word.[15] Heidegger's nearly exclusive emphasis on the equipment of work neglects, as I mentioned in the introductory chapter, the aesthetics of the natural world, things as provocative of authentic curiosity and genuine wonder. For the spectrum of poetic seeing from Rimbaud to Rilke, the mysteriousness and elusivity of Being is authentically approached in a rupture of the exclusively prosaic interpretation of the world. This suggests that ordinary experience already shelters, though does not emphasize, possibilities of poetic vision—the glimpse that beckons the imagination beyond the ordinary grasp of things, possibilities that are neglected by Heidegger in his account of world in *Being and Time*, despite its call for poetical expression.

5. Poetical truth, and I would like to retain that term, is one that *troubles the ordinary distinctions between the real and the imaginary, the verifiable and the elusive*. When the poetic subject, either in disorientation or in a heightened clarity, approaches the unknown, it does so not in order to abandon knowledge, but rather to expand its boundaries toward the source of those reverberations of the uncertain and the mysterious. This does not mean that poetry is characterized by mere fantasy. Even here poetic Dasein shares something in common with certain forms of scientific cognition, such as when theoretical physicists speculate in advance of the mathematically verifiable, or must grapple with competing, and equally verifiable, views of the universe. I have in mind multiple models of string theory, or the cognitive imagination required to hold together and attempt to overcome, such as in a possible unified field theory, incompatible and incomplete views of the universe in relativity theory and quantum mechanics. In chapter 2 I argued for a

formal resonance between the poetical articulation of Heidegger's *Ereignis* through Hölderlin's poetry of rivers and the withdrawal of absolute cognition prescribed by Heisenberg's uncertainty principle. While poetical truth cannot be adequate to the scientific aim (and scientific truth might inspire but will not satisfy the poet), the work of the imagination in both poetry and science is at some specific intersections indistinguishable. Thus I reject both Heidegger's polarization of poetry and science and Kristeva's view that poetic speech forever abandons the realm of knowledge. Rather, poetry might serve in resolving the opposition between modernist conceptions of (absolute) truth and postmodern deconstruction thereof. This resolution, however, requires attendance to the notion of a poetical imagination, to which I will turn shortly.

6. On both ends of the Rimbaudian-Rilkean spectrum described earlier, the unknown is approached with the hope of grasping it in some form of what I will call *poetical cognition*. Poetical *cognition* should be defined as a grasp of something that is not, as in ordinary cognition, univocal and final, in the sense of being conceptually settled — subsumed under a final legislation of the understanding to use Kantian terms — but rather remains open-endedly reverberant. The content, as well as the form, of that cognition must be perhaps ascertained in the case of each individual poetic structure, though in principle categorization of varying types should be possible.

7. Poetically understood, we must be able not to escape ontology such as Levinas prescribes,[16] but rather to *admit within an ontology an account of the unforeseeable*. Heidegger's association of Being and thought certainly suggests rigorous pathways of approaching the "unthought" or the "unsaid" within poetic utterance. Yet it does not acknowledge to a sufficient extent, I think, the possibility that the unknown will elude even the most rigorously poetic thinking, a possibility expressed by Rimbaud in his acknowledgment of the potential failure of the poetic vision, and certainly by Hölderlin when I have indicated his sense of poetic subjectivity as "analeptic." The acute possibility of failure eludes the heroism in Heidegger's account of the poet as founder of truth, yet it is an aspect of the provisional nature of poetical seeing. The history of Being and its logic prescribes a fate that obliterates the singularity of what is unforeseen, what is not of the origin but nevertheless might demand poetical articulation.

8. A theory of language — of the unsaid that is tapped into by poetic thinking — ought not eclipse the *specificity of the specific content of original speech*. The specific loss, the specific joy, an accusation, the very particular texture of the subject matter of poetry are in danger of

absorption into a general theory of the relation of Being to thought. By original speech we mean not speech that arises out of an origin itself accessible to thought, but language that, in its factical specificity, is irreducible to any other utterance than itself. This resonates with Levinas's concern for the "saying" over the "said." Heidegger indicates a hesitation to overwhelm the poem with the thinking that attends it, yet he often enough does not sufficiently recognize the irreducible specificity of the poem's utterance, its "truth content." This occurs particularly when the poem's subjective elements are obliterated. The poem indicates, too, the specificity of the self who speaks, and of course this cannot show up in a theory that refuses the poetic self a perceptible role.

This point might be illuminated by an example. Miklós Radnóti comes to mind: he was a Hungarian Jewish poet who wrote, literally, on the edge of disaster and killed by fascists on a forced march from a labor camp where he had been interred and had also written poems. A notebook of these poems was salvaged from his trench coat when his wife later found his body in an unmarked grave. While I would want to be able to say something general about poetic Dasein that could take into account even Radnóti's extreme distress, his so fragile hold on self (as when he writes: "*Palinode* / But don't leave me, delicate mind! / . . . Sweet wounded reason, don't / leave me now"), a self sustained by his writing, by poetic language itself, I am certain that the "essence" of his poetry would be missed in a general theory of the revelation of Being.[17] The specificity of Radnóti's address overrides the categorization into structures of ontological saying, even if those might be relevant; yet this specificity in no way renders Radnóti's poetry unessential, even by Heideggerian measures. Following this, a poetics of Dasein, must be only as self-assured and scientific, to adapt Aristotle's prescription for ethics, as its subject allows. Poetic theory is at best only a scaffolding through which the structures of poetical experience and meaning become visible.

9. An account of poetical Dasein must *reclaim the imagination,* for all the merits of Heidegger's rejection of egological aesthetics. I have shown in previous chapters that Hölderlin locates within traditional aesthetics points of departure from an ego-centered or idealist metaphysics. In Rilke, too, the imagination is essential to the attainment of poetical clarity; it is by virtue of the imagination that we allow room for what might be, as he suggests in one of the *Sonnets to Orpheus* about a nonexistent creature posited by the imagination (a unicorn) as the object of love. For Rilke what "scarcely needed to be" ("brauchte kaum

zu sein") provides a horizon for the actual which immeasurably enriches it.[18] Here I will argue that the imagination is a necessary element of poetic subjectivity and poetical existence, and that it is the imagination, not as merely reproductive but initiative, which preserves the freedom of the poetical self within the specific nature of its experience. I will turn to the problem of the imagination again in this chapter, in a discussion of the structure of poetical Dasein.

For in a new poetics of Dasein, some account must be given of the *structure* of poetical Dasein, for an account of which we will interweave the theses presented earlier. Here revised concepts from *Being and Time* can serve as initial formulations of existential structures. We remember that for Heidegger, Dasein is characterized by *Sorge,* the unity of the temporal ecstases, the past, present, and future brought together; Dasein is characterized by *Befindlichkeit* or thrownness, discourse, and projective understanding. As Heidegger writes, "when fully conceived, the care-structure includes the phenomenon of Selfhood" (BT 370/323); and it is through care that the world appears to Dasein. If we are to retain certain existential and phenomenological features of selfhood, the ecstases must be reexamined poetically; the relationship between care and world is at issue here. Phenomenologically speaking, world is not the given material substrate within which we dwell, nor merely a spatiotemporal nexus of localities, but is structured by how Dasein finds itself (*Befindlichkeit*), what it has to say, its interpretive and projective understanding. When that understanding is poetical in nature, rather than primarily practical as in Heidegger's account of equipmentality, the elusive nature of existence which recedes from direct appearances — the relation of things to presence and absence and to thus to what is not directly graspable — comes into play. A world is projected that is inherently poetical in nature, keeping in mind that the provisionality of poetical truths prevents reification of world into any univocal mythos. We would speak not of poetical features, but perhaps of poetical undertones or nuances, of world related to its receding into the unknown and unknowable. This is explicit in Rilke, for instance, whose poetical practice involves sustained formal indication of what he refers to as the "other side" of things,[19] and in Rimbaud's persistent reference to the "unknown."

Projection (*Entwerfen*), is for us the activity of interpretation of the given, which is aided by discourse (*Rede*) as a creative relation of poetical Dasein to its world. As I indicated in chapter 6, projection is here understood in terms of transformation and transcendence. Rather than cognitive-rational organization of likenesses and types, informed by practical use (equipmentality) or scientific examination, poetical language breaks with ordinary taxonomy to reveal surprising connections between prosaically disparate things, feelings, and events. Such language remains rational in the original sense of logos as linguistic order, but this ordering is accomplished only as an indication, rather than as a definitive cognitive possession, of truth. Thus poetical cognition is brought about by use of, for instance, metaphor, wherein a "truth" of connectedness between two logically disparate entities is presented in a compelling but elusive way. In terms of motivation, rhythmic and phonic characteristics of language are at play with imagistic denotation. Through the engagement of poetic language, Dasein discursively interprets and as such also transcends the given, initiating a level of meaning that is both part of world, as reflective of it, and self-referential. However, poetic interpretation limits the "truth-claims" of its language to an acknowledged finitude, that is, circumscribes them as specifically poetical truths. Such truths are revealed in their disclosive, and thus partial, nature, as we have discussed in previous chapters. The imaginative and linguistic casting of world as poetical in nature opens up a reception of its wondrous and elusive, familiar and "other," plurisignificant nature. The futural temporality of projection is preserved by its infinite deferral of *telos* or finality; this sustains meaningfulness for the present without achieving total disclosure of the Being of the world. For us the poetical initiation of projective interpretation, the spontaneous accomplishment of composition and "building," or, as Heidegger calls it, "setting-up" of truth, cannot serve as a founding of historical truth. As *of* the world, poetical truths are subject to the same features—elusivity, finitude, provisionality—that characterize the world itself poetically understood. Thus they are continually subject to revision, sincere and yet decidedly irresolute.

In the same tone, we might also then reconsider *Befindlichkeit* and *Stimmung:* the first concerns the manner in which poetical Dasein is "thrown" into factical life and how it "finds" itself within such life, its "state of mind" (as in the Macquarrie/Robinson translation of *Sein und Zeit*) or state of being; the second is its "mood" or being attuned (*gestimmt*), a situation which is inherently disclosive; here these elements are closely related. Given that we include Dasein's embodied life as integral to its conscious situation, we will use the term "state of being" rather than "state of mind" for *Befindlichkeit*. Poetical Dasein's state of being is situated by its concerns, and these make up both the subject matter and procedures of poetry. Poetical concerns include: (1) the concerns of factical life in its mundane happenings or in its extraordinary moments, both transformed through the receptive-experiential mode of poetical attention as described earlier; (2) attunement can also be focused upon language itself, to words themselves, their sound, feel and tone, their multiple capacities realized as sources of provisional revealing of Being; or (3) upon the imaginative initiation that stirs within the locus of Dasein's sense of self. Here the horizonal possibilities attending things are mirrored in the horizonal reverberations on the part of the subject, indicating its provisional identity as well as other ways to be. Of course, engagement with poetic language is various, and these variations, in the main, can be distinguished by the magnification of one or more of the three aforementioned elements of poetical state of being or attunement; a compelling poem is likely to engage all three, as in a complex of alterations of tone. As a matter of tenor, poetic language can be colored by many specific feelings: for instance, as in Radnóti, a sense of radical loss (of immediacy and specificity of something once possessed or known) or by the joy of reconciliation, as in Whitman—or, characteristic of Hölderlin, an alteration of both. The fundamental authentic mood that characterizes poetical Dasein includes a heightened sense of its own finitude, brought about less by a confrontation with death as by awareness of Dasein's rootedness in its own materiality, irreducible to an empirical substrate alone, to an anthropology of instinct or a psychology of drives. This materiality is reflected in its formal structure in the makeup of the lifeworld as it is perceived and lived through by Dasein. Perhaps Rilke's notion of intimacy as it pertains both to the inner self and the things of the world can be seen as indicating this materiality; in Rimbaud it involves a relationship to the disoriented senses. Such materiality poetically understood is subject to accident and unforeseeability, insofar as it is not strictly circumscribable within the empirical or the predictable logic of instinct or the traceable unconscious. Such materiality poetically understood is unforeseeable through the logic of a *Seinsgeschichte*. The materiality of poetic Dasein joins Dasein intrinsically to what underlies and makes possible utterance but is not fully revealed there. Grounded in the flesh of the world, the poet accepts the radical limitations of its access to the world inasmuch as its own finitude is already co-given in such acceptance. The self need not signify, in René Char's words, the "intimate unfolding of the irreparable" ("l'intime dénouement de l'irréparable").[20] Yet the finitude of language is correlate to Dasein's own.

As indicated in the preceding theses, the notion of existential authenticity must be revisited. Authentic repetition (*Wiederholung*) occurs not in seizing the past in a moment of vision toward a totality of self or an identification with history, but in a genuinely Hölderlinian *Andenken,* the remembrance that locates the elusive and other within the deferred promises of poetic language. The revolutionary features of language, while limited also by the productive nature of poetry, are preserved in the impossibility of expulsion of alterity from the sphere of self, even by means of absorption, in appropriative resoluteness. Poetical language breaks up the illusion of a totality of self, as well as the illusion of the totality of a people or *Volk,* nationalist uses and abuses of poetry notwithstanding. Along with the absolute self-certainty of the subject, prohibited is the closed identity of any cultural signification such as a "people" or "nation." As enacted by certain poets—not only by the poetry of later Hölderlin but also Celan and Radnóti—the poetical self seems to be a tentative accomplishment resulting from the very unraveling of self-possession, a radical decentering that paradoxically holds together a fragile grasp of the world in the wake of destruction of one's ordinary faith in it. Thus I take issue with Kristeva's notion, discussed in chapter 6, that poetic language must be understood as an "outright destruction" of the speaking self. Rather, it seems to enact the self in such a way as to articulate a challenge to self-possession. One also thinks here of the poetry of Anna Akhmatova and Osip Mandelstam, whom Stalin terrorized, knowing that the meaning of poetry, though powerful in its ideological potential, could not be unequivocally tethered to a constituted object-pole; language was always slipping out of reach.[21] Poetical joy, such as in some of Rilke's writings, also suggests the loss of self-possession: Rilke's Orpheus must lose everything to attain the ultimate promise of is poetic gifts. Even in less catastrophical poetry (consider Robert Frost or Wallace Stevens and Christian Morgenstern) the sense of self achieved is either courageously tentative (Frost's "Here are your waters and your watering place / Drink and be whole again beyond confusion") or playfully mocked (Stevens and Morgenstern), or, in the case of Walt Whitman, dilated in breadth beyond a singular location. Authentic repetition is an analeptic process: not a gathering of self to itself from distraction in the "they," but recovery that is never total or final and from which the "other" is never fully expelled. Thus existential repetition is inadequate for the *Kampf* of founding history.

We must include in a discussion of Dasein's structure its peculiar specificity, thus marking as provisional many of our generalizing concepts. Although we accept these quasi-phenomenological structures as a general account of poetical subjectivity, we can locate no transcendental ego that can be named as the guarantor of its truth content. Moreover, the history of Being to which Heidegger tethers the essence of language can be taken only as one possible and partial model of interpreting the relationship between language and Being in its historical unfolding. Even the designation of "Being" for what precedes and engenders language is only a tentative identification in the absence of any absolute designation. The specificity of the being who speaks always in some way resists enclosure within conceptual designation of "existence as such" even if it is subject to its finitude.

Perhaps most importantly, we need to expand the sketch of poetical Dasein to include creative production and its ontological spontaneity. Contrary to Kristevian poetics, poetic Dasein is not principally shattered and unsettled—and Hölderlin's poetic subject always aims at recovery from loss—and its initiative movement toward creation and composition need not be reduced to a psychoanalysis of drives. Insofar as poetical Dasein has certain capacities, this might be analyzed in a nonmetaphysical—that is, not merely representing–phenomenology of the poetic imagination. While featuring, of course, the phenomena of linguistically motivated images, the imagination is for us not primarily representative but intuitive, disclosive, and productive. By means of projecting and connecting cognitively dissimilar elements, for instance in metaphor but also in neologism, the imagination creates provisional unity within difference. Peculiar to poetic language is its relation to rhythm, the carrying-through of the undercurrents of natural and embodied life into poetical grammar, a passage that is facilitated, again, by the poetical imagination in its creative projection of the noncognitive levels of experience. Although the deliberate strategies of poetic practice enable the compositional unity of formal poetry, we find implied there the fragility of human memory and the destructive entropy of history. Although much of my discussion pertains to modern poetry, perhaps the most elemental examples are Shakespeare's sonnets concerning the brevity of beauty, the necessity of formal means to retain in language a preserving memory of such. Poetical "recovery"—as transcending the given state of dissolution by virtue of a projected wholeness, a recovery I have argued is essential to Hölderlin's poetics—is indebted to the possibilities of the poetical imagination. Yet, as we have seen, a phenomenology of the imagination, in its resonance with metaphysical aesthetics, was necessarily excluded from Heidegger's theory of art and language. This is contrary not only to Hölderlin's procedure but also to Rilke's conception of poetry. In reference to Orpheus, Rilke declares: "Mag auch die Spieglung im Teich / oft uns verschwimmen: / Wisse das Bild" ("The reflection in the pool may / often make us swim: / know the image").[22]

Although Heidegger provides a generous ontological account of the imagination in *Kant and the Problem of Metaphysics*, he generally abandons the terminology of the imagination when he attends later to art and poetic language, because he is unable to dissociate the imagination from metaphysical (Cartesian) subjectivity. And while Heidegger occasionally refers to images in poetry, he also expresses (in GA 13, as I have discussed previously in this book) hesitation with regard to the visualizable element of poetic language, a hesitation no doubt due to the metaphysical alliance between images and representational consciousness. Yet *Kant and the Problem of Metaphysics* might contribute to our theory of poetic Dasein: according to Heidegger, Kant discovered that the imagination is not merely a mediation between sense and understanding. It does not only reproduce or represent but also "intuit[s] 'images' which it forms itself, rather than relying upon representations of empirical perceptions."[23] The productive imagination is responsible for original "images" that form the conditions of possibility of presenting objects for understanding: for instance, that of continuous substance. This can be related to my earlier suggestion about the capacity of poetic Dasein, by virtue of imagination, to project wholeness or permanence on the basis of the fragility of memory and finitude of its world. For this reason a new phenomenology of the imagination must be outlined in response to Heidegger's disqualification. The poetical imagination, understood not in subordination and service to cognition, is not part of a static anatomy of the subject; it is not a "faculty." Rather, I argue that the imagination signifies the multiplicity of those disclosive strategies by which for Dasein a world—and Dasein as self, appear with features of being both knowable and unknowable, both present and ungraspable, and by which competing possibilities are held in abeyance in order to enrich an understanding of the real. Within the self's response to world, it is a locus for spontaneity and productive creation. This imagination is poetic, but it is not limited to poetry and art; it is engaged in theoretical science, in religious experience, and perhaps even in moral cognition.

If I am right concerning the possibilities for the productive imagination in this new poetics of Dasein—that it is a locus for spontaneity not exhausted by service to rational cognition—such might also be the source of freedom that poetic language, in its resistance to fixed truths, continually suggests. Freedom would then not be described as rational autonomy or deliverance from phenomenal causality, but rather the suspension of *telos*, which governs thought toward absolute rational expression. Freedom is in this sense, against Hegel, aligned with alterity and unforeseeability, with a preservation of that which eludes the realm of absolutes. Freedom thus described, admittedly, can no longer serve as a basis of a Kantian moral reason, but it need not be opposed to moral thinking either, just as poetry, in attending to the mysteriousness of the world, does not erase knowledge but forces a confrontation with its finitude.

Assembling together these features of the structure of poetical Dasein with our nine theses above, my new poetics of Dasein can be summed up as follows: Poetical Dasein is the existence of a conscious being aware of itself in reference to a world poetically understood. Poetical projection is the means by which, in compositional spontaneity, imaginative understanding presses forward into possibilities in transcendence of the given. Poetical mood signifies a stance toward presence for which the distinction between the real and the illusory is provisional, such that reality exceeds graspable or delineable presence, such that the elusive and the receding can be included within its sphere. Poetical attunement is the generosity of the receptive imagination in its attention to beings in suspension of cognitive legislation. Yet mood and attunement are not primarily states of "mind" but of embodied being-in-the-world. Repetition as poetical remembrance is correlate to the granting of plurisignificant images to shelter lost elements of the past in an always-deferred reinscription of their belonging the unity of life or Being. Poetical cognition is never final or total, not of the order of possession as it is said that one can "possess" knowledge. Dasein is, moreover, specific, this specificity resisting absorption by historical ontology or even by an ontology of language; what needs be said in poetic language can be indicated formally by poetological theory, as a second-order indication of the formal indication that poetic language itself articulates in relation to the known and the unknown. Because of its productive spontaneity and its relation to the unknown, phenomenology of poetical Dasein includes an account of the poetic imagination that must be recovered from the model presented by modern philosophy and Heidegger's rejection of it.

This new poetics of Dasein confirms Heidegger's critique of the metaphysical subject, without, however, abandoning the structure of the self. The self that Heidegger outlines in *Being and Time* is not that of absolute cognition nor of a "thinking thing" whose own static presence serves the basis for its relation to the world. Heidegger had already intimated, though in *Being and Time* had not fully laid out, the extent to which hearing, and therefore listening, is constitutive of language (BT 206/163), as well as the fact that poetic language is "a disclosing of existence" (BT 203/160). In our poetics of Dasein, *Geworfenheit*, extricated from the law of return that characterizes authentic Dasein's resolute, self-possessed totality, is subjected to the principle of *Gelassenheit*. Thus the poet's precariousness might admit the very equivocality that Heidegger in the "Der Ister" lecture, and even in *Being and Time* in the discussion of ambiguity (BT §37), attempts to avoid. Indirectness and ambiguity, rather than inauthentic indecisiveness, are essential to the transcendence of the given that is imaginative projection, so what is inherited is subject to variable interpretation and only tentative reinscription within a present understanding of the world. While poetic language does not leave altogether the "abode" of the speaking subject, it reveals a fundamental deferral of *telos*, and an alterity that cannot be eliminated by self-possessed resoluteness. The subject of poetic language is eccentric in the sense that it is never a self-contained or circumscribed totality and cannot stand in for or "found" one; it cannot be the center of a gathering (*Versammlung*) essence of what is its own; it is characterized, rather, by excendence. The poet is set on a course which never completes its arrival — and this has been associated in studies of Hölderlin with the "failure" of mourning or *Andenken*.[24] It is in not arriving — being not-at-home — that poetic dwelling is indirectly accomplished. As poets have long expressed, the "feeling of life" — and here we mean the factical life of Dasein, the phenomenological lifeworld, as much as the principle of life per se — is preserved only in not being pinned down determinatively by ordinary cognition, but rather in being "formally indicated" in poetical discovery and preservation. Exposed here is the incapacity of the self to ground its relation to the world in direct statement. Véronique M. Fóti accordingly claims, "Hölderlin, indeed, immediately adduces the obstacles which resist and frustrate preservation and remembrance: in being drawn into conflagration, the 'captive elements' go wildly astray; and above all, 'a longing' tends ever toward the boundless."[25] This longing indicates the poetical reverberation of the unknown beyond what can be grounded in rational cognition or grasped with poetical immediacy.

As it is formally indicated in poetry, the world, though inscribed in language, continually evades description even when the poet, such as Rilke, achieves the "clarity" of poetic seeing. This is because poetic language attests to the inexhaustibility of the real, an inexhaustibility that language approaches only when absolute distinctions between the real and the imagined are suspended. Blanchot thus refers to the poet who, unlike the traditional subject of metaphysics, anchored in the geometric certainties of cognitive consciousness, finds no settled home. The "caesura," which is so important for Hölderlin's poetic logic, perhaps symbolizes the disruption of the subject's guarantee of return, a disruption that leaves one fragile, ever-in-process. The poetic Dasein, set adrift, maintains a precarious oscillation between identity and rupture—and so the moment arises when it can be indicated that, as Rimbaud claimed, "I is someone else," or I is an "other."

This transformation is associated with tragedy and the formal notion of the caesura, which in Hölderlin, however, is involved in what Lacoue-Labarthe calls the "deconstruction of the speculative matrix of tragedy,"[26] which I take to mean the dissociation of tragic poetry from a grasp of the absolute. For, as I discussed in previous chapters, the tragic turn occurs when the "Sign = 0." In *The Writing of the Disaster*, Blanchot gives a terse reading of the tragic in Hölderlin, which refutes any inscription of the tragic within a logic of history or destiny:

> "All is rhythm," he is supposed to have said. . . ."All" does not mean
> . . . any already ordered totality which it would be rhythm's job
> to maintain. Rhythm does not belong to the order of nature or of
> language, or even of "art," where it seems to predominate. Rhythm
> is not the simple alteration of Yes and No, of "giving-withholding,"
> of presence-absence or of living-dying, producing-destroying.
> Rhythm, while it engages the multiple form of its missing unity,
> and while it appears regular and seems to govern according to a
> rule, threatens the rule. . . . The enigma of rhythm—dialectical-
> nondialectical, no more the one than the other is other—is the
> extreme danger. That we should speak in order to make sense of
> rhythm, and to make rhythm, which is not sensible—perceptible
> and meaningful: such is the mystery which traverses us.[27]

Rhythm, which Hölderlin thinks as the course of a tragic poem, ends in rupture before arrival, at that moment when arrival, the authentic grasp of Being, seems to be announced. At this moment the oppositions merely "appeared to be resolved" in the transcendence of the "ordinary and human boundaries of knowledge" (ELT 58, 60). In this rupture the poetic word is silenced; the "eccentric path" finds no essential origin, as Blanchot describes how "a circle, uncurled along a straight line rigorously prolonged, reforms a circle eternally bereft of center."[28]

Here, resoluteness on the part of poetic Dasein results not in authenticity but in disaster. This disaster, escaping the play of Being and nothingness, is not, however, the singular goal of poetic language, even when it aims, as in the poetry of Celan and Radnóti, at expressing inexpressible loss. Even in Radnóti, who writes from the vortex of disaster, one finds that poetic language maintains a grasp on life that, however fragile, exceeds the actual by virtue of a poetically enflamed possibility (of survival, of life). In the title poem of *Clouded Sky*, he writes in the final stanza:

> Clouds pour across the moon. Anger
> leaves a poisonous dark-green bruise on the sky.
> I roll myself a cigarette,
> slowly, carefully, I live.[29]

This tentative, slow maintenance despite the sky's raging bruises and the horrible absence of the familiar and the good suggests an initiative element of projective transcendence in poetic engagement that evades simple designation. For Radnóti's poetry, along with Hölderlin's insistence on the "feeling of life," shows that poetry's tasks exceed both Kristeva's negative revolutionary poetics and Heidegger's historical ontology. In Radnóti remembrance of the past necessitates first the struggle to preserve a hold upon the present; and yet his poems indicate also that the past, things in the world worth loving, preserves the present by appearing in glimpses through the oblivion.

In the new poetics there is a place for Dasein's self, albeit fragile, as the eccentric ungrounded self among beings in the world, a self not merely statically present, but a horizontal-imaginative nexus of possibility, creation, and preservation. In being itself, poetic Dasein accepts this nexus as the space of its own specificity and freedom. If denied its resolute self-grounding, Dasein finds no closure even in overcoming death by radically accepting it. Dasein does not embrace the nothing in a heroic struggle, does not reach the absolute in a tragic collision or shattering, but lives precariously alongside its constant insinuation. This fragility, as emphasized in Radnóti, clings to life in the face of extinction. He writes, "This is how this poem walks up to you —/ the words stamp quietly, then they fly up and crash, / just like death. And afterwards, a full, whishing / silence listens."[30] But possibility and joy are also illuminated, for instance in Hölderlin, as our creative access to the "feeling of life," and in Radnóti most tentatively in the poetic recollection of beings in the world worth living for.

Rhythm conceived as the unsaid layer of embodied materiality might too find a place in a poetics of Dasein, if it is released from the strict confines of the Freudian notion of repression. If Kristeva, in her predominantly negative notion of revolution, does not think this ontologically enough (except perhaps in reference to the chora) — as that otherness that precedes, but exceeds, even human corporeality, psychic and social life, as that closer, then, to what Hölderlin calls "life as such" — her view nevertheless opens poetic Dasein to an alterity often obviated in favor of the determination of "home." There is, here, another kind of anamnesis to be discovered: that of the fragility of the subject at the grounds of saying — by whom the world, disclosed in the shelter of language, is encountered. Here a poetics of Dasein is opened to an account of interconnected embodied life that had been left behind in Heidegger's insistence on the purity and isolation of the poet's mission. Released from the destiny of return, the "tongue" of poetic language — its hovering, ringing, trembling — is given flesh[31] in a postmetaphysical subject, and is opened to an *Ereignis* that, recalling no singular origin, brings poetic language into a more radical, and more poetic, sphere of thinking. Thus in poetic language, Blanchot writes, "we do not repel the earth, to which, in any event, we belong; but we do not make of it a refuge" for the being who speaks.[32]

The earth, conceived as the site for being's poetic disclosure, is indeed one substrate of poetical articulation; but the notion of spontaneity for which I have been arguing in conclusion demands rather a complex of points of departure that cannot be foreseen in any singular conscription of the earth. If poetry expresses a rootedness to the earth, how can we address the poetry of the refugee and the persecuted, the uprooted, who as in Celan or Radnóti sees "lead in the winter sky," and smells "the odor / of scorched human flesh"?[33] Or when, as Anna Akhmatova writes, "the grave I go to will not be my own."[34] The earth is only one point of departure; others include accident as I have written it from Hölderlin's terminology, as a locus of the unforeseeable; the intervention of spontaneity; fragile memory; and the seeking inscription into language of fragile life. Beyond the earthly, here Rilke's suggestion from *Sonnets to Orpheus* rings authentic:

Und wenn dich das Irdische vergass,
zu der stillen Erde sag: Ich rinne.
Zu dem raschen Wasser sprich: Ich bin.

And if the earthly has forgotten you,
to the quiet earth I say: I flow.
To the rushing water I say: I am.[35]

It must not be forgotten that, even at its most ontological, even at its most revolutionary, poetry is above all an act of creation. Poetry is—and perhaps this is the measure of authentic poetry—a tentative, never ontologically final, preservation of the mysteries and possibilities of (being-in-) the world.

Notes

Introduction: The Dialogue Between Poetry and Thinking

1. See Otto Pöggeler, *Martin Heidegger's Path of Thinking*, trans. Daniel Magurshak and Sigmund Barber (Atlantic Highlands, N.J.: Humanities Press International, 1987), 16.

2. In citing the German I sometimes alter the case of adjectives and nouns from genitive, accusative, or dative to nominative case for the sake of consistency with the English. I also leave out articles when they appear awkward in the English sentence.

3. Heidegger here links poetic language with *Befindlichkeit:* "Die Mitteilung der existenzialen Möglichkeiten der Befindlichkeit, das heißt das Erschließen von Existenz, kann eigenes Ziel der 'dichtenden' Rede werden" (SZ 162). Heidegger, further, refers to this passage in the *Letter on Humanism* (LH b222). On the passage in *Being and Time,* see Friedrich-Wilhelm von Hermann, *Subjekt und Dasein: Interpretationen zu 'Sein und Zeit.'* (Frankfurt am Main: Vittorio Klostermann, 1984), 179–180.

4. See Michel Haar, *The Song of the Earth: Heidegger and the Grounds of the History of Being,* trans. Reginald Lilly (Bloomington: Indiana University Press, 1993), 102–104. Compare with von Hermann, *Subjekt und Dasein,* 181–185.

5. On the "turn" in Heidegger, see Werner Marx, *Heidegger and the Tradition,* trans. Theodore Kisiel and Murray Greene (Evanston, Ill.: Northwestern University Press, 1971), 173–179. The "turn" in Heidegger refers to the transition from metaphysics to the thinking of the *Ereignis,* which is brought about in the danger of the oblivion of Being that arises with modern technology. Yet as it refers to the transitions in Heidegger's thinking of Being—which Hans-Georg Gadamer claims was already incipient in 1924—this transition is generally located after *Being and Time* and in Heidegger's turn to poetic language. We attempt here not to place a division in Heidegger's thinking between *Being and Time* and the discussion of poetry and technology, which would obscure the developments of as well as the continuities in Heidegger's thinking, but rather attempt to see both the continuities and the transitions along the way.

6. This essay-lecture from 1949 was first published in *Die Technik und die Kehre* (Pfullingen: Günter Neske, 1962) and in English translation in QT.

7. See Beda Allemann, "Martin Heidegger: Die Kehre," in *Hölderlin und Heidegger* (Zürich and Freiburg: Atlantis Verlag, 1956), 69–72.

8. In *Being and Time* Heidegger already refers to "listening" (*Zuhören*) as constitutive for language (*die Rede*). "We can make clear the connection of discourse with understanding and intelligibility by considering an existential possibility which belongs to talking itself—hearing . . . listening to . . . is Dasein's existential way of Being-open as Being-with for Others. Indeed, hearing constitutes the primary and authentic way in which Dasein is open for its ownmost potentiality-for-Being—as in hearing the voice of the friend whom every Dasein carries with it. Dasein hears, because it understands. . . . Being-with develops in listening to one another [*Aufeinander-hören*]" (BT 206/163).

9. This reference is a somewhat cryptic passage in the *Beiträge zur Philosophie* wherein Heidegger links Hölderlin particularly with Kierkegaard and Nietzsche as those who have suffered most deeply the unrootedness of modernity (GA 65, 204).

10. Reiner Schürmann gives an account of Heidegger's differentiation between *Beginn* and *Anfang/anfänglich*—the latter of which "designates a point of departure" and a thinking of the "event" (*Ereignis*) and the former of which refers to the beginning of metaphysics in Plato and Aristotle or the beginning in the sense of the beginning of an era, a "first step." In the *Seinsgeschichte* Heidegger designates several beginnings as *Beginn* (premetaphysical, metaphysical, and the transition to the overcoming of metaphysics), but *Anfang* refers to the inception of a thinking which is anticipatory (*Vordenken*) and remembrance (*Andenken*) at once. See Reiner Schürmann, *Heidegger on Being and Acting: From Principles to Anarchy*, trans. Christine-Marie Gros (Bloomington: Indiana University Press, 1987), 120–125. Although we will concentrate here more particularly on the notion of *Andenken,* it is to be noted that both *Andenken* and *Vordenken* arise in Heidegger's readings of Hölderlin—as in the echo of the lost gods and the waiting of an arrival. Inception (*Anfang*) belongs to this "between."

11. See Aristotle, *Poetics* 1451b1, 1456b1; *Politics* 1341b32–1342a18.

12. Hölderlin writes of a "poetic logic" in his essay "Remarks on Antigone" (ELT 109).

13. Given the importance of Heidegger's critique of logical and grammatical accounts of language for his own theory, claims of "contradiction" would have to be put into context and in a careful discussion of Heidegger's method, which will be discussed particularly in chapter 2.

14. Marx, *Heidegger and the Tradition*, 231.

15. For example, Véronique M. Fóti, *Heidegger and the Poets: Poiésis, Sophia, Techné* (Atlantic Highlands, N.J.: Humanities Press International, 1992); and "Textuality, Totalization, and the Question of Origin in Heidegger's Elucidation of *Andenken,*" *Research in Phenomenology* XIX (1989): 43–58; Paul de Man, *Romanticism and Contemporary Criticism*, ed. Kevin Newmark, Andrzej Warminski, and E. S. Burt (Baltimore: Johns Hopkins University Press, 1993), 55–56, 65.

While Fóti charges Heidegger with "totalization," de Man claims that Heidegger demands an "absolute totality" and a truth that "no longer lies in the poem." See also Jacques Derrida, *Points . . . Interviews, 1974–1994*, trans. Peggy Kamuf and others; ed. Elisabeth Weber (Stanford, Calif.: Stanford University Press, 1995), 316, 325–326, on the question of Heidegger's method of elucidation.

16. I am citing Paul de Man, "Heidegger's Exegesis of Hölderlin," and Otto Pöggeler, "Heidegger's Political Self-Understanding," reprinted in *The Heidegger Controversy*, ed. Richard Wolin (Cambridge, Mass.: MIT Press, 1993), 235.

17. Derrida refers to a "catastrophe" in "Che Cos'é la poesia?" in *Points*, an essay which implicitly critiques many facets of Heidegger's account of poetic language; Derrida charges, in the interview "Istrice 2: *Ick bünn all hier*," an "undeniable" "thematacist tendency in Heidegger." *Points*, 314.

18. See Derrida, *Points*, 324; compare with de Man, *Romanticism and Contemporary Criticism*, 124.

19. See Fred Dallmayr, *The Other Heidegger* (Ithaca, N.Y.: Cornell University Press, 1993), 141. Dallmayr suggests that Heidegger's use of Hölderlin is not political but rather a "counterpolitics, signaling a radical change of political course" (143). Compare with Robert Bernasconi, *Heidegger in Question* (Atlantic Highlands, N.J.: Humanities Press International, 1993), 136.

20. See Marx, *Heidegger and the Tradition*, 321.

21. Karl Jaspers, "Letter to the Freiburg University Denazification Committee," in *The Heidegger Controversy*, 148. See also Otto Pöggeler, "Heidegger's Political Self-Understanding," 203; Christoph Jamme, "Dem Dichter vordenken: Aspekte von Heideggers 'Zwiesprache' mit Hölderlin im Kontext seiner Kunstphilosophie," *Zeitschrift für philosophische Forschung* 38 (1984): 19; and Berel Lang, *Heidegger's Silence* (Ithaca, N.Y.: Cornell University Press, 1996), 63–64.

22. See Robert Bernasconi, "Poet of Poets: Poet of the Germans," in *Heidegger in Question*, 136.

23. Joseph J. Kockelmans, "Heidegger on Time and Being," in *Martin Heidegger: Critical Assessments*, ed. Christopher Macann (London and New York: Routledge, 1992), 1:156.

24. The essay "Time and Being," written in 1961, gives an account of the *Ereignis*, but follows insights Heidegger had already seen in the early 1940s at the time of the last lecture course on Hölderlin. (See chapter 1.) There is little consensus on whether or not Heidegger, in thinking *Ereignis*, remains within insights which could be called phenomenological. See Emmanuel Levinas, *Ethics and Infinity* (Pittsburgh: Duquesne University Press, 1985), 42, where he speaks of the "disappearance in [Heidegger's later thought] of phenomenology properly speaking." See Joan Stambaugh's introduction to *On Time and Being*, x, where she claims that Heidegger here is "far removed from phenomenology . . . describing sheer occurrence without reference to a thing occurring." Samuel Ijsseling calls this thinking "the realization and radicalization of the original idea of phenomenology" and yet claims that Heidegger

thinks a concept "which can only be justified phenomenologically with great difficulty." See Samuel Ijsseling, "The End of Philosophy as the Beginning of Thinking," in *Martin Heidegger: Critical Assessments*, 388, 396. Compare with Otto Pöggeler on Heidegger's transition from phenomenology to ontology and then to topology, in Otto Pöggeler, "Being as Appropriation," in *Martin Heidegger: Critical Assessments*, 284, 295, 303.

25. See Lyotard, *Heidegger and "The Jews,"* trans. Andreas Michael and Mark Roberts (Minneapolis: University of Minnesota Press, 1990), 4, 7.

26. See John D. Caputo's account of the influence of Meister Eckhart, *The Mystical Element in Heidegger's Thought* (New York: Fordham University Press, 1986), esp. 11, 119.

27. Nevertheless, de Man points out in *Romanticism and Contemporary Criticism* that Hölderlin research is still dominated by Heidegger (54), as does Dieter Henrich, *The Course of Remembrance and Other Essays on Hölderlin*, ed. Eckart Förster (Stanford, Calif.: Stanford University Press, 1997), 159, 282.

28. See de Man, *Romanticism and Contemporary Criticism*, 60.

29. Wilhelm Scherer, "Friedrich Hölderlin," in *Vorträge und Aufsätze zur Gesichte des geistigen Lebens in Deutschland und Österreich* (Berlin, 1874), 346–355.

30. August Sauer, *Friedrich Hölderlin: Sammlung gemeinnütziger Vorträge. Nr. 189* (Prague, 1894).

31. Josef Nadler, *Literaturgeschichte der deutschen Stämme und Landschaften*, 2d ed. (Regensburg: J. Habbel, 1923–28).

32. For an overview of Hölderlin reception through the time of Heidegger's interpretations, see Alessandro Pellegrini, *Friedrich Hölderlin: Sein Bild in der Forschung* (Berlin: de Gruyter, 1965). For a more recent account see Jochen Schmidt, "Hölderlin im 20. Jahrhundert," in *Hölderlin und die Moderne*, ed. Gerhard Kurz (Tübingen: Attempo-Verlag, 1995), 105–125.

33. Dilthey begins his treatment of Hölderlin with a high romanticization, perhaps essentialization, of the empirical life of the poet (a biographical gesture Heidegger rejects): "Hölderlin lived in such piously preserved purity (*Reinheit*) and in even greater beauty of essence (*Schoenheit des Wesens*)." Wilhelm Dilthey, *Das Erlebnis und die Dichtung* (Leipzig: Reclam, 1988), 287.

34. Goethe, letter to Schiller, July 1, 1797; cited in Friedrich Beißner, *Hölderlin Heute: Der lange Weg des Dichters zu seinem Ruhm* (Stuttgart: W. Kohlhammer, 1963), 34. See also Lawrence Ryan, *Friedrich Hölderlin* (Stuttgart: J. B. Metzlersche Verlagsbuchhandlung, 1962), 39.

35. See Richard Unger, "Hölderlin and his German Readers," in *Friedrich Hölderlin* (Boston: Twayne, 1984), 131.

36. On the politics surrounding Stefan George and his poetry, see Franz-Karl von Stockert, "Stefan George und sein Kreis: Wirkungsgeschichte vor und nach dem 30. Januar 1933," in *Literatur und Germanistik nach der 'Machtübernahme': Colloquium zur 50. Wiederkehr des 30 Januar 1933*, ed. Beda Allemann (Bonn: Bouvier Verlag Herbert Grundmann, 1983), 52–89.

37. Georg Lukács, "Hölderlins *Hyperion*," in *Goethe and his Age*, trans. Robert Anchor (New York: Grosset & Dunlap, 1969), 147–149. Lukács describes the appropriation of Hölderlin by the Third Reich as a "disfigurement of his memory."

38. See Helen Fehervary, *Hölderlin and the Left: The Search for a Dialectic of Art and Life* (Heidelberg: Carl Winter Universitätsverlag, 1977).

39. Beda Allemann explains what Hölderlin called the *Vaterländische Umkehr* with reference to the Empedocles tragedy in its several versions and to the essay "Remarks on Antigone." It is, most simply put, to be understood as the principle of return to earth, or homeward, for the conscious, finite human being, rather than Greek antiquity's embrace of the "fire from the heavens." This involves as well the distinction between German (or modern) and Greek (or ancient) that Hölderlin makes in the letter to Böhlendorff of 1801, to which we will turn in the following chapters. Allemann defines the *Umkehr* according to the third version of Empedocles or *"Empedocles auf dem Ätna,"* wherein the kingly principle (for in this version Empedocles's brother is king) and the Empedoclean are at odds. The former involves the acceptance of law and rule and is associated with art (for Hölderlin the organic); while the latter involves the demand for inclusion or fusion with the divine and infinite, and is associated with nature (for Hölderlin the aorgic). The *Umkehr* is a turning-away from Empedoclean hubris (a term used by de Man in his reference to Empedocles in *Romanticism and Contemporary Criticism*) — *"in* diese Welt, *auch* Erde *genannt."* Beda Allemann, *Hölderlin und Heidegger,* 13–34, here 28. According to Allemann, it is also this distinction or opposition between nature and art that defines for Hölderlin *Schicksal,* 21. On the distinction between organic (*organisch*) and aorgic (*aorgisch*), see Thomas Pfau, "Critical Introduction" to ELT, 168.

40. See de Man, *Romanticism and Contemporary Criticism,* 124. De Man argues that Hölderlin's term the "national" (*das Nationelle*) "has nothing in common" with twentieth century nationalism. This applies as well to the *vaterländisch,* which we will take up in detail in chapters 5 and 6.

41. Heidegger maintains the term phenomenology as "responding to the claim of what is to be thought," which has been considered both a move beyond phenomenology (toward the thinking of *Ereignis*) and phenomenology's radicalization. See his essay "My Way to Phenomenology," in *On Time and Being.*

42. That Heidegger's reading has been criticized as a literary interpretation of Hölderlin is not overlooked, but must be taken into context of Heidegger's own critique of *Literaturwissenschaft,* which is discussed and cited, though not taken up thematically, in the following three chapters. Beda Allemann gives an account of this in "Heidegger und die Literaturwissenschaft," *Hölderlin und Heidegger,* 185–202. This does not mean that Heidegger's procedures are immune to philosophical criticism, as Adorno first supplied in his essay "Parataxis: On Hölderlin's Late Poetry," in *Notes to Literature,* trans. Shierry Weber Nicholsen (New York: Columbia University Press, 1992), 2:109–149. Other philosophically oriented criticisms are taken up or cited in the following chapters.

43. While Heidegger claims that his discussion of Hölderlin is beyond "the political" (GA 39, 214), Bernasconi argues that "Heidegger is quite explicit about the political significance" of Hölderlin's institution of "German Being (*Seyn*) by projecting it into the most distant future" (GA 39, 220).

44. "Abandonment of humanism" does not mean that Heidegger advocates the inhumane. On Heidegger's "Letter on Humanism," see John D. Caputo, *The Mystical Element of Heidegger's Thought* (New York: Fordham University Press, 1986), 240–244. See also Dallmayr, *The Other Heidegger,* 130–131.

45. John D. Caputo argues that there is a loss of "life," a "displacement of living," in Heidegger's discussion of poetry. See Caputo, *Demythologizing Heidegger* (Bloomington: Indiana University Press, 1992), 164.

46. See Henrich, *The Course of Remembrance; Grund im Bewusstsein: Untersuchungen zu Hölderlins Denken (1794–1795)* (Stuttgart: Klett-Cotta, 1992); and *Hegel im Kontext* (Frankfurt am Main: Suhrkamp, 1971). See also Manfred Frank, *Einführung in die frühromantische Ästhetik* (Frankfurt am Main: Suhrkamp, 1987); and "'Intellektuelle Anschauung': Drei Stellungnahmen zu einem Deutungsversuch von Selbstbewusstsein: Kant, Fichte, Hölderlin/Novalis," in *Die Aktualität der Frühromantik,* ed. Ernst Behner and Jochen Höfisch (Paderborn: Verlag Ferdinand Schöningh, 1987); and "Hölderlins philosophische Grundlagen" in *Hölderlin und die Moderne.* See also Friedrich Strack, *Ästhetik und Freiheit: Hölderlins Idee von Schönheit, Sittlichkeit, und Geschichte in der Frühzeit* (Tübingen: Niemeyer, 1976).

47. In original German, see J. C. F. Hölderlin, *Theoretische Schriften,* ed. Johann Kreuzer (Hamburg: Felix Meiner Verlag, 1998). The text is based on those of the *Frankfurter Ausgabe.* In English translation, see Friedrich Hölderlin, *Essays and Letters on Theory,* trans. and ed. Thomas Pfau (Albany: SUNY Press, 1988). This version is based on the *Grosse Stuttgarter Ausgabe,* but refers to the *Frankfurter Ausgabe* in cases of "conflicting editorial principles." I refer to these editions of Hölderlin's writings to avoid the difficult philological issues that arise in the presentation of Hölderlin's writings in the two larger critical editions upon which they are based, particularly the inclusion of complicated transcriptions and facsimiles. Although both editions are of great worth for Hölderlin scholarship and for interpretations of the poetry, for our purposes they would overburden the attempt to access Hölderlin as a thinker of poetic language.

48. Yet there is already copious scholarship to which I refer in elucidating these writings. See n. 46 above. Here I will attempt to present a line of interpretation which cannot cover all dimensions of Hölderlin's thought, but takes up the problem of poetic language in its relation to philosophical systematicity and conceptuality and to the problem of the subject, as emergent in Hölderlin's discussion of reflection, sensitivity (*Empfindsamkeit*), consciousness (*Bewusstsein*), understanding (*Verstand*) and judgment (*Urtheil*), which I do not discuss systematically but as moments of Hölderlin's incomplete and emerging, that is to say, incipient theory of the subject. This involves a laying-out of notions of the feeling of life, freedom, and remembrance (both *Erinnerung* and *Andenken*), and

involves a discussion of Hölderlin's relation to Kant, Fichte, Hegelian idealism, and to some extent Platonic *anamnesis*.

49. As had been shown in Ernst Cassirer's 1918 study "Hölderlin und der deutsche Idealismus," in *Idee und Gestalt: Goethe, Schiller, Hölderlin und Kleist* (Darmstadt: Wissenschaftliche Buchsgesellschaft, 1971), 113–155.

50. See chapter 5.

51. Hans-Jost Frey, *Studies in Poetic Discourse: Mallarmé, Baudelaire, Rimbaud, Hölderlin*, trans. William Whobrey (Stanford, Calif.: Stanford University Press, 1996), 187.

52. Henrich, *The Course of Remembrance*, 72, 88.

53. Reinhard Mehring notes that Heidegger's tendency to read Hölderlin along Nietzschean lines was already a theme of the George circle. Mehring, *Heideggers Überlieferungsgeschick: Eine dionysische Inszenierung* (Würzburg: Königshausen and Neumann, 1992), 58.

54. Henrich, *The Course of Remembrance*, 282. See Beda Allemann, *Hölderlin und Heidegger*, on whom Henrich comments. See de Man on Allemann's book, *Romanticism and Contemporary Criticism*, 126–127.

55. Adorno, "Parataxis."

56. Including Henrich, *The Course of Remembrance;* Véronique M. Fóti, *Heidegger and the Poets* and "Textuality, Totalization, and the Question of Origin"; Annemarie Gethmann-Siefert, "Heidegger and Hölderlin: The Over-Usage of 'Poets in an Impoverished Time,'" *Research in Phenomenology* XIX (1989): 59–88; Christoph Jamme, "Hölderlin und das Problem der Metaphysik: Zur Diskussion um 'Andenken,'" *Zeitschrift für philosophische Forschung* 42 (1988): 645–665; and John D. Caputo, "Heidegger's Poets," in *Demythologizing Heidegger*, 148–168.

57. For an overview of literature on Heidegger's Hölderlin, in addition to the sources cited in this introduction, see Jamme, "Dem Dichter vor-denken," 191 ff.

58. To note a few examples: Michel Haar, in his otherwise excellent study of Heidegger's later philosophy, writes, "The Hölderlinian Sacred echoes anew Heraclitean thought. . . . Heidegger's position can neither be separated nor even distinguished from that of Hölderlin," *The Song of the Earth*, 55. Philippe Lacoue-Labarthe identifies Heidegger's *Ereignis* with the "caesura in the sense Hölderlin accorded this term"; Lacoue-Labarthe, *Heidegger, Art, and Politics*, trans. Chris Turner (Oxford: Basil Blackwell, 1990), 41–46. Werner Marx claims that "this essence, of poetizing, which the new type of thinking had thought and Hölderlin had poetized, determines for Heidegger the role of the essence of man"; Marx, *Heidegger and the Tradition*, 233. Jacques Derrida writes that whether in reference to "Heidegger or Hölderlin" the path of poetry aims at a "home port" that is specifically German. (See chapters 5 and 6 for a discussion of the "German" and the "proper" as regarding Heidegger and Hölderlin and their differences.) Derrida, *Points*, 324. Another such example is found in Bernasconi, *Heidegger in Question*, 110.

59. Jamme, "Hölderlin und das Problem der Metaphysik," 661.

60. De Man, *Romanticism and Contemporary Criticism*, 71.

61. J. M. Bernstein argues this thesis—that in Heidegger's account of art Being takes on the function of "genius" once granted to subjectivity—in *The Fate of Art: Aesthetic Alienation from Kant to Derrida and Adorno* (University Park: Pennsylvania State University Press, 1992), 66–135.

62. Ibid.

63. De Man, *Romanticism and Contemporary Criticism*, 127.

64. Hölderlin's 1793 *Abgangszeugnis*, on display in the permanent collection at the Hölderlin-Turm in Tübingen, reads: "seine theologische Studien hat er mit viel Erfolg betrieben . . . die Philologie, vornehmlich die griechische, die Philosophie, vornehmlich die von Kant, und die schönen Wissenschaft hat er mit Ausdauer gepflegt." In original Latin: "Philologia, imprimis gracae, et philosophio imprimis Kantiano, et litterarum elegantiorum assiduus cultor." Permanent exhibition, room 1, box 2, piece 10.

65. Derrida, *Points*, 321.

66. See de Man, *Romanticism and Contemporary Criticism*.

67. Friedrich-Wilhelm von Hermann, for example, in his treatment of Heidegger's critique of the philosophical subject-object distinction, reads the existential-ontological analytic of Dasein in terms of setting up the problem of thinking as it learns from poetry's phenomenological revealing, and poetic dwelling is considered in terms of Being-in-the-world and *Befindlichkeit*. See von Hermann, *Subjekt und Dasein*, 178–188.

68. The lecture courses on "Germanien," (GA 39) "Andenken," (GA 52) and "Der Ister" (GA 53; DI) are all examined in detail.

1. Heidegger's Critique of Subjectivity and the Poetic Turn

1. See Schürmann, *Heidegger on Being and Acting*, 65–77.

2. Kockelmans, "Heidegger on Time and Being," 146.

3. Pöggeler, *Martin Heidegger's Path of Thinking*, 2. Hans-Georg Gadamer also notes the continuity of Heidegger's "one path," in *Reading Heidegger from the Start*, ed. Theodore Kisiel and John van Buren (Albany: SUNY Press, 1987), 25. Frederick Olafson argues for a deeper continuity that underlies the "turn" in Heidegger's thinking. See Olafson, "The Unity of Heidegger's Thought," in *The Cambridge Companion to Heidegger*, ed. Charles B. Guignon (Cambridge: Cambridge University Press, 1993).

4. See Haar, *The Song of the Earth*, 75.

5. Gadamer claims that the "other beginning" is initiated for Heidegger in reading Nietzsche and Hölderlin. "Martin Heidegger's One Path," 29.

6. I am citing François Raffoul, who discusses these elements of Heidegger's critique of the modern subject in *Heidegger and the Subject*, trans. David Pettigrew and Gregory Rocco (Atlantic Highlands, N.J.: Humanities Press International, 1998), 47, thus laying out the following passage

from Heidegger (GA 24, 173/123): "The motive of this primary orientation toward the subject in modern philosophy is the opinion that this being which we ourselves are is given to the knower first and as the only certain thing, that the subject is accessible immediately and with absolute certainty, that it is better known than all objects. In comparison, objects are accessible only by way of a mediation."

7. Compare with Michel Haar, "Heidegger and the God of Hölderlin," *Research in Phenomenology* XIX (1989): 89–91.

8. *Aletheia*, as unconcealment, is also intrinsically connected in Heidegger's usage to forgetting (*lethe*) and un-forgetting, or remembrance. This connection will be made only implicitly here but will become obvious in the reading of the notion of *Andenken* or recollection, remembrance, in chapter 2.

9. Gadamer, "Martin Heidegger's One Path," 24.

10. Giorgio Agamben, "The Passion of Facticity," in *Potentialities: Collected Essays in Philosophy*, ed. and trans. Daniel Heller-Roazen (Stanford, Calif.: Stanford University Press, 1999), 189.

11. Ibid., 192.

12. Ibid., 189.

13. Gadamer describes the "hermeneutics of facticity" this way: "The 'hermeneutics *of* facticity' is thus a possessive and not object genitive, meaning 'facticity's hermeneutics.' . . . Facticity, which lays itself out, which interprets itself, does not bring interpretive concepts to bear on itself, rather it is a kind of conceptual speaking that wants to hold onto its origins and, thus, onto its own life's breath, once it is translated into the form of a theoretical statement." Gadamer, "Martin Heidegger's One Path," 25.

14. Gadamer argues that the "formal indication" is significant for understanding the whole of Heidegger's thought. Ibid., 33.

15. Gadamer makes this connection in ibid., 25–26.

16. Agamben, "The Passion of Facticity," 202.

17. On this aprioricity, see Schürmann, *Heidegger on Being and Acting*, 63.

18. See Agamben, "The Passion of Facticity," 200–201.

19. Rudolph Bernet, "The Phenomenological Reduction and the Double Life of the Subject," in *Reading Heidegger from the Start*, ed. Theodore Kisiel and John van Buren (Albany: SUNY Press, 1987), 247.

20. Ibid.

21. See Kockelmans, "Heidegger on Time and Being," 154.

22. Otto Pöggeler, "Being as Appropriation," 291.

23. Haar, *The Song of the Earth*, 79.

24. See Pöggeler, "Being as Appropriation," 291.

25. Agamben, "The Passion of Facticity," 203.

26. On the shift from Dasein as individual to a "collective" destiny or history, see Schürmann, *Heidegger on Being and Acting*, 72; Caputo, *Demythologizing Heidegger*, 80–81.

27. Pöggeler, *Martin Heidegger's Path of Thinking*, 259, 287.

28. For an account of Heidegger's representation of language as the "flower of the mouth," see Friedrich Wilhelm von Hermann, "The Flower of the Mouth: Hölderlin's Hint for Heidegger's Thinking of the Essence of Language," *Research in Phenomenology* XIX (1989): 27–42.

29. J. M. Bernstein argues that Heidegger's theory of art is nevertheless indebted to "Kant's discovery of a new philosophical subject" and that Heidegger's account of the artwork depends on Kant's theory of subjective freedom. Nevertheless, Heidegger and Kant are to be radically distinguished with regard to "how 'subjects' are connected to such works." See Bernstein, *The Fate of Art*, 14, 18, 117.

30. The nature of this "submission" oscillates in Heidegger's account, particularly with regard to the notion of the question (*die Frage*). Heidegger both demands a listening which submits, does not ask questions (OWL 71, 75, 76), and claims that questioning is the "piety of thought" (QT, first and last paragraphs).

31. Bernstein, *The Fate of Art*, 128.

32. Ibid., 14.

33. See Haar, *The Song of the Earth*, 81.

34. Heidegger's answer in the "Letter on Humanism" refers to a more "originary" ethics; in some sense the *Gelassenheit* structure, which I am arguing is fundamental to Heidegger's theory of poetic language and phenomenological disclosure, might be called a dimension of this ethics. Yet the concerns that I will unfold in the considerations of Heidegger and Hölderlin include ones that are political-philosophical and that also deal with the problem of humanism itself, which I argue takes a different form of articulation in Hölderlin. Thus we leave aside the question of "originary ethics," but refer to Haar, *The Song of the Earth*, 90–91, who argues that the ethical question is taken up in Heidegger as the "more explicitly ethical" question of technology; and to Johanna Hodge, *Heidegger and Ethics* (New York: Routledge, 1995), who takes up this question in depth.

35. Werner Marx poses this question in *Heidegger and the Tradition*.

36. Bernstein, *The Fate of Art*, 117.

37. Derrida calls this a "thematizing tendency" in Heidegger in *Points*. See also Derrida, *Of Spirit: Heidegger and the Question* (Chicago: University of Chicago Press, 1991). On the notion of totality, see Haar, *The Song of the Earth*, 72.

38. As argued by Marx in *Heidegger and the Tradition* and Bernstein in *The Fate of Art*.

39. Marx, *Heidegger and the Tradition*, 233–234.

40. This might be described as a "generalized" *Gelassenheit* in which "the task is to let all things be as they are," thus as an "ethics of liberation, toleration, and solidarity." John D. Caputo, *Radical Hermeneutics: Repetition, Deconstruction, and the Hermeneutic Project* (Bloomington: Indiana University Press, 1987), 288.

41. "Poeticization" here, as we shall see in chapter 3, involves not merely an aestheticization of the rational subject but also its destabilization.

42. Marx, *Heidegger and the Tradition*, 234.

43. A critique of narrative (as Hegelian or, less directly, Heideggerian historicality) is given in Eric L. Santner, *Friedrich Hölderlin: Narrative Vigilance and the Poetic Imagination* (New Brunswick, N.J.: Rutgers University Press, 1996).

44. Hölderlin discusses the problem of the accidental in a letter to Ludwig Neuffer of July 1799, in the context of the problem of poetic form. While tragic poetic form has been developed to "advance in a harmonious alteration" in a "proud denial of anything accidental," this denial has threatened the tragic form: "it had become dead like all other forms when they lost the living soul whom they served like an organic structure out of which they originally developed." Hölderlin juxtaposes this traditional tragic form to the sentimental (lyric) form, which, likewise in harmonious alteration, can proceed with "this gentle shyness of the accidental" which is then apt to "present the ideal of a living whole, to be sure, not with this strained force of parts and this onrushing progression" but with an "intimate brevity." Hölderlin then asks in what form this could be most naturally achieved (ELT 142–143). In accordance with Hölderlin's theory of poetic forms, each form (lyric, tragic, epic) must include, in addition to its basic mood, the alternating tones of the other (ELT 83–88). Accident is also treated as an element of subjectivity in Hölderlin's short essays on Kant, which will be discussed in subsequent chapters.

2. Heidegger's Hölderlin

1. See also *Die Geschichte des Seyns* for a sketched-out version of this "history" in the context of the saying of the "simple" word (GA 69, 2–5).

2. Gregory Fried, *Heidegger's Polemos: From Being to Politics* (New Haven: Yale University Press, 2000), 17.

3. Ibid., 16.

4. Ibid., 29.

5. Cited in ibid., 17.

6. See ibid., 162–163.

7. Some counterexamples are given in the introductory chapter, "The Dialogue Between Poetry and Thinking," above; see also PR 102–103; EHD 113, 183.

8. Compare Heidegger's use of this term (*überdichtet*) to the play on its prefix in *Being and Time*: *überantwortet, überkommene, übergibt* (BT 43/21).

9. Walter Benjamin, "Zwei Gedichte von Friedrich Hölderlin," in *Sprache und Geschichte*, ed. Rolf Tiedemann (Stuttgart: Philipp Reclam, 1992).

10. Compare with Heidegger's critique of Dilthey's *Literaturgeschichte* in *Being and Time*: BT, 450/398.

11. See Schmidt, "Hölderlin im 20. Jahrhundert."

12. See Fehervary, *Hölderlin and the Left*.

13. For competing discussions of the relation of Heidegger's thought to Hegel, see Robert Bernasconi, *The Question of Language in Heidegger's History of Being*

(Atlantic Highlands, N.J.: Humanities Press International, 1993), 7–8; Haar, *The Song of the Earth*, 80; and Dennis J. Schmidt, *The Ubiquity of the Finite: Hegel, Heidegger, and the Entitlements of Philosophy* (Cambridge, Mass.: MIT Press, 1988).

14. See John D. Caputo's exegesis in *The Mystical Element of Heidegger's Thought*, 60–66.

15. See Caputo, *Demythologizing Heidegger*, 96–97.

16. Nevertheless, see Rainer Schürmann's discussion of the Greek categories in *Heidegger on Being and Acting*, 168–181.

17. The principle of hubris as informing Hölderlin's understanding of tragedy and his own tragic writings will be discussed in the next chapter.

18. Hölderlin's essay "Judgment and Being," and the critique of transcendental idealism therein, is of importance for his drama *Empedocles* and the tragic conflict in which the title character is involved; see chapter 3, below.

19. See Dieter Henrich, *The Course of Remembrance* and *Der Grund im Bewusstsein*, for a discussion of Hölderlin's critique of Fichte and transcendental idealism. See chapter 3, below.

20. Bernasconi, *The Question of Language*, 6.

21. Ibid., 7.

22. Jochen Schmidt calls this an "ontologization" in "Hölderlin im 20. Jahrhundert."

23. See Franz Gabriel Nauen, *Revolution, Idealism, and Human Freedom: Schelling, Hölderlin and Hegel and the Crisis of Early German Idealism* (The Hague: Martinus Nijhoff, 1971), 53–54, 65.

24. See Strack, *Ästhetik und Freiheit*, for a sustained discussion of Hölderlin's relation to the principles of Kantian freedom.

25. See Friedrich-Wilhelm von Hermann's description of poetic dwelling in *Subjekt und Dasein: Interpretationen zu 'Sein und Zeit.'* (Frankfurt am Main: Vittorio Klostermann, 1984), 178; the chapter "Heidegger as Friend of the Earth" in Fred Dallmayr, *The Other Heidegger;* and Haar, *The Song of the Earth*, 139–140.

26. On this point see Véronique M. Fóti, "Textuality, Totalization, and the Question of Origin in Heidegger's Elucidation of Hölderlin's *Andenken*," *Research in Phenomenology* XIX (1989): 52.

27. One would note here as well Heidegger's interest in Paul Klee, whom he mentions in "Time and Being" which we take up below as an articulation of *Ereignis*. Siegbert Peetz argues for the inclusion of Paul Klee next to Hölderlin in the development of Heidegger's concept of earth. See "Welt und Erde: Heidegger und Paul Klee," *Heidegger Studies* 2 (1995): 167–187, esp. 186.

28. Cf. Allemann, *Hölderlin und Heidegger*, 23. Paul de Man criticizes the identification of heroic, historical action with the poet in *Romanticism and Contemporary Criticism*.

29. We might note hear Heidegger's preference for a "listening" thinking over the metaphysics of vision–the absolute "gaze" of cognition to which Hegel refers. This preference, while affording a reconception of language beyond

the utterance of a representational subject, aids Heidegger's avoidance of images as discussed above.

30. Heidegger makes clear that this relation to the Greek is not to be thought according to the classicism of Goethe and Schiller, who can be said to have influenced Hölderlin. GA 52, 78; DI 50.

31. The problem of the foreign and the proper as the theme of the Böhlendorff letter is taken up in the third and sixth chapters.

32. See Dieter Henrich's critique of this identification of the poet and the seafarers in *The Course of Remembrance*. In the next chapter we will discuss Henrich's alternative reading in detail.

33. Paul de Man argues against Heidegger's identification of the poet in "Wie wenn am Feiertage" with historical founding and with the historical hero, and argues that the poet's role is shown to be far more modest. See "Temporality," 68. We will take up this debate in chapter 3.

34. Christoph Jamme's discussion of this lecture course focuses in part on a critique of Heidegger's reading of the greeting. See "Hölderlin und das Problem der Metaphysik," 645–665.

35. Among other passages from Hölderlin's poems and essays.

36. Bernet, "Phenomenological Reduction and the Double Life of the Subject," 245–268.

37. See Dieter Henrich, *The Course of Remembrance*. We will turn to this reading of "Andenken" in the next chapter.

38. See Otto Pöggeler, "Being as Appropriation," and Kockelmans, "Heidegger on Time and Being."

39. Pöggeler, "Being as Appropriation," 281.

40. Ibid., 295.

41. Friedrich-Wilhelm von Hermann gives an account of Heidegger's reading of Hölderlin here in "The Flower of the Mouth: Hölderlin's Hint for Heidegger's Thinking of the Essence of Language," *Research in Phenomenology* XIX (1989): 27–42.

42. Heidegger refers here to Novalis and his notion of "monologue," which must be taken into account when assessing Heidegger's notion of language as "dialogue." (See OWL 134.) If language is a dialogue between poet and thinker, it is a monologue in the sense that both dimensions of saying issue from and return to language itself.

43. On the thinking of the withdrawal, see Samuel Ijsseling, "The End of Philosophy as the Beginning of Thinking," in Macann, ed., *Martin Heidegger: Critical Assessments*, 4:383–397.

44. Pöggeler, "Being as Appropriation," 296.

45. Heidegger connects his readings of "Andenken" and "Der Ister" in GA 52, 39 and in DI 151.

46. The name of Hölderlin's poem was given by the editor Norbert von Hellingrath.

47. See Hölderlin, ELT 112.

48. Compare with Bernasconi, *The Question of Language*, 39.

49. See ibid., 40.

50. Which recalls as well the "simplicity" (*Einfachheit*) granted to *Schicksal* when Dasein achieves a resolute *Wiederholung* of *das Gewesene*, our fates, which "have already been guided in advance" (BT 436/383). This simplicity excludes inauthentic "ambiguity" (*Zweideutigkeit*) (BT 435/383).

51. See also GA 52, 72–73 for Heidegger's remarks on Hölderlin's engagement with the Oedipus and Antigone plays of Sophocles.

52. See chapter 5, "The Poetic Politics of Dwelling."

53. See chapter 1, "Heidegger's Critique of Subjectivity and the Poetic Turn," and chapter 3, "Poetic Subjectivity and the Elusiveness of Being."

3. Poetic Subjectivity and the Elusiveness of Being

1. Compare with Levinas's views of language in *Totality and Infinity*, trans. Alphonso Lingis (Pittsburgh: Duquesne University Press, 1969) (wherein Levinas rejects poetic language in favor of "prose," which guarantees language's "sincerity and veracity" and its communicative function—that is, its relation to the "Other"); and in *Otherwise than Being*, wherein Levinas admits that language, even communication, includes an "enigmatic ambivalence," the "diachronic ambivalence" of inspiration.

2. On the relation of poetic language and "earth," see Haar, *The Song of the Earth*, 111–117; and von Hermann, "The Flower of the Mouth." See also Dallmayr, *The Other Heidegger*.

3. See Fóti, *Heidegger and the Poets*.

4. Paul de Man in *Romanticism and Contemporary Criticism*, and Adorno in "Parataxis," for instance.

5. Stanley Corngold, *The Fate of the Self: German Writers and French Theory* (Durham, N.C.: Duke University Press, 1994), 51–53.

6. Samuel Ijsseling claims that the *Seinsgeschichte* or Heidegger's "concept of 'history' (*Geschichte*) is . . . a concept which can only be phenomenologically justified with great difficulty." "The End of Philosophy as the Beginning of Thinking," 396. Otto Pöggeler, in "Being as Appropriation," claims that "the later Heidegger does not wish to have his thought understood as phenomenological research" (294), but rather that "Heidegger's latest endeavors of thought . . . form a topology, i.e., they are designations of the place, or sayings of the place of Being's truth, with the help of a selection of loci or a collection of the guiding concepts and principles of Western thought." "Topology" is to be understood as "a saying of the place, and thus a thinking of the truth, of Being" (306). If this involves a relationship to beings, which Pöggeler claims "is already posited along with the thinking of Being" (304), this means that "thought no longer moves from beings to Being, but rather from Being to beings" (296). At times, including in the "Time and Being" essay to which we referred in the last chapter, Heidegger presses thinking beyond beings

and not back toward them, such that the *Ereignis* as the *withdrawing* event can come to word.

7. See Friedrich-Wilhelm von Hermann's account of Heidegger's overcoming of the notion of artist as subject and master of a work: von Hermann, *Subjekt und Dasein: Interpretationen zu "Sein und Zeit"* (Frankfurt am Main: Vittorio Klostermann, 1984), 190.

8. Beda Allemann follows to some extent Heidegger's reading here in *Hölderlin und Heidegger,* 13, 16; cf. 23.

9. Compare with Bernasconi, *The Question of Language,* 39.

10. That Heidegger's choice of "essential" poets are all male poets (with the exception of Sophocles's character Antigone whom Heidegger identifies with "the poet" figure in DI), and that his characterization of the poet explicitly rejects femininity (GA 39, 17), I maintain Heidegger's use of the masculine poet (*der Dichter*), his (*sein, seine*), and him (*ihn, ihm*). Below, in the penultimate chapter on Kristeva, Heidegger, and Hölderlin, this problem becomes more explicit.

11. Werner Marx claims that Heidegger's understanding of the "creative man" leaves behind direction for everyday dwelling. See Marx, *Heidegger and the Tradition.*

12. See Heidegger's discussion of Mozart in *The Principle of Reason.*

13. See Fried, *Heidegger's Polemos,* and chapter 2, above.

14. See Christopher Fynsk, *Language and Relation* (Stanford, Calif.: Stanford University Press, 1996), 39–40.

15. Christoph Jamme argues that "Andenken" is, however, a unification of autobiographical and poetic-theoretical discourse. Jamme, "Hölderlin und das Problem der Metaphysik," 645. This argument is followed in depth in Dieter Henrich, *The Course of Remembrance.*

16. Heidegger elsewhere appeals to what Hölderlin meant or did not mean — for example, that where Hölderlin writes of Rousseau, Hölderlin means not Rousseau but the becoming homely that the river poem poetizes (DI).

17. Paul de Man argues so in *Romanticism and Contemporary Criticism,* as does Adorno in "Parataxis."

18. Compare with von Hermann, *Subjekt und Dasein,* who gives a somewhat compatible reading of *Being and Time's* Dasein in terms of the later phenomenological-poetic insights. Most contemporaneous with *Being and Time* in terms of a phenomenological-poetic insight is Heidegger's discussion of a page from Rilke in *The Basic Problems of Phenomenology,* trans. Albert Hofstadter (Bloomington: Indiana University Press, 1982). See introduction, "The 'Dialogue' Between Poetry and Thinking," above.

19. As for René Char, Mallarmé, Valéry, and others. See Haar, *The Song of the Earth,* 118.

20. Frey, *Studies in Poetic Discourse,* 190.

21. See Adorno, "Parataxis."

22. See Lawrence Ryan, *Hölderlins Lehre vom Wechsel der Töne* (Stuttgart: Kohlhammer, 1960).

23. On hubris, see de Man, *Romanticism and Contemporary Criticism*, 42; and Lawrence Ryan, *Friedrich Hölderlin*, 52. The quotation is from Corngold, *The Fate of the Self*, 36.

24. Frey, *Studies in Poetic Discourse*, 187.

25. Ibid., 184.

26. Corngold, *The Fate of the Self*, 51.

27. Frey, *Studies in Poetic Discourse*, 186.

28. Richard Unger, in *Hölderlin's Major Poetry: The Dialectics of Unity* (Bloomington: Indiana University Press, 1975), traces the problem of the *hen kai pan* throughout Hölderlin's work.

29. This text was available in Hölderlin's collected works only in 1951; thus it was unavailable to Heidegger during the main years of Heidegger's Hölderlin interpretations.

30. See Henrich, *Der Grund im Bewusstsein.*

31. Henrich, *The Course of Remembrance*, 73, 126–128.

32. Ibid., 86.

33. See Manfred Frank, "Hölderlins philosophische Grundlagen," in *Hölderlin und die Moderne*, ed. Gerhard Kurz, (Tübingen: Attempto-Verlag, 1995).

34. See Henrich, *The Course of Remembrance*, 126.

35. Johann Gottlieb Fichte, *Introductions to the Wissenschaftslehre and Other Writings*, trans. and ed. Daniel Breazeale (Indianapolis: Hackett, 1994), 86.

36. Ibid., 46.

37. Ibid., 9.

38. Ibid., 113.

39. It is to be noted that the title is an editorial insertion, judgment discussed on one side of the original page, Being on the other.

40. This representation relies upon Dieter Henrich's account in *The Course of Remembrance*, 104–105.

41. Ibid., 104.

42. Ibid., 107.

43. Ibid., 75.

44. Frank, *Einführung in die frühromantische Ästhetik*, 152.

45. Henrich, *The Course of Remembrance*, 75.

46. Fichte, *Introductions*, 21.

47. Which is incipient in *Being and Time* as the hearing and silence that ground the possibility of *Rede*. See von Hermann, *Subjekt und Dasein*, 192–197.

48. Fichte, *Introductions*, 86.

49. Adorno, "Parataxis," 144.

50. Lawrence Ryan, "Zur Frage des 'Mythischen' bei Hölderlin,' in *Hölderlin ohne Mythos*, ed. Ingrid Riedel (Göttingen: Vandenhoeck & Ruprecht, 1973).

51. Compare with Santner, *Friedrich Hölderlin*, 136.

52. In the following I am referring principally to the second draft of *Empedocles*, unless otherwise noted.

53. De Man, *Romanticism and Contemporary Criticism*, 69–71.

54. On "founding" see Frey, *Studies in Poetic Discourse*, 188.

55. Thomas Pfau uses the language of "ontological skepticism" in the context of Hölderlin's "Judgment and Being" and his departure from philosophy. See his "Critical Introduction," *Friedrich Hölderlin: Essays and Letters on Theory*, trans. Thomas Pfau (Albany: SUNY Press, 1987), 21.

56. Adorno, de Man, and Hans-Jost Frey claim this.

57. Blanchot, *The Space of Literature*, trans. Ann Smock (Lincoln: University of Nebraska Press, 1982), 238.

58. Frey, *Studies in Poetic Discourse*, 189.

59. Blanchot, *The Space of Literature*, 247.

60. Ibid., 237.

61. Haar, *The Song of the Earth*, 142.

62. See Stanley Corngold, *The Fate of the Self*, 51; and Gaston Bachelard, *On Poetic Imagination and Reverie*, trans. Colette Gaudin (Dallas: Spring Publications, 1971), 20.

63. De Man, *Romanticism and Contemporary Criticism*, 51. Compare with Anselm Havercamp, *Leaves of Mourning: Hölderlin's Late Work*, trans. Vernon Chadwick (Albany: SUNY Press, 1996).

64. Henrich, *The Course of Remembrance*, 244.

65. Adorno, "Parataxis," 122.

66. Friedrich Strack, *Ästhetik und Freiheit*, 118.

67. Santner, *Friedrich Hölderlin*, 28, 5. Santner argues for the undermining of narrative structure particularly in Hölderlin's late poetry, which he calls a "poetry of shards," and yet I would argue that the grounds for this are set up in Hölderlin's earlier essays and in *Hyperion* and *Empedocles*.

68. Adorno, "Parataxis," 123.

69. Strack, *Ästhetik und Freiheit*, 111.

70. Jacques Derrida, *Points*, 321; see also 256–257, 280–281, 320. See also *Mémoires for Paul de Man* (New York: Columbia University Press, 1986).

71. Derrida, *Points*, 321.

72. Ibid., 322.

73. Bernstein, *The Fate of Art*, 165.

74. Derrida, *Mémoires for Paul de Man*; Jean-Paul Sartre, *The Transcendence of the Ego: An Existentialist Theory of Consciousness*, trans. Williams and Kirkpatrick (New York: Farrar, Straus & Giroux, 1987), 89.

75. See Bernstein, *The Fate of Art*, on "Kant's discovery of a new philosophical subject"; see also Philippe Lacoue-Labarthe and Jean-Luc Nancy, *The Literary Absolute*, trans. Philip Barnard and Cheryl Lester (Albany: SUNY Press, 1988), and Jacques Taminiaux, *Poetics, Speculation, and Judgment: The Shadow of the Work of Art from Kant to Phenomenology*, trans. Michael Gendre (Albany: SUNY Press, 1993).

76. Strack, *Ästhetik und Freiheit*, 110–111.

77. Haar, *The Song of the Earth*, 56.

78. Dieter Henrich, *The Course of Remembrance*, 148.

79. See "Introduction: The Dialogue Between Poetry and Thinking."

80. Henrich, *The Course of Remembrance*, 145; his explication of the relation of Fichtean synthesis to Hölderlin's theory of the modulation of tones is at 135. See also Ryan, *Hölderlins Lehre über den Wechsel der Töne*.

81. Ryan, *Friedrich Hölderlin*, 53–54.

82. Heidegger identifies the seafarers with the speaker of the poem who greets them (GA 52, 137) and with the (in this poem unmentioned) fatherland: (GA 52, 86): "Die Schiffer sind die kommenden Dichter Germaniens"; whereas Henrich shows this reading to be untenable in light of the structure of the poem in *The Course of Remembrance*. Christoph Jamme criticizes Heidegger's identification in "Hölderlin und das Problem der Metaphysik," 657.

83. Haverkamp, *Leaves of Mourning*, 87.

84. See Santner, *Friedrich Hölderlin*.

85. See Haverkamp, *Leaves of Mourning*.

86. Blanchot, *The Space of Literature*, 247.

87. Henrich, *The Course of Remembrance*, 188.

88. Santner, *Friedrich Hölderlin*, 136.

89. See Adorno, "Parataxis"; Frey, *Studies in Poetic Discourse*.

90. Blanchot, *The Space of Literature*, 237, 247.

91. Henrich, *The Course of Remembrance*, 203.

92. Ibid., 209.

93. Eric L. Santner argues that the preservation (implied by "was bleibet") is not an attempt to counter the flux of time, but to feel it more deeply, to "celebrate" it. Santner, *Friedrich Hölderlin*, 136.

94. Henrich, *The Course of Remembrance*, 217.

95. Ibid.

96. Haverkamp, *Leaves of Mourning*, 54, 75. Haverkamp thinks that the "old" Hölderlin (who, in "madness" in the Zimmer house, signed his poems Scardanelli, and whose writings we do not take up) moves "beyond" cryptic subjectivity.

97. Blanchot, *The Space of Literature*, 237.

98. Haverkamp, *Leaves of Mourning*, 66, 68.

99. Ibid., 89.

100. De Man, *Romanticism and Contemporary Criticism*, 51–52.

101. Haverkamp, *Leaves of Mourning*, 77.

102. Adorno, "Parataxis," 136–137.

103. Ibid., 137.

104. Ibid., 135.

105. De Man, *Romanticism and Contemporary Criticism*, 68.

106. Ibid., 69–73.

107. Ibid., 69.

108. Ibid., 71.

109. Marx, *Heidegger and the Tradition*, 255.

110. Henrich, *The Course of Remembrance*, 216.

111. Ibid., 218–219.

4. The Critique of Technology and the Poetics of "Life"

1. See Haar, *The Song of the Earth*, 14.

2. This is also the problem of temporality, which is contrasted for ancient Greek and modern German poetry. Beda Allemann comments on the latter: "Unsere, der Abendländischen Bahn liegt umgekehrt. Ausgefahren in der Richtung auf das himmlische Feuer, müssen wir zurück zur Erde." See Friedrich Hölderlin, "Remarks on Antigone" (ELT 112) and Beda Allemann thereupon, *Hölderlin und Heidegger,* 31.

3. See Hans-Jost Frey's discussion of the impossibility of the poet's naming, *Studies in Poetic Discourse,* 180.

4. See Thomas Pfau, "Critical Introduction," 21.

5. CJ 204. Kant uses both "das Lebensgefühl" and "das Gefühl des Lebens" in the "General Comment on the Exposition of Aesthetic Judgments."

6. See Kant, *Groundwork to the Metaphysics of Morals,* VI:211.

7. See Frank, *Einführung in die frühromantische Ästhetik,* 31.

8. Ibid., 101–102.

9. Friedrich Strack treats the aesthetic idea in Hölderlin's relation to Kant in *Ästhetik und Freiheit.*

10. Frank, *Einführung in die frühromantische Ästhetik,* 101.

11. Novalis, *Schriften II: Das Philosophische Werk* (Stuttgart: Kohlhammer), 647, n. 473. See also Frank, *Einführung in die frühromantische Ästhetik,* 104–105, 137, 142.

12. See Friedrich Schlegel's *Philosophical Fragments,* trans. Peter Firchow (Minneapolis: University of Minnesota Press, 1995), 32, 38–39.

13. Paul Valéry, *The Art of Poetry* (Princeton, N.J.: Princeton University Press, 1992), 64.

14. This text is called "Sieben Maximen" or "Seven Maxims" in the *Frankfurter Ausgabe* and is thought to have been written in 1799, much in the style of Novalis and Schlegel.

15. On the relation between Hölderlin and Schiller, see Henrich, *The Course of Remembrance,* 123–125; Friedrich Beissner, *Hölderlin Heute: Der lange Weg des Dichters zu seinem Ruhm* (Stuttgart: W. Kohlhammer, 1965), 24–27, 30–31; Frank, *Einführung in die frühromantische Ästhetik,* 104–136. On their differences, see E. L. Stahl, "Hölderlin's Idea of Poetry," *The Era of Goethe* (Oxford: Oxford University Press, 1959), 155.

16. Influences on Hölderlin's theory include Plato and what Dieter Henrich calls the "side-stream thought of neo-Platonic philosophy" that accompanied the empiricism and metaphysics of the eighteenth century, particularly in Shaftesbury and Herder. See Henrich, *Hegel im Kontext,* 12–14.

17. See Strack, *Ästhetik und Freiheit,* 121.

18. So Hennig Bothe claims in *Hölderlin zur Einführung* (Hamburg: Junius, 1994), 69.

19. See Strack, *Ästhetik und Freiheit,* 107–118.

20. Ibid., 111–118.

21. Bothe, *Hölderlin zur Einführung*, 88.

22. Henrich, *Hegel im Kontext*, 18.

23. See Strack, *Ästhetik und Freiheit*, 118.

24. Lacoue-Labarthe and Nancy, *The Literary Absolute*, 32.

25. Friedrich Nietzsche, *The Birth of Tragedy*, trans. Walter Kaufmann (New York: Random House, 1967), 37.

26. See the "Preface" to the Thalia Fragment of *Hyperion*, WB, I.

27. *Ahndung* or *ahnden* is, according to the notes of Thomas Pfau in ELT 169–170, the eighteenth-century spelling for *Ahnung*, which has connotations of presentiment, mental delusion, and remembrance. As remembrance, it is linked to Kant's use. Of Kant's use in the *Anthropology from a Pragmatic Point of View*, the translator Victor Lyle Dowdell writes: "Ahnden is equivalent to 'keep something in mind' [*Gedenken*]. Used with the dative, it means that something presents itself vaguely to my mind. Used with the accusative it means to remember someone's deed with malicious intent. . . . It is always the same notion only used in different ways." Cited in Pfau, "Critical Introduction," 169. *Andenken* is thus "structurally cognate" with *Ahndung*, as used by Hölderlin in this essay.

28. Paul de Man, *Rhetoric of Romanticism* (New York: Columbia University Press, 1986), 59.

29. See chapter 3, "Poetic Subjectivity and the Elusiveness of Being," above, and Henrich, *The Course of Remembrance*, 22, 121–125, 132.

30. Henrich, *Hegel im Kontext*, 34.

31. Pfau, "Critical Introduction," 11.

32. Henrich, *Hegel im Kontext*, 12.

33. Pfau, "Critical Introduction," 26.

34. Santner, *Friedrich Hölderlin*, 51.

35. See Henrich, *Der Grund im Bewusstsein.*

36. Adorno, "Parataxis," 129.

37. From the preface to the penultimate version of *Hyperion*. See Santner, *Friedrich Hölderlin*, 51.

38. Santner, *Friedrich Hölderlin*, 118.

39. These citations are from Henrich, *The Course of Remembrance*, 244–247.

40. Pierre Bertaux links the increasingly estranged account of nature to Hölderlin's political disappointments. He notes that freedom appears less frequently as a theme in the writings after 1799, and links this to a crackdown on the prerevolutionary activity of Hölderlin's circle of friends. See Bertaux, *Hölderlin und die französische Revolution* (Frankfurt am Main: Suhrkamp, 1961), 121.

41. Frederic Prokosch's translation has been helpful here; *Some Poems of Friedrich Hölderlin*, 6.

42. Fred Dallmayr, *The Other Heidegger*, 41. See also Jennifer Anna Gosetti, "Feminine Figures in Heidegger's Theory of Poetic Language," in *Feminist Interpretations of Heidegger*, ed. Nancy Holland and Patricia Huntington (University Park: Pennsylvania State University Press, 2001), 196–218.

43. See Haar, *The Song of the Earth*, 53.
44. Ibid., 52.
45. Adorno, "Parataxis," 143.
46. Ibid., 143.
47. Ibid., 145.
48. Ibid., 143.
49. Ibid., 143.

5. The Politics of Sacrifice

1. Johanna Hodge marks three forms of homelessness in Heidegger's account. See Hodge, *Heidegger and Ethics*, 131–133.

2. Werner Marx points out that everydayness, even that of the early Greeks on whom Heidegger's views rely, does not appear in this account. See Marx, *Heidegger and the Tradition*, 245.

3. The content of "original ethics," if it can be described as content, is met with debate. In *The Song of the Earth*, Michel Haar argues that Heidegger's critique of technology is this content. Compare with Marx, *Heidegger and the Tradition*, 245–249, 255, who argues that Heidegger's directives for poetry lend little guidance to how to dwell within everyday life; but see also Marx's subsequent treatment of phenomenology as a realm of the ethical in Werner Marx, *Towards a Phenomenological Ethics* (Albany: SUNY Press, 1992). See Frank Schalow's claim that Heidegger's "appeal to poetry orients the ethical concern for humanity's welfare from the wider expanse of manifestation" in "Language and the Tragic Side of Ethics" in *International Studies in Philosophy* XXVII, no. II (1996): 49–63, here 50–53. See also Dennis J. Schmidt, "Poetry and the Political: Gadamer, Plato, and Heidegger," in *Festivals of Interpretation*, ed. Kathleen Wright (Albany: State University of New York Press, 1990). David Carr claims that Heidegger's philosophy both before and after the turn to poetic themes is governed by the lack of a social philosophy. See David Carr, "Die fehlende Sozialphilosophie Heideggers," in *Zur philosophischen Aktualität Heideggers*, ed. Dietrich Papenfuss and Otto Pöggeler (Frankfurt am Main: Vittorio Klostermann, 1989), 1: 239, 244. Annemarie Gethmann-Siefert challenges Heidegger's identification of dwelling with destiny and claims that Heidegger thus overlooks a "'practical' dimension" of dwelling. See Gethmann-Siefert, "Heidegger and Hölderlin," 66–68.

4. On this violence, see Marx, *Heidegger and the Tradition*, 231.

5. See Michel Haar on the world-earth relation in *The Song of the Earth*, 95–98.

6. Marx, *Heidegger and the Tradition*, 185.

7. See Jean-François Lyotard, *Lessons on the Analytic of the Sublime*, trans. Elizabeth Rottenberg (Stanford, Calif.: Stanford University Press, 1994), on the violence involved in the economy of strife among the faculties, particularly the imagination and reason.

8. Marx, *Heidegger and the Tradition*, 234.

9. Hölderlin's notion of genius is, then, also set aside. Annemarie Geth-mann-Siefert comments on this in "Heidegger and Hölderlin," 71.

10. Haar, *The Song of the Earth*, 106.

11. Elsewhere, as in *On the Way to Language*, Heidegger no longer under-stands poetic language as arising out of the language of a people, but rather poetic language as the original language out of which human speaking within a world would arise. See OWL 59, 120. Yet Heidegger does not abandon the notion that essential language is fundamentally connected to the speakers of a landscape or region, even to dialect. See his 1955–60 essays "Sprache und Heimat" (GA 13, 155–180), "Hebel—der Hausfreund" (GA 13, 133–150), and "Die Sprache Johann Peter Hebels" (GA 13, 123–125).

12. Reinhard Mehring examines the Nietzschean dimensions of Heideg-ger's tragic rendering of the present, particularly in the early 1940s; Mehring argues that Heidegger has not abandoned Nietzsche's *Übermensch* in the notion of sacrifice he reads in Hölderlin. See Reinhard Mehring, *Heideggers Überliefer-ungsgeschick: Eine dionysische Inszenierung* (Würzburg: Königshausen and Neu-mann, 1992), 64, 112–113. Johanna Hodge gives and account of Heidegger's relation to Hölderlin via an account of the importance of Nietzsche for Hei-degger's development. See her chapter "Heidegger and Hölderlin: Together on Separate Mountains," in *Heidegger and Ethics*.

13. Haar, *The Song of the Earth*, 106.

14. Ibid., 107. Haar claims further that disclosedness, in this antagonism, is itself a matter of conflict (169 n. 60).

15. On the role of Hölderlin in "The Origin of the Work of Art," compare with Mehring, *Heideggers Überlieferungsgeschick*, 68.

16. As we saw in chapter 1, wherein poetic language was described in its relation to a phenomenological account of truth.

17. Haar, *The Song of the Earth*, 117.

18. Haar reads *Gewalt* and *gewaltig* not so much as a matter of "violence" but of "extreme power," and gives a careful rendering of what might be the difference between them. Yet he also describes this *Gewalt* in terms that are difficult to distinguish from violence: "art lies in ambush for being; it takes possession of it, wrenching it from familiar beings in a climate of rapture and struggle on the brink of the abyss." Ibid., 107.

19. Christoph Jamme argues that Heidegger's turn to Hölderlin is both a "politische Selbstkorrectur" and "eine Fortführung der Politik mit anderen, nämlich kunstdeutenden Mitteln." Jamme, "Hölderlin und das Problem der Metaphysik," 653; Annemarie Gethmann-Siefert, "Heidegger and Hölder-lin," 59 n. 2, points out that Otto Pöggeler first expressed the line of interpre-tation that Heidegger's turn to Hölderlin was a correction of his political involve-ments in *Philosophie und Politik bei Heidegger* (Freiburg: Niemeyer, 1972), which was, in Gethmann-Siefert's words, "revised in several important areas on the basis of new materials, which depart from Heidegger's self-interpretation" in

Pöggeler, "Den Führer führen? Heidegger und keine Ende," *Philosophische Rund-schau* 32 (1985). Fred Dallmayr's thesis is that Heidegger turns from politics to a "counterpolitics," in *The Other Heidegger.*

20. See the introduction to this book.

21. It is worth noting the ambivalence Heidegger expresses with regard to Rilke. "What Are Poets For?" (PLT 91–142) gives a long treatment of Rilke's notion of the "open," which Heidegger employs in thinking the problem of representational consciousness in its opposition to poetic language. Yet Rilke, Heidegger argues, "still thinks of nature metaphysically in terms of the nature of will" (PLT 102), and Heidegger favors Hölderlin over Rilke as the most essential of poets (PLT 141–142). In the "Der Ister" lectures, Heidegger explicitly rejects an association of his thinking with Rilke's poetry (DI 91 n. 2), despite the fact that Heidegger had first expressed the phenomenologically disclosive possibilities of poetic language with regard to Rilke. (GA 24, 244). It is possible that Heidegger overlooks some "metaphysical" similarities between Rilke and Hölderlin, with regard to the relation between the "open" (which Heidegger locates in both poets) and the problem of consciousness.

22. See Peter Szondi's essay on the Böhlendorff letter, wherein Szondi emphasizes that Hölderlin's theory—in which Greek and German poetry are contrasted—marks a decided and even unbridgeable difference between Greek and German. This is to overcome the tendency of German classicism to mimic Greek poetic forms. See "Überwindung des Klassisismus: Hölderlins Brief an Böhlendorff vom Dezember 1801," in Peter Szondi, *Schriften I* (Berlin: Suhrkamp, 1977).

23. Anne Gethmann-Siefert argues that Heidegger's interpretation of Hölderlin is "premodern," that Heidegger "skips over this difference" between antiquity and the modern in Hölderlin's view. See Gethmann-Siefert, "Heidegger and Hölderlin," 69, 86. Beda Allemann argues for the difference between antiquity and the modern in Hölderlin's view, in "Hölderlin zwischen Antike und Moderne," in *Hölderlin-Jahrbuch* 25 (1984–85), 29–62. See also Allemann's discussion of the Böhlendorff letter and the "Remarks on Antigone" in *Hölderlin und Heidegger,* 28–34, wherein the Greek and German are situated as contrasting paths between Orient and Occident.

24. Jacques Taminiaux argues that the nostalgia for Greece makes sense only when a "radical rupturing" between it and the present epoch is revealed. Taminiaux, *Poetics, Speculation, and Judgment,* 74–75. It is implicit in my argument here, and explicit elsewhere, that Hölderlin's longing for Greece is to be differentiated from Heidegger's; while Heidegger aims for an authentic *Wieder-holung* of a possibility of thinking and Being lost in the advent of metaphysics and humanism, Hölderlin's "romanticization" of Greece belongs to the context of his devotion to the modern, Kantian ideal of freedom, even though he disparages, as does Heidegger, what we now call the technological component of humanism—its lack of reverence for nature. To put it tersely, the difference between Heidegger and Hölderlin on the question of Greece is, then, Kant. For

Heidegger, despite his important readings of Kant, Kant belongs to metaphysics. For Hölderlin (who, Heidegger admits, also belongs to metaphysics), Kant is "the Moses of our nation" and the point of departure for an aesthetic philosophy, for a poetology, for a thinking—and feeling—of freedom.

25. As in the *Wiederholung* of an inheritance (*eines Erbes*) of Dasein who, "under the eyes of death," is thrown back upon its having-been (*Gewesene*) in a destinal-historical way, which yields the simplicity (*Einfachheit*) of *Schicksal*. See *Being and Time*, §74.

26. Paul de Man argues that Hölderlin's own use of the national "has nothing in common" with twentieth-century nationalism. De Man, *Romanticism and Contemporary Criticism*, 124.

27. As Allemann argues, *Hölderlin und Heidegger*, 21. On the law of succession as that of art, see ibid., 19, 34.

28. Dallmayr, *The Other Heidegger*.

29. In *Theoretische Schriften* this text appears under the title "Fragment philosophischer Briefe" (TS 10–15).

30. See Paul de Man, "The Image of Rousseau in the Poetry of Hölderlin" in de Man, *The Rhetoric of Romanticism* (New York: Columbia University Press, 1984), 19–45. On Hölderlin's relation to the classicism of Goethe and Schiller, see Taminiaux, *Poetics, Speculation, and Judgment*, 73, 76. See Henrich, *The Course of Remembrance* and *Der Grund im Bewusstsein;* and Friedrich Strack, *Ästhetik und Freiheit*, for sustained readings of Hölderlin's philosophical-poetic relation to his Enlightenment context.

31. Lacoue-Labarthe, *Heidegger, Art, and Politics*.

32. Lyotard argues against treating the two dimensions outlined here as extricable from each other: "one cannot be satisfied with simply acknowledging the coexistence of the two faces of Heidegger, one venerable, the other ignoble, and diagnose a split between the two"; Lyotard further argues, however, against a sensationalism about Heidegger's politics and for the urgency to think both "the importance of Heidegger's thought" as well as his "deliberate, profound, and in a certain way persistent" politics. Lyotard, *Heidegger and "the Jews,"* 52, 53.

33. Reinhard Mehring calls Heidegger's interpretation of Hölderlin's awaiting the gods a sublime *Stimmung*. Mehring, *Heideggers Überlieferungsgeschick*, 64.

34. Bertaux, *Hölderlin und die französische Revolution*.

35. Lukács, "Hölderlin's *Hyperion*."

36. Véronique M. Fóti argues that Heidegger "literalizes" the Hölderlinian figure of Germania; *Heidegger and the Poets*, 66. I do not dispute this, but add that Heidegger is aware of the discordance between what Hölderlin "meant" (*meinte*) and his own vision of Germania, as I argue in the following paragraphs.

37. And yet it brings up again the question of the "supplement" added by the thinker in elucidating the poem, which Véronique M. Fóti locates in Heidegger's reading of "Andenken." See "Textuality, Totalization, and the Question of Origin," 43–45.

38. Compare with Hölderlin's letter to his brother, written in Jena on April 13, 1795, in which Hölderlin discusses the possibility of promoting to a professorship (he was indeed the only one of the Tübingen *Stift* circle of himself, Hegel, and Schelling, to be invited to promote at Jena). Hölderlin hopes that he can teach on the basis of exams rather than the defense of a *Habilitationsschrift*. He writes: "Schiller will presumably stay on. If I stay here, I will probably take my exams next autumn. This is the only condition that allows me to hold lectures. The title of a professor is of no importance to me, and a professor's salary is fair only for a few" (ELT 129). Hölderlin leaves Jena without this accomplished, and writes to Schiller that the reason for his leaving is the too-great proximity to Schiller's influence.

39. When Friedrich Beissner edited a book of Hölderlin's poetry for soldiers during the National Socialist regime, to be printed in 100,000 copies as a "field selection," he included this passage. Jochen Schmidt reports that Peter Szondi ("who, on the grounds of his own Jewish ancestry and the fate of his family in the concentration camp at Bergen-Belsen could not be accused of being an apologete for the Nazis"), called the inclusion of this passage an act of "civil courage." Schmidt, "Hölderlin im 20. Jahrhundert," 118–120.

40. Henrich, *The Course of Remembrance*, 83.

41. See Johann Kreuzer, "*Einleitung*" to Hölderlin, *Theoretische Schriften*, viii–ix.

42. Lyotard, *Lessons on the Analytic of the Sublime*, 187.

43. As Lyotard argues in ibid.

44. Class inequality is also defended by Kant in the service of the rational system, for, Kant claims, "it is hard to develop skill in the human species except by means of inequality among people." Since the human being is the "ultimate purpose of nature here on earth, the purpose by which all other things constitute a system of purposes," the class inequality of a culture, though miserable, has to do with the "development of man's natural predispositions." "Civil society" is the only formal condition under which nature can achieve its final aim, and the impairment to freedom that civil society must entail is justified as perfecting the human being as the perfection of nature. Kant thinks that the inequality of classes is requisite to develop higher specimens who must, in order to promote their own skills and perfection, "keep the majority in a state of oppression, hard labor, and little enjoyment." Yet civil society must curb the freedom of these lower classes whose misery, unfortunate as it may be, contributes to human progress as a whole. Kant, *Critique of Judgment*, trans. Werner S. Pluhar (Indianapolis: Hackett, 1987), 430, 433.

45. Thomas Pfau, "Critical Introduction" to Hölderlin, *Essays and Letters on Theory*, 13.

46. Ibid.

47. For Heidegger it is death or mortality that primarily issues eccentricity (DI 28), a view that is not opposed to Hölderlin, but that shifts the focus away from the limits of knowledge and understanding (*Erkenntnis, Verstand*)

to which Hölderlin's view refers. We will take up the difference between Heidegger's and Hölderlin's views on this in the next chapter.

48. See ELT 102.

49. For an account of this discovery, see Schmidt, "Hölderlin im 20. Jahrhundert."

50. Adorno, "Parataxis," 113.

51. Ibid., 112.

52. Ibid., 70.

53. Ibid., 112.

54. Lacoue-Labarthe, *Heidegger, Art, and Politics,* 43.

55. Lacoue-Labarthe and Nancy, *The Literary Absolute,* 30.

56. Adorno, "Parataxis," 114–115.

57. Lacoue-Labarthe, *Heidegger, Art, and Politics,* 41.

58. Ibid., 45.

59. I would ask, without aiming here to provide an answer, whether the language of "pure" and perhaps also that of an "event" is appropriate, as if an event must be "pure" in order to be singular.

60. A failure that Lyotard calls a "leaden silence" "observed on the extermination of the Jews," a "mute silence that lets nothing be heard." Lyotard calls it a "scandal" that Heidegger neglected this question "in a thought so devoted to remembering," and implicates Heidegger in a "politics of forgetting." Lyotard, *Heidegger and "the Jews,"* 52, 54, 57.

61. In "Remarks on Oedipus," Hölderlin writes that in "such moments the human being forgets himself and the god and turns around like a traitor, naturally in a saintly manner. In the utmost form of suffering, namely, there exists nothing but the conditions of time and space. Inside it, man forgets himself because he exists entirely for the moment, the god because he is nothing but time; and either one is unfaithful, time, because it is reversed categorically at such a moment, no longer fitting beginning and end; the human being, because at this moment of categorical reversal he has to follow and thus can no longer resemble the beginning in what follows" (ELT 108).

62. As discussed in other chapters, tragedy's principles for Hölderlin include that of hubris. On hubris in Hölderlin's *Empedocles,* see de Man, *Romanticism and Contemporary Criticism,* 69.

63. See Blanchot's discussions of Hölderlin in *The Writing of the Disaster,* trans. Ann Smock (Lincoln: University of Nebraska Press, 1995).

64. Lacoue-Labarthe, *Heidegger, Art, and Politics,* 44.

6. Revolutionary Poetics and the Subject-in-Process

1. By "intersubjective communal experience" I mean the community to which Hölderlin refers in "On Religion" (ELT 90–95). Hölderlin's unique pantheism provides a different access to religious feeling than the one Kristeva here criticizes, though the differences here must be noted. For whereas

Kristeva thinks poetry is profoundly "a-theological" (RPL 61), Hölderlin's poetic practice supports a proliferation of representations of "religious" feeling as expressions of the "feeling of life." (See chapter 3.) Yet for Hölderlin, religion is close to myth, which he calls essentially "poetic," and Kristeva likewise links myth to the practices of art and poetry (RPL 22). Kristeva rejects an aesthetic religion (DL 112) as, for example, practiced by the French revolutionaries, and Hölderlin's poetry, as well as the essay "On Religion," cannot be wholly divorced from that kind of practice. Yet for Hölderlin it is a uniquely poetic one that requires a rigorous, poetic logic and is wholly incompatible with monotheism.

2. It is not my task to discuss here in detail Kristeva's notion of sexual difference, which is fundamental to the psychoanalytic dimensions of her theory. Nevertheless, the debate about the gendered subject in Kristeva is of central importance here, in that Kristeva takes on the traditionally male subject of psychoanalysis and yet undermines, at the same time, the Freudian-Lacanian accounts of sexual difference. Two issues, peripheral to this discussion, arise here. First, Kristeva's relation to traditional psychoanalysis, for Kristeva remains within the boundaries set by Freud despite her transgression thereof. For a critical account of Freud's usefulness for feminist analysis, see Kate Millet, *Sexual Politics* (New York: Doubleday, 1969); Juliet Mitchell claims that Freud is useful if his account of feminine sexuality is rejected in *Psychoanalysis and Feminism* (New York: Random House, 1975). See also Jessica Benjamin's *The Bonds of Love* (New York: Pantheon, 1988). On Kristeva's relation to Freud and Lacan, see Kelly Oliver, *Reading Kristeva: Unraveling the Double-Bind* (Bloomington: Indiana University Press, 1993), 29–34, 73–74, 77–81, 94, 190 n. 5. Second, the question of biology and psychology in Kristeva's account of gender- and subject-formation. Kristeva argues for the "relativity of the symbolic as well as biological experience" in WT 210. Elizabeth Grosz argues that Kristeva ignores the specific sexual difference of women by denying sex and identity before gender, by denying "the sexed body" as the site of difference; see Grosz, *Sexual Subversions* (Boston: Allen and Unwin, 1989), 96. Judith Butler has argued that identity politics cannot be based on sex, which is always-already gender, and that gender itself is a performative construction; see Butler, *Gender Trouble* (New York: Routledge, 1990). My analysis and employment of Kristeva's theory does not treat these issues directly.

3. See Santner, *Friedrich Hölderlin*, 25–26.

4. See especially Adorno, "Parataxis"; Hans-Jost Frey, *Studies in Poetic Discourse*; and Santner, *Friedrich Hölderlin*.

5. Christopher Fynsk analyzes this listening as itself a performance "enacted in Heidegger's text." *Language and Relation*, 40.

6. This is not to be confused with a "reification" of language as charged by Richard Rorty in *Essays on Heidegger and Others*, vol. 2, *Philosophical Papers* (Cambridge: Cambridge University Press, 1991). Heidegger gives the revealing character of language a primary function outside the sphere of speaking

subjects—and I call this move here into question—but this does not make Heidegger guilty of granting an intentionality to Being. Rather, Heidegger accounts for how the world—the fact and way in which beings can be said to be, and are presenced—beckons me to speak, and challenges thinking to make this fact primary, or to think it primordially.

7. Werner Marx calls for an account of practice in Heidegger's late philosophy, one that he claims is absent from the exclusive address to the poetic. *Heidegger and the Tradition*, trans. Theodore Kisiel and Murray Greene (Evanston, Ill.: Northwestern University Press, 1971), 245.

8. Kelly Oliver analyzes this "double bind" throughout *Reading Kristeva*.

9. In Valéry, *The Art of Poetry*, 55–56.

10. Ibid., 55.

11. Ibid.

12. Ibid., 64.

13. Fynsk, *Language and Relation*, 20.

14. See Hölderlin's complaint about the grammatical period, which is of "seldom use to the poet," for it demands the stasis of completion, which is unpoetic (ELT 45).

15. Other modern examples include the proliferation of text in Cervantes's *Don Quixote de la Mancha*, in which a text "found" is weaved into the plot; and Kierkegaard's *Either/Or*, which employs a fictional editor to assemble "found" texts, themselves poetic fictions but also philosophical treatises, veiled diaries, and letters. Kierkegaard's *Repetition* is also such an interweaving. This passage among economies, according to Kristeva's theory, throws the author's position into displacement, for the "thetic" is continually articulated according to a new economy and toward a shifting "object" (RPL 60). Contemporary examples include Siegfried Lenz's *The German Lesson* and Italo Calvino's *If on a Winter's Night a Traveler*.

16. This stands in contrast to Michel Foucault, for whom subjectivity is a product of discourse, of "confessional technologies," of institutions and the matrix of power.

17. On the non-Hegelian character of "dialectic" in Kristeva, see Oliver, *Reading Kristeva*, 99–100.

18. The relation of the poem "Mnemosyne" to "Andenken" as treated by Heidegger in GA 52 is contested by both Dieter Henrich, in *The Course of Remembrance*, and Véronique M. Fóti, in *Heidegger and the Poets*.

19. See Santner, *Friedrich Hölderlin*, 11, 98.

20. As to Hölderlin's own "madness," I leave aside here speculation on Hölderlin's own biography and the meaning of its details for Hölderlin's writings and refer to the debate thereupon only in footnotes. For philosophical-theoretical accounts of Hölderlin's madness, as well as on the significance thereof for Hölderlin's late works, see Pierre Bertaux, who denies the account accepted by Hölderlin scholarship at large in *Friedrich Hölderlin* (Frankfurt am Main: Suhrkamp, 1978). Compare with Haverkamp, *Leaves of Mourning*; Michel Foucault, "Le

nom du père," in Jean Laplanche, *Hölderlin et la question du père* (Paris: Presses Universitaires de France, 1961); and D. E. Sattler, *"Al rovescio:* Hölderlin nach 1806" in *Individualität* 21 (March 1989): 44–53. See also Blanchot, *The Space of Literature,* 276. Heidegger makes reference to Hölderlin's madness as his being "taken into the protection of his gods," (ST, 39) and occasionally treats it as the consequence of the proximity of exposure to Being, but largely refuses reference to Hölderlin's biography as a tactic of *Literaturwissenschaft.*

21. Oliver, *Reading Kristeva,* 101.

22. Compare with Philippe Lacoue-Labarthe and Jean-Luc Nancy in "The Nazi Myth," *Critical Inquiry* 16, no. 2 (winter 1990): 291–312.

23. On this "other" in the context of fascism, see Lyotard, *Heidegger and "the Jews."*

24. On the principle of hubris in Hölderlin, see de Man, *Romanticism and Contemporary Criticism;* Ryan, *Friedrich Hölderlin,* 52–55.

25. Nietzsche, *The Birth of Tragedy,* 36, 38.

26. Ibid., 47.

27. Ibid., 43.

28. See Michel Haar on Heidegger's discussion of death in *Introduction to Metaphysics* (EM 121) in *The Song of the Earth,* 107.

29. Oliver, *Reading Kristeva,* 13–14.

30. A phrasing I find fortuitous and relevant was provided by Mark Strand in his comment on Jennifer Anna Gosetti-Ferencei, *After the Palace Burns* (Lincoln, Neb.: Zoo Press, 2003).

31. In this letter Hölderlin meditates on the relation between German and Greek poetry and claims that their strengths are reverse. While the Greeks know the "fire from the heavens," German poetry possesses "clarity of presentation." Each element must learn to master what it does not intrinsically possess; and yet what each does possess is in fact the "most difficult" to learn. See Peter Szondi, "Überwindung des Klassizismus: Der Brief an Böhlendorff vom. 4. Dezember 1801" in *Schriften 1* (Stuttgart: Suhrkamp, 1977), 345–366. For what we here call "the proper" Hölderlin uses the term *das Nationelle,* which Heidegger renders *das Eigene,* which resonates with *das Ereignis* and *das Eignen.* While Hölderlin's term is translated as "the national," this is not to be misinterpreted according to later, problematic developments in "nationalism"; it is to be kept in mind that for Hölderlin the "national" was not a reality but a promise for a future democratic society. See chapter 5.

32. See Unger, *Hölderlin's Major Poetry,* on the *hen kai pan* as the guiding thread of Hölderlin's poetics.

33. Heidegger understands this problem of consciousness in the human being's "turning away" from the "open," which he derives from Rilke. See "What Are Poets For?," in PLT. Yet Heidegger begins to reject Rilke in favor of Hölderlin, and in some sense obscures their "philosophical" similarities. See Heidegger's footnote, DI 91.

34. Fynsk, *Language and Relation,* 95.

35. Heidegger here implicitly criticizes the "arbitrary willfulness of dictators" in a discussion of the political, which is evidence of his distance from the reign of National Socialism in what Pöggeler calls its "externalized" form; this despite Heidegger's reference to National Socialism's "historical uniqueness" (DI 86) and his troubling discussion of the political. See chapter 5.

36. I wonder if this refers to Heidegger's own "expulsion" from politics.

37. See Beda Allemann, *Hölderlin und Heidegger,* 13–34.

38. Heidegger rejects all Enlightenment influences on Hölderlin's understanding of the "German" or the "national." He explicitly rejects the appearance of Rousseau in Hölderlin's poem and argues that Hölderlin's views have nothing to do with the cosmopolitanism of Goethe or of Lessing, whose writings were to teach religious tolerance. See DI 50, 65, 70. Hölderlin prays for the victory of the French against Austria-Prussia in 1792 (letter to his sister, *Werke und Briefe,* 806) as the "defenders of human rights." We have seen in chapter 4 that Hölderlin's political views strongly favored freedom in a democratic sense.

39. Here Derrida suggests this both of Heidegger and Hölderlin but does not make efforts to distinguish their views of the "German" and, furthermore, of the return "home." Derrida, *Points,* 324. Derrida writes, "Whether one is talking about that Hölderlin or this Heidegger, there is always some address to the German people, if not a speech to the German nation." In the previous chapter I made efforts to contextualize Hölderlin's understanding of the "German" and to distinguish that from Heidegger's politics.

40. See Haar, *The Song of the Earth,* 142.

41. On Hölderlin's experience of meeting with Goethe, see the letter to Hegel in ELT 124–125. On the considerable and self-admitted influence of Schiller on Hölderlin see David Constantine, *Friedrich Hölderlin* (Oxford: Oxford University Press, 1988), 11, 168–169; Dieter Henrich, *The Course of Remembrance,* 120–125.

42. Hölderlin studied not only Greek but also several other foreign languages from a very early age, including Latin, from which he also translated (see Constantine, *Friedrich Hölderlin,* 81), and Hebrew. He also knew French. Hölderlin's imagination about the landscape of Greece was informed by both French and English authors, including Count Choiseul Gouffier's *Voyage de la pittoresque de la Grèce,* George Foster's *Journey Around the World 1772–1775,* Adm. George Anson's *Voyage Round the World in the Years 1740–44,* and Richard Chandler's *Travels in Asia Minor and Greece,* the last three probably in translation. See Santner, *Friedrich Hölderlin,* x, 287.

A New Poetics of Dasein

1. See Rimbaud's letters in *Illuminations and Other Prose Poems,* trans. Louise Varèse (New York: New Directions, 1957), xxvii and xxix.

2. Ibid., 12–13.

3. Ibid., xxx–xxxi.

4. Ibid., xxxi.

5. Ibid., 132–133.

6. Ibid., xxvii.

7. For a discussion of attunement in Rilke, see Jennifer Anna Gosetti, "Phenomenology of the Mysterious: A Reading of Rilke's Sonnets to Orpheus," *Phenomenological Inquiry* 26 (fall 2002): 87–98; and "Phenomenological Literature: From the Natural Attitude to 'Recognition,'" *Philosophy Today*, summer supplement (2001): 18–27.

8. For a discussion of the breakdown of the prosaic or mundane by poetic seeing in the literary writings of Sartre, Rilke, and Francis Ponge, see Jennifer Anna Gosetti, "The Ecstatic Quotidian," *Journal of the Association of the Interdisciplinary Study of the Arts* 7, no. 1 (2001): 51–61.

9. Valéry, *The Art of Poetry.*

10. The most obvious examples are from Rilke's *New Poems*, such as "The Archaic Torso of Apollo"("Archaïscher Torso Apollos") and "Black Cat" ("Schwartze Katze"), but this double movement can also be seen in *Sonnets to Orpheus.*

11. Two poems, among many, come to mind. See Rilke's poems "Das Roseninnere" and the uncollected poem that begins, "Durch den sich Vögel werfen, ist nicht der / vertraute Raum" ("What birds plunge through is not the intimate space"). Translation of the latter is found in *The Selected Poetry of Rainer Maria Rilke*, ed. and trans. Stephen Mitchell (New York: Vintage Books, 1984).

12. Paul Verlaine, *Selected Poems*, trans. C. F. Macintyre (Berkeley: University of California Press, 1948), 114–115.

13. Valéry, *The Art of Poetry*, 75.

14. Levinas, *Ethics and Infinity*, 42.

15. The quotation is from T. E. Hulme, "Bergson's Theory of Art," in *Speculations: Essays on Humanism and the Philosophy of Art* (New York: Routledge, 1987), 149.

16. See Emmanuel Levinas, *On Escape*, trans. Bettina Bergo (Stanford, Calif.: Stanford University Press, 2003), 73, where Levinas proposes "getting out of being by a new path."

17. Miklós Radnóti, *The Clouded Sky*, trans. Stephen Polgar (New York: Harper & Row, 1972), 18.

18. Rainer Maria Rilke, *Sonnets to Orpheus*, trans. M. D. Herder Norton (New York: Norton, 1942), 76–77.

19. For a discussion of Rilke in this context, see Gosetti, "Phenomenology of the Mysterious."

20. René Char, *Selected Poems*, ed. Mary Ann Caws and Tina Solas (New York: New Directions, 1992), 32–33.

21. A poetical enactment of Stalin's terrorization of these poets has been given in a recent book by Tony Brinkley, *Stalin's Eyes* (Orono, Maine: Puckerbush Press, 2003).

22. Rilke, *Sonnets to Orpheus*. I have not employed M. D. Herder's translation here.

23. I am quoting here from Richard Kearney's brief account of the "ontological imagination" in *Poetics of Imagining: Modern to Post-Modern* (New York: Fordham University Press, 1998), 47.

24. On this "failure" see Fóti, *Heidegger and the Poets*, 69. Paul de Man claims that failure marks the interstice between present and past, past and future, the gods and human kind. He writes: "The future is present in history only as the remembering of a failed project that has become a menace." *The Rhetoric of Romanticism* (New York: Columbia University Press, 1984), 58–59.

25. Fóti, *Heidegger and the Poets*, 68.

26. Phillipe Lacoue-Labarthe, "'La césure du spéculatif' dans Friedrich Hölderlin," in *L'Antigone de Sophocle* (Paris: Christian Bourgeois, 1978), 43, cited in Fóti, *Heidegger and the Poets*, 74.

27. Blanchot, *The Writing of the Disaster*, 112–113.

28. Ibid., 2.

29. Radnóti, *The Clouded Sky*, 17.

30. From the poem "Like Death," ibid., 15.

31. Akin to what I am suggesting here is Maurice Merleau-Ponty's notion of "flesh" in *The Visible and the Invisible* (Evanston, Ill.: Northwestern University Press, 1968).

32. Blanchot, *The Writing of the Disaster*, 113.

33. From the poems "Like Death" and "Suddenly," Radnóti, *The Clouded Sky*, 15, 51.

34. From "This Cruel Age Has Deflected Me," in Anna Akhmatova, *Poems of Akhmatova*, trans. Stanley Kunitz et al. (Boston: Houghton Mifflin, 1967), 129.

35. Rilke, *Sonnets to Orpheus*, my translation.

Selected Bibliography

Adorno, Theodor W. *Notes to Literature*. 2 vols. Trans. Shierry Weber Nicholsen. New York: Columbia University Press, 1992.

Agamben, Giorgio. "The Passion of Facticity." In *Potentialities: Collected Essays in Philosophy*, trans. and ed. Daniel Heller-Roazen, 185–204. Stanford, Calif.: Stanford University Press, 1999.

Akhmatova, Anna. *Poems of Anna Akhmatova*. Trans. Stanley Kunitz. Boston: Houghton Mifflin, 1967.

Allemann, Beda. *Hölderlin und Heidegger*. Zürich and Freiburg: Atlantis, 1954.

———. "Hölderlin zwischen Antike und Moderne." *Hölderlin-Jahrbuch* 24 (1984–85): 29–62.

Bachelard, Gaston. *On Poetic Imagination and Reverie*. Trans. Colette Gaudin. Dallas: Spring Publications, 1971.

Beissner, Friedrich. *Hölderlin Heute: Der lange Weg des Dichters zu seinem Ruhm*. Stuttgart: W. Kohlhammer, 1965.

Benjamin, Walter. "Zwei Gedichte von Friedrich Hölderlin." In *Sprache und Geschichte: Philosophische Essays*, ed. Rolf Tiedemann, 5–29. Stuttgart: Reclam, 1992.

Bernasconi, Robert. *Heidegger in Question*. Atlantic Highlands, N.J.: Humanities Press International, 1993.

———. *The Question of Language in Heidegger's History of Being*. Atlantic Highlands, N.J.: Humanities Press International, 1985.

Bernet, Rudolph. "The Phenomenological Reduction and the Double Life of the Subject." In *Reading Heidegger from the Start*, ed. Theodore Kisiel and John van Buren, 245–268. Albany: SUNY Press, 1987.

Bernstein, J. M. *The Fate of Art: Aesthetic Alienation from Kant to Derrida and Adorno*. University Park: Pennsylvania State University Press, 1992.

Bertaux, Pierre. *Friedrich Hölderlin*. Frankfurt am Main: Suhrkamp, 1978.

———. *Hölderlin und die französische Revolution*. Frankfurt am Main: Suhrkamp, 1961.

Blanchot, Maurice. *The Space of Literature*. Trans. Ann Smock. Lincoln: University of Nebraska Press, 1982.

———. *The Writing of the Disaster*. Trans. Ann Smock. Lincoln: University of Nebraska Press, 1995.

Bothe, Hennig. *Hölderlin zur Einführung*. Hamburg: Junius, 1994.

Brinkley, Tony. *Stalin's Eyes*. Orono, Maine: Puckerbush Press, 2003.

Brogan, Walter. "The Place of Aristotle in the Development of Heidegger's Philosophy." In *Reading Heidegger from the Start*, ed. Theodore Kisiel and John van Buren, 213–227. Albany: SUNY Press, 1994.

Cadava, Eduardo, Peter Connor, and Jean-Luc Nancy, eds. *Who Comes After the Subject?* New York: Routledge, 1991.

Caputo, John D. *Demythologizing Heidegger*. Bloomington: Indiana University Press, 1992.

———. *Heidegger and Aquinas: An Essay on Overcoming Metaphysics*. New York: Fordham University Press, 1982.

———. *The Mystical Element in Heidegger's Thought*. New York: Fordham University Press, 1986.

———. *Radical Hermeneutics: Repetition, Deconstruction, and the Hermeneutic Project*. Bloomington: Indiana University Press, 1987.

Carr, David. "Die fehlende Sozialphilosophie Heideggers." In *Zur philosophischen Aktualität Heideggers*, ed. Dietrich Papenfuss and Otto Pöggeler, 234–246. Frankfurt am Main: Vittorio Klostermann, 1991.

Cassirer, Ernst. "Hölderlin und der deutschen Idealismus." In *Idee und Gestalt: Goethe, Schiller, Hölderlin und Kleist*. Darmstadt: Wissenschaftliche Buchsgesellschaft, 1971.

Char, René. *Selected Poems*. Ed. Mary Ann Caws and Tina Jolas. New York: New Directions, 1992.

Constantine, David. *Friedrich Hölderlin*. Oxford: Oxford University Press, 1988.

Corngold, Stanley, *The Fate of the Self: German Writers and French Theory*. Durham, N.C.: Duke University Press, 1994.

Dallmayr, Fred. *The Other Heidegger*. Ithaca, N.Y.: Cornell University Press, 1993.

De Man, Paul. *The Rhetoric of Romanticism*. New York: Columbia University Press, 1984.

———. *Romanticism and Contemporary Criticism*. Ed. Kevin Newmark, Andrzej Warminski, and E. S. Burt. Baltimore: Johns Hopkins University Press, 1993.

Derrida, Jacques. *Mémoires for Paul de Man*. New York: Columbia University Press, 1996.

———. *Of Spirit: Heidegger and the Question*. Trans. Rachel Bowlby and Geoffrey Bennington. Chicago: University of Chicago Press, 1991.

———. *Points . . . Interviews, 1974–1994*. Trans. Peggy Kamuf and others; ed. Elisabeth Weber. Stanford, Calif.: Stanford University Press, 1995.

———. *The Truth in Painting*. Trans. Geoff Bennington and Ian McLeod. Chicago: University of Chicago Press, 1987.

Descartes, René. *Philosophical Writings*. Trans. and ed. Elizabeth Anscombe and Peter T. Geach. New York: Macmillan, 1971.

Dilthey, Wilhelm. *Das Erlebnis und die Dichtung*. Leipzig: Reclam, 1988.

Fehervary, Helen. *Hölderlin and the Left.* Heidelberg: Carl Winter Universitätsverlag, 1977.

Fichte, Johann Gottlieb. *Introductions to the Wissenschaftslehre and Other Writings (1797–1800).* Trans. and ed. Daniel Breazeale. Indianapolis: Hackett, 1994.

Figal, Günter. *For a Philosophy of Freedom and Strife: Politics, Aesthetics, Metaphysics.* Trans. Wayne Klein. Albany: SUNY Press, 1998.

_____. "Heideggers Hölderlin: Die Götter, der Gott, und die dürftige Zeit." In *Heidegger zur Einführung,* 135–151. Hamburg: Junius, 1992.

Fóti, Véronique M. *Heidegger and the Poets: Poiēsis, Sophia, Technē.* Atlantic Highlands, N.J.: Humanities Press International, 1992.

_____. "Textualization, Totalization, and the Question of Origin in Heidegger's Elucidation of 'Andenken.'" *Research in Phenomenology* XIX (1989): 43–58.

Frank, Manfred. *Einführung in die frühromantische Ästhetik.* Frankfurt am Main: Suhrkamp, 1989.

_____. "Hölderlins philosophische Grundlagen." In *Hölderlin und die Moderne,* ed. Gerhard Kurz et al., 174–194. Tübingen: Attempto-Verlag, 1995.

_____. "'Intellektuelle Anschauung': Drei Stellungnahmen zu einem Deutungsversuch von Selbstbewusstsein — Kant, Fichte, Hölderlin/Novalis." In *Die Aktualität der Frühromantik,* ed. Ernst Behler and Jochen Hörisch, 96–126. Paderborn: Ferdinand Schöningh, 1987.

Frey, Hans-Jost. *Studies in Poetic Discourse: Mallarmé, Baudelaire, Rimbaud, Hölderlin.* Trans. William Whobrey. Stanford, Calif.: Stanford University Press, 1996.

Fried, Gregory. *Heidegger's Polemos: From Being to Politics.* New Haven: Yale University Press, 2000.

Fynsk, Christopher. *Language and Relation.* Stanford, Calif.: Stanford University Press, 1996.

Gadamer, Hans-Georg. *Gadamer on Celan.* Trans. and ed. Richard Heinemann and Bruce Krajewski. Albany: SUNY Press, 1997.

_____. *Heidegger's Ways.* Trans. John W. Stanley. Albany: SUNY Press, 1994.

_____. *Literature and Philosophy in Dialogue: Essays in German Literary Theory.* Trans. Robert H. Paslick. Albany: SUNY Press, 1994.

_____. "Martin Heidegger's One Path." In *Reading Heidegger from the Start,* ed. Theodore Kisiel and John van Buren, 19–34. Albany: SUNY Press, 1987.

_____. *Philosophical Apprenticeships.* Trans. Robert R. Sullivan. Cambridge, Mass.: MIT Press, 1985.

Gehmann-Siefert, Annemarie. "Heidegger and Hölderlin: The Over-Usage of Poets in an Impoverished Time." *Research in Phenomenology* XIX (1989): 59–88.

Gosetti, Jennifer Anna. "The Ecstatic Quotidian." *Journal of the Association of the Interdisciplinary Study of the Arts* 7, no. 1 (2001): 51–62.

_____. "Phenomenological Literature: From the Natural Attitude to 'Recognition.'" *Philosophy Today* 45 (2001): 18–27.

_____. "Phenomenology of the Mysterious: A Reading of Rilke's Sonnets to Orpheus." *Phenomenological Inquiry* 26 (fall 2002): 87–98.

_____. "Feminine Figures in Heidegger's Theory of Poetic Language." In *Feminist Interpretations of Heidegger,* ed. Nancy Holland and Patricia Huntington, 196–218. University Park: Pennsylvania State University Press, 2001.

Gosetti-Ferencei, Jennifer Anna. *After the Palace Burns.* Lincoln: Zoo Press, 2003.

Grondin, Jean. "Hermeneutics in *Being and Time.*" *Epoché: A Journal for the History of Philosophy* 4, no. 2 (1996): 1–21.

Haar, Michel. *Heidegger and the Essence of Man.* Trans. William McNeill. Albany: SUNY Press, 1993.

_____. "Heidegger and the God of Hölderlin." *Research in Phenomenology* XIX (1989): 89–99.

_____. *L'Oeuvre d'art: Essai sur l'ontologie des oeuvres.* Paris: Hatier, 1994.

_____. *The Song of the Earth: Heidegger and the Grounds of the History of Being.* Trans. Reginald Lilly. Bloomington: Indiana University Press, 1993.

_____. *Towards a Phenomenological Ethics.* Albany: SUNY Press, 1992.

Hamburger, Michael. *Contraries: Studies in German Literature.* New York: E. P. Dutton, 1970.

Haverkamp, Anselm. *Leaves of Mourning: Hölderlin's Late Work.* Trans. Vernon Chadwick. Albany: SUNY Press, 1996.

Heidegger, Martin. *Aus der Erfahrung des Denkens. Gesamtausgabe* 13. Ed. Hermann Heidegger. Frankfurt am Main: Vittorio Klostermann, 1983.

_____. *The Basic Problems of Phenomenology.* Trans. Albert Hofstadter. Bloomington: Indiana University Press, 1982.

_____. *Basic Writings.* Ed. David Farrell Krell. New York: Harper & Row, 1977.

_____. *Being and Time.* Trans. John Macquarrie and Edward Robinson. New York: Harper & Row, 1962.

_____. *Discourse on Thinking.* Trans. John M. Anderson and E. M. Freund. New York: Harper & Row, 1966.

_____. *Einführung in die Metaphysik.* Tübingen: Niemeyer, 1953.

_____. *The End of Philosophy and the Task of Thinking.* Trans. Joan Stambaugh. New York: Harper & Row, 1969.

_____. *Erläuterungen zu Hölderlins Dichtung.* Frankfurt am Main: Vittorio Klostermann, 1971.

_____. *Existence and Being.* Trans. Werner Brock. Chicago: Henry Regnery, 1949.

_____. *Gelassenheit.* Pfullingen: Verlag Günter Neske, 1959.

_____. *Die Grundprobleme der Phänomenologie. Gesamtausgabe* 24. Frankfurt am Main: Vittorio Klostermann, 1989.

_____. *Hölderlin's Hymn "The Ister."* Trans. William McNeill and Julia Davis. Bloomington: Indiana University Press, 1996.

_____. *Hölderlins Hymne "Andenken." Gesamtausgabe* 52. Ed. Curd Ochwadt. Frankfurt am Main: Vittorio Klostermann, 1982.

_____. *Hölderlins Hymnen "Germanien" und "Der Rhein." Gesamtausgabe* 39. Ed. Susanne Ziegler. Frankfurt am Main: Vittorio Klostermann, 1980.

_____. *Hölderlins Hymne "Der Ister." Gesamtausgabe* 53. Ed. Walter Biemel. Frankfurt am Main: Vittorio Klostermann, 1984.

_____. *Holzwege.* Frankfurt am Main: Vittorio Klostermann, 1972.

_____. *An Introduction to Metaphysics.* Trans. Ralph Manheim. New York: Anchor, 1959.

_____. *On the Way to Language.* Trans. Peter D Hertz. New York: Harper & Row, 1971.

_____. *On Time and Being.* Trans. Joan Stambaugh. New York: Harper & Row, 1972.

_____. *Ontologie (Hermeneutik der Faktizität). Gesamtausgabe* 63. Frankfurt am Main: Vittorio Klostermann, 1988.

_____. *Pathmarks.* Trans. William McNeill. Cambridge: Cambridge University Press, 1998.

_____. *Phänomenologie des religiösen Lebens. Gesamtausgabe* 60. Ed. Matthias Jung, Thomas Regehly, and Claudius Strube. Frankfurt am Main: Vittorio Klostermann, 1995.

_____. *Poetry, Language, and Thought.* Trans. Albert Hofstadter. New York: Harper & Row, 1971.

_____. *The Question Concerning Technology and Other Essays.* Trans. William Lovitt. New York: Harper & Row, 1977.

_____. *Sein und Zeit.* Tübingen: Niemeyer, 1979.

_____. *Unterwegs zur Sprache.* Pfullingen: Verlag Günter Neske, 1959.

_____. *Wegmarken. Gesamtausgabe* 9. Ed. Friedrich-Wilhelm von Hermann. Frankfurt am Main: Vittorio Klostermann, 1976.

_____. *Zur Sache des Denkens.* Tübingen: Niemeyer, 1969.

Henrich, Dieter. *The Course of Remembrance and Other Essays on Hölderlin.* Ed. Eckhart Förster. Stanford, Calif.: Stanford University Press, 1997.

_____. *Der Grund im Bewusstsein: Untersuchungen zu Hölderlins Denken (1794–1795).* Stuttgart: Klett-Cotta, 1992.

_____. *Hegel im Kontext.* Frankfurt am Main: Suhrkamp, 1971.

Hodge, Johanna. *Heidegger and Ethics.* New York: Routledge, 1995.

Hölderlin, Friedrich. *Essays and Letters on Theory.* Trans. and ed. Thomas Pfau. Albany: SUNY Press, 1988.

_____. *Hymns and Fragments.* Trans. Richard Sieburth. Princeton, N.J.: Princeton University Press, 1984.

_____. *Hyperion and Selected Poems.* Trans. Willard R. Trask; ed. Eric L. Santner. New York: Continuum, 1994.

_____. *Poems and Fragments.* Trans. Michael Hamburger. London: Anvil Press, 1994.

_____. *Selected Poems*. Trans. David Constantine. Newcastle upon Tyne: Blood-axe Books, 1990.

_____. *Theoretische Schriften*. Ed. Johann Kreuzer. Hamburg: Felix Meiner, 1998.

_____. *Werke und Briefe*. Vols. I–II. Ed. Friedrich Beissner and Jochen Schmidt. Frankfurt am Main: Insel, 1969.

Hulme, T. E. "Bergson's Theory of Art." In *Speculations: Essays on Humanism and the Philosophy of Art*. New York: Routledge, 1987.

Huntington, Patricia J. *Ecstatic Subjects, Utopia, and Recognition*. Albany: SUNY Press, 1998.

Husserl, Edmund. *Cartesian Meditations*. Trans. Dorion Cairns. Dordrecht, The Netherlands: Kluwer Academic, 1993.

_____. *Ideas Pertaining to a Pure Phenomenology and to a Phenomenological Philosophy, First Book*. Trans. F. Kersten. Dordrecht, The Netherlands: Kluwer Academic, 1982.

Ijsseling, Samuel. "The End of Philosophy and the Task of Thinking." In *Martin Heidegger: Critical Assessments*, ed. Christopher Macann, 4:383–397. London: Routledge, 1992.

Jamme, Christoph. "Dem Dichter vor-denken." *Zeitschrift für philosophische Forschung* 38 (1984): 191–218.

_____. "Hölderlin und das Problem der Metaphysik: Zur Diskussion um 'Andenken.'" *Zeitschrift für philosophische Forschung* 42 (1988): 645–665.

Kant, Immanuel. *Critique of Judgment*. Trans. Werner S. Pluhar. Indianapolis: Hackett, 1987.

_____. *Critique of Pure Reason*. Trans. Norman Kemp Smith. New York: St. Martin's, 1965.

_____. *Kritik der Urteilskraft*. Hamburg: Felix Meiner, 1993.

Kearney, Richard. *Poetics of Imagining: Modern to Post-Modern*. New York: Fordham University Press, 1998.

Kisiel, Theodore. *The Genesis of Heidegger's Being and Time*. Berkeley: University of California Press, 1993.

Kockelmans, Joseph J. "Heidegger on Time and Being." In *Martin Heidegger: Critical Assessments*, ed. Christopher Macann, 141–169. London: Routledge, 1992.

Krell, David Farrell. *Daimon Life: Heidegger and Life-Philosophy*. Bloomington: Indiana University Press, 1992.

Lacoue-Labarthe, Philippe. *Heidegger, Art, and Politics*. Trans. Chris Turner. Oxford: Basil Blackwell, 1990.

_____, and Jean-Luc Nancy. *The Literary Absolute*. Trans. Philip Barnard and Cheryl Lester. Albany: SUNY Press, 1988.

Lang, Berel. *Heidegger's Silence*. Ithaca, N.Y.: Cornell University Press, 1996.

Laplanche, Jean. *Hölderlin et la question du père*. Paris: Presses Universitaires de France, 1961.

Levinas, Emmanuel. *Ethics and Infinity.* Trans. Richard A. Cohen. Pittsburgh: Duquesne University Press, 1985.

———. *On Escape.* Trans. Bettina Bergo. Stanford, Calif.: Stanford University Press, 2003.

———. *Totality and Infinity.* Trans. Alphonso Linis. Pittsburgh: Duquesne University Press, 1969.

Lukács, Georg. *Goethe and His Age.* Trans. Robert Anchor. New York: Grosset & Dunlap, 1969.

Lyotard, Jean-François. *Heidegger and "the Jews."* Trans. Andreas Michel and Mark Roberts. Minneapolis: University of Minnesota Press, 1995.

———. *Lessons on the Analytic of the Sublime.* Trans. Elizabeth Rottenberg. Stanford, Calif.: Stanford University Press, 1994.

Marx, Werner. *Heidegger and the Tradition.* Trans. Theodore Kisiel and Murray Greene. Evanston, Ill.: Northwestern University Press, 1971.

———. *Towards a Phenomenological Ethics: Ethos and the Life-World.* Albany: SUNY Press, 1992.

Mehring, Reinhard. *Heideggers Überlieferungsgeschick: Eine dionysische Inszenierung.* Würzburg: Königshausen and Neumann, 1992.

Merleau-Ponty, Maurice. *The Visible and the Invisible.* Evanston, Ill.: Northwestern University Press, 1968.

Nadler, Josef. *Literaturgeschichte der deutschen Stämme und Landschaften. 2d ed.* Regensburg: J. Habbel, 1923–28.

Nauen, Franz Gabriel. *Revolution, Idealism, and Human Freedom: Schelling, Hölderlin and Hegel and the Crisis of Early German Idealism.* The Hague: Martinus Nijhoff, 1971.

Nietzsche, Friedrich. *The Birth of Tragedy.* Trans. Walter Kaufmann. New York: Random House, 1967.

Olafson, Frederick. "The Unity of Heidegger's Thought." In *The Cambridge Companion to Heidegger,* ed. Charles B. Guignon, 67–106. Cambridge: Cambridge University Press, 1993.

Oliver, Kelly. *Reading Kristeva: Unraveling the Double-Bind.* Bloomington: Indiana University Press, 1993.

Peetz, Siegbert. "Welt und Erde: Heidegger und Paul Klee." *Heidegger Studies* 2 (1995): 167–187.

Pellegrini, Alessandro. *Friedrich Hölderlin: Sein Bild in der Forschung.* Berlin: de Gruyter, 1965.

Pöggeler, Otto. "Being as Appropriation." In *Martin Heidegger: Critical Assessments,* ed. Christopher Macann, 284–305. London: Routledge, 1992.

———. "Den Führer führen? Heidegger und keine Ende." *Philosophische Rundschau* 32 (1985).

———. *Martin Heidegger's Path of Thinking.* Trans. Daniel Magurshak and Sigmund Barber. Atlantic Highlands, N.J.: Humanities Press International, 1987.

_____. *Philosophie und Politik bei Heidegger.* Freiburg: AlberBroschur Philosophie, 1972.

Radnóti, Miklós. *The Clouded Sky.* Trans. Stephen Polgar. New York: Harper & Row, 1972.

Raffoul, François. *Heidegger and the Subject.* Trans. David Pettigrew and Gregory Rocco Atlantic Highlands, N.J.: Humanities Press International, 1998.

Rilke, Rainer Maria. *Die Aufzeichnungen des Malte Laurids Brigge.* Ed. Manfred Engel. Stuttgart: Reclam, 1997.

_____. *Selected Poetry of Rainer Maria Rilke.* Ed. and trans. Stephen Mitchell. New York: Vintage Books, 1984.

_____. *Sonnets to Orpheus.* Trans. M. D. Herder. New York: Norton, 1942.

Rimbaud, Arthur. *Illuminations and Other Prose Poems.* Trans. Louise Varèse. New York: New Directions, 1957.

Rorty, Richard. *Essays on Heidegger and Others.* Vol. 2, *Philosophical Papers.* Cambridge: Cambridge University Press, 1991.

Ryan, Lawrence. *Friedrich Hölderlin.* Stuttgart: J. B. Metzlersche, 1962.

_____. *Hölderlins Lehre vom Wechsel der Töne.* Stuttgart: Kohlhammer, 1960.

_____. "Zur Frage des 'Mythischen' bei Hölderlin." In *Hölderlin ohne Mythos,* ed. Ingrid Riedel. Göttingen: Vandenhoeck & Ruprecht, 1973.

Sallis, John. *Echoes After Heidegger.* Bloomington: Indiana University Press, 1990.

Santner, Eric L. *Friedrich Hölderlin: Narrative Vigilance and the Poetic Imagination.* New Brunswick, N.J.: Rutgers University Press, 1986.

Sartre, Jean-Paul. *The Transcendence of the Ego: An Existentialist Theory of Consciousness.* New York: Farrar, Straus & Giroux, 1987.

Sattler, D. E. "Al rovescio: Hölderlin nach 1806." *Individualität* 21 (March 1989): 44–53.

Schalow, Frank. "Language and the Tragic Side of Ethics." *International Studies in Philosophy* XXVII, no. II (1996): 49–63.

_____. "Why Evil? Heidegger, Schelling, and the Tragic Side of Being." *Idealistic Studies* 25, no. 1 (winter 1995): 151–167.

Schlegel, Friedrich. *Philosophical Fragments.* Trans. Peter Firchow. Minneapolis: University of Minnesota Press, 1995.

Schmidt, Dennis J. "Poetry and the Political: Gadamer, Plato, and Heidegger." In *Festivals of Interpretation,* ed. Kathleen Wright, 209–228. Albany: SUNY Press, 1990.

_____. *The Ubiquity of the Finite: Hegel, Heidegger, and the Entitlements of Philosophy.* Cambridge, Mass.: MIT Press, 1988.

Schmidt, Jochen. "Hölderlin im 20. Jahrhundert." In *Hölderlin und die Moderne,* ed. Gerhard Kurz, 105–125. Tübingen: Attempto-Verlag, 1995.

Schürmann, Rainer. *Heidegger on Being and Acting: From Principles to Anarchy.* Trans. Christine-Marie Gros. Bloomington: Indiana University Press, 1987.

Silverman, Hugh J. "The Text of the Speaking Subject: From Merleau-Ponty to Kristeva." In *Merleau-Ponty Vivant*, ed. M. C. Dillon, 183–194. Albany: SUNY Press, 1991.

Stahl, E. L. *The Era of Goethe*. Oxford: Oxford University Press, 1959.

Stockert, Franz-Karl. "Stefan George und sein Kreis: Wirkungsgeschichte vor und nach dem 30. Januar 1933." *Literatur und Germanistik nach der 'Machtübernahme': Colloquium zur 50. Widerkehr des 30 Januar 1933*, ed. Beda Allemann, 52–89. Bonn: Bouvier Verlag.

Strack, Friedrich. *Ästhetik und Freiheit: Hölderlins Idee von Schönheit, Sittlichkeit, und Geschichte in der Frühzeit*. Tübingen: Niemeyer, 1976.

Taminiaux, Jacques. *Heidegger and the Project of Fundamental Ontology*. Trans. and ed. Michael Gendre. Albany: SUNY Press, 1991.

_____. *Poetics, Speculation, and Judgment: The Shadow of the Work of Art from Kant to Phenomenology*. Trans. and ed. Michael Gendre. Albany: SUNY Press, 1993.

Unger, Richard. *Friedrich Hölderlin*. Boston: Twayne, 1984.

_____. *Hölderlin's Major Poetry: The Dialectics of Unity*. Bloomington: Indiana University Press, 1975.

Valéry, Paul. *The Art of Poetry*. Princeton, N.J.: Princeton University Press, 1992.

Van Buren, John. *The Young Heidegger: Rumor of the Hidden King*. Bloomington: Indiana University Press, 1994.

Verlaine, Paul. *Selected Poems*. Trans. C. F. Macintyre. Berkeley: University of California Press, 1948.

Von Hermann, Friedrich-Wilhelm. *Der Begriff der Phänomenologie bei Heidegger und Husserl*. Frankfurt am Main: Vittorio Klostermann, 1981.

_____. "The Flower of the Mouth: Hölderlin's Hint for Heidegger's Thinking of the Essence of Language." *Research in Phenomenology* XIX (1989): 27–42.

_____. "Kunst und Technik." *Heidegger Studies* 1 (1985): 25–62.

_____. *Subjekt und Dasein: Interpretationen zu "Sein und Zeit."* Frankfurt am Main: Vittorio Klostermann, 1984.

Wolin, Richard, ed. *The Heidegger Controversy*. Cambridge, Mass.: MIT Press, 1993.

Zimmerman, Michael E. *Eclipse of the Self: The Development of Heidegger's Concept of Authenticity*. Athens: Ohio University Press, 1981.

Index

expression, poetic, 160, 162–163; language as, 106

factical life, 171, 240; as transformed in poetry, 215
facticity, 29, 31, 135; hermeneutics of, 32–33, 267; and fallenness, 33; and singularity, 129–130
fallenness, 37, 244
fascism, German, xii, 63, 176, 200, as cultural hysteria, 223–224
fate, 28, 197, 245
feeling, 14, 66, 83,105, 107–108; as site of synthesis of phenom and noumenal, 133, 158–159; 162–163, 165–166, 205
Fehervary, Helen, 263, 269
feminine, notion of the, 166, 189, 273; and violence, 224
feminist theory, 285
Fichte, Johann Gottlieb, 15, 18, 70, 79, 111, 116, 120, 121–122, 133, , 134, 138, 169, 195, 219, 226, 274
finitude, of consciousness, 17
focus imaginarius, 220
forgetting, politics of, 33, 200–201, 203, 239, 243, 253, 254
Fóti, Véronique M., 254, 260–261, 265, 282
Foucault, Michel, 202, 207, 286
Frank, Manfred, 119, 264
freedom, 28, 38, 68, 80, 89, 121, 129, 150, 157; as submission to destiny, 46, 51, 71, 77; as autonomy, 52; as spontaneity, 52–53, 220; and sacrifice, 186; and revolution, 189; as beyond the state, 190; and imagination, 195, as autonomy, 142; democratic, 182–183; in religion, 184; and poetic Dasein, 256; symbolized in *Hyperion*, 185, 189; poetic, 228; in Kantian aesthetics, 132–133; and nature, 132, 164; and necessity, 133; and unforseeability, 253; and difference, 120; and reflective judgment, 150–156; and necessity, 161, 163; and precariousness of, 168; sensible presentation of, 191; and nature 193,

195; and aesthetic ideas, 204; less frequent appearance in Hölderlin's writings after 1799, 278.
French Revolution, 182, 185, 188–189, 190, 205, 218
Freud, Sigmund, 208, 211 (*see also* Freudian theory)
Freudian theory, 24, 205, 208, 211–212, 214, 228, 257, 285
Frey, Hans-Jost, 16, 126, 138, 265
Fried, Gregory, 62, 269, 273
"Friedensfeier," 196
Frost, Robert, 240, 250
Fynsk, Christopher, 273

Gadamer, Hans-Georg, 259, 266, 267
Gelassenheit, xiii, 7–10, 12, 16, 17, 21, 22, 24–26, 40, 49, 52, 97, 98, 142–143, 147, 150, 161–162, 171, 173, 176, 185, 187, 202, 204, 210, 212, 218, 220, 228, 243, 254, 268
genius, 51, 103, 105, 121, 131, 149, 150–151, 155, 157 158, 159,160–161, 175, 185, 203, 238, 266
George, Stephan, 6, 9, 10, 11, 16 85, 90, 146, 262
German romanticism, 205
German history, violence in, 223 (*see also* Holocaust; Auschwitz; *and* fascism)
German people, xii, 18, 48, 51, 57, 59,176, 184–186, 236 (*see also* Volk)
German destiny, Hölderlin as poet of, 62, 97, 180, 184, 235
German idealism, 13, 14, 16, 17, 18, 116, 204
Germania, figure of, 189, 282
"Germanien," 13, 75, 77, 85, 189–190
Germany, 172, 173,175, 180, 184, 189, 218, 235
Gethmann-Siefert, Annemarie, 265, 279, 280
Geworfenheit, 135
Goethe, Johann Wolfgang von, 11, 48, 105, 184, 168, 236, 262; classicism of, 271; cosmopolitanism of, 288; Hölderlin's meeting with, 288
Gontard, Suzette, 72

147, 149–164, 166–169, 171, 175,
184, 191–198, 204, , 219–220, 223,
278; ideal of freedom of, 281–282; on
class inequality, 283
Kearney, Richard, 290
Keats, John, 105, 128, 140, 155, 168,
207, 228, 239, 240
Kierkegaard, Søren, 2, 3, 4, 37, 68, 140,
221, 260, 286
Klee, Paul, 85, 155, 270
Knowledge, and poetry, 203, 205–207,
214; poeticization of, 220–221; and
power, 207, 220; and alterity, 218;
limits of, 234
Kristeva, Julia, xii, 24, 106, 141, 199,
202, 205–218, 220–221, 230, 236,
238, 242, 245, 250, 251, 256, 257,
284–285

Lacan, Jacques, 208, 211
Lacoue-Labarthe, Philippe, 158, 197,
199–201, 223, 255, 265
Lang, Berl, 261
language, as expression, 66, 67, 162,
208, 210, 213; reification of, 285; as
signification, 210–211; and social
structures, 210; and materiality,
209–210, 213–214; as communication, 211; poetics vs. ordinary, 211;
and the symbolic, 205, 211–212; and
the semiotic, 205, 211–212; scientific
vs. poetic, 212–214; and cognition,
159–161
"Lebensalter," 102–103
Leibniz, Gottfried Wilhelm, 3, 10, 29
Lenz, Siegfried, 286
Lessing, Gotthold Ephraim, 288
Levinas, Emanuel, 239, 241, 242, 245,
246, 261, 272
life, feeling of, 24, 188, 132, 136–138,
148–151, 154, 156–163, 166, 188,
190, 194, 199, 218–219, 221, 228,
254, 256; and spontaneity, 218; and
the Dionysian, 224
lifeworld, 32, 171, 203, 244, 249, 254
linguistics, structural, 208, 210
literature, modern, 216–217 (*see also*
poetry, modern)

Literaturwissenschaft, 62, 65, 263; notions
of symbol and metaphor in, 74, 94
loss, notion of, 18, 25, 59, 119–120, 126,
131, 136 161–163, 166, 197, 217,
220, 249, 251; and longing, 114, 128,
137, 140
Lukács, Georg, 11, 166, 188, 189, 218,
263
Lyotard, Jean-François, 10, 193, 200,
262, 279, 282

madness, of Hölderlin, 71, 73, 241,
286–287; as psychosis, 213, 217, 222;
and poetry, 226
Mandelstam, Osip, 240, 250
Marx, Werner, 7, 143, 259, 261, 265,
269, 273, 279, 286
maternal, notion of the, 209, 211, 214,
224
Mehring, Reinhard, 265, 280, 282
Merleau-Ponty, Maurice, 290
metaphor, 248, 251
mimesis, 215, 225
"Mnemosyne," 221
modern poetry, 225
modernism, 203–204
modernity, 17, 30, 37, 50, 165, 168, 172,
180, 217
moral feeling, 194
moral law, 161, 226, 234; as contingent
132–134
Morgenstern, Christian, 250
mourning, 131, 134, 140, 150, 162–163,
166, 168–169, 227, 254
Mozart, Wolfgang Amadeus, 273
music, 44–45

Nadler, Josef, 11, 262
Nancy, Jean-Luc, 158, 197
narrative, 269
National Socialism, 8, 9, 11, 179, 199,
233, 283, 288
nationalism, 49, 50, 127, 263; in Heidegger's thought, 24, 54, 82, 180; in literary theory, 11, 179; and Hölderlin,
287–288 (*see also* fascism *and*
National Socialism)
natural attitude, 238, 242, 244

nature, 23, 79–80, 112–115 124–125, 222; and causality, 53; Japanese conception of, 50; unity with, 198; unity of, 120; as sacred, 172, 198, 199; and the poetical, 147, 278; and poetic receptivity, 119; and the overpower of Being, 175; law of remains unsaid, 134, 141; poet's relation to, 142; and imagination, 195; and feeling of life, 144, 148, 156–159, 190; as physis, 147; and the Dionysian, 224; and subjectivity, 205, 220; and technology, 145–150172; and the sublime, 192–194; aesthetically neglected in Heidegger, 241; and freedom, 149, 161–164; and reflective judgment, 150–156; and causality, 154; and organicity, 157; and genius, 161
negative capability, 155, 207, 239
neo-Platonism, 158, 277
Neuffer, Ludwig, 157, 188, 191
Niethammer, Immanuel, 112
Nietzsche, Friedrich, 2, 4, 18, 31, 62, 63, 68, 158, 163, 166, 175, 224–226, 239, 260, 265, 280
Novalis, 147, 155, 166, 271

objective correlative, 123
Oedipus, 234
Olafson, Frederick, 266
ontological difference, 37, 39, 103, 168, 229
ontology, fundamental, 38, 44, 64
Orpheus, 243, 250

pacifism, 168, 189–190
painting, 44–45, 75, 155
paradox, 196, 197, 200, 220
Parmenides, 2
Paul, 19, 130
perception, 14, 238
Pfau, Thomas, 275
physics, modern, 96, 97; Aristotelian, 96
physis, 146–147, 168, 177
Pindar, 236
Planck's constant, 96
Plato, 3, 4, 34, 92, 94, 100, 124, 146, 162, 260

poeisis, and techne, 145–147
poetic Dasein, structure of, 247–253; imagination of, 244–245, 246–247, 251–253; projection, 247; materiality of, 249, 253, 256–257; authenticity of, 250; specificity of, 245–246, 250–251, 253
poetic experience, 85, 106,110, 121–122, 127, 137, 143, 154, 239, 240, 241–242, 246
poetic form, 100–101, 107, 108–128, 130, 138, 140, 155–156, 159–160, 164, 182–184, 197, 221, 269
poetic image, 123, 128, 189, 229
poetic knowledge, 234
poetic language, and alterity, 229–236; and violence, 223
poetic logic, 164
poetic meter, 200 (*see also* poetic form)
poetic receptivity, 20–21, 24, 82, 100, 102, 107, 117, 119, 159, 161, 185–186, 188, 219–221
poetic reflection, 107, 115, 121–122, 130 134, 137, 157, 159–163, 221
poetic subjectivity, as poetic Daesin, 203; and alterity, 204; and analepsis, 217
poetic time, 90, 93
poetic truth, 202, 207, 214–215
poetical cognition, 25, 27, 155, 242, 245
poetical expression, 244
poetical intuition, 243
poetry, modern, 215, 239–241 (*see also* literature, modern)
Pöggeler, Otto, 8, 49, 259, 261, 262, 266, 272, 280
poiesis, 69
polis, 179–180, 230
Ponge, Francis, 289
postmodernism, 172, 203–204
power, 175, 286; and language, 178
projection, 203
Prokosch, Frederic, 278
Proust, Marcel, 105
punishment, 133
purposivity, in reflective judgment, 151–154, 158

quantum mechanics, 96, 244